ANJALI DESA

ASSISTED BY VIVEK KHADPEKAR

INDIA ◈ GUIDE

INDIA GUIDE PUBLICATIONS | AHMEDABAD • HOUSTON

India is not just a place.
India is not just a people.
India is the celestial music,

And inside that music
Anybody from any corner of the globe
Can find the real significance of life.

Sri Chinmoy

Legend
- ■ Country Capital
- ◉ State Capital
- ● Other Places
- —·—·— International Border
- ——— State Border

AFGHANISTAN

JAMMU & KASHMIR

HIMACHAL PRADESH

PUNJAB

HARYANA

UTTARANCHAL

DELHI

CHINA

NEPAL

PAKISTAN

RAJASTHAN

UTTAR PRADESH

BIHAR

SIKKIM BHUTAN

ARUNACHAL PRADESH

ASSAM

NAGALAND

MEGHALAYA

MANIPUR

MT ABU

UDAIPUR

AHMEDABAD

GUJARAT

MADHYA PRADESH

INDORE

I N D I A

JHARKHAND

WEST BENGAL

BANGLADESH

TRIPURA

MIZORAM

MYANMAR

CHHATTISGARH

ORISSA

MUMBAI

MAHARASHTRA

ARABIAN SEA

ANDHRA PRADESH

BAY OF BENGAL

GOA

KARNATAKA

LAKSHADWEEP

TAMILNADU

ANDAMAN AND NICOBAR ISLANDS

KERALA

INDIAN OCEAN

N

NOT TO SCALE

SRI LANKA

The international boundaries on this map are neither claimed to be correct nor authenticated by the Survey of India directives.

iii

PAKISTAN

GREAT RANN OF KACHCHH

BANASKANT

Khavda

Dholavira

Lakhpat
Koteshwar

PATAN

Hodka

Rapar

LITTLE
RANN
OF
KACHCHH

Jhinjhuwada

KACHCHH

BHUJ

Wild Ass
Sanctuary

Gandhidham

Halvad   Dhrangadhra

Mandvi
Mundra

Bhadreshwar

Morbi

SURENDRANAGAR

GULF OF KACHCHH

Wankaner

SURENDRANAGAR

Beyt Dwarka

Marine
National Park

Chotila

JAMNAGA R

Dwarka

JAMNAGAR

RAJKOT

RAJKOT

Velavadar
National P

Ghumli

Barda
Sanctuary

PORBANDA R

PORBANDAR

Virpur

Jetpur

Gondal

BHAVNAGA

BHAVNAG

AMRELI

Shiho

JUNAGADH

Palitana

Madhavpur

JUNAGADH

AMRELI

AMRELI

Tala

Khijadia Sanctuary

Sasan Gir

ARABIAN
SEA

Gir National Park

Veraval
Somnath

Ahmedpur Mandvi

Diu
Union Territory

N

NOT TO SCALE

iv

TABLE OF CONTENTS

The inspiration for India Guide surfaced from a conversation between a small group of friends who have been living in India for some time. We intently discussed our desire to share with others the deep bond and affection that we have for the country, while also communicating the colorful, often incredible experiences that we encounter on a daily basis. And so we planted the seeds for India Guide—a travel guide written by people that are largely local or possess first-hand knowledge of India. One that draws attention to destinations off the beaten path, places that encompass the essence of all that is amazing in this country. India Guide is for the traveler who wants to connect with local people, explore the stretches between major cities and major sights and immerse all five senses and sensibilities into a space that demands reflection and offers new perspective. Although the Taj Mahal and scenic beaches of Goa offer a glimpse into the splendor of India, they do not encompass the complete spectrum of her majesty. India Guide is a humble endeavor to highlight the hidden treasures of India while cheering on the spirit of exploration and discovery.

For the first of the India Guide series, we selected Gujarat, a state we know intimately and one that is rarely seen as a travel destination. Beyond its kaleidoscope of attractions, Gujarat hosts a unique culture of enterprise, hospitality and diversity. Just as Gujaratis have spread around the world, they have openly welcomed people, ideas and customs of various backgrounds into their own land. India Guide Gujarat is a celebration of this warm ethos.

India Guide Publications is a team of passionate travelers (supported by a network of topic experts) who speak the local language and understand the culture. Our values are strongly rooted in knowledge-based traveling and built upon four principles: cultural sensitivity, supporting the local economy, respecting nature and reducing the negative impact of our footprint wherever we may tread. We encourage self-reliance and empowerment through information and cheer on those who take the road less traveled.

As each journey extends into the world around us, it reaches an equal distance into the world within.
Anonymous

RESPONSIBLE TOURISM

As the globe grows increasingly smaller, we must each do our part in taking care of it. Since our choices and attitudes impact the world of tomorrow we have highlighted a few guidelines that promote conscious traveling in an effort to preserve the treasures of today for the next generation of travelers.

Cultural Sensitivity Travel with an open mind to really immerse in a new culture. Make it a habit to always look, listen and learn in order to better understand and internalize the local way of life. Try to do some research and get to know the area—its history, customs and cultural norms. The proper context will help enhance your sensitivity towards the place. Take the time to learn a few phrases of the language to really connect with people. Respect the appropriate dress codes and norms of each environment.

Support the Local Economy Stay at locally owned accommodations, eat foods native to the area and purchase products made with indigenous materials. Help support local artisans and preserve craft traditions by buying handcrafted goods. And when time allows, get to know the person behind the craft.

Respect Nature Make the effort to conserve your water and power use. Recycle whenever possible. Minimize the use of plastic by keeping a cloth bag on you to carry your purchases. Avoid water pouches when possible. Hold on to your waste until you have access to proper disposal facilities. Do not remove anything from its natural environment, and when in nature, follow trails and travel in small, unobtrusive groups.

Reduce the Negative Impact of your Footprint Always try to be aware of your actions and their possible affects. When taking photos, especially of women, ask for permission first since it can be obtrusive and disrespectful; in some communities it may even be taboo. Try not to make promises to people such as return visits and sending pictures if you can not follow through with them. Giving money to beggars only reinforces their behavior. Instead donate to or get involved in local social organizations that know and work with the area's underprivileged communities.

THE ULTIMATE
GUJARAT EXPERIENCE

THE ULTIMATE GUJARAT EXPERIENCE

The following is a selection of some of Gujarat's highlights, which promise to offer you an unforgettable experience. For more information refer to the page number listed after each highlight.

SOMNATH Junagadh district

Visit this omnipotent shrine, which has been destroyed and rebuilt six times and houses one of India's 12 sacred *jyotirlingas*. *(p 263)*

PAVAGADH AND CHAMPANER
PANCHMAHAL DISTRICT
From majestic mosques to a hilltop fort, this heritage sight resonates with history and legend. *(p 177)*

HERITAGE HOTELS Across Gujarat
These converted palaces and royal estates offer an experience filled with warm hospitality, old world charm and regal splendor. *(p 383)*

NAVJIVAN NATURE CURE CENTRE Kachchh district
Cleanse your mind, body and spirit with a few days of yoga, natural spa treatments and nourishing food. *(p 332)*

DIU The southern coast of Saurashtra
Relax on the beaches of this serene coastal town and delight in the distinctive fusion of Gujarati and Portuguese cultures. *(p 264)*

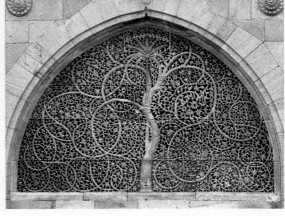

⑦

AHMEDABAD'S WALLED CITY
AHMEDABAD CITY
Wander through labyrinthine streets studded with immortal masterpieces of Islamic influence while imbibing the local lifestyle that buzzes with a charm unique to the city. *(p 88)*

⑤

GANDHI ASHRAM
AHMEDABAD CITY
Reflect in the tranquil spirit of a powerful landmark, from where Mahatma Gandhi started his movement for India's freedom through non-violence. *(p 96)*

⑥

VADODARA
VADODARA DISTRICT
A vibrant art scene, imposing palaces and one of India's leading universities make this metropolis Gujarat's "City of Culture". *(p 165)*

 8   **9**

GIR NATIONAL PARK
JUNAGADH DISTRICT
Take a safari into the Gir Forest, the last remaining habitat of the Asiatic Lion, and hope for a meeting with this King of the Jungle. *(p 260)*

PATAN
PATAN DISTRICT
This quintessential medieval town boasts of an extensive fort wall, a millennium-old stepwell, Solanki monuments from its days as the former capital of Gujarat and fabulous Patola weavers. *(p 215)*

10

JUNAGADH CITY
JUNAGADH DISTRICT
Travel through time in this ancient city, where King Ashoka inscribed his edicts, Buddhist monks carved caves and the Muslim Nawabs reigned for several centuries. *(p 251)*

 11

SHOOLPANESHWAR SANCTUARY
NARMADA DISTRICT
Trek through the enchanting bamboo and teak forests of this wildlife sanctuary. *(p 153)*

THE LAW GARDEN
AHMEDABAD CITY
Bargain like a local while strolling down this vibrant street bazaar lined with open stalls that display bright costumes, embroidered handbags, silver jewelry and other local crafts. *(p 98)*

A GUJARATI THALI
ACROSS GUJARAT
Pamper your taste buds with a traditional feast, which offers unlimited quantities of vegetables, dals, breads, pickles and peppers, side dishes and sweets. *(p 365)*

UTTARAYAN IN AHMEDABAD
AHMEDABAD CITY
Feel the magic as you celebrate this whimsical festival on the rooftops of Ahmedabad where people of all ages fill the sky with colorful kites to commemorate the passing of winter. *(p 66)*

14

MASALA CHAI
ACROSS GUJARAT
Experience a favorite "time pass" of Gujarat and sip on a cup of warm spiced tea while taking in the exuberance of daily life. *(p 369)*

ADALAJ STEPWELL
GANDHINAGAR DISTRICT
Roam about the five stories of this exquisite 15th c. stepwell, which served as a resting place for weary travelers. *(p 109)*

TEXTILES
ACROSS GUJARAT
Many places around Gujarat have their own distinctive traditions in handcrafted textiles. From tie-and-dye and block printing to weaving and embroidery, there is something to excite every taste. *(p 360)*

 15
SURYA TEMPLE, MODHERA
MAHESANA DISTRICT
Walk around this majestic
shrine, one of the most
magnificent Sun temples in
India. *(p 225)*

 16
CALICO MUSEUM
AHMEDABAD CITY
Tour this exquisite collection of
Indian textiles that ranges across five
centuries. *(p 86)*

 17
MANDVI
KACHCHH DISTRICT
Marvel at the colossal wooden boats
built by craftsmen along the banks of
the Rukmavati River and take a stroll
on the serene stretch of the
Mandvi Beach. *(p 328)*

18
VIJAYNAGAR AND POLO FORESTS
SABARKANTHA DISTRICT
This picturesque countryside,
strewn with ruins of ancient
temples, lies nestled in the
undulating foothills of the
Aravali Mountains. *(p 192)*

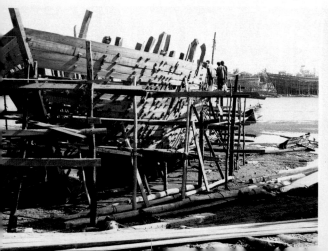

WILD ASS SANCTUARY
LITTLE RANN OF KACHCHH
Take an excursion into the Little Rann of Kachchh for an exciting adventure filled with sightings of the Wild Ass, a drive through salt flats and a glimpse of a unique pastoral culture. *(p 305)*

PALITANA
BHAVNAGAR DISTRICT
Climb 3000 steps up to this enchanting abode of the Gods, which has more than 860 Jain temples. *(p 247)*

 NAVRATRI
AHMEDABAD AND VADODARA CITIES
Celebrate this nine-night festival by dancing with locals into the early mornings. *(p 73)*

 **HANDICRAFTS OF BANNI**
KACHCHH DISTRICT
From vibrant embroidery to finely engraved wood, almost every community in this rustic region boasts of a colorful craft that demands the skill of a dexterous hand. *(p 322)*

 SARKHEJ ROZA
AHMEDABAD DISTRICT
This elegant composition of architecture sits on the banks of a lake and glitters with the sun's rays peering through latticed windows, a medley that makes for an incredible retreat. *(p 106)*

24 25 HOLI IN CHHOTA UDEPUR   VADNAGAR

HOLI IN CHHOTA UDEPUR
VADODARA DISTRICT
Revel in this festival of colors, when tribal fairs erupt in every community along the eastern belt of Gujarat. *(p 176)*

VADNAGAR
MAHESANA DISTRICT
Famous for its *toran*, this town predates history and is a living museum of ancient architecture and beautiful relics. *(p 226)*

26 DWARKA
JAMNAGAR DISTRICT
Steeped in myths of the legendary Krishna, Dwarka is one of the seven sacred cities of Hinduism. *(p 285)*

 27

BIRDWATCHING AT NAL SAROVAR
AHMEDABAD DISTRICT
Enjoy birdwatching in this picturesque wetland sanctuary, which attracts more than 200 species of migratory birds in the winter. *(p 107)*

 28

LOTHAL
AHMEDABAD DISTRICT
This archaeological site showcases one of the prominent cities of the 5000-year-old Indus Valley Civilization. *(p 108)*

 29

BARDA HILLS SANCTUARY
PORBANDAR AND JAMNAGAR DISTRICTS
Trek along the hidden treasures of temple ruins tucked away in these rolling hills. *(p 275)*

 30

EUROPEAN TOMBS
SURAT CITY
Marvel at imposing mausoleums that jet out amidst daily life to tell of European trade in the city's flourishing past. *(p 118)*

 SURENDRANAGAR DISTRICT
Explore between charming stepwells, haunting memorial stones and ancient ruins scattered across this vast region. *(p 298)*

32 **THE DANGS**
This region stands apart for its thick jungles pulsating with wildlife, tribal culture and stunning natural beauty. *(p 137)*

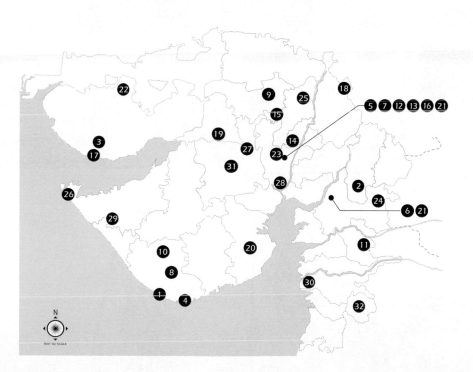

N

NOT TO SCALE

ABOUT GUJARAT

FACTS AT A GLANCE

LAND AREA	196,024 sq km	**FOREST AREA**	7.6%
POPULATION	50,671,000 (about	**COASTLINE**	1659 km
	5% of India's	**WILDLIFE SANCTUARIES**	21
	population)*	**NATIONAL PARKS**	4
RURAL POPULATION	31,741,000*	**MAJOR RIVERS**	Narmada, Tapi,
URBAN POPULATION	18,930,000*		Mahi, Sabarmati
OFFICIAL LANGUAGES	Gujarati, Hindi	**RELIGIOUS DIVERSITY**	
BEST TIME TO VISIT	October through	**HINDU**	89.09%*
	March	**MUSLIM**	9.06%*
CLIMATE	Summer 27°C - 42°C	**JAIN**	1.04%*
(AVG RANGES)	Winter 14°C - 29°C	**OTHER**	0.81%*
LATITUDE	20°02'N - 24°39'N	**RAIL NETWORK**	5,268 km
LONGITUDE	68°10'E - 74°37'E	**MAJOR CROPS**	Groundnut, Cotton,
CAPITAL	Gandhinagar		Tobacco
MAJOR CITIES	Ahmedabad, Surat,	**MAJOR INDUSTRIES**	Chemicals,
	Vadodara, Rajkot,		Petrochemicals,
	Bhavnagar,		Pharmaceuticals,
	Jamnagar, Junagadh		Textiles, Diamonds,
NUMBER OF CITIES	27		Consumer goods
TOWNS	242	**LITERACY RATE**	69.14%*
VILLAGES	18,539	**FEMALE/MALE RATIO**	920/1000*
DISTRICTS	25	**INFANT MORTALITY RATE**	57/1000

* Facts and figures are based on Census of India 2001

GEOGRAPHY

Gujarat rests on the western coast of India, bounded by the Arabian Sea to the west and surrounded by the states of Rajasthan on the north, Madhya Pradesh on the east and Maharashtra on the south. To the northwest, it shares an international border with Pakistan. The southern tip of the Aravali Mountain Range extends into northern Gujarat, the Satpura and Vindhya hills occupy parts of the eastern belt and the Sahyadri Range (Western Ghats) reaches over into the Dangs. The state has the country's longest coastline at more than 1600 kilometers. The Tropic of Cancer passes through the north of Gujarat.

Traditionally, Gujarat is subdivided into four geographic regions with distinguishable socio-cultural characteristics. The divisions include mainland Gujarat, which stretches from the southern end of the Aravali Mountains to the northern tip of the Western Ghats; Saurashtra, formerly known as Kathiawad; Kachchh; and the eastern tribal belt. Gujarat also reveals some striking attributes shaped by its shared history with Rajasthan and the Sindh region of Pakistan.

HISTORY

Indus Valley Civilization

The significant archeological record of Gujarat begins some 5000 years ago with the Indus Valley Civilization, also known as the Harappan Civilization, which evolved around the Indus River and its tributaries. Today, more than 2500 Harappan cities and towns have been unearthed, of which a few dozen are in Gujarat (Dholavira in Kachchh and Lothal near Ahmedabad are most noteworthy). Studies and archeological findings have shown that this society practiced advanced urban planning and built efficient drainage systems, baths and mud brick houses. It may have been a single state, as indicated by its standardized system of weights and measures, and the similarity in design of many of the artifacts found at sites separated by vast distances. Excavations have also uncovered red ware pottery, similar to today's terracotta craft. The Indus period started to decline due to factors such as climate change, deforestation and flooding.

Ancient History

The documented history of Gujarat begins with the incursion of Maurya (322-185 BC) rule in Saurashtra, which, for the first time, brought most of the subcontinent under a central authority based in North India. This empire also introduced Buddhism across its realm. The edicts of the third Maurya emperor, Ashoka (273-237), inscribed on rock, still exists at the foot of Mt Girnar (Junagadh). Numerous rock-cut Buddhist caves from this period can be found in different parts of Saurashtra. After the death of Ashoka, the Maurya Empire was split into several factions; Saurashtra fell under a grandson of Ashoka who spread Jainism throughout the region.

After 137 years of Maurya rule, much of present-day Gujarat was controlled by successive waves of invaders from the northwest. Of these, the Guptas (415-470) consolidated their hold over Saurashtra, which became an important province in their kingdom until their vassals, the Maitrakas (473-788), took independent control of the region. They established Valabhi as their capital, and it prospered as a port and a center of learning. The period from 788 to 942 saw another succession of changes in ruling dynasties, except in western Saurashtra, where the Saindhavas remained firmly in control. The prominent religion from the end of Maurya rule to the end of the Maitraka period also shifted from Buddhism to Jainism to Sun worship to Shaivism.

The Golden Age

The Solanki era (942-1304) marks what many consider the Golden Age of Gujarat's history. The center of power shifted from Saurashtra to North Gujarat, with Anahilvada Patan as the capital. This period saw the emergence of an integrated Gujarat, more or less corresponding to the geo-cultural region and the state as we know it today. Architecture and sculpture matured to produce works that, nearly a thousand years later, still count among the masterpieces of these forms in India. An era of intellectual ferment began. Jain scholars made great contributions to the world of knowledge and script, under the joint patronage of the kings and the Jain mercantile community from Rajasthan. During this time, the Jain community established roots in Gujarat and greatly influenced its cultural ethos.

This period also marks the beginnings of Islamic contact, in both peaceful and violent ways. The trade with west Asia had already brought Muslims to coastal Gujarat. Small Muslim communities had begun forming in Bharuch, Khambhat and Veraval, and local rulers facilitated

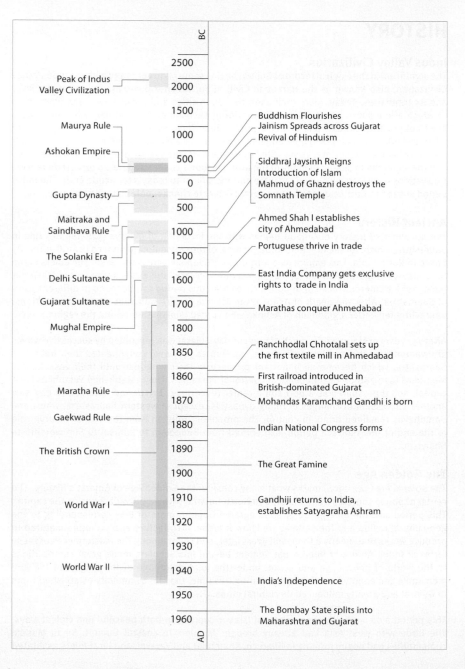

BC

2500

2000 — Peak of Indus Valley Civilization

1500

Maurya Rule

1000 — Buddhism Flourishes
Jainism Spreads across Gujarat
Revival of Hinduism

Ashokan Empire

500 — Siddhraj Jaysinh Reigns
Introduction of Islam

0 — Mahmud of Ghazni destroys the Somnath Temple

Gupta Dynasty

500

Maitraka and Saindhava Rule

1000 — Ahmed Shah I establishes city of Ahmedabad

The Solanki Era — Portuguese thrive in trade

1500

Delhi Sultanate

1600 — East India Company gets exclusive rights to trade in India

Gujarat Sultanate

1700 — Marathas conquer Ahmedabad

Mughal Empire

1800

1850 — Ranchhodlal Chhotalal sets up the first textile mill in Ahmedabad

1860 — First railroad introduced in British-dominated Gujarat

Maratha Rule

1870 — Mohandas Karamchand Gandhi is born

Gaekwad Rule

1880 — Indian National Congress forms

The British Crown

1890

1900 — The Great Famine

1910 — Gandhiji returns to India, establishes Satyagraha Ashram

World War I

1920

1930

World War II

1940

1950 — India's Independence

1960 — The Bombay State splits into Maharashtra and Gujarat

AD

the creation and endowment of mosques for them. At the same time, the sixteenth (1025) of the seventeen invasions of India by Mahmud of Ghazni was marked by the plunder and desecration of the Somnath Temple and by large-scale massacre.

Delhi Sultanate

In the 12th and 13th c. the Arabs, Turks and Afghans invaded Northern India and eventually established the Delhi Sultanate (1206-1320). In 1299, the army of Sultan Alauddin Khilji from Delhi invaded Gujarat. They besieged Patan and looted Somnath for a second time. After this, the army split; one part sacked Junagadh and the other the port of Cambay (Khambhat). After plundering several more cities, they returned to Delhi. Alauddin Khilji dispatched his troops once more in 1304, this time to seize Gujarat. Rajput power was displaced by the Turks, although a few lingering kingdoms continued to herald power. From the 8th c. until Muslim occupancy, the ports of Bharoch (Bharuch), Cambay (Khambhat), Rander and Sindan (Sanjan) thrived on trade. Over the next several years, the power of Delhi over Gujarat weakened under the Tughlaq Dynasty.

Gujarat Sultanate

After the fall of the Tughlaqs, the independent Gujarat Sultanate was proclaimed in 1403 from Patan. In 1411, the third Sultan in the line, Ahmed Shah I, founded the city of Ahmedabad and shifted the capital there. His 31-year rule witnessed the consolidation of the Sultanate. The peak of the Gujarat Sultanate came under Mahmud I, who ruled for a period of 52 years (1459-1511). His conquests of Junagadh in 1469 and Pavagadh in 1484 earned him the title "Begada" (conqueror of two forts). He strengthened the fortifications of Champaner, renamed it Muhammadabad (after the Prophet) and shifted the capital there, which remained so until 1535. He also conquered Daman, raided Kachchh and Sindh and contained piracy around the ports of Dwarka and Ghogha. Mahmud's lasting contribution to Gujarat is the magnificent monuments he built, especially at Champaner, Sarkhej and Ahmedabad. No single reign in India until Akbar's, nearly 150 years later, contributed so much to architecture.

The last important ruler of Gujarat was Bahadur Shah (1526-1537), who granted the Portuguese permission to build a fort in Diu in return for their support against the Mughals. He lost several territories to Humayun in 1534 until the Mughals were forced to return to Delhi to protect the empire against the invading forces of Sher Khan. Bahadur Shah regained most of his territories, but was later slain by the Portuguese at Diu. By 1573, the Mughals had taken over Gujarat, which was reduced to the status of a province in the Empire.

Mughal Era

With a few exceptions, the Mughal rulers integrated with Indian culture and tolerated, if not patronized, other religions. They married local royalty and allied with kings. They continued the synthesis of Turko-Persian and Indian culture, which further enriched architecture, music and art, and ignited theological and philosophical discourse. This is one reason why the Mughal Empire was a greater success than the short-lived regimes of the Delhi Sultanate. Emperor Akbar visited Patan in 1572 to secure the submission of Gujarat nobles and establish a relationship with the Portuguese to restore commercial traffic and protect pilgrims. In the 16th and 17th c., Gujarat was largely peaceful. The region grew famous for its silk and cotton textiles. Sarkhej, near Ahmedabad was the main center for indigo dyeing. At the turn of the 17th c., the Dutch arrived and built a factory in Surat. The English and the French soon followed.

During 1630-32, a drought brought about horrible famine in Gujarat, which was followed by a year of floods. It took a decade to restore prosperity. Shah Jahan's final years were marked by internal fighting among his sons for the throne. After his death, his son Aurangzeb ruled from 1658 to 1707, a period infamous for severe bigotry and iconoclasm against Hindus. After Aurangzeb's death, the Mughal Empire steadily declined over 150 years. By 1818 the British had taken de facto control of India, including 600 princely courts, which were reduced to mere spectacle and ceremony.

The Portuguese

Vasco da Gama, the Portuguese explorer, discovered a new sea route to India in 1498. The Portuguese set up bases at several places along the west coast and took over maritime trade in the Indian Ocean and Red Sea. They also paved the road to European colonization of the country. In the 16th c. their growing influence undermined trade at Cambay, where many Portuguese traders settled and married local women. They also implemented a system of *cartas-armada-cafila*, which required all ships sailing in Asian waters to have a pass issued by them.

Post-Mughal Era The Marathas and Colonialism

In 1615 the Mughals and the East India Company signed a treaty giving the latter exclusive rights to reside and build factories in the country, including Surat, in exchange for goods and rare objects from the European markets. The English soon eclipsed the Portuguese. The enterprise started as a joint stock company to favor trade privileges in India and dealt mainly in cotton, indigo, tea and silk. In the course of 21 years, it established a monopoly on all trade in the country. As its auxiliary powers grew, so did the need to protect itself. The Company organized armies, drawing mainly from the local population. As this switch from trade to politics took place, it set up Agencies to monitor the affairs of princely states and help enforce law and order. Eventually they operated as controlling bodies under the British monarchy. The states had nominal jurisdiction over civil and criminal powers, but real power was vested in the Agent.

In 1664, Shivaji, the founder of the Maratha Empire in western India, led an army into the thriving port of Surat and plundered it dry. He returned in 1670 to loot it once more. The Marathas encountered stiff opposition from the British East India Company and left the English factory untouched. Some 125 years later, the British would split control of Gujarat, barring the Kathiawad peninsula, with the ruling Maratha dynasty, the Gaekwads.

In 1674, after consolidating control over his territories in the Deccan, Shivaji declared war on the Mughal Empire during Aurangzeb's rule and gained popular support against the intolerant Emperor. In 1758 the Marathas took over Ahmedabad, ending Mughal rule in Gujarat. They conquered central and eastern Gujarat in the 18th c. Their representatives in Gujarat, the Gaekwads, proclaimed themselves as rulers and set up Baroda (now Vadodara) as their capital. During this period, many parts of Kathiawad and Kachchh reverted to rule by independent local kings, most of whom paid tribute to the Marathas. After the Anglo-Maratha war in the early 19th c., the British took over much of Gujarat. The Gaekwads signed a special treaty, which gave Baroda a degree of autonomy while most of Gujarat was under direct or indirect British control. When the East India Company shifted its center of commerce from Surat to Bombay (now Mumbai), many Gujaratis also migrated there for business opportunities and played a major role in establishing Bombay as the economic capital of India.

After 1857, when armed uprisings and rebellions in northern and central India against the British took place, the British Crown took direct control of India, with a Viceroy at the helm of affairs. Except for scattered instances of rebellion and, from 1915 onwards, Gandhiji's sustained but principled opposition to British rule, Gujarat witnessed 90 years of peace, law and order, and socio-economic reform that helped it leap from medieval feudalism to a modern industrial society. Unlike many other parts of India, Gujarat wrought this change largely by indigenous initiative and entrepreneurship. The 90 years of British rule saw the beginnings of transformation in fields as varied as education, culture, social reform, commerce, industry, industrial relations and governance.

Mohandas Karamchand Gandhi ("Gandhiji"), born in 1869, went on to become one of the most profound spiritual and political leaders and social activists of the 20th c. He played a pivotal role in securing India's independence from British rule while also building on the contributions of those who preceded him.

By 1864, the first railroad had been introduced in British-dominated Gujarat. Some princely states followed the example, but without giving much thought to the integrated overall network that extended beyond their own territories. In 1861, the American Civil War sent the price of cotton, Gujarat's cash crop, soaring. The British invested heavily in India at the time and a large percentage was flowed to Gujarat. Also in 1861, Ranchhodlal Chhotalal set up the first textile mill in Ahmedabad, marking the emergence of a new economy in Gujarat based on modern industry. By 1946, Ahmedabad had 74 mills, giving it the title "The Manchester of the East".

In 1896 ships from Hong Kong brought the bubonic plague to Bombay, which spread all the way up to Mahesana in Gujarat. Soon after, the Great Famine of 1900 spread across western India, followed by epidemics of cholera and influenza. These calamities took the lives of millions and affected many more. Along with the growth of the textile industry and railways, these factors induced the first wave of migration from rural Gujarat to urban centers. Both peasant communities and Dalits participated in the migration and diversified from agriculture to the modern sectors of commerce, industry and technical education.

Meanwhile, in 1885, eminent leaders formed the Indian National Congress, with people such as Dadabhai Naoroji emerging as the voice of Indian autonomy. Although the British allowed it in order to secure liberal, pro-British support from Indians, the Congress soon evolved into a voice for Independence.

In 1915, Gandhiji returned to India from South Africa and established the Satyagraha Ashram in Ahmedabad. He organized several non-violent non-cooperation campaigns for mill workers and farmers and popularized the idea of *swaraj* (self-rule) and *swadeshi* (local production and exclusive support of local economy). Gandhiji promoted non-violence and truth as the only means for liberation from British occupation. He also tried to reduce increasing Hindu-Muslim tensions. The Muslim League, established in 1906 as a political party dedicated to promoting the interests of Muslims in India, became a major driving force behind the creation of Pakistan as a Muslim state. In 1913, Muhammad Ali Jinnah, the son of an affluent Gujarati merchant from Kathiawad, joined the League after leaving the Congress due to disagreements with Gandhiji. Jinnah eventually became the founder of Pakistan.

In 1942, the British involved India in World War II without consulting the people. Indians were divided over the issue, some hoping that assistance to the British would lead to independence while others thought that the British had coming to them what they deserved. In July 1942, Congress passed a resolution demanding complete independence from Britain, threatening civil disobedience. Soon after, the Quit India Movement commenced and the nation plunged into intense non-violent civil disobedience. Although the movement dwindled after a year, by 1946, the British had opened dialogue with Congress about a transfer of power.

On August 15 1947, India split into two independent states under British dominion—a secular India and a Muslim Pakistan. On the same day the British surrendered power. The partition of the subcontinent saw the largest mass migration in modern history when over twelve million people moved across the new international border. Sindhi and Gujarati Hindus migrated into Gujarat from Sindh, but due to its relatively small and dispersed Muslim population at the time, Gujarat did not experience the bloody post-partition violence that ensued in Bengal and Punjab.

After independence the princely states began to cede power, either to the Union of India or to Pakistan. The dethroned rulers were allowed to retain their titles and many of their privileges. They were given privy purses, which were retracted in 1975. All of the states in the territory that now forms India agreed to join the Union, except Junagadh, Kashmir and Hyderabad. The Nawab of Junagadh was a feeble leader whose Diwan was a strong ally of Jinnah. The Diwan had convinced the Nawab to refute the accession of Junagadh to the Indian Union as a political move to secure the Muslim dominated Kashmir. Junagadh's choice caused uproar in Kathiawad. Thousands of people crossed into Junagadh, and the Nawab fled with his entourage to Pakistan. The Diwan waited for assistance from Pakistan, but eventually turned the state over to India. In 1948, the 222 princely states of Kathiawad were organized as the United States of Kathiawad while Kachchh was established as an independent state. Mainland Gujarat merged with the State of Bombay.

Mahagujarat Movement
The term Mahagujarat encompassed the whole Gujarati speaking area including Gujarat, Saurashtra and Kachchh. In 1948, a Mahagujarat conference took place to integrate the entire Gujarati speaking population under one administrative body and on May 1, 1960, the Bombay State split into the states of Maharashtra and Gujarat. For the first time after the Sultanate, Gujarat was once again autonomous.

As a new political entity, Gujarat's elite had the freedom to initiate their own ideas for development. Many took to Nehru's model, which emphasized modernization and technology as the instrument for change. It encouraged tapping human and natural resources to develop agriculture and promote industrial growth. The 1960s, associated with the Green Revolution, witnessed cash crop agriculture spurred on by new technologies and policies such as hybrid seeds, irrigation projects and subsidized electricity for farmers. This was followed by the White Revolution, which was characterized by a cooperative dairy movement. The state government then introduced schemes supporting small and medium scale industries and granted land and tax benefits to entrepreneurs for setting up units in designated industrial estates. By the 1980s, Gujarat was one of the most industrialized states in the country. Industrialization led to rapid urbanization, the rise of an entrepreneurial middle class, ecological degradation and the marginalization of a portion of society living below the poverty line.

Gujarati Diaspora

In the early 19th c., several Gujarati communities such as the Bohra, Khoja and Memon had already settled in East Africa, largely as traders. Orthodox Hindus were restricted from overseas travel due to social taboo. It was only around the early 20th c., after reforms within the castes eased these restrictions, that people from the Jain, Vaniya and Brahmin communities traveled abroad.

The Famine of 1900 induced the first major wave of westward migration as people searched for job alternatives. Many migrated to Africa as the construction of the East African railways offered employment opportunity. Some Gujarati emigrants eventually established enterprises while professionals also resettled there. The future looked promising until 1970, when Idi Amin evicted Asians (mostly comprised of Gujaratis) from Uganda. This resulted in an exodus of Gujaratis to the United Kingdom. Many had to rebuild their lives, running small businesses and corner shops.

In the 1960s, the United States reformed its immigration laws lifting the restriction on Asian professional migrants. Gujarati doctors, engineers, scientists and pharmacists led the migration, followed by businessmen, who eventually turned to small enterprises such as motels and convenience stores. Today, the Gujarati Diaspora continues to invest money in the state, especially in areas such as health, education and new business ventures.

ECONOMY

Quick Facts (statistics from ca. 2004-05)

GDP of Gujarat	: 39.8 billion USD
Contribution to the national GDP	: 6.64%
Per Capita Income	: 485 USD (415 USD is the national average)
Contribution to Indian exports	: 14%
Industrial Growth Rate	: 15%

Gujarat is one of the most economically advanced states in India. It is a fertile ground for investment, attracting nearly nine percent of all foreign direct investments in India. The famous entrepreneurial spirit of its people and the integration of India with the global economy, along with recent government initiatives to spur economic development, have led to a booming business environment. Gujarat's larger cities are now experiencing an onslaught of fresh construction with malls, entertainment complexes, restaurants, commercial property and housing complexes springing up in record time. Real estate prices are rocketing and the sense of a state and nation on the move is palpable. Globalization has brought about many new job opportunities for the educated, urban middle classes and though the effects of growth are spreading wider and more deeply into all sectors, there are undoubtedly some sections of society for whom progress is all too slow.

Agriculture and Animal Husbandry
The agriculture sector accounts for about 15 percent of the state's GDP (Gross Domestic Product). Most agriculture depends on the rains of the southwest monsoon (Jun-Sep). However, these rains are erratic and crop output fluctuates from year to year. The major food crops in Gujarat

are wheat, maize, *tuver* (red gram), gram, *jowar* (sorghum), *bajra* (pearl millet), oilseeds, rice and peanuts. Fruits and vegetables such as mango, banana, *chikoo* (sapota), sugarcane, citrus fruits, potato, onion, aubergine, tomato, okra, cucumber, squashes and pumpkins are also grown in abundance. The principal non-food crops include tobacco and cotton. Gujarat produces 57 percent of India's tobacco, 30 percent of its peanuts and 18 percent of its cotton. It is also the world's largest producer of cumin and fennel.

India's milk revolution began in Gujarat with the birth of the Gujarat Cooperative Milk Marketing Federation in Anand, also known as the Amul Cooperative. This is the country's largest food product marketing association and launched what is often referred to as India's "White Revolution". Among animal husbandry-related economic activities, Gujarat also has a thriving poultry industry and is a significant producer of wool, from both sheep and camel.

Industry

One of the leading industrialized states in India, Gujarat's industrial output includes chemicals and petrochemicals, textiles, food processing, engineering and metallurgy. Modern industry began in Gujarat during the second half of the 19th c. with the establishment of the first cotton textile mill in Bharuch. By the early 20th c., Ahmedabad was known worldwide as the "Manchester of the East" for its flourishing textile mills. At its peak in 1946, it had 74 mills. Today Arvind Mills, Ashima Textiles, Soma Textiles and Asarwa Mills are significant players in Gujarat's textile market. The state is also Asia's largest denim supplier and India's leading cotton producer. Textiles account for 23 percent of Gujarat's GDP and 12 percent of India's total textile exports.

Share Mania

The American Civil War changed the face of the cotton industry in western India. America was the main supplier of cotton to England, but when the war interrupted supplies, the demand for Indian cotton suddenly skyrocketed. Several cotton trading companies were floated in Mumbai and Ahmedabad between 1863 and 1865, and many Gujaratis tried to make a quick fortune by investing in their shares. People even left secure jobs hoping for a slice of the pie.

The Share Mania was led by a Surti, Premchand Raichand, considered the Napoleon of the Share Bazaar. A wealthy opium and cotton merchant, he was a shrewd entrepreneur who single-handedly controlled the market. When he bought or sold a share people would follow suit, and if he stepped into a bank, they assumed its shares would rise. In 1866 the market crashed. Premchand's power and wealth declined, but because of his philanthropy during his prime he is still remembered fondly in Gujarat.

Gujarat accounts for more than 20 percent of India's chemical production. Indian Petrochemicals Corporation Ltd (IPCL), now part of Reliance Industries Ltd, established the country's premier petrochemical complex near Vadodara. IPCL helped initiate the country's petrochemical revolution. Reliance Industries, India's leading petrochemical company, set up the world's largest integrated refinery and petrochemicals complex near Jamnagar in 1999.

About 40 percent of the country's pharmaceutical production comes from Gujarat, which supports approximately 3200 registered pharmaceutical industrial units such as Cadila and Torrent. The state is also at the forefront of exporting pharmaceutical research services with companies such as Dishman, Claris, Zydus and Oxygen Healthcare Research leading the way. A number of pharmaceutical Special Economic Zones (SEZ) are set to become a feature in the development of this sector and Gujarat as a whole.

Surat is the hub of the diamond cutting and polishing industry in India, with more than 10,000 processing units in and around the city. Other major diamond units are located in Ahmedabad, Palanpur, Bhavnagar, Valsad and Navsari. Gujarat administers the processing of eight out of every ten diamonds in the world. A major part of the diamond business in Antwerp, Belgium is controlled by Gujaratis from Palanpur.

More than 70 percent of India's salt is produced in Gujarat. Industries related to salt, such as bromine, soda ash, caustic soda, chlorine gas, gypsum, potassium and magnesium production are located in Mithapur (Jamnagar) as well as Bharuch, Kachchh, Valsad and Surendranagar. Gujarat produces about 94 percent of the country's soda ash.

Small Scale Industries
There are approximately 300,000 small scale industries spread throughout Gujarat and nearly half of them are concentrated in Ahmedabad, Surat and Rajkot districts. A large number of these are involved in textiles, textile machinery, chemicals and plastic processing. Industrial clusters are based in different areas: textiles in Ahmedabad, Dholka and Surat; tobacco processing in Anand; oil engines and machine tools in Rajkot; ceramics in Morbi, Thangadh and Wankaner; ship breaking in Alang; dyes in Ahmedabad, Vadodara and Vapi; pharmaceuticals and plastic processing in Ahmedabad and Vadodara.

Infrastructure
Besides possessing rich reserves of natural resources that sustain various industries, Gujarat has more highly developed infrastructure than many states in India. It has a network of nearly 75,000 km of roads, which the government continues to strengthen. It generates 55,727 MWh of power. Gujarat presently has one international and eight domestic airports and 41 ports. Three-quarters of India's private port cargo passes through Gujarat. The state accounts for seven percent of the country's natural gas production (valued at 100 million USD). It has the most extensive gas pipeline network in the country; the state also leads the nation in natural gas-fired power generation.

The Government's Role in Economic Growth
In an effort to accelerate economic growth, the state government has established many corporations that span the industries common to Gujarat. They provide infrastructure, finances, adequate research and administration to new or existing ventures. The Gujarat Industrial Development Corporation (GIDC), one of the larger corporations, develops industrial estates equipped with essential infrastructure such as power, water, drainage and roads. These estates also provide additional facilities such as banks, schools, shopping complexes, accommodation and other essential support to assist business people in setting up and running industries.

Tourism
The state government is making substantial efforts to develop the state as a prime tourist destination. Medical tourism is seen as having a particularly high growth potential because of the availability of high-quality, low-cost treatment in cardiology, neurology, orthopedics and ophthalmology. Gujarat already has the advantage of a well-planned transportation network,

a strong culture of hospitality and a safe and secure environment. Projects have been proposed to develop the coastline and restore heritage and pilgrimage areas.

Prominent Business Houses in Gujarat

ADANI The Adani group began business in 1988 with Adani Exports Ltd and has now expanded into infrastructure development and fast moving consumer goods. It also excels in varied areas such as distribution of natural gas, production of edible oil, operation of call centers and management of retail centers. Gujarat Adani Port Ltd developed India's first private port at Mundra in Kachchh.

ARVIND MILLS In 1931, the three Lalbhai brothers—Chimanbhai, Narottambhai and Kasturbhai—established Arvind Mills under the Lalbhai Group. The indigenous textile mill was established with a mere 55,000 USD at a time when the Swadeshi Movement was sweeping across India. Today Arvind Mills is one of the leading producers of denim in the world.

RELIANCE The Ambani brothers, Mukesh and Anil, respectively head Reliance Industries Limited (RIL) and the Reliance–Anil Dhirubhai Ambani Group. RIL is a Fortune Global 500 company that trades in sectors such as textiles, polyester, plastics, fiber intermediates, petrochemicals, petroleum refining and oil/gas exploration and production. Meanwhile, the Reliance–Anil Dhirubhai Ambani Group is involved in the power sector, telecommunications and financial services. Reliance Communications Ltd, headed by Anil Ambani, revolutionized telecommunications in India and made mobile phones commonplace. The company is the largest private sector information and communications entity in India.

TORRENT The Torrent Group set up its pharmaceutical operations in 1959 and later ventured into the power sector. Today the company has a generation capacity of 1271 MWh and distributes power to Ahmedabad, Surat and Gandhinagar.

ZYDUS CADILA One of the leading pharmaceutical companies in India today, Zydus Cadila was founded in 1952. About forty years later, the company restructured its operations and reemerged as Cadila Healthcare under the name Zydus Cadila. The company invests heavily in research and development and offers a range of healthcare products and services.

The Nirma Story

In 1969, a young scientist by the name of Karsanbhai Patel worked at a government lab, but dedicated all free time to making his dream a reality. Patel spent endless hours mixing soda ash with various chemicals in the hope of creating a new detergent. After a successful experiment, he packed his product into polythene bags and marketed the soap from door to door. At three rupees per kilogram, people readily purchased the product. It was a bargain compared to 13 rupees demanded by the cheapest brands in the market. Thus began the huge enterprise, Nirma, now a leading detergent manufacturer in India and a competitive player in the global market. Nirma continues to offer low-cost, quality products while revolutionizing the market for the middle class. The corporation has also given back to the community by setting up several institutes of higher learning, such as the reputed Nirma Institute of Management near Ahmedabad.

ECOLOGY

Gujarat's diversity in habitats includes the arid grasslands and scrub forests in Saurashtra and Kachchh; salt flats in the Ranns of Kachchh; deciduous forests along the eastern periphery of the state; and river-systems such as Narmada, Sabarmati, Mahi and Tapi. An abundance of wetlands scattered across the state attract an impressive range of migratory birds and a long coastline nurtures extensive marine ecosystems, including tidal mudflats, estuaries, reefs and sandy coasts. Along coastal areas of the Saurashtra peninsula, there are also mangrove forests and coral reefs, which are essential to supporting marine biodiversity.

These rich ecosystems nurture more than 2700 species of animals and 4300 species of plants. To protect this biodiversity, the state has set up four national parks (including the first marine reserve in the country) and 21 wildlife sanctuaries. The Gir National Park in Junagadh is the only remaining habitat of the Asiatic Lion. The Wild Ass Sanctuary in the Little Rann of Kachchh is home to the endemic Ghudkhar, a member of the horse family. Species indigenous to India and found in Gujarat include Nilgai (Blue bull), Chowsingha, Sloth bear and Blackbuck.

Ranns of Kachchh

The Little and Great Ranns of Kachchh form a subsection of the Indian desert zone. In strong contrast to the neighboring sandy Thar Desert of Rajasthan, the Ranns comprise of salt flats surrounded by widespread grasslands and thorny scrub, forming an exceptional ecosystem. During the monsoon, the Ranns are prone to flooding by sea water; and therefore, nurture plant species that have adapted to a saline-marshy environment. The area also hosts a number of bird species. The Great Rann is best known for its vast breeding colony of Lesser flamingoes while avifauna such as Houbara bustards and sand grouse inhabit the Little Rann.

Wetlands & Forests

Wetlands cover about 27,000 sq km of Gujarat. These low-lying ecosystems have water tables near the surface and serve as mating and feeding grounds for many animal and plant species. They also help to regulate the water cycle, recharge ground water, filter the water supply, prevent soil erosion and absorb floodwaters.

The forest cover, 7.7 percent of the total geographic area, is largely concentrated along Gujarat's eastern border (from the Dangs up to Sabarkantha) and the hilly portion of Saurashtra. More than 60 percent of Gujarat's population lives in rural areas and depend directly on forest resources, including fodder, timber and wood, for their daily needs. This has challenged the government's ability to maintain and regenerate forest areas. As a result, the State Department of Forestry promotes a Social Forestry Program, encouraging citizens and organizations to plant trees on non-forested land to increase the green cover of Gujarat.

Who's Who

Asiatic Lion (*Panthera leo persica*) Currently, only three hundred Asiatic lions roam the Sasan Gir Sanctuary. Listed amongst the most endangered species in the wildcat family, these lions are distinguished from their African cousins by their smaller mane, tufts of hair on the knees and a lighter colored coat. The female usually hunts, but the male assists when she faces an unrelenting enemy.

Sloth Bear (*Melursus ursinus*) This mammal is a nocturnal bear with a heavy coat of fur, a long muzzle and a protruding lip. Found only in the forests of South Asia, it is identifiable by a "V" mark on its breast. The Sloth bear feeds primarily on termites, fruits, insects and tubers. It hunts during the day, and can be spotted in trees searching for honeycombs in the summer. Its population is concentrated in the Jessore, Balaram-Ambaji (both in Banaskantha) and Ratanmahal (Dahod) sanctuaries.

Blackbuck (*Antilope cervicapra*) A graceful creature, this endangered antelope has a rich black coat with a white underbelly and white circles around its eyes. The male has spiral horns with three to four turns, while the female is usually hornless. When she does have horns, they are not ringed. Blackbucks can run almost thirty kilometers per hour when needed, as a natural defense against predators. This mammal can be seen at the Velavadar National Park and Sanctuary in Bhavnagar.

Chowsingha (*Tetracerus quadricornis*) The Chowsingha males are the world's only four-horned antelope. The shorter pair of horns rise from the front of the forehead, with the longer set placed between the ears. The female is hornless. These antelopes, the smallest in Asia, have a dull, yellow-brown coat, a white belly and thin legs marked by a prominent black stripe down the front.

Sambar (*Cervus unicolor*) This is the largest deer found in India. It has impressive antlers that can grow up to one meter long. It has a shaggy and coarse, dark brown coat and grows hair on its neck. Extremely shy, the Sambar lives in forest dense areas and prefers to graze or feed late in the evenings. It generally travels in small groups of two to five.

Nilgai (*Boselaphus tragocamelus*) Found only in India, the Nilgai is a member of the bovine family and is closely related to the spiral-horned antelopes found in Africa. It has the face of a deer and the body of a bull, lending to its other name—Blue bull. The males are grey or blue-black in color, while the females have a yellow to light brown coat. Strong in build, both genders have a small mane at the back of the neck and a beard dangling from the front.

Ghudkhar (*Equus hemionus khur*) The Little Rann of Kachchh is the only place where the critically endangered Ghudkhar or Indian Wild Ass can be found. It belongs to the horse family, but resembles a donkey. Physical characteristics include toes completely encased in hooves, a gray-brown coat, a coarse dark mane and a short tufted tail with a black tip. It does not like to be approached and generally avoids human contact. Locally, the animal is prized for its hide and excellent meat—one of the reasons for its dwindling numbers.

Flamingoes (*Phoenicopterus sp.*) The flamingo has a long neck, tall legs with webbed feet and black flight feathers on its wings. It obtains its pink color from a diet of shellfish and algae, which are rich in carotenes. These birds bend their heads backwards to dip their beaks into shallow water to capture food. The beak siphons the food while filtering out mud and silt. Flamingoes build cone-shaped mud nests about 30-60 cm high and with a depression on top. The female lays only one to two eggs at a time. Both parents take turns incubating the eggs by straddling the nest with their legs folded flat on either side. The commonly found species in Gujarat are the Greater flamingo (*Phoenicopterus ruber*) and the Lesser flamingo *(Phoeniconaias minor)*, respectively the largest and smallest of the species.

Great Indian Bustard (*Ardeotis nigriceps*) The Great Indian Bustard, the most endangered group of the bustard family, is found in the deserts and grasslands of Gujarat and Rajasthan. It has a black head, brown cover and white underbelly. The male can measure over a meter tall and has an additional black band across the breast, while the female is slightly smaller. There are less than 1000 Great Indian Bustards in existence today; their numbers are declining on account of habitat loss.

Sarus Crane (*Grus antigone*) Considered the world's tallest flying bird, the Sarus Crane is nearly extinct in Gujarat. It lives in grasslands and around fresh water and nests on the ground, laying two to three eggs at a time. Both the male and the female take turns sitting on the eggs, although the male is the main protector. An adult crane is grey in color with a white crown on its bare red head.

Birds

Gujarat lies on the migratory route of thousands of bird species, making it a birdwatcher's paradise. The annual southwest monsoon (mid-Jul to Sep) brings desperately needed rains that replenish water bodies and regenerate grasslands, creating perfect habitats for avifauna such as the flamingo, stork, ibis, goose, duck, Sarus crane, bustard, florican and pelican. A sizeable population of the world's Demoiselle and Common cranes spend their winter in Gujarat and about half the world's Lesser florican, an endangered species, breeds in the grasslands of Kachchh, Saurashtra and Dahod districts during the monsoon. The vulnerable Imperial and Greater-spotted eagles also migrate to the state during winter. The only known breeding area of the Lesser flamingo is found in the Ranns of Kachchh. For a complete listing of resident and migratory bird species found in Gujarat, visit www.birdsofgujarat.net.

In addition to water bodies across the state, the Banni grasslands (Kachchh), Gir National Park and Wildlife Sanctuary (Junagadh), Khijadiya Bird Sanctuary (Jamnagar), Marine National Park (Jamnagar), Little Rann of Kachchh, Nal Sarovar (Ahmedabad District), Thol (Mahesana) and Velavadar National Park (Bhavnagar District) are excellent for birdwatching.

Challenges

Gujarat faces several ecological challenges, primarily posed by urbanization and industrialization. Both factors have started to strain natural resources before ecological zones can regenerate their supplies. Populations in urban centers use more resources and produce more pollution. Communities dependent on specific habitats like the grasslands also contribute to their depletion. Changes in land-use patterns, deterioration of grasslands, pressures of increasing livestock, invasion of exotic flora and fauna species, desertification and pollution all create threats to Gujarat's ecosystems.

RELIGION

Throughout its history, Gujarat has welcomed and embraced settlers and merchants from all corners of the world and adapted their ideologies, belief systems and practices to its own. The traditions of one faith seamlessly merge with those of another, where Hindus worship Muslim saints and Muslims celebrate traditionally Hindu festivals. Followers of the seven major faiths of the world can be found in Gujarat. They not only live in harmony, but also embody the philosophy of *sarva dharma samabhava*—respect for all religions.

Hinduism

Hinduism claims no single founder or definitive holy book, nor does its origin date back to any single point in time. Considered by historians to be the world's oldest religion, Hinduism has been in practice for at least 5000 years. In Gujarat, it was the dominant religion until the introduction of Buddhism in the 3rd c. BC, which was then succeeded by Jainism. Hinduism borrowed strongly from both these faiths and resumed as the prevailing religion after the 2nd c. AD. Hindus make up about 89 percent of Gujarat's population. Two of the most sacred pilgrimage places for Hindus are situated in Gujarat: the seaside temple of Somnath, dedicated to Shiva and the Dwarkadeesh Temple of Krishna in Dwarka. Other auspicious sites include the Ranchhodrai temple dedicated to Krishna in Dakor; the Shakti temples of Pavagadh, Ambaji and Chotila; and the Swaminarayan temples in Ahmedabad, Bochasan and Vadtal.

Derived from the Vedic phrase *sanatana dharma*, which means "the eternal religion", Hinduism is perpetual and open to everyone and does not adhere to any specific doctrine. Hindus ultimately seek *moksha* or liberation from the cycles of rebirth. The three paths shown by scriptures to attain this salvation are *bhaktiyoga* (devotion), *karmayoga* (selfless action) and *jnanayoga* (self knowledge and meditation). Reincarnation is governed by the law of *karma*, which states that every action, word or thought produces a corresponding reaction. This cycle of cause and effect spawns *samsara* (cycle of life and death). In order to maintain good *karma*, one must live according to their *dharma*, moral law combined with spiritual discipline that guides each individual life.

Although Hinduism is widely perceived as polytheistic (the worship of more than one God), it actually asserts one cosmic force that has 330 million manifestations. Many Hindus practice idol worship, in which the deity helps the individual concentrate and prepare the consciousness for its search of the eternal truth. It represents a means and not the end itself. The Hindu tradition has a number of sacred texts, classified into two categories: *shruti* (that which is heard and of divine origin) and *smriti* (that which is remembered and of human origin). *Shruti* texts include the four *Vedas* (*Rigveda, Yajurveda, Samaveda and Atharvaveda*) along with the *Upanishads*. *Smriti* writings include the *Puranas*, the famous epic stories of the *Ramayana* and the *Mahabharata* and the epic poem, the *Bhagavad Gita*.

More on Hinduism

PUJA AND AARTI Chanting (*mantra*), prostrations, meditation (*dhyana*), singing devotional songs (*bhajans*), austerity (*tapas*), offering food (*prasad*) and reading of scriptures (*svadhyaya*) are all various forms of *puja* or worship practiced by Hindus. These may be performed individually or in groups. It is also common to see people's foreheads marked with different variations of sandalwood, ash and vermilion. These markings, called *tilak*, symbolize respect for the divine within and differ based on the sect to which the follower belongs.

ROADSIDE SHRINES Rocks smeared with vermilion, trees wrapped in string, earthen horses as offerings alongside roads—these are just a few of the many examples of roadside shrines that turn up at every corner. Hinduism is deeply rooted in respecting the natural elements and all forms of life, and the infinite styles of worship signify the acknowledgment of God in all of these representations.

RIVERS Hindus consider water a cleansing medium and hold rivers in high esteem for their powers of ablution. Participating in cleansing baths, submerging idols and sacred objects into bodies of water on significant occasions and releasing the ashes of the dead into flowing water are just a few of the Hindu rituals associated with water.

COWS The cow is compared to a mother, who gives her milk to sustain her children. Milk is also used to process clarified ghee and curd, which are important elements in Hindu rites. After the hunter-gatherer stage, but before settled agriculture became the norm, cattle was the main commodity used to measure wealth. Cows in particular were valued because of their multiple uses and came to be seen as holy. These are a few of the reasons that cows have the freedom to wander as they please.

In theory, Hinduism is divided into three major factions: Vaishnavism, Shaivism and Shaktism. Vaishnavas conceive Vishnu as the supreme manifestation. During the Bhakti Movement (900-1700), which promoted reverence and adoration for God, several of Gujarat's most popular Vaishnav cults took birth. One of the most prominent followings is Pushtimarg, established by

Vallabhacharya (1471-1531) and spread through Gujarat by his son Vithalnathji. Its followers believe that God and his creations are one in the same, and therefore, the joy and grace associated with God exists in every being. They worship Lalji and Shreenathji, the child and adult forms of Krishna respectively. Another prevalent sect is Swaminarayan, which was founded by Swami Sahajanand at the turn of the 19th c. He spent eight years in deep penance before arriving in Gujarat, where he spent his life teaching the importance of unity during a time of excessive religious division. Breaking through class and caste divisions, he also combined spiritual development and social service. Swaminarayan followers give prominence to gurus as the medium between God and humans. It is divided into several sects including BAPS, which has a large following among Gujaratis. On the other hand, Shaivas perceive Shiva as the principal deity. Shiva is often represented by a *linga,* which is encompassed by a *yoni,* the combination of which represents the balance between the masculine and feminine. Followers of Shaktism worship the Goddess Shakti as the cosmic energy of the universe. She is often called by various names (Kali, Durga, Chamunda and more) that depict a range of conflicting attributes, but comprehensively represent the ultimate divine force. Each clan also has a *kuldevi,* a goddess who protects them. Most Hindus, however, give respect to all forms of divinity, which in many instances include the Godheads of other religions.

Islam

Islam was introduced to India by Arab traders long before Muslims invaded the country. Islam was introduced to Gujarat in a significant way in the 13th c. when Alauddin Khilji conquered the region and brought it under the Delhi Sultanate and Sufi saints played a considerable role in spreading the faith. Today, Muslims represent about nine percent of the state's current population.

The term Islam means "submission" and the followers of Islam are Muslims, or those who submit to God. It propounds one God, Allah, and his prophets. The holy book is the *Koran,* which contains revelations of God as dictated to Muhammad, the last prophet. Islam believes that each Muslim will reap the fruit of his actions on judgment day (*qayamat*). All Muslims have five obligations: believing in only one God, Allah and in his messenger, Muhammad (*shahadat*); fasting during the holy month of Ramzan (*swam*); offering charity (*zakat*); making at least one pilgrimage to Mecca if possible (*hajj*); and offering *namaz* or prayer five times a day (*salah*). The call for prayer echoes from the minarets of mosques (Islamic place of worship) to summon the faithful. There are no depictions of God in the mosque. Muslims are subdivided into two major sects in India – Sunni (those who follow the traditional interpretation of Islam) and Shia (those who believe that Ali, the son-in-law of Mohammad, and Ali's descendants are the leaders of the Muslims). Sufism, which spread in Gujarat around the 12th c., is a sect of Islamic mysticism that deems all occurrences as a single manifestation of one truth. In India, this sect fuses elements of Islam and Hinduism. Major Islamic festivals include Ramzan (the ninth month of the lunar year during which many Muslims fast from dawn to dusk), Id-ul-Fitr (the last day of Ramzan celebrated with feasting), Muharram (see **Fairs and Festivals**) and Id-ul-Zuha (celebrated with sacrificing goats and offering prayers in commemoration of Hazrat Ibrahim, who almost sacrificed his own son to prove his faith to Allah).

Jainism

Although Jainism accounts for just over one percent of Gujarat's population, it has always wielded a strong influence, which continues to pervade the local culture. *Ahimsa* (non-violence), a central principle in everyday Jain life, was later adopted by modern sects of Hinduism. The Jain influence also accounts for the high percentage of vegetarians in the state. Unlike Buddhism, the Jain faith did not spread beyond the subcontinent, but it was a dominant religion throughout the history of medieval Gujarat. It also gave rise to the power of the mercantile class in the state, a social feature that sets Gujarat apart from most Indian states. Mahatma Gandhi also internalized many values of Jainism and implemented them in his life and actions.

The term Jain comes form the Sanskrit word *jina*, which means "he who conquers". Jain philosophy is based upon universal truths governed by natural laws and declares that each human being has the capacity to reach the ultimate state of liberation solely by his deeds. Jains follow five vows to help them along their path to liberation: non-violence (*ahimsa*), truth (*satya*), non-stealing (*asteya*), chastity (*brahmacharya*) and non-possession (*aparigraha*). Non-violence is practiced through strict vegetarianism and positive thinking while self-discipline is considered a means to attain nirvana (*moksha*). Compassion and equality for all life is central to Jainism. The fundamental principles of the faith include religious tolerance, moral purity, harmony between self and environment and spiritual contentment. One can eliminate *karma* and attain salvation by following the path of right faith (*samyak-darshana*), right knowledge (*samyak-jnana*) and right conduct (*samyak-charitra*). Right knowledge is considered the proper knowledge of the six universal substances (*dravya*) and the nine fundamental truths (*tattva*), while right faith is determined by conviction in that knowledge. Right conduct includes non-violence, self-purification, compassion, penance, austerity and meditation. Jains worship the *tirthankars* or liberated souls. Mahavir ("the great hero"), who lived in 6th c. BC, was the 24th *tirthankar* in his era and is considered the founder of Jainism. He was a near contemporary of the Buddha and rejected the caste system, along with the Hindu belief in the cycle of births.

The two primary sects in Jainism are Shvetambar (who wear white clothes and believe that women can attain salvation) and Digambar (who wear no clothing and deny that women can reach liberation). Gujarat hosts a larger concentration of Shvetambars. Important Jain festivals include Paryushan, an eight-day period where followers practice a strict routine of meditation and self control, and Mahavir Jayanti, the birth anniversary of the last *tirthankar*. Jain temples can be found all over Gujarat, and are usually known for their stone structures and intricate carvings. The temples on Shetrunjaya Hill in Palitana are considered to be the most auspicious pilgrimage site for Jains. Mt Girnar, Khumbaria and Taranga are also important destinations.

The Jain Dilemma

Originally, Jains did not transcribe the teachings of Mahavira or the main principles of the faith in observation of *aparigraha* (non-possession). In fact they abstained from all documentation and refrained from carrying books, instead depending entirely on oral history. About 800 years after Mahavir, around 2nd c. AD, a series of consecutive droughts plagued the region for several years and led to the malnutrition and memory loss of Jain monks. In an urgency to record the wisdom of these men, a council was called to Valabhipur (in present day Bhavnagar District) and all monks were asked to recite and scribe the knowledge they could recollect. Even conflicting information was documented and accredited to the respective monk.

Sikhism

Sikhism is based on the teachings of ten gurus who lived between the 15th and 17th c. in India. These gurus are believed to have directly received the word of God. The founder of the Sikhism was Guru Nanak, who was born in 1469 and preached a message of love and understanding.

He criticized the blind rituals of other religions. The last guru, Gobind Singh, institutionalized Sikhism. Before his death he designated, as the eleventh and the eternal guru, the *Guru Granth Sahib*, the sacred text containing the words of the ten gurus. Sikhism decrees that there is one God, who still exists in the world, but cannot take human form. During Mughal rule, many non-Muslims were persecuted, this led Guru Gobind Singh to teach Sikhs to defend themselves and he prescribed five sacred symbols to create a unified identity. The five sacred symbols (*panj kakkar*) include: uncut hair (*kesh*), comb (*kangha*), dagger (*kirpan*), bracelet on the right hand (*kara*) and shorts (*kachchha*).

Unlike other religions, Sikhism does not aim at salvation, but instead teaches that people should live a life of duty and learn to control anger, greed, attachment, lust and pride. The Sikh population in Gujarat is very small and consists of largely recent migrants to the state. Two historical *gurudwaras* (Sikh temples) can be found in Gujarat, at Lakhpat in Kachchh and the Chadar Saheb in Bharuch.

Christianity
Saint Thomas, one of the twelve disciples of Jesus, carried Christianity with him to Kerala in 52 AD. It spread through Gujarat and Maharashtra with the arrival of the Portuguese. Most Gujarati Christians belong to the Church of North India. In Gujarat, Christians make up 0.6 percent of the total population. The main Christian festivals celebrated in Gujarat include Christmas and Easter.

Buddhism
Founded in India in 525 BC by Siddhartha Gautama or Buddha (the enlightened one), the faith is based on his teachings. Buddhism spread far and wide through the subcontinent in the 3rd c. BC under the efforts of Emperor Ashoka, who commissioned the erection of rock edicts documenting the teachings of Buddha across his empire. Some of these Ashokan edicts still exist at Junagadh. In Gujarat, Buddhism was mainly centered in Saurashtra and Kachchh, where Buddhist caves and remains of ancient monasteries can still be seen. In the subsequent centuries, the faith faced a decline in popularity in western India because of the Hindu revival and the growing influence of Jainism. However, Buddhism flourished in many other parts of Asia, where it continues to thrive. Today, a small percentage of the Gujarat population practices this faith. Many of them are Neo-Buddhists who converted in 1956 along with Dr Babasaheb Ambedkar, an ex-Harijan, prominent jurist and the Architect of the Constitution of India, who led a mass movement for the eradication of untouchability.

Buddhism is a philosophy coordinated with a code of physical and intellectual morality. Buddhists seek nirvana, the release from the cycle of rebirth and suffering. The basic doctrines of Buddhism include the four noble truths: Truth of suffering (*dukkha sacca*), truth of the origin of suffering (*samudaya sacca*), truth of the cessation of suffering (*nirodha sacca*) and truth of the path leading to the cessation of suffering (*magga sacca*). These truths are achieved by following the eight fold path which leads to the removal of suffering and the attainment of wisdom (*panna*) through righteous aspirations and understanding, following the precepts (*sila*) of right speech, right action and right livelihood and the concentration of mind (*samadhi*) attained by right exertion, right attentiveness and right concentration. Buddhism accepts the presupposition of *samsara*, in which living beings are trapped in a continual cycle of birth and death based on their previous physical and mental actions (*karma*). Buddhism is strongly based on meditation and the observance of a moral code. The sacred text of Buddhism is the *Tripitaka* (the three baskets), which comprises *Vinaya Pitaka* (monastic law), *Sutta Pitaka* (words of the Buddha) and *Abhidhamma Pitaka* (philosophical commentaries). Buddhism gave rise to two major sects: Hinayana (dominant in Sri Lanka and Southeast Asia) and Mahayana (based in China, Mongolia, Korea and Japan).

Zoroastrianism

When the Arabs invaded Persia in 650 AD, a group of Zoroastrians, the followers of the prophet Spitaman Zarathushtra or Zoroaster, fled persecution and sailed to India, initially landing on the Gujarat coast. They quickly integrated with the local community, adopted the local language and lifestyle, but maintained their distinct culture. Their important holy centers include Sanjan and Udwada. Known as Parsis, their settlements still exist in some towns in south Gujarat, but most of the community resides in Mumbai and Pune. Their numbers are dwindling because of a low birth rate, growing inter-community marriages and stringent rules against recognizing mixed-blood children as Parsis.

Only Parsis may enter the *agiari* (fire temple) where they worship Ahura Mazda, their God. An eternal flame *(aatash)* helps them concentrate on their worship. The holy book of Zoroastrianism is called the *Avesta,* which includes the *gathas*, a series of five hymns that compose the original words of Zoroaster. Adherents follow a three fold path founded on good thoughts, good words and good deeds. Parsis believe in a dualist ideology where the omnipotent God Ahura Mazda represents good and Angra Mainyu embodies evil. Together, the two represent the entire universe, including mankind who must choose between good and evil. The faith also claims that in the afterlife the human soul is judged by God as to whether it did more good or evil in its life and is sent to heaven or hell accordingly. The Parsis dispose of their dead by exposing the corpse on stone towers called Towers of Silence, where the remains are devoured by vultures. Their key festivals include Pateti (the Parsi New Year) and Khordad Saal (the birth anniversary of Zoroaster).

Judaism

The largest community of Jews in India belongs to the sect called Bene Israel, who arrived on the subcontinent sometime in the first millennium AD. History holds that their ancestors were shipwrecked and the few surviving members swam to a village on the Konkan coast (from the southern tip of Gujarat to Goa) where they resettled. In the 19th c., the community migrated to major cities across the northwestern regions, including Ahmedabad, in search of better jobs. Gujarat still hosts a small population of Jews in Ahmedabad; however, since 1950 the community has mostly migrated to Israel. The Magen Abraham Synagogue in Ahmedabad, built in 1933, is the only synagogue in the state. India is one of the very few countries where Jews were never persecuted.

ARCHITECTURE

The earliest surviving architecture in Gujarat is from the period of the Indus Valley Civilization (IVC). At its peak, about 4500 years ago, it covered a vast area stretching from Punjab in North India to the Pakistan-Iran border and into Rajasthan and Gujarat. Although contemporaneous with ancient Egypt, Mesopotamia and China, it was more extensive and had sophisticated urban characteristics such as baked brick houses with courtyards, networks of brick-lined drains and uniformity in urban form and character across a large territory. Its script, so far found only in short legends on seals and a few other objects, is yet to be deciphered.

Lothal, 80 km from Ahmedabad, and Dholavira in the Great Rann of Kachchh are the most remarkable of the IVC sites discovered in Gujarat. Lothal is easier to reach and has been more extensively excavated. It is the only IVC port found with a dock, possibly the world's first.

Roughly between the decline of the IVC (around 1400 BC) and the advent of Buddhism in Saurashtra (3rd c. BC), Krishna and his Yadav clan colonized Dwarka and its surrounding areas in Saurashtra. The only significant relics from this period lie undersea off the Dwarka coast, accessible only to marine archeologists at this time.

Architecture from the Buddhist period mainly consists of rock-cut caves, water cisterns and a few primitive stepwells in some parts of Saurashtra. The most easily accessible of these are at Uparkot in Junagadh and Talaja, near Bhavnagar.

The oldest existing constructed temple in Gujarat stands in Gop (Jamnagar District). It is dedicated to the sun and belongs to the 7th c. AD when the Maitraka dynasty (5th-8th c.) ruled Saurashtra. The temple stands on a high platform and has the distinctive Maitraka feature—a layered pyramid-shaped roof embellished with horse-shoe shaped *chaitya* arch motifs. The largest temple of this period is Bileshvar, about 30 km south of Gop. Many other Maitraka temples lie scattered over Saurashtra. Together with those of the Saindhava period (8th-10th c.), they mark the evolution of the pyramidal roof into a *shikhara* or spire with gradually curving edges, shaped like an inverted beehive.

Under the Solankis, temple architecture climaxed. The inverted beehive-shaped *shikhara* grew more elaborate and refined. The walls, columns and the *shikhara* were profusely adorned with carvings of abstract, floral and animal motifs. Niches were assigned to gods and goddesses, and other celestial beings. The *toran*, a symbolic, free-standing gateway with ornate columns and a beam across the top, was built in front of some temples.

Of the major ancient Solanki temples in Gujarat, none of them are both pristine and intact. Damage caused by time, natural disaster and invasions along with the tradition of rededicating a temple to a deity other than its original (often from the Sun to Shiva) have led to the rebuilding and repairs of these structures, often with additions and alterations. The Sun Temple at Modhera, completed in 1027 AD, is one important temple that comes close to being in its original condition, though not entirely intact.

During early Solanki rule, Hindu and Jain temples were architecturally similar. It was under royal patronage that the latter started acquiring a distinct personality. Like their Hindu counterparts, Jain temples were also subject to frequent alterations. Together they represent an elegant synthesis of architecture, sculpture and ornamentation. The significant difference is the heavy use of marble in Jain temples, whereas Hindu temples are largely built in sandstone or limestone.

After the founding of Ahmedabad in 1411 AD, the greatest contribution of Gujarat to what some refer to as "Indo-Saracenic" architecture is the integration the Sultanate achieved between Islamic form and Jain and Hindu detail work in the design of mosques and tombs. In the Muslim world, these two building types tend to be monumental in scale and simple in the use of ornamentation. In Ahmedabad and elsewhere in the Sultanate, while the spatial organization of the buildings was essentially Islamic, the mutually compatible scale and the adornment were determined entirely by local master craftsmen who had a long tradition of executing fine temples. Many motifs used here, especially those representing nature, would be frowned upon by orthodox Islam, which favored abstract geometric patterns. In Gujarat the new motifs were not only accepted, but actively encouraged. This revolutionary achievement influenced Mughal architecture in North India from the reign of Akbar onward.

Even though at least three of the initial six "great" Mughal emperors had close associations with Gujarat, they made very few significant architectural contributions, and nothing comparable to the internationally known masterpieces built in Agra, Delhi, Lahore and Fatehpur Sikri.

The Marathas held sway over considerable parts of Gujarat after the disintegration of the Mughal Empire in the early 18th c., but were generally engaged either in internal feuds or in plundering the province. Only the Gaekwads, who ruled from Vadodara, made architectural contributions of any consequence. Consisting mainly of civic buildings, mansions and palaces, these bore European influences, as did most of the architecture patronized by royalty all over India from the 19th c. onwards. They were encouraged by the British, the then de facto rulers. Outstanding instances of such European-influenced architecture and urban design from that period exist in many capitals of princely states all over Gujarat. Jamnagar, Morbi and Gondal offer some of the more impressive examples, especially of urban design.

Water Structures

An important architectural form is the stepwell or *vav*. Gujarat offers the finest examples of these subterranean structures that were usually built by a patron for a village or for travelers along country roads. They are maintained by the local communities, store drinking water and function as a space for social interaction. Flights of steps form a long corridor descending to the main well shaft. To prevent the side walls from caving in, braces are introduced at the landings. In many *vavs* these are elaborated into pavilions, adding one story at each landing and form cool places to retreat from the heat on summer afternoons. The earliest rudimentary *vavs* predate the Solanki period, but the greatest examples are from the 10th to the 16th c. The most magnificent example from the Solanki period is the Ranki Vav at Patan (1063) while the Rudabai Vav (1499) at Adalaj near Ahmedabad exemplifies the craftsmanship of the Sultanate era. Although *vavs* were essentially secular, the sanctity of water drove the builders to incorporate a variety of idols and religious symbols into the structures.

Another water structure, usually rectangular in plan, is the *kund*—a pond surrounded by short flights of steps leading to the water. Normally built near a temple, its function was ritualistic, and it often had small shrines on its periphery or steps. Like stepwells, the earliest *kunds* precede the Solanki era, but climax during it, such as the one at Modhera.

The *talav* or *sarovar* is the third type of water body, usually polygonal in plan and often upgraded from older irrigation tanks by adding masonry steps, elaborate sluices, ramps and some decorative elements. Outstanding examples from the Solanki period are the Sahasralinga in Patan and Munsar in Viramgam. From the Sultanate era we have Kankaria in Ahmedabad, the tank at Sarkhej, Khan Sarovar in Patan and the Malav and Khan Talavs in Dholka. Unlike the *vav* and the *kund*, the *talav* was used for mundane purposes such as bathing and washing and as a water source for cattle. An exceptional feature of some of the finest *talavs* is the sluice gate, an exquisitely adorned water inlet with three round circular openings.

Secular Architecture

Most of the surviving ancient and medieval architecture is monumental, civic or institutional, but hardly any notable examples of secular architecture remain today. This is because temples, water structures and monasteries were built to be permanent, but shelters, even of the most elevated people, were, like human life itself, considered transient. They were built largely in wood, brick-and-mud and tiles. Lower down the economic scale the materials used may have been adobe, wattle-and-daub (mud and grass), loose stone masonry and thatch. Routine maintenance and repair were part of living in these buildings and when abandoned, they would fall apart and the debris would be used elsewhere.

Even today, a large part of rural Gujarat lives in these types of shelters, which include some exceptional examples of vernacular architecture, definitive statements of the environments and cultures that produce them. These include the *bhunga,* a round hut, with mud walls and a thatch roof that belongs to pastoral and semi-nomadic communities of Kachchh. It was one structural form that largely survived the 2001 earthquake. Also noteworthy are the rich variety of traditional house forms, built with materials from the surrounding forests, found in different communities along the tribal belt. Frequent repairs and rebuilding mean that some features are continually changing. For example thatch roofs may be replaced by tile or tin sheet, and mud walls by brick. However, the essential design, the use of space and the rich embellishment (with prominent mirror work) live on. A special feature of such houses is their mud-and-cow dung floors, known as *lipan,* which need regular maintenance. These are common all over India, but in Gujarat a special effort goes into beautifying them, with arc-shaped patterns impressed by hand into each fresh layer, making even the floor an important sensual element.

The Pols

Pols are a distinctive feature of the important old cities of Gujarat, particularly Patan, Ahmedabad and Palanpur. They are enclosed residential clusters entered by gates, which used to shut at night. Usually there would be just one gate, occasionally two, but there would also be secret passages, known only to the residents, that connected to adjoining *pols.* These were meant for use in periods of strife when the main entrance might be besieged for several days. The essence of a *pol* is a network of small streets, side lanes, shrines and open community spaces with a *chabutro,* a birdhouse raised on a pole to feed birds in the neighborhood. A *chabutro* is an inheritance of the Jain tradition of *jeevadaya* or compassion for all life forms. Historically, each *pol* was specific to a community, caste or occupational group, and each house was a single-family unit. The neighborhood was formed based on cultural homogeneity rather than economic status.

The typical *pol* house, usually two to four stories high, is deep and narrow and shares side walls with its neighbors. Each story projects beyond the one below, minimizes sun and heat penetration and shades the actual streets during the summer. The core of the house is a courtyard, which lets out heated air by convection. Organized around it is a series of semi-open spaces and rooms. In many of the houses the courtyard also forms the roof of the *tanka,* a spacious underground tank that collects rainwater during the monsoon to be used year round. A tacit system based on degrees of privacy governs who can enter the house and how far past the courtyard or up the steep, single-flight stairs they can wander.

The more affluent families owned broader houses called *havelis,* with larger rooms and courtyards and more extensive exteriors. The *havelis,* as well as many of the modest houses, often had exquisitely carved wooden façades with columns, struts, beams, balconies, windows and doors, all lending to the integrated whole. Unfortunately, only a few of these houses have survived the onslaught of modern real estate development in the *pols.* Those that do remain demonstrate an appealing sense of the understated grandeur that was typical of Ahmedabad not so long ago.

Modern Architecture

Beginning in the 1950s, Ahmedabad became something of a Mecca of modern architecture and design. The pioneer was Indian architect AP Kanvinde, whose building for the Ahmedabad Textile Industry's Research Association was the harbinger of the International Style in Gujarat.

Soon after, Le Corbusier, designer of the new city of Chandigarh in Punjab, designed four buildings in Ahmedabad, including the Sanskar Kendra and Ahmedabad Textile Mills Association. Balkrishna Doshi, apprentice to Le Corbusier in Paris, came to Ahmedabad as his site architect and settled in the city. Doshi set up a practice and founded the renowned School of Architecture in 1962. The LD Institute of Indology, Kasturbhai Lalbhai Campus, Amdavad ni Gufa, Gandhi Labour Institute (all in Ahmedabad) and the Gujarat State Fertilizer Corporation (near Vadodara) are a few of his acclaimed works.

A year before the School of Architecture was founded came the National Institute of Design, steered by the vision of the world-renowned designers Charles and Ray Eames. The same year saw the beginning of the Indian Institute of Management, designed by Louis Kahn, another international giant, which was built over the next few years. The site architect, Anant Raje, designed most of the buildings for the IIM campus from 1974 to 1997.

The renowned Indian architect, Charles Correa also did some of his early work in Ahmedabad, such as the museum at the Sabarmati Ashram, characterized by a square modular grid of free-flowing spaces and tiled pyramidal roofs.

The reputation of Ahmedabad as a center for international architecture is largely due to these great works and many others that followed. It is equally important to remember the enlightened and visionary patronage of the local leaders who brought in such outstanding talent and gave them the freedom to express their best work, setting examples for others to follow. This helped to reinstate the excellence of design and execution in the same spirit that the Solankis and the Sultanate did.

LITERATURE

Oral traditions in the form of folk songs, narratives, theater and aphorisms, were the prominent form of literature throughout India, including Gujarat, until modern times. Of course, the stories and messages evolved as they passed through generations, leaving behind numerous versions of each myth and legend.

The earliest literature was based on religious themes. Before Gujarati emerged as its own linguistic identity, the works were in Sanskrit and later in Prakrit. Gujarati literature began to take shape in the 10th c., with Hemachandracharya's grammar book, *Siddha Hema Shabdanushasan*.

The literary tradition in Gujarat is largely linked to the Bhakti Movement, which swept across most of India between the 12th and 17th c. In Gujarat, it began with the poet Narsinh Mehta (1408-80), who spent his life practicing and advocating selfless human compassion while facing immense opposition from his community. The movement continued with Mirabai (1498-1547), one of the foremost woman poets, claimed equally by Gujarat and Rajasthan. She dedicated her life to the worship of Krishna. Mirabai along with a number of other saint-poets (poets who wrote in praise of God) were also great musicians and composers. Akhyana, a form of story telling through verse, was popularized by Premananda (1636-1734). He was also the first Maanbhatt, a poet who sings to the accompaniment of music created by a copper pot (*maan*) struck with ringed fingers. Many medieval oral forms are still popular today.

The 19th c. ushered in a focus on man's relationship with his social environment. Narmad (1833-86) pioneered Gujarati prose and modern literature through his essays on social revolution. He opposed religious orthodoxy and wrote about self-government and establishing a single national language. He published *Dandiyo,* a newsletter to increase community awareness against British rule. He also introduced Western literary forms and developed the Gujarati language by using new phrases to convey his ideas. Govardhanram Tripathi (1886-1907) penned the four-part novel *Sarasvatichandra,* depicting the complexities of society and social reform. It is one of the most popular and influential novels of Gujarati literature.

The beginning of the World War I also marked the beginning of the Gandhian era (1915-45) in Gujarati literature, characterized by nationalism, humanism and a deep social consciousness that attempted to reach out to the masses. K M Munshi (1887-1971) brought history to life with his trilogy based on the Solanki dynasty. Zaverchand Meghani (1897-1947) compiled and published the rich repertoire of oral traditions of Saurashtra. Pannalal Patel wrote of rural Gujarat, while Sundaram highlighted the exploitation of the poor. Umashankar Joshi's (1911-88) most significant contribution was to liberate poetry from the restraints of poetic meter by introducing free verse.

In the post-Gandhian era, new literary trends replaced old conventions, though traditional forms always found their patrons. Diction transformed as old words acquired new meaning and language and imagery became more bold and direct. Literature moved away from addressing social issues, as writers turned their gaze inwards and wrote for personal satisfaction. Many post-war genres of western literature were emulated in Gujarat, often in social and psychological contexts very different than those that gave birth to them in the west.

An important post-Gandhian genre is Dalit literature, which voices the atrocities suffered by this oppressed class. Although many orthodox scholars refuse to acknowledge it as real literature, arguing that it reads like a documentary and lacks creativity, these works offer insight into an otherwise overlooked segment of society.

THEATER

Gujarat has a rich tradition of stage art that often combines theater, music and popular literary or social themes.

Bhavai
One of the most popular forms of theater in Gujarat is Bhavai, which is said to have been started by Asait Thakar, a Brahmin from Mahesana. Ostracized by his community, he used his poetic inclination and the support of his three sons to introduce this folk form that mixes dance, song and drama. It was traditionally performed in the village square and was characterized by farce and satire aimed at certain sections of society. The word "Bhavai" is derived from the Sanskrit root "bhava", which means expression. A typical performance begins with a prayer to the Mother Goddess. Characters known as Rangli and Ranglo introduce the theme and add continuity throughout the performance. Instruments such as the *harmonium, sarangi* (an Indian stringed

instrument), *pakhawaj* (the two faced horizontal drum) and *jhanjh* (cymbals) accompany the play. Dialogues were originally in verse and often sung by the actors. Female roles were played by men in the earlier days of Bhavai. Each episode of a Bhavai is called a *vesh*. Only 60 of the 360 *vesh* that Asait Thakar wrote survive. Some troupes still perform Bhavai while the contemporary street plays, enacted by social activists, have evolved from the Bhavai format.

Modern Drama

Modern theater in Gujarat started in the latter part of the 19th c. Rooted in Parsi theater, which is usually light comedy and borrows from western models, it had no links to Bhavai. The style was spectacular, loud and catered to mass appeal. Ranchhodbhai Udayram (1837-1923), popularly hailed as the Father of Gujarati Drama, tried to counter this trend with plays that promoted awareness. Chandravadan Mehta strengthened this effort with themes that encouraged the use of Gujarati literary sources. This new theater also allowed women to perform. In recent years, theater has faced competition from cinema and TV, but attempts are being made to revive it, particularly in the big cities. Despite the seductions of the new media, theater still has a small but faithful following that has kept it alive.

DANCE

The folk dance culture of Gujarat is a celebration of lively music and colorful costumes. Most dance forms in Gujarat have religious or social significance and are participatory, although sometimes exclusive to one gender or the other.

Garba

Garba is Gujarat's best-known folk dance. Its name comes from a Sanskrit word "garbha deep", which refers to a oil lamp placed in a perforated earthen pot. The dance is performed around the pot in a circle to celebrate the festival of Navratri, which honors Goddess Amba and the nine nights she fought to defeat a demon. A form of worship offered by women, the dance consists of clapping hands and moving feet in various combinations and speeds according to the rhythm of the song. Besides Navratri, Garba is performed at weddings, religious functions and other festive occasions.

While most people associate Garba with the dance form, its essence is actually in the song to which it is performed. Navratri Garbas usually sing praises of the Mother Goddess, but there are hundreds of Garbas, traditional and modern, on a gamut of religious and secular themes. They express emotions that characterize the human condition. Traditionally only women danced Garba. Similarly, the Garbi is exclusively performed by men. It is a very energetic dance that involves circular actions executed with tremendous speed and grace.

Raas

Raas, a dance form that involves beating together *dandiya* or pairs of sticks, was the favorite dance of Krishna, and is immortalized as the theme of various paintings and art forms. Men and women often dance together, which is rare for non-tribal dance in India. These distinctions are disappearing, with men now joining women in Garbas, *dandiya* no longer restricted to Raas, and modern orchestras replacing the traditional drummer accompanied by a wind or string instrument.

Tippani

The roots of Tippani in Gujarat can be traced to the Chorwad region of Saurashtra. It originated from an old practice of beating lime into the foundation of a house with a *tippani,* a long stick fitted at one end with square wooden or iron block. Women invented the dance to enjoy the otherwise tedious and tiring process. They stand in two lines facing one another and beat the *tippani* in rhythm while dancing and singing. It is mostly performed during festivals and weddings.

Dangi Nritya

A beautiful dance form based on pace and formation, the Dangi Nritya originated in the Dangs. It is a tribal dance full of energy, skill and enthusiasm. Men and women interlock hands at the waist to form a chain and dance in sync while maintaining a serpentine movement. There are more than 25 different *chala* or formations, including that of a human pyramid, which are complemented with the music of the *dhol* and *pavri.*

Hudo

Hudo is popularly performed by the Bharvad or shepherd community, especially at the Tarnetar fair in Surendranagar. Dancers face each other in pairs and clap palms with one another while shuffling back and forth on their feet. Their movements are an attempt to mimic those of two sheep ramming their heads. The hand and foot movements create a uniform sound and music does not always accompany the dance.

Matukadi

In this dance form found among the Rabari and Bharvad communities, women rotate brass pots between their palms, using their ringed fingers to create music as they move their feet gracefully.

Siddi Dhamal

This dance form is performed by the men of the Siddi communities in Jafrabad and Jambur (Saurashtra) and migrated with them from East Africa. Adorned with peacock feathers that make both the headdress and the skirt, they dance to the tempo of the *dhol,* and a smaller two-sided drum, known as a *dhamal.* A *mashira* (a coconut casing filled with shells and wrapped in a green cloth) is used as a prop in the dance. Characterized by the vigorous jumping, the tempo of the drums and the fierce facial expressions, the climax is of this dance is the tossing of the *mashira* up in the air, followed by its cracking on the dancer's head.

Gujarat has many other dance forms besides those listed above. Many of them, beyond the popular Garba, Garbi and Raas, are difficult to come across, but are still danced in different communities on particular occasions and sometimes during stage shows.

MUSIC

Gujarat has a rich musical heritage with genres including folk, popular, spiritual and classical. The region has produced outstanding musicians and original melodic forms, and has made many contributions to the range of musical instruments. Most folk instruments of Gujarat resemble those found across many parts of Asia and beyond, and differ only in name, minor details of design and playing technique.

Folk and Devotional Music

In addition to the popular Garba, which combines dance and song, Gujarati folk songs also include devotional melodies, lullabies, wedding songs and funeral songs. *Marsiyo*, for instance, is an elegiac chant particular to Shia Muslim funerals. Bardic communities such as Gadhvi and Charan, who sing about the valorous deeds of kings, warriors and their brave womenfolk, still perform their ancestral music. Many tribal groups have their own music to accompany their dances.

The Vaishnav tradition has a form of devotional music called Haveli Sangeet (*haveli*, literally means "mansion" and also refers to a temple of the Pushtimarg sect). More popular devotional music genres include *bhajans* and *kirtans*. Many saint-poets of the medieval period were also accomplished musicians. Notable among these are Narsinh Mehta, who composed *Vaishnav Jana To*, a favorite of Mahatma Gandhi and one of Gujarat's most beloved songs. He also introduced the *prabhatiyun,* a morning hymn, usually invoking Krishna. Another popular poet is the Rajput princess Mirabai, whose songs evoke the same devout fervor with which she composed them.

Classical Music

Although relatively few Gujaratis are represented in Indian classical music today, Gujarat has made significant contributions over past centuries. Some outstanding *ragas* evolved in Gujarat and are named after the regions or personalities behind their origins.

Several legendary musicians hail from Gujarat. Nayak Baiju (popularly known as Baiju Bawara or "crazy Baiju") was from Champaner. According to legend, he defeated Tansen (court musician to the Mughal Emperor Akbar) in a musical contest and earned the reputation of a great musician.

In recent history, a leading vocalist of Gujarati origin was Omkarnath Thakur, one of the greatest voices of 20th c. Indian classical music. According to an anecdote, he cured Mussolini of insomnia with his singing. Omkarnath excelled as a performer, a theorist and a teacher.

After the eclipse of the Mughals in the mid-19th c., patronage shifted to the princely states scattered across India. Some of the greatest Indian musicians were appointed to major and minor courts in Gujarat. Notable among these is Faiyaz Khan, who was a court musician at Baroda during Sayajirao's reign. Pandit Jasraj, one of the top-ranking musicians in India today, spent his formative years in the tiny princely state of Sanand (near Ahmedabad); the prince of Sanand himself was an accomplished musician and musicologist.

Ghazal

A *ghazal* is a sequence of couplets. Each couplet (called a *sher*) is a complete poetic idea in itself and the sequence forms a larger unified poem. *Ghazals* often weave spiritual themes into secular, often erotic, metaphors. They mostly express beauty, longing, unrequited love, betrayal, death and similar subjects. The *ghazal's* overall mood is one of submission to fate. Originally a recited form, *ghazals* are now usually sung; however, in an authentic rendering, the poetry dominates the music. *Ghazal* performances are generally interactive. The performer seeks the listeners' involvement with its content. A discerning audience responds to the completion of each *sher* with expressions of appreciation and dramatic hand gestures. Stemming from Arab and Persian Sufi traditions, the *ghazal* came to India around the 12th c. AD and first developed in the Urdu language. Towards the latter part of the 19th c., people began to compose *ghazals* in other modern Indian languages, particularly Gujarati.

Music on the Airwaves

The popular FM station across Gujarat is Radio Mirchi, which mostly plays popular Hindi songs, but airs *bhajans* in the mornings. All India Radio, the state owned network, offers a range of music from popular to classical. The best listening hours for classical music are from 2130-2300 on Sat and Sun, 2230-2300 on Mon and Tues, and 1500-1530 on Wed.

Contemporary Popular Music

Bollywood film songs, mostly in Hindi, are composed to accompany blockbuster films, and are the staple in popular music. They are enjoyed by people of all ages. These catchy tunes generally center on the theme of love and often blare from stores, rickshaws and households, adding music to the background of everyday life. There is also a growing number of independent pop artists who release songs with music videos that meet popular demand.

One of Gujarat's first recorded rock bands, Purple Flower, was formed in the early 1970s. Hammersmith, now disbanded, was the first group from Gujarat to appear on an MTV video.

ART

Although Gujarat's art history parallels the general trends that took place in India, the location of Indus Valley sites in the region pushes it to an early date. In Lothal, the port town of Indus Valley, findings include stamps and seals depicting images of animals and women in addition to beaded jewelry and earthenware, all of which demonstrate the people's creative aptitude.

Miniature Painting

India had a rich tradition of wall painting as seen in the caves of Ajanta. The purpose of these paintings was religious and didactic. A new tradition of miniature painting started in eastern India sometime in the 8th c., followed by the west, including Gujarat, in the mid-10th c. Painted onto palm leaves and tree bark, these illustrations initially had ornamental purpose, but soon became visual accompaniments to religious scriptures.

In the beginning, the art of manuscript illustration was confined to the representation of gods and goddesses. These were directly emulated from stone carvings with figures mostly drawn in three-quarter profile and divinities in frontal position as seen in sculptures at places such as the Sun Temple at Modhera and Ranki Vav at Patan. The figures are usually slim and elongated. They share similar features such as squarish faces and tubular limbs bending at acute angles. Faces are characterized by a pointed nose, a pointed chin and the further eye protruding beyond the cheek line of the face in profile. This eye lost its organic context when the style became repetitive in the 15th c.; consequently it appeared to be suspended in air to the extent that it became redundant. This feature became the hallmark of the Gujarat's miniature paintings. The style was used to illustrate various religious texts of the Shvetambar Jains and many other manuscripts of Vaishnav sects. Examples of such Gujarati paintings can be seen on display in the Lalbhai Dalpatbhai Museum and Calico Museum, both in Ahmedabad, and Baroda Museum and Art Gallery in Vadodara. The earliest indigenous examples of highly evolved calligraphy known today are also found in Jain manuscripts produced in Gujarat.

Gujarat also had a rich tradition of wall paintings. The walls of the Lakhota Kotha in Jamnagar and the Darbargarh of Shihor have examples of Kamangari style paintings that include mostly male figures depicted with meticulous detail, such as each fold of their turbans and the shape of their whiskers.

Indian artists received little encouragement during the British rule—to the biased British eye, local art never matched the standards of the West. However, the artists found their patrons in Indian kings. Chief among them was Sayajirao of Vadodara who invited Raja Ravi Varma, one of India's foremost painters of the time, to paint at his court. These paintings are exhibited in the Fatehsinh Museum in Vadodara. Sayajirao played a substantial role in cultivating the tastes of his subjects and spreading a love for the arts.

Folk Art

Folk art largely overlaps with craft, resulting in utilitarian products imprinted with artistic expression. The needle and thread tradition is a common medium for women across the state. They create vibrant expressions related to their community and culture, which are then transformed into clothing, house wares, religious paraphernalia and more. There are dozens of types of embroidery styles in Gujarat, and each is associated with particular communities. Every type of stitch creates a different effect and implicit in each design is the identity of the woman behind the masterpiece. The motifs used in the embroidery are drawn from the environment and culture and reused in other forms such as woodwork and wall paintings.

Tribal art usually expresses the concept of man as part of a larger universe. Unlike most Indian painting traditions that use vibrant colors and fine details, these compositions depict everyday village life using simple bold strokes and a white color made from rice flour. The Warli people decorate their homes with these images in honor of special occasions such as a birth or marriage. The Vaghari community is known for another ritual art form, Mata ni Pachedi, which is created on cloth with an image of the Mother Goddess defeating a demon as the central figure. These are made with a combination of block prints and hand painting. The Meghwals in Pachchham, Kachchh create striking murals on their mud walls using colors such as lavender, yellow and mauve extracted from mineral rocks found in the vicinity. The designs are purely decorative and are dominated by geometric, floral, animal and human motifs.

Modern Art

The Revivalist Movement from Bengal came to Gujarat in the early 20th c. Art began to reflect the influence of Indian philosophy, literature and ancient styles inspired by the Ajanta caves and the Mughal-Rajput paintings. It was with the Progressive Artists' Group in the 1950s that Modern Indian Art really began to acquire a distinct personality. It became more individualistic, experimental and free spirited. Artists began to travel and display their works all over the country and abroad. Galleries were opened, dialogues started happening and art as a whole became more prestigious. The reputed Faculty of Fine Arts at the Maharaja Sayajirao University was also established in this period. Many celebrated artists of the 20th c. were associated with it. Ahmedabad was also an early center of art education in Gujarat with people like Ravishankar Rawal (1892-1977), who was among the earlier artists in the state to create awareness about art. His magazine, Kumar, published paintings that brought several artists into the public eye.

To observe the evolving art scene and meet artists and students, visit MS University (Vadodara) and Kanoria Centre of Art (Ahmedabad). Contemporary art works can be seen at the Picture Gallery (Vadodara), and Sanskar Kendra, Ravishankar Gallery and Contemporary Art Gallery (Ahmedabad).

PEOPLE

Ahir
Kachchh, Bhavnagar, Rajkot

The least nomadic of the pastoral communities, many Ahirs switched to businesses in transport, salt production and carpentry among other areas to sustain their livelihood. They claim lineage to Krishna but are most probably descendants of the Scythians. Although settled across India, a large number of Ahirs have made Gujarat home. They have a rich tradition of folk songs, instruments and dance, including Raas, which they introduced into the Gujarati culture. The women from each sub-community dress in variations of bright tops and black *gaghra*. The black was traditionally worn as a symbol of mourning for Krishna's death. Reputed for their *torans* and wall hangings, the women are adept in embroidery.

Bharvad
Kachchh, Saurashtra

The Bharvads believe that their ancestors migrated with Krishna and the Yadav clan from Mathura to Gujarat. Settled in all corners of the state, this community of cattle breeders congregates at the Tarnetar Fair in Surendranagar every year. The men are known for their vibrant dress, which includes colorful *dhoti*-like bottoms trimmed with hand-work, fully embroidered bold vests and bright turbans. They greet each other with a hearty "Ram, Ram". As a practice to ward of the evil eye, the women crack their knuckles after touching them to another person's temples. Both genders give importance to ornamentation. Tattoos are also significant. They believe that a person who dies without one returns as a camel in the next birth.

Bhil
Panchmahal, Dahod, Vadodara, Narmada, The Dangs, Valsad, Navsari

It is believed that the earliest traditional rulers of Gujarat were Bhils. Their origin can be traced to the Dravidian word Bilu, which means "bow"—the characteristic weapon of the tribe. The Bhil community, settled across the eastern border of Gujarat, comprises of several smaller clans, including Tadvi, Valvi, Vasava Bhil-Garsias and Bhilalas They all live off the forest and rely heavily on bamboo to build their houses, make farming tools and prepare food items like pickled bamboo shoot. Largely agriculturalists, they sell their produce at weekly *haats* (bazaars). The Bhils have a strong relationship with nature. This is reflected in their art forms such as totems, terracotta figures and masks, which are largely tied to rituals. They also have a rich tradition of folk music, instruments and dancing. Bhils consider the Mahuda a sacred tree and distill liquor from its flowers and oil from its seeds.

Dangis
The Dangs

This is a mixed population comprising of the Bhils, Kunbis, Warlis, Gamits and Naikas, all of whom share the forests of the Dangs, while maintaining their own cultural identity. The Bhils, Kunbis and Gamits are aboriginals and the other two groups migrated to the area. Intermarriage between any of the five is not allowed. All Dangi women wear a golden *nath* nose ring and a double chained necklace made of one rupee coins. They also enjoy social and economic equality from childhood.

Jath
Kachchh

Believed to originate from Aleppo in Turkey, this semi-nomadic community is settled along both sides of the once-perennial Indus River. It is subdivided into three main groups, the Garasias (agriculturalists), Dhanetas (herdsmen) and Fakiranis (previously holy men and now landowners). The women wear *aabhos* or long gowns embellished with a beautiful embroidered yoke. Jath embroidery is considered among the finest in India. A distinctive feature of the Dhanetah women is the large gold nose ring they wear, which is held up by a bundle of black threads pinned to their hair just above the forehead.

Meghwal Kachchh

Originally from Marwar, Rajasthan, the Meghwals live in Kachchh and are usually found along the peripheries of villages inhabited by Muslim animal herders. This physical proximity fosters a social synthesis between the two groups, as the Meghwals, expert tanners and wool weavers, depend on the byproducts of their neighbors. Many of the men have switched to wood carving, which they use to embellish furniture and other décor items that they make. The women excel in embroidery and clay relief work, both designed around small pieces of mirror. Married women wear sensual bare-back blouses called *kanjaris*, with the front entirely covered in bold embroidery designs. On special occasions, these women wear an elaborate gold nose ring called *velado* that hangs over the mouth.

Mutwa Kachchh

It is believed that a *hijra* (eunuch) led the Mutwas from Arabia to Kachchh via Sindh about 500 years ago. They still follow the Bedouin culture and practice the Islamic faith. Largely cattle breeders, the Mutwas are also exceptional artisans who create beautiful mud work with *lipan* and mirrors. The women are known for their extremely fine embroidery patterned around tiny mirrors. Like many communities in Gujarat, the wedding trousseau is extensive among the Mutwas and includes silver and gold ornaments, embroidered pieces, dozens of hand made quilts and large metal vessels

Rabari Kachchh, Saurashtra, Patan, Mahesana, Sabarkantha

A pastoral community, the Rabaris hail from Marwar, Rajasthan. According to folklore, a group of Rajput men decided to marry celestial damsels, and the descendants of this union came to be known as Rabari or "those who leave the path". The community, spread across Gujarat, observes all marriage ceremonies on a single day of the year. Many Rabaris are semi-nomadic. The men travel with a caravan of sheep and camel based on a seasonal cycle, returning home just before monsoon breaks. The women manage the home and sell clarified butter and wool to generate income. The traditional Rabari dress is a striking feature. Married women wear black woolen *dupattas* with red dots, black heavily-pleated skirts called *gaghra* and an open back blouse that they embellish with handiwork. Heavy coiled earrings known as *nagla* hang from their ears, stretching their lobes. Tattoos, believed to hold magic powers, often cover their hands and neck. The men dress in all white, from their turbans and *kediyun* (double-breasted top that fans out just below the chest) to a *dhoti*-like bottom. They sometimes throw an embroidered wool shawl over the shoulder. The men also wear heavy earrings known as *toliya*, pierced through the hard part of the ear.

Rathwa Vadodara, Panchmahal, Dahod

The Rathwas are an agricultural community, many of whom supplement their income through wage labor and animal husbandry. They depend on the forest for farm land, wild animals for food and wood for fuel. The Rathwas celebrate a number of festivals linked to the harvest cycle, including the colorful Kawant Mela, which welcomes the arrival of spring. They consider tattoos, especially the snake and scorpion motifs, a form of beautification and protection. The women wear neck ornaments composed of silver rupees or white metal ten *paise* coins.

IN THE FOOTSTEPS OF GANDHIJI

On March 12, 1930, a sixty year-old ex-lawyer clad in *dhoti* and armed with a walking stick set out with seventy-eight of his trusted associates from the banks of the Sabarmati River en route to the sea. They embarked with the implicit intention of liberating their country from English rule. The lawyer himself vowed "till Swaraj is established in India ... Only with complete victory can we return to this place."

In India today, Gandhiji is considered a saint by the masses. Also known as the father of the nation, he graces its banknotes. As with most saints, the essence of his message has been forgotten much more rapidly than the trivia of his deeds.

Mohandas Karamchand Gandhi (1869-1948)

On October 2, 1869, Mohandas Karamchand Gandhi, destined to become the Mahatma, "the great soul", was born in a blue three-story house in Porbandar (Kirti Mandir, now a national memorial). His family moved to Rajkot seven years later (where his father's house, Kaba Gandhi no Delo still stands), married Kasturba at thirteen, and subsequently attended Alfred High School.

As a young man, Gandhiji experimented with impropriety but found sin alien to his concept of truth and duty. He once engaged in theft, immediately confessed to his father, and suffered a silent rebuke of his father's tears that taught him strong lessons in morality and non-violence. Physically and intellectually unimpressive, the young Gandhi attempted to continue his education at Samaldas College in Bhavnagar (his records can still be seen at the Barton Museum). He soon left college and, in 1888, sailed for England to study law, famously promising his mother not to touch "wine, women, or meat".

Like most college students, Gandhiji went through various phases. He was exposed to dissident philosophies (through his friends in the Vegetarian Society), then read a variety of religious texts, and finally dedicated himself to his studies, wholly irrelevant to his being admitted to the bar. He sailed home in 1891 after three years in England, having secured a profession and having upheld his promises.

A familiar story, the young graduate found his theoretical knowledge less than helpful amidst the practical chaos of the real world. Gandhi was unemployed until called to work in South Africa in 1893. But in South Africa, his life changed dramatically. His seeds of stubbornness, dedication to truth and sympathy towards religious sentiment sprouted in the harsh soil of racial oppression. The years witnessed his twin shoots of fearlessness and faith in truth grow side-by-side.

During his time at the Sabarmati Ashram, Gandhiji lived in a very simple cottage called Hriday Kunj.

Gandhiji Returns to India

After 23 years of struggle, public agitation, and community building in Africa, Gandhiji returned to India in 1915 a hero. He wielded weapons of *ahimsa* (non-violence), including *satyagraha* (non-violent resistance) and *swadeshi* (self-sufficiency) against the colonial oppressor.

In 1915, Gandhiji settled down, founding the Kochrab Ashram in Ahmedabad. After the plague spread through the area, the ashram moved to the banks of the Sabarmati, where it continues to effuse goodwill and serenity. (In addition to housing an excellent museum on the life and work of the Mahatma, it is home to a library, school, a non-profit called Manav Sadhna and Gandhiji's well-kept rooms and prayer grounds).

One of the few belongings Gandhiji owned was a small statuette of the three monkeys, who represent "hear no evil, speak no evil, see no evil".

It was in this same year that Gandhiji organized an Ahmedabad mill workers 'strike. The turn of the 20th c. arrived with the plague in Western India and mill owners promised a bonus to workers who risked their lives working in the hazardous environment. Once the plague disappeared, however, so did the promise to increase wages. So Ahmedabad's mill workers congregated under the shade of the Ek Tek Banyan Tree (still standing near the Gandhi Bridge in Ahmedabad) with Gandhiji and Ansuya Sarabhai, the daughter of a textile magnate. Gandhiji also took on a 21-day fast. Finally the mill owners relented and compromised on a raise. It was under this very tree that the victory was announced.

Khadi, handspun on a charkha, was Gandhi's symbol for self-sufficiency. It was his weapon against the British and he strongly promoted it to the masses.

The Journey for Freedom

Four years later, the British Government announced the Rowlatt Act, a statute that granted the colonial powers the right to imprison locals if they appeared a threat to "national security". Gandhiji voiced this as an infringement of freedom and launched a nationwide boycott of English goods by fasting and praying. Although the nation rose to the call, the bloody massacre ordered by Brigadier-General Reginal Dyer of a public gathering at Jallianwala Bagh in Amritsar brought the movement to a screeching halt by the dismayed Gandhiji.

In 1920, Gandhiji joined the Congress as its president and founded the Navjivan Press to reproach the evils of society and anchor ideas for a non-cooperative movement against the English. He founded Gujarat Vidyapith, a learning institute focused on creating leaders to fight for India's independence and work for social development. (Students continue to attend a daily all-religion prayer and spin Khadi.) This was the same year he launched the Non-cooperation Movement, which sang the praises of being *swadeshi,* an economic strategy that encouraged Indians to use indigenously made goods and boycott British products. This was also when Gandhiji began his ritual spinning of the *charkha* and committed to the *dhoti* as his lifetime uniform. Across the country, masses joined in and fed British cloth and books to the flames. The campaign was short-lived when a group of citizens, harassed by local police, lost control and burned down a police station in Chauri Chaura (near Uttar Pradesh). Grief-stricken by the violence, Gandhiji aborted the movement. One late evening in 1922, Gandhiji was arrested at the ashram for sedition. During the trial, which took place in the courtroom of the Ahmedabad Circuit House, Gandhiji pleaded guilty on all counts and gave a speech that moved the entire nation and the judge, who sentenced him to six years in prison after asserting, "...you are a great patriot and a great leader. Even those who differ from you in politics look upon you as a man of high ideals and of noble and even saintly life." Prison afforded Gandhiji a period of reflection and rejuvenation. After two years, he was released for appendicitis surgery.

The year 1928 brought another opportunity to raise the sword of non-violent resistance. The British government decreed a 22 percent increase on taxes in Bardoli, despite the harsh drought farmers had suffered earlier in the year. With the leadership of Sardar Patel, the farmers of Bardoli fought this excessive levy and eventually reaped triumph.

The Salt March (Dandi Yatra)

On March 12, 1930, Mahatma Gandhi walked from the Sabarmati Ashram with 78 dedicated *satyagrahis* in order to break the salt laws and catapult the country into widespread non-violent civil disobedience. The elderly activist and statesman, hardier and faster than most of his disciples, chose to oppose the salt tax because it affected the poorest of India's millions, the very masses to whom he had consciously dedicated his life. When he arrived in Dandi 24 days later, and raised a handful of salt, millions of his countrymen joined him in mass civil action. A new era in the struggle had been born. (A simple museum with large, poignant photographs marks the spot—a nearby high school run along Gandhian values keeps the spirit alive.)

The pilgrims marched 385 km through towns, villages, rivers and ample countryside from Ahmedabad to the sea at Dandi, over a period of 24 days. Everywhere they went, locals joined them and in the evenings Gandhiji would address the crowds about *swaraj*, truth and social unity. The pilgrimage raised consciousness and liberated a nation in chains.

Immediately after Dandi, Gandhiji and many of his associates were sent to jail. After his release, the Mahatma embarked on a new phase. Sabarmati Ashram was handed over to the Harijans (the name, which means "children of God", that Gandhiji gave to what was traditionally known as the untouchable community). A new ashram was developed at Sevagram in Wardha. For the subsequent 18 years the Gandhiji worked to emancipate the nation through non-violence and encouraged communal harmony. He also pursued deeper in his search for truth. Then on August 15, 1947, the British handed over the powers of the country back to its people. Independence had been won. Gandhiji spent the next month trying to maintain peace between the Hindus and Muslims and took on what would be his final fast. On January 30, 1948 the bullets of an assassin seized Gandhiji's last breath and left the nation in grief, without its apostle of peace.

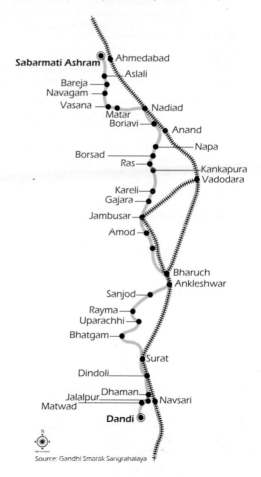

Source: Gandhi Smarak Sangrahalaya

54

Your Freedom Trail

by Ankur Shah

More than 75 years after Gandhiji marched to Dandi, the modern pilgrim would likely have quite different aims. I followed in Gandhiji's footsteps, following his dates, schedule and vows of conduct to the best of my budding ability. My goals, though vague at the start, became clear a few days into the journey: verily, we make the road by walking.

By following the Dandi Yatra, in addition to paying homage to Gandhiji, I had an opportunity to exit the social domain of tourism, to step through my mind into the realm of pilgrimage. Pilgrimage lies at the confluence of three knowings: the self, the road and the journey. Each step led closer to purification (voluntary or not) and I came to know the fragility of my own boundaries. After sheer volume of exposure to a land and its people I gained an understanding of Gujarat simply not available through any other means of transport. And in reflection with my other journeys—on cycles, autos, buses, trains, ships and airplanes—I experienced the understanding that the slower I went, the more I learned; that every person I met was, in fact, infinitely deep, and that he who is really interested in knowledge did not move at all.

In pilgrimage the only rule is Gandhiji's–to be true to Truth. This does not mandate following Gandhiji's precepts, nor blindly obeying our own desires, but rather it requires a deep and continuous attunement to the inner voice. Without her we would certainly be lost.

Practical recommendations for doing the Yatra are surprisingly simple. You don't need to know the language or to articulate why you have started—you need only be armed with faith in the Gujarati people and yourself. However, modern physics still troubles most of us. I suggest the following:

Water is a public good, a public god; ask whenever you are thirsty and you should never be denied. Bottled water is unavailable. The heat will bother you. Stay cool, cover your head, chew *neem* leaves and accept limes when offered.

Mosquitoes came before you and will remain after you leave. In the mean time, they will bother you, but it is a serious *tapasya* to awaken at four and spend a day walking and praying after a bug-ridden sleepless night.

1 **Porbandar**
Kirti Mandir
(Gandhi's birthplace)

2 **Rajkot**
Kaba Gandhi No Delo
(his father's house)
Alfred High School
(his High School)

3 **Bhavnagar**
Samaldas College

4 **Ahmedabad**
Kochrab Ashram
Sabarmati Ashram
Gujarat Vidyapith

5 **Bardoli**
Bardoli Ashram

6 **Dandi**

As a guide for the "inmates" of the ashram and a codification of his life and message, Gandhiji established the observance of eleven vows.

"A vow means unflinching determination. Determination is worth nothing if it bends before temptation."

Truth "Truth is not fulfilled by mere abstinence from telling or practicing an untruth in ordinary relations with fellow men, but truth is God, the one and only reality."

Non-violence "Mere non-killing is not enough. The active part of non-violence is love. The law of love requires equal consideration for all life, from the tiniest insect to the highest man."

Celibacy "Observance of the foregoing principles isimpossible without the observance of celibacy...animal passion must be so controlled as to be excluded even from the mind."

Control of the Palate "The observance of [celibacy] has been found from experience to be extremely difficult so as long as one has not acquired mastery over taste...eating is necessary only for keeping [the body] as a fit instrument for service."

Non-stealing "The fine truth at the bottom of this principle is that nature provides just enough and no more for our daily needs, hence it is also a theft to possess anything more than one's minimum requirement."

Non-possession "One must not possess anything that one does not really need... in observing the principle one is led to a progressive simplification of one's own life."

Swadeshi "Man serves the world best by first serving his neighbor...one must as far as possible purchase one's requirements locally...[Swadeshi] enjoins the sacrifice of oneself for the family, of the family for the village, of the village for the country, of the country for humanity."

Fearlessness "One cannot follow truth or love so as long as one is subject to fear...a seeker of the truth must give up the fear of parents, caste, government, robbers...and he must not be frightened by poverty or death."

Removal of Untouchability "The ashram does not believe in caste, which it considers [injurious to] Hinduism because of its implication of inferior and superior status and of pollution by contact...a person should [follow] the hereditary occupation...and should devote all his spare time and energy to the acquisition and advancement of true knowledge."

Equality of Religions "The ashram believes that the principle faiths of the world constitute a revelation of truth...one can only pray that the defects in the various faiths may be overcome and that they may advance side by side towards perfection."

Physical Labor "Able-bodied adults should do all their personal work themselves and may not be served by others...the service of children as well as the disabled, the old, and the sick is a duty incumbent on every person who has the required strength."

KRISHNA IN GUJARAT

Krishna, heralded as the 8th incarnation of the Hindu deity Vishnu, is popularly worshipped across India. Though exact dates are not known, most evidence indicates that he was a king who lived sometime between 1700 and 700 BC and spent significant time in Gujarat after shifting his kingdom from Mathura to Dwarka, at the tip of the Saurashtra peninsula on the coast of Gujarat.

The Legends of Krishna

Several thousand years ago, an evil king by the name of Kansa ruled over a confederacy of several clans that had their capital in Mathura, about 100 km south of present day Delhi. When a prophecy from the sky informed him that the eighth child of his sister Devaki would slay him, he attempted to kill her. Devaki's husband, Vasudev, prevented this by promising Kansa that they would surrender all their children to him. Kansa imprisoned Devaki and Vasudev and killed the first six children the couple bore. Legend holds that the seventh child was transplanted to the womb of Rohini, the other wife of Vasudev who was hiding in the home of Nanda and Yashoda, the leaders of a pastoral community. The child was known as Balaram. The eighth child was born at midnight, in the midst of a monsoon storm. A divine form appeared and advised Vasudev to carry the child across the Yamuna River and exchange it with the newborn daughter of Yashoda and Nanda in the village of Gokul. The prison doors opened, the guards fell asleep, and the river parted to help Vasudev execute his mission. After exchanging the newborn babies, Vasudev returned to the prison. Immediately, the baby's cries awakened Kansa who snatched the girl to kill her. She transformed into a goddess and revealed that his enemy was still alive. Kansa was outraged and ordered the death of all newborn boys in his kingdom. Krishna, however, managed to slip their notice.

Krishna led a happy childhood in Gokul, spending time with the *gopis* (milkmaids), stealing *makhan*, herding cows, playing his flute and destroying demons sent by Kansa to kill him. When Krishna grew into a young man, he left Gokul to fulfill the prophecy; he killed Kansa and became the king of Mathura.

DWARKA The City of Gold   JAMNAGAR DISTRICT

Jarasandh tried to avenge the death of his son-in-law, Kansa, by attacking Mathura. Krishna and his army defeated Jarasandh seventeen times but suffered heavy casualties. When Jarasandh made his 18th attempt, Krishna knew his clan would not be able to withstand the attack, so he convinced the Yadav dynasty to leave Mathura and follow him to safety. They arrived on the coast of present-day Saurashtra, where they decided to build their capital. Krishna appealed to Vishvakarma, the God of architecture, to help them build their new kingdom. He agreed, provided that Samudradev, the God of the sea, provided the land. Krishna then prayed to Samudradev, who blessed him with land measuring up to twelve *yojanas* (773 sq km). Vishvakarma followed through with his promise and built Dwarka.

Archeological evidence suggests that Dwarka, often called the City of Gold because of its wealth and finery, was built about 3500 years ago. In ancient texts, Dwarka is described as a planned city with a fort wall, 64 gates and a residential quarter for each queen. Dwarka, which means "gate", was considered the entryway to western India. Legend holds that no one could enter the city walls without presenting the sovereign

seal given to each citizen of the kingdom. The empire was surrounded completely by water, relying solely on bridges to connect it to the mainland. It is said to have been a thriving port and a flourishing city in its era.

The World's First Love Letter

Bhishmaka, the king of Vidarbha, located in modern-day Maharashtra, had five sons and a beautiful daughter named Rukmini. Upon hearing stories of Krishna's courage, good looks and virtues, Rukmini decided that Krishna would be her husband. Her eldest brother Rukmi, however, had betrothed her to Shishupal, Krishna's cousin and rival. Upon hearing this, Rukmini wrote what is claimed to be the world's first love letter to Krishna, revealing her affection for him and the situation at hand. Krishna set out to rescue her, reaching her just before the wedding ceremony. The princess joined Krishna on his chariot and took over the reigns as he and his brother Balaram defeated Rukmi, Shishupal and their legion of friends. After the victory, the couple traveled back to Dwarka to commence their married life.

Madhavpur 60 km from Porbandar City   PORBANDAR DISTRICT

A small coastal village called Madhavpur hosts an ancient temple dedicated to Krishna, Balaram and Rukmini. According to legend, Krishna and Rukmini stopped at this holy site to take their wedding vows before continuing to Dwarka. In celebration of this legend, the locals hold a large fair between March and April commemorating Krishna and Rukmini's union.

Defeat of Narakasura

Although Rukmini was Krishna's first and favorite wife, she was only one of many. A powerful tyrant named Narakasura ruled a small province in present- day Nepal, where he kidnapped thousands of women, exploited them and imprisoned them in his palace. Krishna attacked Narakasura to end his tyranny and liberate his kingdom. Upon Narakasura's defeat, Krishna released the women from prison, but they lamented that they could not return to their families after their reputations had been sullied by the evil ruler. To provide them with a life of honor and acceptance in society, Krishna married all 16,000 women, bringing his total number of wives to 16,108. They all lived together in Dwarka.

Rukmini Temple 2 km from Dwarka City   JAMNAGAR DISTRICT

One day, Krishna and Rukmini invited the short-tempered sage Durvasa to dinner. He accepted the invitation on the condition that Krishna and Rukmini pull his chariot. Happily obliging, the couple escorted the sage back to Dwarka. Along the way, Rukmini grew thirsty so Krishna pounded his toe into the ground and released a spring of Ganga water. When Durvasa noticed Rukmini taking a sip, he became outraged at her inhospitality for drinking the water without offering some to him. The sage cursed her that she would be separated from her beloved Krishna. This is the local explanation given for why the Rukmini Temple, embellished with paintings of Rukmini and Krishna, stands two kilometers outside of Dwarka.

Sudamapuri Temple Porbandar City   PORBANDAR DISTRICT

While attending the Sandeepani Ashram as a young boy, Krishna befriended Sudama, the son of a poor Brahmin. After completing their studies, Krishna went on to rule Dwarka while Sudama married a simple girl and led the life of a poor Brahmin householder. When his family expanded, it became difficult for him to make ends meet. His wife encouraged him to visit his childhood friend Krishna and ask for his help. Before he departed for Dwarka, Sudama's wife packed a small pouch of sweet rice for Krishna. In Dwarka, Krishna gave Sudama the royal treatment with lavish meals and hospitality. In jest, Krishna asked his friend if he had brought him anything. After Sudama hesitantly gave the rice, Krishna finished it with great appreciation. Lost in the joy of reuniting with his dear friend, Sudama forgot to ask Krishna for help, and left Dwarka.When he returned home, a mansion stood in place of his small house. When his wife and children, clad in new clothes, came to greet him, Sudama realized that Krishna had known his difficulties all along. The Sudama Temple in Porbandar commemorates the character of Sudama; the town of Porbandar is also known as Sudamapuri.

Shankha Tirtha

After the completion of his education, Krishna asked his guru Sandeepani Muni what he desired for his *gurudakshina* (a token of gratitude and compensation given by a student to his teacher at the end of his education). He asked Krishna to rescue his son from the sea-demon known as Panchajan. Krishna obliged and rescued the boy after he defeated the evil demon at the coastline of Prabhas Patan, during which he acquired his famous conch, known as Panchajanya.

Gopi Talav 20 km north of Dwarka   JAMNAGAR DISTRICT

As a young boy in Mathura, Krishna often danced Raas with the *gopis*. After he left for Dwarka, they missed him so much that they decided to visit him. They all reunited at a lake north of Dwarka and danced once more under the full moon. At the end of the dance, unable to part with Krishna, the *gopis* chose to merge into the earth instead. Legend says that they transformed into a yellow clay called *gopi chandan*, which is still found near the lake and used by devotees of Krishna to mark their bodies.

The Mahabharata War

The entire story of the Mahabharata leads to the Kurukshetra War which took place on a battlefield in the present-day state of Haryana. The war arose from long-standing disputes between the Kauravas and the Pandavas that led to a deceitful game of dice. The Kauravas won the game and forced their Pandava cousins from the throne and into exile for thirteen years. When the Pandavas returned, Duryodhana, the eldest of the Kauravas, refused to return the seat of power. A war was declared and armies from all over the Indian subcontinent joined the two clans. It was on the battlefield that Krishna spoke the words of the *Bhagavad Gita* to Arjun, just before the war commenced.

Bhagavad Gita

A sacred text of Hinduism, the *Bhagavad Gita* is an eighteen chapter compilation of the conversation between Krishna and Arjun on the Kurukshetra battlefield. When Arjun sees his family, friends and teachers on the opposing side he hesitates about fighting in the war. Just then, Krishna guides Arjun on issues relevant to the spiritual and ethical struggles of the human soul. Even today, the text is read in order to understand and overcome the issues of everyday life.

Gandhari's Grief

After the end of the Kurukshetra War, Gandhari (the mother of the Kauravas) was overwhelmed with grief over the death of her 100 sons. She blamed Krishna for her loss since he had assisted the Pandavas as Arjun's charioteer. She cursed him that his entire clan would come to an end in several decades and that the women in his family would suffer just as she had.

Krishna's Death Bhalka Tirth, Near Prabhas Patan   JUNAGADH DISTRICT

On returning to Dwarka, Krishna found that his dynasty had deteriorated into delinquents. Once some of the young men had fallen drunk and decided to fool three revered sages. They disguised one of their friends as a pregnant girl and asked the holy men what "she" would give birth to. Offended by their foolishness, the sages cursed the boys that whatever "she" bore would bring the end of the Yadav clan.

The boy soon produced an iron rod, which they immediately crushed into a powder and threw into the ocean. While the powder sprouted sharp metal grass on the beach, a part of the rod remained intact and sunk to the ocean floor, where it was swallowed by a fish. Later, a fisherman caught the fish and sold it to the wife of a hunter named Jara. She found the metal fragment and gave it to her husband, who fashioned the rod into an arrow tip. Years later, the Yadavas got drunk during a festival on the beach and, after an argument broke out, began fighting with one another using the sharp blades of grass. Krishna tried to stop the bloodshed, but finally accepted that destiny was approaching and departed to the forest nearby. As Krishna played his flute beneath a tree with one leg resting on his bent knee, Jara mistook Krishna's heel for the head of a deer. The hunter shot him with the arrow tip he had shaped earlier. When Jara realized his mistake, he begged for forgiveness. Krishna blessed him and peacefully awaited his death.

Ten Reincarnations of Vishnu

According to Hindu mythology, when mankind is in danger and evil influences devastate law and order on earth, Vishnu takes birth to restore balance and faith. These mortal births are referred to as *avatars* or incarnations. According to Hindu mythology, Vishnu has taken nine earthly forms, while the tenth *avatar*, Kalki, often depicted riding a horse, is yet to be born. Krishna was the eighth *avatar* of Vishnu. The reincarnations of Vishnu also roughly correspond to the evolution of life on earth. Many believe that evolution is one of the deep metaphors contained in these allegories. The *avatars* of Vishnu are: Matsya (fish), Kurma (tortoise), Varaha (boar), Narasimha (half-man, half-lion), Vamana (dwarf), Parashurama (Rama with an axe), Rama (perfect human), Krishna (ultimate statesman), Buddha (enlightened one) and Kalki (crusader of righteousness).

Arjun Cremates Krishna Prabhas Patan   JUNAGADH DISTRICT

Krishna sent his chariot driver to deliver the message of his impending death to Arjun, who eventually cremated Krishna's mortal body in Dehotsarg, which sits at the confluence of three rivers known as Triveni Ghat.

The Ocean Swallows Dwarka

Krishna's death marked the beginning of Kali Yuga, an age of quarrel and chaos. A flood also occurred immediately after Krishna's departure, which swallowed all of Dwarka and submerged the City of Gold to the bottom of the ocean.

The Discovery of Dwarka

The lost city of Dwarka no longer remains a myth as the National Institute of Oceanography found remains of pottery and a fort wall off the coast of Dwarka. Explorers also located a foundation of boulders, which they believe supported the walls of a sea fortress and confirm that Dwarka was indeed reclaimed by the ocean. Through scientific dating, archeologists have dated the pottery to around 1500 BC, also lending insight into the actual time of Krishna's life and the dates of the Mahabharata.

FAIRS &
FESTIVALS

The Rathwa community of Chhota Udepur celebrate Holi.

FAIRS & FESTIVALS

Fairs and Festivals hold an important place in Gujarati culture, illustrated by the many celebrations held around the year. While Gujarat is synonymous with Navratri and Uttarayan, it also celebrates a host of rural fairs and regional events that combine social, cultural and religious values. The celebrations usually mark a change in season, a harvest or a religious occasion. They almost always include dance, music and sumptuous food.

Most of the traditional Hindu festivals are based on the lunar calendar, making it difficult to provide a corresponding date on the Gregorian calendar. For this reason, the following list gives months alone, unless actual dates are known. The Islamic calendar is also based on the lunar cycle, but it has no periodic corrections for the difference with the solar calendars. So the festival dates advance by nearly eleven days each year. Since it is impossible to provide even a range of corresponding months for Muslim festivals, we have listed the Islamic month for these celebrations. Locals can help find the Gregorian equivalents. For exact information about an event, contact one of the Gujarat Tourism offices *(see p 346)* or ask an elder member of any traditional family.

SAPTAK MUSIC FESTIVAL Ahmedabad — JANUARY 1-10

AHMEDABAD DISTRICT

This ten-day festival stages mainly classical music, showcasing both big names and emerging talent. It is currently the longest-running music festival in India. Daily sessions begin around 2100 and extend past midnight. If you would like to listen to Indian music in a local ambience, attend this is event. *For more details contact the Saptak School of Music 079 27540010.*

UTTARAYAN (Kite Festival) Ahmedabad — JANUARY 14

AHMEDABAD DISTRICT

While Uttarayan is celebrated throughout Gujarat, Ahmedabad is especially famous for the kite festival. Thousands of people flock to their rooftops and fill the sky with colorful kites to celebrate the end of winter. The kite-flyers compete to cut one another's kites. Special foods enjoyed on this occasion include *undhiyu* (a mixed vegetable preparation including yam and beans), sesame seed brittle and *jalebi*. After sunset, special paper lanterns called *tukkal* are attached to the kites and raised into the sky, lighting up the cityscape. For a memorable experience, visit the 24-hour kite market in the Old City the night before the festival, and watch kite enthusiasts purchase their gear for the revelry. Some caution is advised since the crowds often include aggressive men. Gujarat Tourism also organizes the three-day International Kite Festival in Ahmedabad, where kite flyers from around the world gather.

MODHERA DANCE FESTIVAL Modhera — JANUARY

MAHESANA DISTRICT

Held against the backdrop of the 11th c. sun temple in Modhera, this mesmerizing three-day classical dance festival invites artists from around india to perform during the third week of January every year.

From Top Left (clockwise): A little boy dressed up for Navratri; playing the flute at Sanskruti Kunj; Janmashtami celebrations in Kachchh; men dancing Garbo; conducting business at the Vautha Mela.

BHAVNATH MELA Mount Girnar JANUARY/FEBRUARY JUNAGADH DISTRICT

Thousands of devotees from all over India congregate at the Bhavnath Mahadev Temple at the base of Mt Girnar for a five-day celebration around Mahashivaratri, the moonless night on which Shiva performed the Tandava, his cosmic dance of destruction and creation. The *puja* for Shiva takes place at midnight on the day of Mahashivaratri, when *naga bavas* (nude sadhus) ride elephants decked in ornaments and lead a procession to the temple, marking the commencement of the religious ceremony. Devotees believe that Shiva himself visits the shrine on this occasion. The festival is filled with dance, Bhavai and music performances.

SANSKRUTI KUNJ Gandhinagar LATE FEBRUARY GANDHINGAR DISTRICT

The Youth and Culture Department of Gujarat sets up a craft village for ten days to showcase the folk culture of Gujarat, Rajasthan, Maharashtra and Goa. Crafts from across western India are featured during the day, and the night comes alive with folk dance, drama and music. Every night has a different lineup of performers, so it is worth going more than once if you have the chance. For exact dates, contact the office of Gujarat Tourism.

KACHCHH MAHOTSAV Bhuj FEBRUARY/MARCH KACHCHH DISTRICT

This desert festival highlights the vibrancy of Kachchhi culture and heritage. The days are filled with excursions to surrounding temples, beaches, craft villages and more. A traditional village is set up to host a variety of music and dance programs, a craft market and food stalls.

DHRANG MELA Dhrang FEBRUARY/MARCH KACHCHH DISTRICT

This two-day festival is in honor of the Saint Mekran Dada, known for helping the hungry and the lost in the Rann of Kachchh with the aid of his dog and donkey. The dog located lost travelers while the donkey carried water and food for them. It is mainly the Rabari and Ahir communities that celebrate this festival, which includes a procession and an overnight gathering, followed by camel and bullock-cart races in the morning.

DANGS DARBAR Ahwa FEBRUARY/MARCH THE DANGS

This vibrant tribal festival, held a few days before Holi, offers a glimpse into the local folk culture of the Dangi communities. The concept of the darbar goes back to the time of British rule when political agents paid an annual tribute to appeal to the local chieftains and retain access to their land. Although the British left in 1947, the celebration continues with dancing, music, folk instruments and theater. The people wear traditional colorful attire and heavy silver ornaments. Merchants flock from all over Gujarat to sell their wares.

HOLI/DHULETI Chotta Udepur MARCH/APRIL VADODARA DISTRICT

There are several legends associated with Holi. The most popular of these tells of the demon king Hiranyakashipu, who tried to kill his son Prahlad because the boy refused to revere his father and instead devoted his life to God. In an attempt to eliminate his son, the king placed Prahlad on the lap of Holika (the king's sister), who possessed a boon that protected her from fire. But when she mounted the pyre of wood, which was set ablaze, Holika was burnt alive while Prahlad remained

Submerging a tazia into the Kankaria Lake in Ahmedabad in honor of Muharram.

unscathed. To celebrate this death of evil, crowds gather in open squares and light bonfires. Holi also denotes the beginning of spring. Dhuleti, on the next day, is filled with fun and mischief as people throw colored powder and water on one another. The excitement is often accompanied by dancing and food.

The period surrounding Holi is an important time for Gujarat's tribal communities, many members of which work as laborers in other cities. They leave their job sites and return to their villages to join the ceaseless folk dancing and festivites. Each community celebrates with its own traditions. For example, at the Dhuleti fair in Bhagoria (Chhota Udepur) people walk on hot ash from the previous night's bonfire. They also observe a tradition called *paanvadi*, where adolescent males offer young women *paan*. If the girl accepts, he initiates a romance. In the Teliyo Mela, women massage their husbands with oil and then push them into the local lake to catch fish. The gesture symbolizes their love while the catch doubles as dinner. You can visit villages around Panchmahal, Poshina, Chhota Udepur, Rajpipla and Saputara to experience a variety of Holi celebrations.

SABARKANTHA DISTRICT

CHITRA VICHITRA Gunbhakhari, Near Khedbrahma   **MARCH/APRIL**

One of the most fascinating rural fairs in Gujarat, this celebration is held a fortnight after Holi. It takes place near the confluence of three rivers situated amid the foothills of the Aravalis. The fair is associated with two brothers, Chitra and Vichitra from the Mahabharata, whose diseases were cured by the water at this site. The festival begins on the eve of the new moon when the women gather at the river and mourn for their dead through the night. The next day,

a huge fair dominated by the Garasia and Bhil communities takes place. More than 60,000 people attend clad in regional costumes and jewelry to celebrate with hours of folk dances and songs. Every group carries its own drums, and the place reverberates with non-stop beats. Hundreds of stalls selling food, drink and various articles are set up. The fair also doubles as a match-making event.

MAHAVIR JAYANTI Palitana   MARCH/APRIL   BHAVNAGAR DISTRICT

The birthday of Mahavir, the 24th Jain *tirthankar*, is celebrated throughout the country. In Gujarat the observance is more fervent because of the concentration of Jains in the state. Followers participate in a pilgrimage around the Shetrunjaya Hill, culminating on the day of Mahavir Jayanti, when Jain pilgrims from all over the country assemble at the ancient shrines of Palitana. Processions of a grand chariot seated with images of Mahavira are taken out simultaneously with religious ceremonies in the temple. Large fairs are organized at these sites and the devout often fast and give alms to the poor.

KAWANT MELA Kawant Village, Near Chhota Udepur   APRIL/MAY   VADODARA DISTRICT

Primarily celebrated by the Rathwas, people from various villages gather at Kawant. To distinguish themselves, the women of each village wear the same colored *dupatta* and skirts, while the men do the same with their shirts and turbans. Everyone dances to drum beats and flute tunes to celebration the harvest. The men, who carry sugarcane, are adorned with traditional silver ornaments and belts covered in small brass bells that create music when they gyrate their hips and bellies. Chhota Udepur and Vadodara are convenient hubs from which to attend the fair.

AHMEDABAD DISTRICT	**RATH YATRA Ahmedabad**	JULY/AUGUST

From the break of dawn, a massive procession of devotees gather at the Jagdish Mandir situated in the Jamalpur quarter of Ahmedabad. Gigantic chariots carrying idols of Krishna, Balaram and their sister Subhadra are pulled by throngs of followers through the Old City. Afterwards the idols are immersed in the Sabarmati River. The parade commemorates Krishna's journey from Mathura to Dwarka and the grieving *gopis* he left behind. Musical bands lead the procession as caparisoned elephants, gymnasts, acrobats and other colorful performers execute astonishing feats. Although extremely crowded, the Rath Yatra is a rich spectacle worth witnessing.

JAMNAGAR DISTRICT

JANMASHTAMI Dwarka   AUGUST/SEPTEMBER

Celebrated throughout Gujarat, the most elaborate festivities of Janmashtami are in Dwarka, the historical kingdom of Krishna. This festival marks the birth of Krishna with day-long *bhajans* and sermons. At midnight, celebrations take on fervor with events reenacting Krishna's childhood, including folk dances like Garba and Raas. Some of the local boys and men form a human pyramid, which a young boy dressed up as Krishna then climbs to break a suspended pot of *makhan* (freshly churned butter). This tradition honors the mischievous Krishna, who would steal *makhan* from the village *gopis*. The Dakor Temple in Kheda District also has a lively celebration.

SURENDRANAGAR DISTRICT

TARNETAR FAIR Tarnetar   AUGUST/SEPTEMBER

This three-day fair commemorates Arjun's arrival in Panchal to win the hand of the beautiful princess Draupadi. First he had to compete in a *swayamvar*. The contest involved shooting an arrow to pierce the eye of a rotating fish suspended from a disc by looking at its reflection in a pond. Arjun accomplished the difficult feat and took home his bride. In this spirit the tribal youth of the area gather near the Trineteshwar Shiva Temple, otherwise known as Tarnetar, to identify a significant other. Unique costumes and hairstyles distinguish the single from the betrothed. The main treat is the intricate, hand-embroidered parasols made and carried by the bachelors. The celebration includes non-stop dancing, music, craft and food. The office of Gujarat Tourism arranges tented accommodation and special packages.

KACHCHH DISTRICT

RAVECHI FAIR Nani Rav   AUGUST (TWO DAYS AFTER TARNETAR)

About 50,000 people gather, mostly from the Charan, Ahir and Rabari communities, to bestow offerings to Ravechi Mata. During this celebration, newlywed couples of the Ahir community come clad in their traditional wedding finery to ask for blessings. In the evenings, the Charan bards narrate folk stories and perform folk music.

AHMEDABAD DISTRICT

GANESH CHATURTHI Ahmedabad   AUGUST/SEPTEMBER

This Maratha tradition arrived in Gujarat with the rule of the Gaekwads. The festival celebrates the birthday of Ganesh, the remover of obstacles. Followers take clay idols of Ganesh home in a procession and offer worship for nine days. On the tenth day, the deities are taken out in a parade and immersed in the nearest water body. This is accompanied with music and dancing. In Ahmedabad thousands flock to the Sabarmati River and Kankaria Lake for the celebration.

Celebrating Navratri.

Firkiwalas prepare manjo (kite string) for Uttarayan.

BHADRAPAD PURNIMA Ambaji   AUGUST/SEPTEMBER

On this full moon night thousands of devotees, especially farmers reaching the end of their busy monsoon season, visit the temple of Ambaji to pay their respect to the Goddess Amba, considered the original power of the universe. The fair is held in the center of the town on the temple grounds, which fill with temporary shops, stalls and rides. Performances of Bhavai and Garba are organized while devotees attend the readings of the *Saptashati*, seven hundred verses in praise of the Goddess.

NAVRATRI Across Gujarat   OCTOBER/NOVEMBER

The world's longest dance festival, Navratri is a nine-day celebration that honors the Mother Goddess and her different forms each night. The celebration takes over the state with the young and old dancing Garba and Raas into the early mornings. Garba consists of people dancing in a circle around a *garbo* (an earthen pot with holes and a lamp lit inside); Raas is a dance played with sticks. The nine nights lead up to Dassera, which honors the victory of Rama over Ravana. In some places effigies of Ravana are stuffed with fire crackers and burnt to represent the triumph. Navratri is celebrated in every village, town and city across Gujarat.

DIWALI Across Gujarat   OCTOBER/NOVEMBER

Known as the "festival of lights", Diwali signifies the victory of good over evil and marks the return of Rama to his kingdom after defeating the evil Ravana. Part of a five-day celebration that includes Dhanteras, Kali Chaudas (rituals to

ward off evil spirits), New Year (among Gujaratis only) and Bhai Bhij, Diwali is celebrated with Lakshmi *puja* (offerings to the Goddess of wealth) and followed with firecrackers. People clean their houses, prepare sweets, make *rangoli* (floor designs created with colored powder) and light up the streets with oil lamps. The following day, family and friends greet one another with good wishes for the New Year. On Bhai Bij, sisters wish their brothers a year of prosperity and happiness and invite them over for dinner. Five days after Diwali is Labh Pacham, an auspicious day to commence business. Most shops remain closed from Diwali to Pacham.

LILI PARIKRAMA FAIR Mount Girnar — OCTOBER/NOVEMBER — JUNAGADH DISTRICT

Performed as an act of thanksgiving after the rains, the Parikrama commences from Dev Uthav Ekadasi (the 11th day of the bright half of the lunar month immediately following Diwali). It is believed that all the deities of the Hindu Pantheon gather at Mt Girnar, known as the holy land of Revantachal from the Vedic period. Over two days, more than 800,000 pilgrims walk clockwise around the mountain in a circuit that covers 32 km. They make two night halts, one at Jina Bawa ni Madhi and the other at Bor Devi. Since this celebration arrives at the end of monsoon, the mountain is lush with vegetation.

SHAMLAJI MELA Shamlaji — NOVEMBER/DECEMBER — SABARKANTHA DISTRICT

More than 200,000 people of various communities visit the Shamlaji Temple in the days leading up to the full moon night of the Hindu month of Kartik. They go to worship the deity and take a dip in the Meshwo River. Many members of the Bhil community attend to pay respect to Shamlaji, whom they refer to as Kaliyo Dev (Dark Divinity). A large number of devotees arrive to the fair on foot, singing devotional songs and carrying banners marked with sacred symbols. Temporary shops and rides add to the ambience of this picturesque site during the two-week celebration.

AHMEDABAD DISTRICT

VAUTHA FAIR Vautha   NOVEMBER/DECEMBER

The only animal trading fair in Gujarat, thousands of donkeys and hundreds of camels embellished with decorations and bright paint are brought to the fair grounds at the Sangam Tirth, where locals believe seven holy rivers once met. Legend holds that on the full moon night of the Hindu month of Kartik, the son of Shiva, Kartikeya, visited this site. In honor of this myth, people bathe in the river and enjoy a week of food, crafts, rides, dancing and folk performances.

AHMEDABAD DISTRICT

MUHARRAM Ahmedabad   ISLAMIC MONTH OF MUHARRAM

Muharram is the first month in the Islamic calendar. During the first ten days, Shia Muslims commemorate the Battle of Karbala in which the grandson of Prophet Muhammad, Imam Hussain, was martyred. The tribute reaches its climax on the tenth day of Muharram, known as Ashurah. The *tazia* procession comprises impressive bamboo and tinsel floats that represent the martyr's tomb, accompanied by devout followers beating their breasts in mourning. Acrobats, singers, dancers and drummers enact scenes depicting the battle.

AHMEDABAD DISTRICT

SHAH ALAM URS FAIR Ahmedabad   ISLAMIC MONTH OF JAMADI-UL-AKHAR

The fair commemorates the death of the saint, Shah Alam, who legend says wielded miraculous powers. The festival begins with a cleansing of the beautiful stone-carved tomb with sandalwood paste. Then for one week, people of all denominations visit the tomb, lighting oil lamps to ask for blessings and to atone their sins. Koran readings take place during the evenings and hawkers set up stalls on the premises.

From Top: International Kite Festival in Ahmedabad; Janmashtami in Kachchh; procession for Ganesh Chaturthi in Vadodara.

SUGGESTED ITINERARIES

All of these itineraries assume Ahmedabad as the starting point. Spend the night at the last place listed for each day. Refer to the relative section of the book for more information about each destination.

KACHCHH

Day 1	Ahmedabad-Bhuj-Bhujodi-Bhuj
Day 2	Bhuj-Banni-Hodka-Bhuj
Day 3	Bhuj-Nirona-Zura-Than-Moti Virani
Day 4	Moti Virani-Nakhatrana (for bus connection)-Koteshwar-Lakhpat-Nakhatrana (for bus connection)-Moti Virani
Day 5	Moti Virani-Nakhatrana (for bus connection)-Mandvi
Day 6	Mandvi-Bhuj
Day 7	Bhuj-Ahmedabad

For anyone interested in the Indus Valley Civilization or archaeology, add Dholavira to the itinerary and give one full day to visit the site. It is best approached by private vehicle.

If you have the time you should add the following to the beginning or end of your Kachchh itinerary.

Day 1	Ahmedabad-Dasada-Jhinjhuwada-Dasada
Day 2	Dasada-Bhuj

SAURASHTRA

Travel in Saurashtra is time consuming because of the long distances between destinations.

Day 1	Ahmedabad-Jamnagar
Day 2	Jamnagar-Dwarka
Day 3	Dwarka-Porbandar
Day 4	Porbandar-Veraval/Somnath
Day 5	Veraval/Somnath-Ahmedpur Mandvi and/or Diu
Day 6	Ahmedpur Mandvi and/or Diu-Sasan Gir
Day 7	Sasan Gir-Junagadh
Day 8	Junagadh-Mt Girnar-Junagadh
Day 9	Junagadh-Palitana
Day 10	Palitana-Shihor-Bhavnagar OR Palitana-Ahmedabad
Day 11	Bhavnagar-Lothal-Ahmedabad

NORTHERN GUJARAT

Day 1	Ahmedabad-Dasada
Day 2	Dasada-Modhera-Patan-Mahesana
Day 3	Mahesana-Vadnagar-Idar
Day 4	Idar-Vijaynagar and Polo-Kadoli Farm (Rent a car to travel the Vijaynagar-Polo Circuit)
Day 5	Kadoli Farm-Shamlaji-Ahmedabad OR Vijaynagar-Udaipur in Rajasthan (160km) OR Vijaynagar-Ambaji-Mt Abu in Rajasthan (137 km)

EASTERN/SOUTHERN GUJARAT

Day 1	Ahmedabad-Vadodara
Day 2	Vadodara
Day 3	Vadodara-Champaner-Pavagadh-Chhota Udepur
Day 4	Chhota Udepur*-Sankheda-Dabhoi-Vadodara
Day 5	Vadodara- Saputara
	(Skip the national highway and take a scenic drive (6 hrs) along the following route: Dabhoi-Tilakwada-Garudeshvar-Rajpipla-Netrang-Mandvi-Valod-Vansda-Saputara. Buses also travel from Vadodara to Saputara.)
Day 6	Saputara-Explore the Dangs-Saputara
Day 7	Saputara-Surat-Vadodara OR
	Saputara-Vansda-Dharampur-Valsad

*It is possible to travel from Chhota Udepur via Dahod to Ujjain/Bhopal in Madhya Pradesh. From Surat and Valsad frequent trains travel to both Ahmedabad and Mumbai.

AHMEDABAD CITY

This is a suggested two-day itinerary for anyone spending some time in the city. Read the Ahmedabad City section for a more details on each place. Rickshaws and buses are the best way to get around the city. A private vehicle would be nice for visits to Sarkhej and Adalaj, but not necessary.

Day 1	0800-1030	Heritage Walk*
	1030-1330	Adalaj Stepwell
	Lunch	Swati Snacks
	1500-1700	Gandhi Ashram
	Dinner	Seva Cafe
	Post-Dinner	Walk through Manek Chowk or Law Garden at night
Day 2	1030-1200	Calico Museum*
	1200-1330	Hutheesing Temple and Siddi Saiyed Mosque
	Lunch	Green House at Lal Darwaza
	1430-1630	Explore Walled City
	1630-1800	Sarkhej Roza (watch sunset)
	Dinner/Entertainment	Vishala/Vechaar Museum (at least 2 hrs)

*These have scheduled tours, so be sure to follow the times listed.

If you are in Ahmedabad on a Sunday, make it to the Ravivari Market (Gujari) under Ellisbridge.

Day excursions from Ahmedabad	Weekend excursions from Ahmedabad
Patan-Modhera-Siddhpur	Dasada-Zainabad-Jhinjhuwada
Idar	Palitana-Shihor
Sojali	Champaner-Pavagadh
Jhinjhuwada (lunch at Zainabad)	
Anand	
Wadhwan and surroundings	

AHMEDABAD

AHMEDABAD

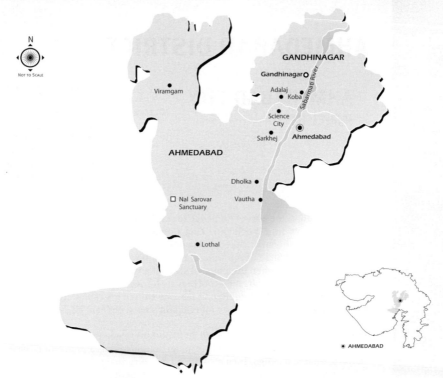

GANDHINAGAR

Gandhinagar○

Adalaj
Koba

Viramgam

Science
City

Sarkhej **Ahmedabad**

AHMEDABAD

Dholka ●

□ Nal Sarovar
Sanctuary

Vautha ●

● Lothal

Sabarmati River

◉ AHMEDABAD

AT A GLANCE

Situated in the heart of Gujarat, Ahmedabad District is home to the city of Ahmedabad, which has a character like no other, defined by a spirit of enterprise. Although Ahmedabad is a bustling metropolitan with reputed institutes and a rapidly growing economy, it is also deeply rooted in tradition. The city is known for its association with Mahatma Gandhi and, in addition to a complex maze of neighborhoods called *pols*, hosts some of the country's finest medieval Islamic architecture. Sarkhej Roza, just outside the city, is a mesmerizing inheritance of the Gujarat Sultanate and makes for an idyllic retreat. For an excursion into nature, Nal Sarovar, an extensive wetland, attracts thousands of migratory birds during winter. The neighboring Gandhinagar District is home to Gandhinagar, the state capital, and Adalaj, a classic example of Gujarat's enchanting stepwells.

AHMEDABAD DISTRICT

AHMEDABAD CITY

અમદાવાદ

	POPULATION	3,694,900
	AREA CODE	079
DISTANCES -	MUMBAI	545 KM
	NEW DELHI	1,025 KM
	VADODARA	110 KM
	SURAT	280 KM
	RAJKOT	225 KM
	BHUJ	395 KM

In the early 11th c. the area of Ahmedabad was known as Ashaval and was ruled by a Bhil chief. In 1074 the Solanki King Karnadev defeated the Bhils and built a neighboring settlement called Karnavati. A little more than three centuries later, King Ahmed Shah of the Gujarat Sultanate was hunting on the banks of the Sabarmati River when the unusual sight of a hare chasing a hound caught his attention. Impressed by the act of bravery he decided that the precinct must possess some miraculous quality. In 1411, he shifted his capital from Patan to Ahmedabad, which would evolve into Gujarat's most eminent city.

The rich mercantile class has played an important role in the prosperity of the city. As traders, they dealt primarily in indigenous materials and commodities—cotton textiles and indigo. They also traded in luxury goods, but promoted local value addition by local craftsmen. This brought prosperity not only to themselves but also to the city and its surroundings. For example, Ahmedabad's famous silk manufacturing process involved eleven sets of workmen, from the import of raw material to the marketing of the finished product. The trading classes were generally Jain and Hindu, while the master craftsmen were Muslims. This led to a comfortable symbiosis between the different communities. By catering to a wide clientele ranging from ordinary people to royalty, the merchants ensured that business never suffered irreversible setbacks. As investors, they supported anything from new enterprises to military campaigns. While ethical in their personal lives, they were indifferent about what they traded in or financed, as long as there was profit to be made.

One of Ahmedabad's greatest contributions from the Sultanate period is its outstanding architecture, which is also testament to the Muslim-Jain-Hindu synthesis of that time. Contrary to the spirit of most Islamic architecture elsewhere, it abandoned sheer monumentality in favor of aesthetics. Ahmedabad probably has the largest number of mosques and tombs of any medieval Indian city.

The city was about business and was well linked to the important port of Khambhat and to flourishing markets in surrounding regions and in faraway Delhi, Agra, Rajputana and Malwa. According to accounts left by some foreign travelers, Ahmedabad was one of the finest cities of the world in the 16th c.

The pioneering spirit of Ahmedabad came to the fore during the 19th c. under British rule. Above all, this included the establishment of a modern textile industry supported entirely by indigenous capital investment and local management. Entrepreneurs adopted technical know-how from other parts of India and from abroad. It was through these efforts that the city earned its nickname, "Manchester of the East".

After returning from South Africa in 1915, Mahatma Gandhi established his ashram in Ahmedabad, and it remained the nucleus of his social and political activities until 1930. The ashram attracted prominent figures from all over the world who joined his non-violent struggle to free India from British rule.

One striking feature of modern Ahmedabad is the number of nationally and internationally renowned institutions, all established primarily by local leaders with global vision. Today, the city is quickly "developing", both in area and in population, and has recently been labeled a "mega city", drawing much attention and investment to the region.

Gandhinagar, the state capital, was formed out of Ahmedabad District in the 1960s. The combined area of Ahmedabad and Gandhinagar districts marks a transition between the fertile lands of the east, the desert of the north and the scrub and grassland vegetation of the west and south. Other than a short stretch of coastline to the southeast along the Gulf of Khambhat, the district is land-locked. However it includes the 4000 year-old Harappan port of Lothal, once accessed from the Gulf, the only known port town of the Indus Valley Civilization.

PLACES OF INTEREST

The Sabarmati River divides Ahmedabad into two distinct parts. The east of the river includes the original Walled City. In 1875 the city began expanding to the west of the river, where many educational institutions, residential suburbs and commercial complexes are found.

EAST OF SABARMATI RIVER
North of the Walled City

The Calico Museum
This is one of the best textile museums in the world. It is managed by a charitable trust, founded by a pioneering business family that is also active in conserving cultural heritage. If you are interested in Indian textile traditions, this is the place to visit. It has a marvelous and well-labeled collection of textile artifacts, designs and technology covering a period of three to four centuries

from most parts of India, and some from neighboring regions in Asia. Museum publications, some reproductions, posters and greeting cards are also available. The timings and numbers of visitors are strictly limited to two daily guided tours, which last 75-90 minutes each. The morning tour (limited to 30 people) is of the textile collection, and the afternoon session (limited to 15 people) focuses on religious relics and bronze statues. *For current information on entry timings call 22865995.* To ensure that you do get in, arrive strictly before the given time. **OPEN Morning** 1030; **Afternoon** 1445. **Closed** Wed and public holidays. **Entry** free. No children below 10 allowed. **Photography** and **cell phones prohibited.**

The museum is situated in a wooded area that is startling to find in a city as dry and dusty as Ahmedabad. The palatial old mansion of the Sarabhai family not only houses part of the museum but is also an outstanding piece of architecture from the early 1930s.

The Sardar Vallabhbhai Patel National Memorial

The palace housing the memorial was originally built for the crown prince Khurram, Mughal governor of Gujarat who later became Emperor Shah Jahan. Legend narrates that the dignitary was riding an elephant to enter the new palace when he struck his head against the gateway. Considering it an ill omen, he left and never returned to live in the palace, one of the few Mughal monuments in the city. In 1878 the Nobel laureate poet and writer, Rabindranath Tagore, stayed here as the house guest of his brother, who was the administrative head of Ahmedabad District. It is said that this was the building that inspired his story *The Hungry Stones*. Today it is a memorial to Sardar Patel. A chronological exhibition of portraits and biographical descriptions of Patel's life, and a presentation of the Sardar Sarovar Project are on display. **Open** 0900-1800 **Closed** Sun and public holidays. **Entry** free.

Miyan Khan Chishti's Mosque

This mosque is slightly difficult to locate. It is situated on the river bank alongside Chinubhai Baronet Mansion at the southern end of Subhash Bridge. The structure, lavishly embellished for the era it belongs to, is totally enclosed without a courtyard, an uncommon feature in Indian mosques. The plain, dome-shaped tops of the minarets are probably part of the repairs done after damage caused by an early 19th c. earthquake.

Tomb of Daria Khan

This 15th c. tomb, about 1 km south of the Chishti Mosque, is built entirely of brick, with slightly tapering walls, arches and domes. The central dome is said to be the largest of its kind in Gujarat. The building stands apart in design from most Sultanate period architecture in the city. Although totally void of adornment, it compensates with its bold monumental appearance.

Hutheesing Jain Temple

This beautiful temple, built in 1848 by one of the influential families of Ahmedabad, stands near the Delhi Darwaza on the road to Shahibaug. Its presence is heralded by the "victory tower" standing in front of it. The presiding deity is Dharmanath, the 15th *tirthankar*. Made entirely of sandstone, its design motifs draw inspiration from the style of woodwork found in local architecture. It is covered with extraordinary carvings and sculptures.

Dada Hari ni Vav

Also known as Bai Harir ni Vav, this stepwell was built in 1500 AD in the area of Asarwa and is named after Sultan Mahmud Begada's harem supervisor, who was probably a eunuch. The *vav* marks an important transition to Indo-Islamic architecture of Gujarat defined by its use of elements from both Hindu and Islamic styles. The small but elegant mosque and tomb of Bai Harir, a short distance to the north of the well, are also worth visiting.

Shaking Minarets

The shaking minarets of Ahmedabad are often cited as unresolved mysteries of local medieval engineering genius. They come in pairs, in which the swaying of one causes vibrations in the other. The city has two well-known pairs of shaking minarets, one next to the Kalupur railway station built in brick during the 16th c., and the other as part of the 15th c. **Siddi Bashir Mosque** opposite Sarangpur Gate. Demonstrations of the shaking phenomenon are no longer allowed. The minarets at the railway station are in better condition and probably the tallest in Ahmedabad, but the mosque they once belonged to no longer remains.

The Wealth of Ahmedabad

According to legend, a guard at Bhadra Gate saw an elegantly dressed woman leaving the city late one night. He stopped her, asked who she was and what she was doing out alone so late. She explained that she was Lakshmi, the Goddess of Wealth, and was leaving the city. The guard said he would need the king's permission first, and asked her to wait till he returned. He realized that without Lakshmi the city would be doomed, so he beheaded himself. Lakshmi, living up to her promise, remains in the city.

EAST OF SABARMATI RIVER

Walled City - North of Gandhi Road

Dabgharwad

From Kalupur Gate, head east to Dabgharwad located in Dariapur. Here craftsmen make traditional Indian percussion instruments—the *dhol, tabla* and *nagara,* which conventionally consist of leather stretched across wooden or metal frames. Today plastic is increasingly used, altering the sound of the instruments. During the rainy season, these same craftsmen make umbrellas!

Swaminarayan Temple

The Kalupur Swaminarayan Temple, south of Dabgharwad, past Khajuri Pol, was built in the 19th c. in honor of Swami Sahajanand. It resembles something out of a fairy tale with all its color and opulent carvings that profusely embellish every wooden bracket, column and arch. The temple is notable for the attractive dresses and ornaments of gods and goddesses. The costumes of the Krishna

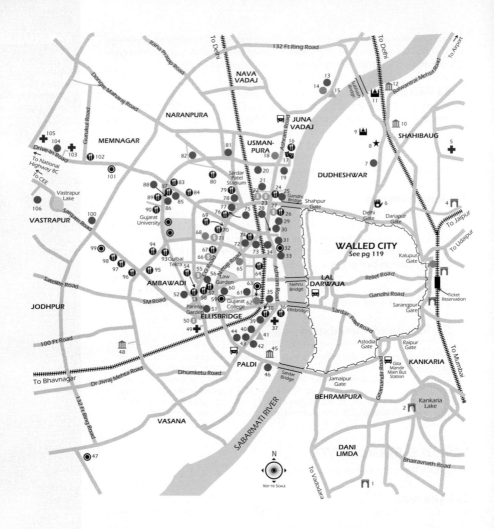

Ahmedabad City

Legend

Accommodation
3	Moti Mahal
14	Toran Guest House
18	Fortune Landmark
62	Inder Residency
65	Nalanda
68	Nest

Food & Drink
16	Café Natarani
24	Oshwal
26	Kandoi Bhogilal Mulchand
36	Gopi
38	Pakwan
47	Vishala Village
53	Asharfi Kulfi
53	Honest
54	Havmor
57	Swati Snacks
58	Café Coffee Day
64	Indu Ben Khakrawala
67	La Feasta
69	Sankalp
70	Seva Cafe
74	Mint Café
76	Mirch Masala
79	Jayhind Sweet
80	Derani-Jetani
83	Barista
83	Havmor
83	Tea Centre
84	Honest
87	Ek One Uno
89	Café Upper Crust
90	Kanubhai chaiwala
93	Café Coffee Day
94	Cellad Eatery
95	R K Eggwala
96	Birmies

and Radha idols are changed seven times every day and are never repeated. This is one of the most important temples of the Swaminarayan sect. **Open** 0600-1900.

The Heritage Walk

This is an excellent walking tour of the Old City organized by the Heritage Cell of the Ahmedabad Municipal Corporation (AMC). The tour includes examples of *pols* and *havelis* as well as some important historical monuments. It commences from the office above the main gate of the Swaminarayan Temple at Kalupur at 0800 and ends at the Jama Masjid at 1030. **TICKETS Indian** Rs. 30, **Foreigner** Rs. 50. *For more information contact 25391811.*

Tankshala

Ahmedabad's 400-year-old mint is situated across Relief Road from the Swaminarayan Temple, opposite the Shantinath Pol. Its elaborately carved teak wood façade is an excellent example of the old splendor of Ahmedabad's wood craftsmanship. The structure was recently refurbished by the Ahmedabad Heritage Centre, a partnership between the Municipal Corporation and the French Government to renovate and restore structures around the Old City.

Mata ni Pachedi

In Mirzapur, behind the main post office, and in Vasna, opposite the Swaminarayan Temple, you can watch artisans from the Vaghari community prepare Mata ni Pachedi (see **Resource Guide, Craft**), a textile art composed

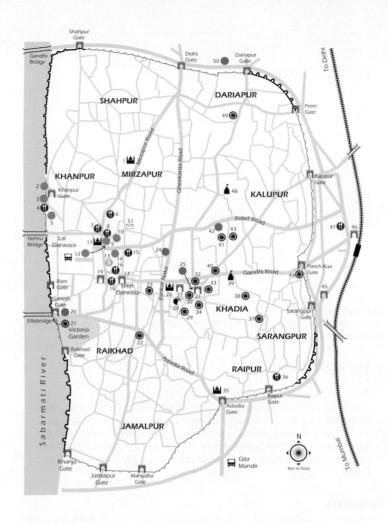

using the traditional techniques of hand painting and block printing. The cloth is used as a shrine to venerate the Mother Goddess. The peak season to watch these artisans at work is in the months preceding Navratri.

Rani Rupvati's (Roopmati's) Mosque

This is another example of Ahmedabad's exquisite mosque architecture. It has a central arch standing between two gracefully carved minarets that were truncated by the earthquake of 1819. You can see the blend of Hindu and Islamic styles in features like the temple-style balconies supported by brackets. Rupvati's tomb lies to the north-east of the mosque.

EAST OF SABARMATI RIVER
Walled City - South of Gandhi Road

Dhalgarvad
Dhalgarvad, near Teen Darwaza, is a lively cloth market selling a wide variety of fabrics at reasonable prices. From here travel southward to Khamasa Chowki, where within a 1 km radius, there is a place of worship for almost every religious faith in India. Ahmedabad's only synagogue is just north of this *chowki*.

Jama Masjid
This magnificent Friday mosque stands to the east of Dhalgarvad, off Gandhi Road. It was built during the reign of Sultan Ahmed Shah I and during its period, it is believed to have been the largest mosque in the subcontinent. The massive courtyard is surrounded on three sides by a colonnaded hallway. In the center is the conventional ablution tank. The prayer hall on the western side is divided into five bays, with 256 columns and roofed with 15 domes. The monument is a milestone in the evolution of mosque architecture in Gujarat. It successfully integrates the universal elements of mosques with ornamentation introduced by local Hindu and Jain master craftsmen in the form of floral motifs, *toran*-like portals inside the three central arches and free standing structures that resemble lampposts in the court.

Badshah no Hajiro (King's Tomb)
The King's Tomb is to the east of the Jama Masjid and is accessed by a connecting doorway. This mausoleum, dating from 1451, houses the tombs of Ahmed Shah I, his son Muhammed Shah II and grandson Ahmed Shah II. It was built during the reign of Muhammed Shah. Each of the four corners of the central hall is occupied by a smaller domed chamber with perforated stone screens set in arches.

Naubat

In the alley leading to Badshah no Hajiro, a *naubat khana* (drum room) sits above the entrance gate to the King's Tomb. A narrow entranceway immediately after the gate leads to a series of stairs. Every day 70-year-old Banubhai Sherbhai and his two sons, the 9th generation of *naubat* musicians, give a 15-minute performance of the *nagara* and *shehnai*. This Persian tradition was introduced to Ahmedabad when Sultan Ahmed Shah established the city in 1411. The orchestra announced the arrival and departure of the king, heralded dignitaries, accompanied festivals and occasions such as royal births, marriages and deaths and marked the beginning of war. The capture of the *nagara* signified the defeat of its army. The *naubat* musicians also served as the timekeepers of the city, indicating the time of the day through their music. The evening orchestra signaled *maghrib* (sunset) while the day's final *naubat* motioned the closing of the city's twelve gates. Today *naubat* commemorates the memory of Ahmed Shah. You can catch a performance Sat-Wed around 1930 (or sunset) and 2300 and on Thu-Fri around 0900, 1200, 1500, 1930 (or sunset) and 2300.

Rani no Hajiro (Queen's Tomb)

The Queen's Tomb is east of Badshah no Hajiro, across the street leading to Manek Chowk. Although squatters have considerably encroached on the surroundings, they add a lot of color with the bright buntings and decorative objects that they make and display. They are also the de facto caretakers and guides of the monument. Unlike most memorials of this kind, the tomb is in a courtyard, not a chamber. It is a nice surprise to find such a serene place in the center of an otherwise bustling area. You can sometimes catch artisans building *tazias* (large floats made from bamboo and paper) in preparation for Muharram (see **Fairs and Festivals**).

Manek Chowk

The heart of Ahmedabad, Manek Chowk is an experience for all of your senses. The main square, filled with various activities throughout the day, is connected by roads that branch off into assorted markets selling silver, cloth, utensils, produce and more. The area transforms into a popular late night eatery where you can enjoy excellent street food. Go past the old **Ahmedabad Stock Exchange** to get to **Muhurat Pol,** claimed to be the city's premier *pol* (see **About Gujarat, Architecture**). This is also where the **Baba Maneknath Temple** is located.

Baba Maneknath

Manek Chowk, Ahmedabad's oldest quarter, is named after the 15th c. Hindu saint, Baba Maneknath. According to legend, he used his magic to thwart Ahmed Shah's plans to build the new capital on his own turf, the east bank of the Sabarmati. Every day while the builders erected the fortress wall, Manek Baba would weave a mat. Then at night he would unravel it, and by morning, the fort wall would also have collapsed. On learning about this, the Sultan invited Baba to demonstrate his magical powers by entering into a small jar. When Baba did, Ahmed Shah sealed and buried the jar. Manek Chowk commemorates Baba Maneknath. In his honor the King also laid the foundation stone of the city in a bastion named Manek Burj.

South of Manek Chowk is **Mandvi Pol,** the largest *pol* in Ahmedabad with some 55 smaller ones located within it. Further ahead is a red-brick, colonial-influenced building with wrought iron gates that shelters the fruit market. Inside columns hold the ceiling high, leaving below open galleries for showcasing the produce. Behind the market, a few steps up to the left lead into the **Kansara Pol.** Here sounds of hammering fill the air as various households continue their family trade of molding metal sheets into pots and vessels.

From the eastern side of Manek Chowk, head north to **Chandla Ol,** an entire street that sells religious paraphernalia. The main product line continuously changes according to the demand of the season. On the way, there are a number of workshops where goldsmiths melt and remold old gold and silver. You can walk into one and ask to watch the process. Their products are sold in stores across the river, mainly along CG Road. Further down the lane, to the west, is the **Kandoi Ol,** which once boasted of 80 sweet shops. Today, there are only about half a dozen left. Head straight on Gandhi Road to the Fernandes Bridge, where there is a busy used book market. It mainly deals in textbooks, but you may find the occasional treasure. Travel further east along Gandhi Road, turn right at the Bala Hanuman Temple and follow the street southward to reach **Moto Suthar Vado.**

Moto Suthar Vado is an excellent neighborhood to wander around and explore the distinct character of the *pol* culture. **Jagdip Mehta's House,** another Ahmedabad Heritage Centre project, is a good example of a typical *pol* residence. It has a colonial-influenced façade with Italian tiles on the floors and a rainwater harvesting system. The ceiling in the sitting room is a 16th c. Italian design. The inner courtyard has also been redone and accentuated with mosaic tiling. Jagdipbhai and family will gladly show you around. The area has several more Heritage Centre initiatives and the owners are generally hospitable. Continuing towards the southeast, you will land in **Desai ni Pol,** where the conservation program had its most visible initial success. Some of the residents are quite open to letting visitors into their houses.

Rani Sipri (Sabrai) Mosque
Just inside Astodia Gate, at the southern fringe of the walled city, this mosque is small in scale, but its elegant simplicity has led some art historians to name it one of the finest mosques in Ahmedabad. At the northern and southern ends of the prayer hall are pairs of balconies, each supported by four brackets. Its slender minarets are solid and purely ornamental. Rani Sipri is said to have been a widow of Mahmud Begada. Her tomb stands west of the mosque.

Siddi Sayid Mosque
This mosque was the last significant monument of the Sultanate period. Although it was not completed, the exquisite stone grilles of its arched windows (especially the second and fourth in the western wall) are famous across the world for their fine tracery work. The delicate "tree of life" motif has become the distinguishing symbol of Ahmedabad. The builder, whose grave is in the forecourt, was a noble belonging to the Siddi community.

Ahmedabad Gates

Like many medieval towns across the world Ahmedabad had a citadel known as Bhadra. When the Marathas took over the city, they converted one of the citadel chambers into a temple for Goddess Badhra Kali, their *kuldevi*. Between Bhadra Gate and Teen Darwaza was a vast open space with gardens, fountains and possibly a few houses belonging to nobility. Beyond Teen Darwaza, where the common people lived, the city expanded and was eventually fortified to become what is known today as the Walled City. The city walls had twelve gates, three on each side facing the cardinal directions. Two more gates were added in the 19th c. The walls have largely disappeared except in a few places. The gates that still exist are now traffic islands, though you also have the choice to drive through some of them. A sign at Sarangpur Gate, however, officially forbids you to take an elephant through!

Ravivari Market (Gujari)

Held every Sunday in the river bed below Ellisbridge (Vivekanand Bridge), the Ravivari Market is a flea market that sells everything from second hand clothes, books, antiques and electronics to chickens and goats. The market has been around since the 15th c. and was originally known as Khaas Bazaar. It is a great way to spend part of your Sunday, rummaging for interesting finds while enjoying the chaos and character of it all. **Open** 0800-sunset. Nearby is **Manek Burj**, the foundation stone of the city. The adjacent **Ganesh Gate** leads in from the riverbank and is symbolic of Ganesh, the remover of obstacles in the Hindu tradition.

Amrutvarshini Vav

Near Panchkuva Darwaza, there is a simple stepwell. The steps lead downwards and then turn left towards the well shaft. Situated next to a small public building, the *vav* is easy to miss, but look for the signboard.

EAST OF SABARMATI RIVER
South of Walled City

Kankaria Lake and Naginavadi

Located 1 km from Astodia Gate, this man-made lake dates from 1451. It is a 34-sided polygon with a 1.25 km circuit and steps leading down to the water level. On the eastern side is an elaborately carved water inlet with three circular openings. This feature, common to several reservoirs in Gujarat, is a monument in its own right. In the center of the lake on an artificial island is the pleasure pavilion known as Naginavadi. The promenade around Kankaria is one of the few places in Ahmedabad to enjoy a walk without the fear of being hit by a vehicle. In the evenings it fills with crowds, food stalls and informal entertainment. There is also a water and light show. A zoo, a natural history museum, a special garden for children called Bal Vatika, and an open air theatre are placed around the lake.

Dutch Tombs

The Dutch and Armenian Tombs stand to the west of Kankaria Lake, on the One Tree Hill embankment. They are a reminder of the presence of the Dutch East

India Company in Ahmedabad during the 17th and 18th c. One of the lesser-known facts of history is that for a brief period between the arrival of the Portuguese and the consolidation of British power, the Dutch had a stronger trade presence and had penetrated deeper into India than any other European power. However, their main center of operations was in present-day Indonesia, and India was peripheral to their interests. The Armenians, fleeing from persecution in their homeland, found allies in the Dutch and entered their service.

Shah Alam Roza

The *roza* includes the mausoleum of Sultan Mahmud Begada's spiritual guide Shah Alam, a mosque, some other tombs and an assembly hall with minor buildings to house pilgrims. Dating from the late-15th and early-16th c. the complex is one of the largest of its kind in the city. Its ambience combines spirituality, worship, learning and community space. This is also where the Shah Alam Urs (see **Fairs and Festivals**) takes place.

The mausoleum has a central tomb chamber surrounded by a finely perforated marble screen and covered with a large dome jeweled from the inside with semi-precious stones and mother of pearl. The mosque has two *minars* with spiral staircases that lead to the roof and further up to the balconies. Beneath the northeastern quarter of the courtyard floor is a large vaulted water tank approached by a flight of steps. It provides water to the ablution tank.

WEST OF SABARMATI RIVER
Along and around Ashram Road

Gandhi Ashram

In 1917, Mahatma Gandhi established the Satyagraha Ashram along the Sabarmati River. He chose a barren location so that he could experiment with farming, livestock and other ideas. The land was also situated between a jail and a crematorium, a position that Gandhiji thought reflected where a *satyagrahi* should be prepared to end up. It was from this ashram that Gandhiji began his non-cooperation movement and evolved from Mohandas to the Mahatma. After the Salt March, Gandhiji moved his center of activity to Wardha and handed the ashram to the Harijan Sevak Sangh, which works for the empowerment of Harijans.

Gandhiji's sparse living quarters have been preserved as a small museum. The **Gandhi Smarak Sangrahalaya**, designed by the famous architect Charles Correa, hosts an excellent pictorial and documented record of the major events in Gandhiji's life, a library of Gandhian literature and paintings. The museum also has an archive of over 34,000 letters written by Gandhiji. Every single one is written on the back of used paper. The Hridaykunj (Gandhiji's simple living quarters), Vinoba-Mira Kutir (where Vinoba and Mira resided, during their separate visits to the ashram.) Prarthana Bhumi (prayer grounds), Nandini (guest house) and Udyog Mandir (training center for small industries) are also preserved for visitors. Behind Udyog Mandir stands a living memorial to Gandhiji—the non-profit organization Manav Sadhna, which works with people from the margins of society. They also run a small store that sells handmade paper products, handicrafts and items promoting Gandhiji's philosophies. The ashram is at its best in the early morning when parrots flutter through, the sun rises just across the river and people come to meditate in the serenity. **Open** sunrise to sunset, daily.

The **Kalam Khush** factory, where you can watch handmade paper being processed, is nearby. It also has a small sales outlet. The stretch of Ashram Road that parallels the ashram is dotted with several Khadi Gramudyog stores where you can pick up handspun cloth and other handmade goods.

Kochrab Ashram

When Gandhiji returned from South Africa in 1915, he established the Kochrab Ashram in the bungalow of a barrister friend in Paldi. It had to be abandoned due to a breakout of plague in the city. The ashram houses a small picture exhibition of Gandhiji, his *charkha* (spinning wheel) and a small library with an extensive collection of books written by and about Gandhiji. Parts of the former ashram, such as the guest houses, kitchen, store-house and rooms for inmates still exist. There is also the open air prayer hall where Gandhiji conducted his daily prayers. Although there is not much to see, the ashram maintains a positive energy.

Sanskar Kendra and City Museum

The Sanskar Kendra building, designed by eminent French architect Le Corbusier, is situated near Sardar Bridge. It includes the **City Museum,** which highlights Ahmedabad from various angles including history, craft, architecture, religion and fine arts. Take note of the world's tallest incense stick at 4.5 m. **The Kite Museum** downstairs has an interesting timeline on the history of kites, but the visuals are lacking. **Open** 1000-1800, Tues-Sun. **Closed** Mon.

Vechaar Museum

The **Vechaar Museum,** located in Vishala, displays a great collection of more than 3000 utensils, including metal vessels and a collection of nutcrackers. **Open** 1100-2200, daily.

WEST OF SABARMATI RIVER
Further West in Ahmedabad

Kasturbhai Lalbhai (KL) Campus and surrounding areas

This campus is home to a number of institutions that are usually buzzing with activity. In particular, the Schools of Architecture and Interior Design, both part of the CEPT University, are among the most versatile student communities in the city. Also on campus are the **Hutheesing Visual Arts Center**, a venue for art exhibitions and performances, and the **Kanoria Centre of Arts**, with interesting sculptures by resident artists displayed outdoors. With permission you can observe sculptors and painters at work. **The Vikram A Sarabhai Community Science Centre**, a pioneering effort in hands-on learning, encourages children to explore science and mathematics.

Amdavad Ni Gufa (Ahmedabad's Cave), also on KL Campus, is the combined genius of two world-renowned artists, painter M F Husain and architect B V Doshi. Actually a subterranean art gallery, its only feature seen above the ground is a series of interconnected and ribbed ferro-cement domes covered in white china mosaic and punctured with round windows. It is a whimsical and engaging piece of modern architecture. Right next door is the **Herwitz Gallery**, where occasional exhibitions are held. *For more information contact 26308698.* **Open** 1600-2000 **Closed** Mon. **Entry** free.

The **N C Mehta Collection of Miniature Paintings** at the L D Institute of Indology, has good examples of Indian miniature paintings. **Open** 1100-1700, in summer 0800-1300. **Closed** Mon and public holidays. **Entry** free. **The L D Museum of Art and Archeology** is on the same premises. Its collection spans several centuries and includes works in stone, bronze and wood. It also has miniatures and cloth paintings, scrolls, Indian coins and rare manuscripts. There are two galleries with a rich exhibition of idols from the 3rd-11th c., pre-Mughal paintings and rare wooden covers for palm leaf manuscripts. The museum runs a variety of programs and activities, usually announced in the newspapers. **Open** 1030-1730, in summer 0800-1300. **Closed** Mon and public holidays. **Entry** free.

Gulbai Tekra
Larger than life replicas of Ganesh and other icons of the Hindu Pantheon dominate the roadsides of University Road, along Gulbai Tekra. These deities are molded from plaster of paris and coated with kitschy colors. It is a treat to watch the artists at work, especially in the months preceding Ganesh Chaturthi (see **Fairs and Festivals**).

Law Garden
After dusk, the sidewalks around the Law Garden transform into a vibrant open market where you can purchase jewelry, apparel and handicrafts. It is a good place to get *chaniya cholis* (traditional Gujarati dress worn in Navratri). Remember to start your bargaining at about one-third of the asking price.

Modern Architecture
Ahmedabad has been graced by the presence and works of celebrated architects such as Le Corbusier, Louis Kahn, Balakrishna Doshi and Charles Correa. For anyone interested in exploring modern architecture it is worth visiting the Ahmedabad Textile Millowner's Association (ATMA, Corbusier 1954), Indian Institute of Management (Louis Kahn, 1962) and Gandhi Labour Institute (Balkrishna Doshi, 1984).

Shreyas Folk Art Museum and Performing Arts Museum
Based on the Shreyas Campus the **Folk Art Museum** displays Gujarat folk culture, including embroidery, beadwork, wood carvings, metalwork and utensils, costumes and animal decorations collected from Gujarat villages. **The Kalpana Mangaldas Children's Museum** (Performing Arts Museum), located in the same premises, is meant for children but is worth a visit for all. Its collection incorporates puppets, dance, drama costumes, paintings, recorded

music of traditional shows from across the world and more, with a special focus on southern and eastern Asia. **Open** 1030-1330 and 1400-1730. **Closed** Mon. **ENTRY** Children Rs. 7, **Adults** Rs. 10, **Foreigners** Rs. 90.

Art Galleries
Contemporary Art Gallery is a short walking distance from the Gujarat College railway crossing. Owned by renowned Ahmedabad artist Amit Ambalal, it encourages emerging talent to display their work. **Ravishankar Art Gallery** near Ellisbridge Gymkhana also displays works by local artists. Exhibitions at both are sporadic. Check newspaper listings to find out if anything is on.

ENTERTAINMENT

Natarani
This open air amphitheater is set against the backdrop of the Sabarmati River and hosts a variety of performing art programs. Although most events are exclusively for members, there are occasional shows open to the public. *For more information contact 27551389.*

Drive-In Cinema
Located on Drive-in Road, this cinema is a bit of American heritage in India. Catch a Bollywood movie at what is considered the largest open air screen in Asia.

NUTS & BOLTS

In and Out
The international and domestic airports are located about 10 km to the northeast of town. A rickshaw to Lal Darwaza costs about Rs. 85. You can also get a prepaid taxi at the airport. Ahmedabad is connected by air with Delhi (around 10 daily flights), Mumbai (16 daily flights), and other cities across India. There are at least a dozen daily express trains connecting with Mumbai. The Shatabdi and the Karnavati, the fastest day trains between the two cities, run six days a week. Gujarat Mail is the best overnight train. Delhi also has two daily trains. Foreign quota is available from Ahmedabad. Except for remote areas in the eastern districts, the highway network across the state is well developed, providing good connectivity between cities and towns. There are also plenty of ST and luxury buses that connect Ahmedabad and Mumbai (8 hrs), Udaipur (7 hrs), Mt Abu (7 hrs) and Indore (8 hrs). **Shrinath Travels** *25625351, Crosschamber, Opp Navchetan High School, Paldi;* **Bonny Travels** *2657658, Paldi Char Rasta* and **Ashwamegh Travel Agency** *26579978 Gopal Bhuvan, Opp Bonny Travels* offer bus services to other parts of the state and the country. The Gujarat Tourism Office (see below) carries a comprehensive list of bus companies.

Getting Around
Rickshaws are the best form of transportation around the city. The minimum meter charge is Rs. 7. Always make sure that the meter reading is set to zero

when you begin and check the meter against the rate card carried by drivers. From 2300-0600 rickshaws charge one and a half times the daytime fare. Rickshaw drivers in this city generally do not overcharge (except for those at the airport and train station). Ahmedabad has almost entirely phased out its petrol rickshaws in favor of CNG (compressed natural gas), distinguished by their yellow and green bodies. This has had a positive impact on the air quality of the city. There is also a shared rickshaw and a public bus system that cover most areas. **Dial a Cab** *32920000* offers 24-hour AC taxi service and charges by the hour (Rs. 150 for 1 hr or 15 km, up to Rs.1200 for a full day or 250 km). The meter only starts running once they pick you up. They also offer transportation to or from the airport (Rs. 250) and railway station (Rs. 200).

Tourist Information

The Gujarat Tourism Office *26589172, HK House, Opp Bata, Ashram Rd.* **Open** 1030-1800. **Closed** Sun, 2nd and 4th Sat of every month and public holidays. There is also a travel desk in the Law Garden managed by the AMC. The House of MG has created an 80 min audio walking tour of the Old City that you can pick up at the hotel (Rs.100/person and Rs. 2000 deposit for the MP3 player).

Travel Agents

The following agents book international and domestic tickets, organize travel packages and car rentals. **Guru Randhawa** *9825039108* of **Gateway International** offers dependable and personal service. You can also contact **Parshwanath Travels** *27544143, Dhan Laxmi Cmplx, Nxt to Gujarat Vidyapith, Ashram Rd;* **Goodwind Travels** *26466292, 102 Aniket, CG Rd;* or Manish Sharma at **Akshar Travels** *26440626, City Centre, Nr Swastik Char Rasta, CG Rd.*

Money

ATMs Citibank *26425757, Rembrandt Bldg, CG Rd;* **HDFC Bank** *27545504, Ashram Rd;* **HSBC** *26402083, Maradia Plaza, CG Rd;* **ICICI** *26402330, JMC House, Parimal Garden, CG Rd;* **SBI** *25506800, Lal Darwaza.* **Bank of Baroda** *27545504, Income Tax Char Rasta, Opp Akashwani* also has a **Western Union.**
Foreign Exchange **Thomas Cook** *26409191, Super Mall, CG Road; 7541564, Sakar, Nr Gujarat High Court;* **LKP Forex** *26403760, Maradia Plaza, CG Rd;* **Weschel** *26444425, Samudra, CG Rd.*
Money Transfer **Western Union** is in the General Post Office *Relief Rd.*

Communication

Internet **Reliance World** *Maradia Plaza, CG Rd; Raja Cmplx, Vijay Char Rasta; Ideal House, Nr Padshah ni Pol, Relief Rd; Advance Plaza, Opp Swaminarayan Temple, Shahibaug.* **Sify Iway** *Om Cmplx, Swastik Char Rasta, CG Rd.*
Wi-Fi Several places offer wireless facilities, charges vary at each. **Tea Centre** *Vijay Char Rasta;* **Subway** *Mithakali Chho Rasta;* **Mocha** *IIM Rd;* **Lounge 9** *IIM Rd;* **Mint Cafe** *Mithakhali Chho Rasta.*
Couriers **Blue Dart** *22860725, Embassy Centre, Ashram Rd.*

Medical

HOSPITALS Civil Hospital *22683721*; V S Hospital *26577621*; Sterling Hospital (Private, multi-specialty) *40011155, Memnagar Rd, Gurukul;* Apollo Hospitals City Centre *66305800, Tulsibaug Society, Opp Doctor House, Ellisbridge;* Sal Hospital *26845600, Opp Doordarshan Kendra, Drive-in Rd.*
MEDICAL STORE Deepak Medical Store (24 hrs) *26462949, Opp Sardar Patel Stadium.*

Photography

Classic Color Lab *Nr Kochrab Ashram, Paldi;* Rama Color Lab *27682614, Gitanjali Shopping Centre, Darpana Char Rasta;* RK Color Lab *26574871, Nr VS Hospital, Ellisbridge.* One Hour Photo *Vijay Char Rasta; Ashram Rd, Nr Wadaj* has a good photo lab and also prints digital photos.

Bookstores

Crossword *Mithakali Chho Rasta* is a national chain with a good selection of English fiction and non-fiction books, maps and music. Art Book Centre *Madalpur, Nr Town Hall* is a one-of-a-kind dealer in art books, especially miniature paintings. Granthagar *26587949, Gujarat Sahitya Parishad, On Riverbank, Nr Mt Carmel School, Ashram Rd* carries a wide selection of English books related to social sciences and humanities. In addition to Gujarati books and literature, it stocks English translations of literature from other Indian languages. Kitab Kendra *26422136, Sahitya Seva Sadan, Nr Gujarat College* sells a large variety of fiction and nonfiction English books. Mapin *27545390, 10 B, Vidyanagar Soc, Opp Usmanpura Garden Gate* publishes Indian art books and also sells them from the office.

Libraries

Hazrat Pir Mohammed Shah Library *located in Hazrat Pir Darga Cmplx* is one of India's oldest libraries and has an extensive collection of rare and original manuscripts in Arabic, Persian, Urdu, Sindhi and Turkish. The Gujarat Vidyapith Library houses one of the city's largest collections, including books on the social sciences, Gandhian literature and works in different Indian languages. M J Public Library *Nr Town Hall, Ellisbridge* has a good stock of english books.

Markets

Reliance Supermarket *Mithakali Chho Rasta.*

Shopping

Gramshree *32954140 4th Flr, Shopper's Plaza, Opp Municipal Mkt, CG Rd* sells a beautiful selection of handicrafts including apparel, home furnishings, handmade paper products and more. The profits go back to the artisans and the women running the cooperative. Banascraft *6405784, 8 Chandan Cmplx, Swastik Char Rasta, CG Rd* is a marketing outlet run by the non-profit organization SEWA that sells a selection of Bandhani, embroidered and block printed apparels and accessories. Gurjari *26589505 Opp La Gajjar Cmplx, Ashram Rd* is the state emporium and has a nice collection of Gujarati and Indian crafts. Gamtiwala *Nr Rani no Hajiro, Manek Chowk* is a must for anybody who appreciates

Gujarat's textiles. The owner, Ahmed Gamtiwala, and his friendly staff will gladly show you their stock of good quality, often innovative, block printed, hand-woven and natural-dyed ranges. **Kapasi Handicraft Emporium** *27541986, Jitendra Chambers, Nr Income Tax Office, Behind Ajanta Centre* is famous for its selection of traditional Indian handicrafts including excellent bronze statues, sandalwood carvings, stone and marble idols, temples, wall hangings and more. **Sanskruti** *2644334, Suryarath, Panchavati* is split into two shops that carry a great assortment of fabrics, sheets, *dupattas* and home furnishings. **Fab India** *26852482 Judges Bunglow Rd, Commerce House II, Bodakdev* is a popular, country-wide retail outlet that offers a large selection of ready to wear eastern and western apparel, made with handwoven and printed textiles. They also carry a selection of home furnishings. **360 Home Store** *26409200, Sera, Law Garden* is a lifestyle store that sells a variety of contemporary home accessories produced in India and abroad. **NIDUS**, *National Institute of Design (NID)* is a retail outlet largely for products made by design students. **Bhujodi** *Mithakali Chho Rasta* carries a variety of Kachchhi crafts including shawls, dress pieces and more.

For unique souvenirs, visit **Bobby Mud Flaps** *Dariapur Darwaza*, where Bobby paints and sells the neon-colored, Bollywood-themed mud flaps you see adorning the bottoms of rickshaws. The red-cloth-bound account books found around **Fernandes Bridge** also make for great gifts. There are plenty of **Khadi Udyog Bhandars** around town that sell handspun cotton and other handmade goods, like soap and *chappal*. The stretch from Pankor Naka past Jama Masjid, often collectively referred to as **Manek Chowk** is Ahmedabad's largest open market where you can find everything from silver jewelry and *mukhwas* (Indian mouth fresheners with digestive properties) to plastic house wares and just about any trinket you can imagine. **Law Garden** is good for costume jewelry, traditional Gujarati dresses, bags and more.

Courses
Darpana Academy of Performing Arts *27551389, Usmanpura, Ashram Rd*, founded by the renowned dancer Mrinalani Sarabai, teaches Bharatanatyam, Indian folk dances, Carnatic vocal and instrumental music and the Kalari martial arts of Kerala; **Kadamb Centre for Dance** *26442886, Opp Parimal Garden*, started by eminent Kathak dancer Kumudini Lakhia, teaches Kathak dance, choreography and related art forms. **Saptak School of Music** *27544124, Shri Vidyanagar High School, Usmanpura Rd* is the place to go to learn Hindustani classical music, especially *tabla, sitar* and vocal music. **Rhythm Riders** *27477666, Abhirath Cmplx, Sardar Patel Colony* teaches *tabla, sitar,* keyboard and music.

ACCOMMODATION

Taj Residency Ummed *22869999 Airport Circle, Hansol* is one of Ahmedabad's few 5-star hotels and conveniently located next to the airport. **Facilities** swimming pool, 24-hour coffee shop/restaurant, laundry, car rental, money exchange, Wi-Fi. **Single** 5500-15,000 **Double** 6000-15,000.

House of MG *25506946, Opp Siddi Sayid Mosque, Lal Darwaza* is in the heart of the city. This refurbished mansion has 12 rooms that retain an old-world charm with all the modern amenities. Each room has its own character and most come with a traditional Gujarati swing. If you are going to indulge while in Ahmedabad, this is the place. **Facilities** Wi-Fi, TV, DVD/VCD/MP3 players, airport pick up, specialized tour packages, two excellent in-house restaurants. **Rooms** 3000-8000.

Fortune Landmark *39884444, Usmanpura, Ashram Rd* offers excellent rooms with good service. **Facilities** airport pick up, three restaurants, gym, Ayurvedic spa. **Single** 5500-10,000 **Double** 6100-10,000.

Cama Park Plaza *25601234, Lady Vidyagauri Rd, Khanpur* is one of the oldest hotels in Ahmedabad and offers lavish rooms overlooking the Sabarmati. All rooms are single occupancy with an additional Rs. 500 for an extra person. **Facilities** courtesy transfer, complimentary breakfast, a terrace pool, permit room for alcohol. **Rooms** 4300-5300 **Extra Bed** 500.

Inder Residency *26425050, Opp Gujarat College, Nr Ellisbridge* has modern interiors and a pleasant ambience, but rooms are slightly cramped. **Facilities** pool, courtesy transfer, health club, travel desk, good restaurant. **Single** 4000-6500 **Double** 4600-7100 **Extra Bed** 600.

Hotel Good Night *25506997, Lal Darwaza,* though slightly stale, has basic rooms that are good value for the money. **Facilities** western toilets, hot water, AC options, room service, TV. **Single** 450-650 **Double** 600-750 **Extra Bed** 125.

Hotel Volga *25509497, Nr Electricity House, Relief Rd* is a decent option. **Facilities** western toilets, 24-hour hot water, car rental. **Single** 450-650 **Double** 600-750 **Extra Bed** 125.

Hotel Balwas *25507135, Opp Relief Cinema, Relief Rd* has well-kept rooms. **Facilities** AC option. **Single** 450-550 **Double** 550-650 **Extra Bed** 150.

Toran Guest House *27559342, Ashram Rd, Opp Gandhi Ashram* offers a range of rooms from bare-basic to spacious and comfortable. **Facilities** running hot water, AC options, TV, restaurant, travel help. **Single** 330-920 **Double** 540-1100.

Stay Inn *255005724, Nath Chambers, Khanpur* has clean and bright rooms with a friendly staff. **Facilities** western toilet, running hot water, AC option, TV. **Single** 550 **Double** 630-1260.

Moti Mahal *22121881, Kapasia Bazaar, Nr Railway Stn* has well-kept spacious rooms with nice interiors. It is conveniently located near the station. **Facilities** western toilet, AC options, running hot water TV, good non-veg restaurant. **Single** 400-500 **Double** 450-630 **Extra Bed** 100.

Nest *26426265, 37 Sardar Patel Road, Behind Telephone Exchange, CG Rd* has a contemporary feel. **Facilities** AC option, TV, running hot water. **Single** 1700 **Double** 2300 **Extra Bed** 400.

Ambassador *25502490, Khanpur Rd* has very basic but tidy rooms, all with AC. **Facilities** western toilet, running hot water and restaurant. **Single** 900-1400 **Double** 1000-1700 **Extra Bed** 300.

Nalanda *26426262, Mithakali Chho Rasta, Nr Ellisbridge* although lacking in character, it is a clean and good option. **Facilities** AC option, running hot water. **Rooms** 2300-3750 **Extra Bed** 530.

FOOD & DRINK

Ahmedabad is full of good restaurants, many of which shut down soon after they start up. The following is a list of places that offer tasty food and have withstood the test of time.

Green House *in House of MG, Lal Darwaza* is set in an open courtyard with wooden tables and plenty of greenery. This place is recommended for its extensive menu of traditional Gujarati foods. Their drinks and *lassis* are excellent. Although prices are slightly higher, the food is worth it. For experiential dining, **Agashiye** *House of MG, Lal Darwaza* tops the list with its rooftop sitting and unlimited traditional Gujarati spread for Rs. 190.

Vishala Village, located in Vasna, was conceptualized by one of Ahmedabad's prominent architects, Surender Patel. It offers a dining experience in a traditional Indian village setting, where you sit on the floor to enjoy the extensive spread of Indian items served on leaf plates. The food is accompanied by folkdance, music and puppetry. **Lunch** Rs. 105, 1100-1400; **Dinner** Rs. 215, 2000-2300.

For Gujarati *thalis*, **Gopi Dining Hall** *Nr VS Hospital, Ashram Rd* is a popular spot that offers excellent options at affordable prices. **Pakwan** *Opp VS Hospital, Nr Ellisbridge; SG Hwy, Nr Judge's Bungalow* is a more upscale *thali* place.

Seva Cafe: Living is Giving

Though the home cooked food and open-rooftop ambience is some of the very best Ahmedabad has to offer, Seva Cafe is much more than just a restaurant. At the cafe, you are not a customer but a "guest," made to feel at home by a dedicated staff and team of volunteers. When you enter this space, which honors the Indian philosophy of Athithi Devo Bhava, or "Guest is God", you automatically become a participant in a social experiment. Each meal is cooked and served with love. It is offered as a gift – there are no bills! It's up to each guest to "pay from the heart," experiencing the joy of giving and allowing this experimental gift economy to continue. The space is a conscious celebration of *seva*, or service, where all proceeds support charitable causes, and everyone is encouraged to serve in their own community. The menu changes daily, offering local and continental items based on seasonal ingredients. Come early, as it only serves 60 customers a day. To volunteer, you must sign up in advance. There is also a small lending library and the Satya gallery with rotating art exhibitions. Open 1900-2200 Closed Mon. *Seva Cafe 32954140, 4th Flr, Shopper Plaza, Opp Municipal Mkt, CG Rd, www.sevacafe.org.*

Swati Snacks *Panchvatti Rd, Law Garden* serves an excellent selection of simple, healthy Gujarati, Rajasthani and Marathi dishes in a modern setup. Try the *mitha paan* just outside the parking lot. **Cellad Eatery** *Panjrapole Rd, Passport Office* offers a good unlimited salad bar for Rs. 135 and several a la carte options, which can be hit or miss. **Ek One Uno** *Vijay Char Rasta, HSG House,* is one of the best options for pizza in town. The dough is fresh and served with a variety of toppings. They also make good calzones, nachos and falafels. If you want authentic Italian food visit **La Feasta**, *4th Flr, Crystal Sq, Girish Cold Drinks Char Rasta*, which prepares tasty wood fired pizzas, a variety of excellent pastas and more. The prices are chic but worth it. **Sankalp** *Samir Bldg, CG Rd* cooks a delicious variety of *dosas* and other South Indian fare. **Coconut Grove** *501 Heritage Plaza, Drive In Rd* serves tasty South Indian dishes, both a-la-carte and *thali*, with the option of open rooftop dining. **Café Upper Crust** *Aarohi Complex, Vijay Cross Rd* is one of few bakeries in town that sells whole wheat bread in addition to indulgent desserts. They have an extensive menu that includes a variety of sizzlers and fish on the weekends. **Mirch Masala** *CG Rd* cooks great vegetarian and non-veg Punjabi fare, though slightly spicy. The best part is the ambience, a mix of Bollywood and the street-side *dhaba*. **Honest** *Panchvati, CG Rd; Vijay Char Rasta* is popular for its *pav bhaji* and *pulav* (rice dish). **Birmis 13** *Antriksh, Nr Polytechnic* musters up tasty stuffed *parathas* along with other Indian and Chinese items, all at affordable prices.

Meat lovers can try **Moti Mahal** *Kalupur,* one of Ahmedabad's popular choices, especially for its chicken *biryani* and kebab dishes. **Court Hyderabadi** *approx 100 m from Green House, Lal Darwaza* offers non-veg Hyderabadi options but at steeper prices. The dessert Qubani-ka-meetha is recommended. **Decent Hotel** *in Ellis Hotel* is recommended for its chicken *bhuna* and Afghani *tangdi* kebabs. **Z K** *Relief Rd* is another excellent choice. **Simrans** *Nxt to Hotel Le Meridien*, posh in its prices, prepares tasty *tandoori*, *pahadi* fish and mutton *biryani*. If money is no issue, **Khyber** in *Fortune Landmark Hotel* serves delicious vegetarian and non-veg Mughlai dishes. **Bhatiyaar Gali** *Nxt to Teen Darwaza* is an entire alley lined with non-veg eateries concocting Muslim cuisine specialties. The chicken *masala* fry is claimed to be a recipe from the Shah's Court. The *bara haandi*, a choice of 12 delectable meat stews left to simmer over hot coals, and the *seekh* kebabs served with freshly diced onions, lime and herb chutney are also good. The alley doubles as a meat market during the day, so it is best to go after 1900.

If you want coffee and dessert try **Mocha**, *IIM Rd*, a popular hangout with a variety of drinks, snacks and hookahs. **Mint Café** *Nr Crosswords, Mithakali Chho Rasta,* is also a good place to hang out and enjoy some continental snacks and a variety of drinks. To sip on a variety of hot and iced teas, **Tea Centre** *Above Barista, Vijay Char Rasta* is the place. They also have vegetarian and non-veg snacks. There is always **Barista** *Vijay Char Rasta; Rudra Square, Bodakdev* and **Café Coffee Day** *Opp Passport Office, University Rd; Nxt to Swati Sancks, Nr Law Garden*. **Café Natarani**, *Usmanpura, Nr Darpana Academy* offers a range of Indian food and snacks.

LOCAL SPECIALTIES **Raipur Bhajiya House** *Nxt to Raipur Gate in Blue Bldg* is popular for its potato, chilly and onion *bhajiya*. Always ask for a freshly fried batch. **Lucky Tea Stall** *Dinbai Tower, Lal Darwaza* was made famous by artist M F Husain, who used to walk barefoot to this old city joint for a tea break. It is known for its *masala chai* and *maska* bun with jam combo. The quirky décor includes a tree, tables flanked by anonymous Muslim tombs that predate the popular hang out, and a painting by Husain himself. For egg dishes, land up in front of NID to sample **RK Omelet**, run by Rajubhai "Kajal", who prepares more than 50 varieties of egg items, at about Rs.120 a dish. He also has a restaurant on Polytechnic Road. **Oswal Restaurant**, *Ashram Rd*, has been making *fafda, jalebi and gota* for three generations. Try the *jalebi* with homemade ice cream. You can also go upstairs for a full *thali* at Rs. 70. **Girish Cold Drinks** *Ashram Rd, Neptune Cmplx; CG Rd* is one of the many establishments that started in Manek Chowk and expanded westward. This is a local favorite for juice, ice-cream and snack foods. **Indu Ben Khakhrawala** *Mithakali Village* is a local legend for her variety of *khakhra* and other Gujarati snack items. **Manek Chowk**, in the heart of old city, transforms into a street food heaven in the evenings (1900-0200). Its role as an eatery evolved at the turn of the 20th c. from the demand of hungry workers returning home late from the mills. For the definitive *chai* experience, enjoy a quick cup of *masala chai* at **Kanubhai Chaiwala**, *Dada Saheb Pagla Char Rasta, University Rd.*

Some of the city's historical sweet shops (still found in Kandhoi Ol) have branched out to the west of the river, including **Kandoi Bhogilal Mulchand** *Opp Nutan School*, known for its fresh *mohanthal* and **Jayhind Sweet** *Nr Stadium Crossroads*, which specializes in *magas, dry fruit halva* and *penda*.

Ahmedabad has a range of ice-cream places. For a homemade taste try **Derani-Jethani** *Stadium Rd* and **Asharfi Kulfi** *White House, Panchvati*. **Havmor** *Vijay, Stadium, Panchvati* is always crowded for its variety of flavors. The popular **Amul** parlors and **Vadilal** outlets are found everywhere. **Gandhi Cold Drink House** *Khaas Bazaar, Nr Nishat Restaurant* is known for its *faloodas, lassis* and *kesar* (saffron) milk.

EXCURSIONS

Sarkhej   10 km from Ahmedabad

Sarkhej Roza is a mosque, tomb and royal complex dedicated to the memory of Shaikh Ahmed Khattu Ganj Baksh, the spiritual advisor of Ahmed Shah. It was under his advice that the Sultan decided to establish his capital in Ahmedabad. The Shaikh's mausoleum is the largest in Gujarat. To the west of his tomb is the simple and graceful Jama Masjid, and to the south, lies the tomb of Mahmud Begada. Though initiated by Ahmed Shah's son in 1146, the complex was finished a decade later under the hands of Mahmud Begada, whose prominent contributions include the Queen's Pavilion to the west, the palace to the south and an elaborate three-ringed water gate to the north of the lake. The *roza* was a retreat for successive rulers, each one adding a garden or pavilion. Sarkhej is another excellent example of a structure that combines Hindu and Islamic design. The best time to visit is around sunset. Even though partly in ruins, the *roza* is both majestic and serene. Buses leave from Lal Darwaza and travel directly to Sarkhej.

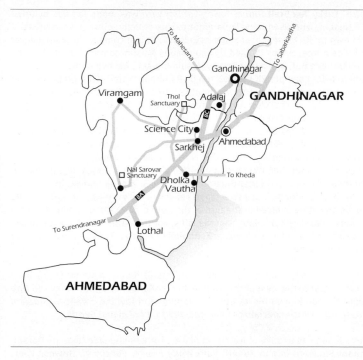

GANDHINAGAR

AHMEDABAD

The Azam-Mu'azzam Tomb will be sure to catch your eye when you pass Vasna, located on the way between Ahmedabad and Sarkhej. It is an all-brick monument from the Sultanate period that is believed to contain the remains of the two men who built Sarkhej Roza. Its four domed corner bastions make it look like a small fort.

Nal Sarovar Lake   65 km from Ahmedabad
The Nal Sarovar Lake is a freshwater body that fills up during the rains and turns saline during the summer. The area covers 120.82 sq km and includes a total of 360 islands of varying sizes. Ten villages, mostly inhabited by the Padhar community, are settled along the lake's peripheries. It has a rich biodiversity including 19 types of fish, various vegetation, algae and medicinal plants. It also has eight different types of habitats for birds and gives shelter to more than 250,000 birds (based on the Feb 2006 Census). Species include the Sarus crane, flamingo, stork, warbler, Red wattled lapwing, Fishing eagles, harriers, owls and hawks. You can hire a **punt** (Rs. 100/person/hour, rates decrease as group size increases) to get a closer view of the birds nesting in the reeds. The season runs from November through February. There are no food or water facilities in the sanctuary, but just outside, there is a **Toran Restaurant** and local herdsmen selling delicious millet *rotla* with freshly churned butter and *chaas*. *For more information contact the Assistant Conservator of Forests, Sanand 02717 223500.*

Viramgam
62 km from Ahmedabad

Viramgam was the official transit point between the Bombay Presidency and Saurasthra during British control. A place of interest is the **Munsar Lake**, built by Minaldevi in 1100 AD. It is surrounded by about 350 shrines in varying condition. Those to the east and south are mostly dedicated to Shiva while those to the north honor Vishnu. The lake is enclosed by a *ghat* that is poorly maintained. Viramgam can be reached by ST buses and trains from Ahmedabad.

Dholka
40 km from Ahmedabad

The town abounds in monuments built over the second millennium AD. It has three exceptional mosques from the 14th-15th c., each in a different style. The **Hilala Khan Qazi Mosque**, the smallest of the three, has fine filigree work. The **Tank Mosque** is profusely carved with Hindu motifs. The **Alif Khan Mosque** shows a strong Islamic influence in its design. Next to it is the **Khan Talav**, a large octagonal lake with stepped sides, named after Sultan Mahmud Begada's general. To its west is a sluice gate with three circular openings for water to enter. Several ST buses ply between Ahmedabad and Dholka.

Vautha
55 km from Ahmedabad

Situated on a confluence of seven rivers, this place comes alive with the annual Vautha Fair—a colorful donkey and camel trade fair (see **Fairs and Festivals**). From Dholka, catch a *chakkada* to Vautha.

Lothal
80 km from Ahmedabad

Of the several Indus Valley Civilization sites in Gujarat, Lothal is the most exhaustively excavated. It is believed to have been a flourishing sea port and trade center between 2900-2400 BC. The city was divided into a raised citadel and a lower town. On the eastern periphery are the remains of a dockyard, believed to be the first of its kind in the world. To protect from the neighboring sea and river, the city was built on a 2-m high platform. The ruins of 12 bath houses and drains suggest a concern with hygiene and sanitation that was far ahead of the times. The lower town was where the artisans lived, and where the bazaar and warehouses were located. The small but informative museum on site (**Open** 1000-1700. **Closed** Fri. **Entry** Rs. 2) displays the artifacts unearthed here, such as seals, terracotta, beads and an excellent set of weights and measures. There is also an artist's impression of how the town must have looked in its heyday.

While Lothal is a fascinating place, lack of proper guides, blazing sun and lack of drinking water on the site can make the excursion exhausting. Carry your own food and water on you and wear a hat. Buses from Ahmedabad take three hours. **Open** from dawn to dusk, daily. **Entry** free.

Science City

Located off Sarkhej-Gandhinagar Hwy in Hebatpur Village, this government initiative promotes science education through hands-on learning in the Hall of Science. It has an Energy Park that promotes renewed energy sources, an Imax Theater and a water, sound and light show. *For more information contact 079 65220111.* **Open** 1500-2100, daily. **ENTRY Children** Rs. 5, **Adult** Rs. 10.

Adalaj
15 km from Ahmedabad

One of the best stepwells in Gujarat, Adalaj Vav was built in 1499 by Queen Ruda, the wife of Vaghela Chief Vikramsinh, as a resting place for travelers. It incorporates both Hindu and Islamic design elements. The entrance, at the south end, can be approached from three directions by steps, which converge on a court crowned with an octagonal opening. The steps descend five stories, passing beams, columns and brackets that are elaborately carved with geometric, floral and animal designs. There are images of human beings engaged in daily activities, such as churning buttermilk. At the north end is the main well shaft and preceding it a *kund*, with beautiful balconies looking over it. Two kissing fish adorn the shaft, perhaps to welcome the visitor to their world. ST buses travel directly to Adalaj. A rickshaw for a round trip journey from Ahmedabad costs around Rs. 150-200.

Gandhinagar City
28 km from Ahmedabad

Named after Mahatma Gandhi, this has been the state capital since 1970. Similar to Chandigarh (Punjab) in layout, the city of Gandhinagar is divided into sectors formed by roads laid in a rectangular grid. It is also known as the "Garden City" for all its greenery. The city's main tourist attraction is the **Akshardam Swaminarayan BAPS Temple Complex**. Spread over nine hectares, it includes a huge modern temple built in pink stone and white marble. A 3.3 meter idol of Swaminarayan in sitting posture is the central attraction, and the Narayan Sarovar, which surrounds the main monument, contains water from 151 rivers and lakes that the saint is believed to have visited. Interactive dioramas, animatronics and a wide-screen film narrate his life story. A 12-minute boat ride takes you through India's religious history and heritage. The city also hosts Indroda Park, popular for its life size replicas of dinosaurs and animals.

GETTING INVOLVED

Blind People's Association *079 26305082, across from IIM campus, Ahmedabad www.bpaindia.org* works with the visually impaired in areas of education, training, rehabilitation and support. **Contact** Tejal Lakhia.

CEE (Centre for Environment Education) *079 26858002, Nehru Foundation for Development, Thaltej Tekra, Ahmedabad, www.ceeindia.org* is a national organization that focuses on fostering awareness about the environment and promotes sustainable development through various initiatives, research and publications. **Contact** Rasleen Sahni.

Chetna *079 22111405, 3010 Desai ni Pol, Khadia, Ahmedabad, www.chetnaindia. org* works in the fields of nutrition, health, education and development. The organization reaches out to disadvantaged children, adolescents and women from rural, tribal and urban areas of Gujarat and surrounding states.

Drishti Media *079 26851235, Sandesh Press Rd, Bodakdev, Ahmedabad, www. drishtimedia.org* is a human rights and development organization that uses media and the arts to strengthen social movements and organizations while increasing the participation of marginalized communities.

Safai Vidyalay-ESI (Environmental Sanitation Institute) *079 23276127 Gandhi Ashram and Sughad Village, Nr Koba, Ahmedabad-Gandhinagar Hwy, www.esi.org. in* conducts trainings on environment and sanitation. It researches and promotes best practices for sanitation and hygiene, while focusing on the human rights of those involved in these processes. **Contact** Ishwarbhai Patel.

Gramshree *32954140, Shopper's Plaza, Opp Municipal Mkt, CG Rd, Ahmedabad, www.gramshree.org* is a cooperative that works towards the holistic development of underprivileged women and local artisans through projects such as income generation, skill training, creative development, savings, health awareness and education, all of which foster integrity and self-reliance. It also promotes preservation of Indian craft. **Contact** Anar Patel.

Indicorps: Service for the Soul

Driven by a theory that change is a human process, Indicorps develops programs that encourage talented Indians from around the world to participate in India's progress by applying their time and skills to pressing societal challenges. Indicorps, an international non-profit organization based in Ahmedabad, believes that personal development and community development are intertwined. Its intensive volunteer programs simultaneously nurture the leadership potential of individual participants while assisting their efforts to implement innovative grassroots projects. Indicorps' initiatives are part of a long-term strategy to promote a culture of giving that looks beyond monetary contribution. Past projects have included interventions in women's health, livelihood, education, sanitation, community mobilization and youth leadership. Stop by and learn how you can get involved in communities across India. *Indicorps, 079 26574791, 3rd Flr, Pran Vijay, HK House Ln, Ashram Rd, www.indicorps.org.*

Manav Sadhna *079 27561767, Gandhi Ashram, Sabarmati, Ahmedabad, www.manavsadhna.org* is a Gandhian organization that works largely with disadvantaged children to nurture their holistic growth in areas such as education, healthcare, hygiene, income generation and more. Their mission is to serve the underprivileged. **Contact** Jayesh Patel or Viren Joshi.

SEWA (Self Employed Women's Association) *079 25506444, SEWA Reception Center, Opp Victoria Garden, Ahmedabad, www.sewa.org* was founded in 1972 by Ela Bhatt. It is a trailblazer trade union that has made internationally recognized contributions towards promoting self-reliance and empowerment of women through various activities in areas of livelihood, literacy, entrepreneurship development, banking, family planning and health.

SOUTHERN GUJARAT

SOUTHERN GUJARAT

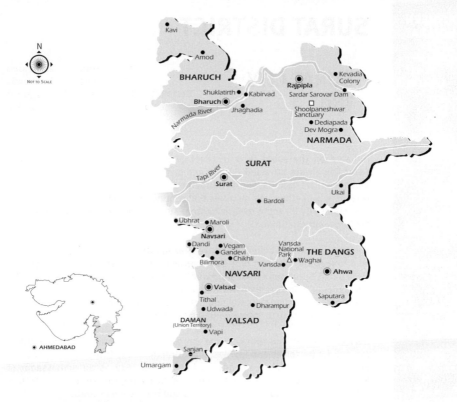

SURAT DISTR

N

NOT TO SCALE

Kavi

Amod

BHARUCH

Shuklatirth ● ● Kabirvad
Bharuch ◉
Narmada River   Jhaghadia

Rajpipla
Sardar Sarovar Dam
▢
Shoolpaneshwar
Sanctuary
● Dediapada
Dev Mogra ●

● Kevadia
Colony

NARMADA

SURAT

Tapi River
● Surat

● Bardoli

Ukai

● Ubhrat ● Maroli
◉
Navsari
● Dandi ● Vegam
● Gandevi
Bilimora ● Chikhli

Vansda
National
Park **THE DANGS**
△
Vansda ● ● Waghai

● Ahwa

NAVSARI

◉ Valsad

Tithal
● Udwada

● Dharampur

Saputara

DAMAN
(Union Territory)

VALSAD

● Vapi

● AHMEDABAD

Sanjan ●

Umargam ●

AT A GLANCE

This region stands apart from the rest of Gujarat for its combination of natural and cultural diversity. The foothills of the Western Ghats enhance the beauty of the Dangs with its vibrant tribal communities and thick forests. The verdant districts of Valsad and Navsari dominate the state's horticulture industry and reflect a distinct Parsi influence. Surat, Gujarat's second largest city, was once a flourishing port known across the old world. Today it thrives as a diamond polishing and textile center. The Narmada River, today popularly linked with the Sardar Sarovar Project, has ancient associations as an area of spiritual pursuit. It flows through the districts of Narmada and Bharuch, which abound in ashrams and temples.

114

SURAT DISTRICT

SURAT CITY
સુરત

	POPULATION	2,800,000
	AREA CODE	0261
DISTANCES -	AHMEDABAD	230 KM
	VADODARA	129 KM
	MUMBAI	282 KM

Situated on the south bank of the Tapi River, about 14 km from the sea, Surat has always attracted traders and merchants from afar. Its finely carved mosques, Parsi *agiaris*, European tombs and colonial houses all testify to the eclectic mix of ethnic communities that continue to live in the city. Surat is the first major city en route to Gujarat from Mumbai, and makes a good base to explore southern Gujarat.

The city is popularly believed to have been founded by Gopi, a Nagar Brahmin, who rose to the position of a governor under the Gujarat Sultanate (15th c.). Most likely, Surat was established well before this period, but flourished under his leadership. In 1572 Emperor Akbar annexed Surat. It then became a major mercantile center and the chief point of entry to the Mughal Empire. All Muslims going on pilgrimage to Mecca embarked from Surat.

Between the 17th and 18th c., Surat was one of India's most prosperous cities, reputed for its spices and textiles, and attracted many Europeans. Sir Thomas Roe of the East India Company landed here in 1612 as an ambassador of King James to seek permission from Emperor Jahangir to set up their factory (warehouse). The Dutch followed in 1616 and the French in 1668.

When the Marathas, led by Chhatrapati Shivaji, invaded the city, they demanded homage from the Mughal administrator and a small army to ensure their security. They were refused both. So the army plundered the Mughal and Portuguese factories. However, the English factory remained unscathed because the agent, George Oxenden, and his men staunchly defended it. The wealth Shivaji collected from Surat was used to strengthen the Maratha Kingdom. In 1759, the English took control of the city.

In 1837, a combination of fire and subsequent floods devastated the city. This, in addition to the financial opportunities of the newly established Bombay (now Mumbai), led many Jains and Parsis to migrate there. The rise of Bombay diminished Surat's importance as a major port and its potential to rank as the most significant city of western India under the British Empire.

Surat was once renowned for its silk weaving and brocade. The city still thrives as a textile center, mainly for its polyester fabrics. As the textile industries declined in Ahmedabad and Mumbai in the 1970s, Surat became one of Gujarat's fastest growing cities and gave rise to several small scale industries.

In 1994 the plague broke out in the city. The municipal commissioner and the citizens joined hands to make it one of India's cleanest cities. In August 2006, a severe flood inundated vast stretches of the city, but Surat proved its resilience once more.

SOUTHERN GUJARAT

▾ DISTRICT
▸ **SURAT**
  Surat City
  Bardoli

VALSAD
NAVSARI
THE DANGS
NARMADA
BHARUCH

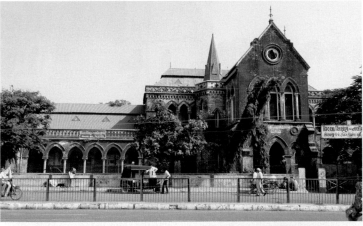

PLACES OF INTEREST

Surat Castle

In 1540 Sultan Mahmud III ordered the construction of the castle on the bank of the Tapi to protect the city against the frequent Portuguese raids. Today it houses government offices, but you can climb the steps to the ramparts, which offer a splendid view of the city and the river. Remains of the fort wall still stand in parts of the old town.

The **Hope Bridge**, built across the Tapi in 1877, helped ease communication with the neighboring districts of Bharuch, Narmada and places further north. **Sir J J Training College**, the imposing building across the main road from the castle, was built in 1872 with funds donated by a wealthy Parsi. Today it is a primary teacher training institute.

Mughalsarai

Built in the mid-17th c. under Mughal Emperor Shah Jahan as a *sarai* or guest house, this building with arcaded verandahs and cornices, served as a jail in 1857. In 1867 the Surat Municipal Corporation moved its offices into the building.

Andrews Library

Donated to the British Collector Andrews in 1850 by the affluent merchant, Naginchandra Zaverchand, the building first served as a hall for meetings and theatrical performances. At one time, large crowds would gather outside it just to listen to Parsi theater being performed. Now a library, it has Gujarati and Hindi novels and Farsi reference books of the historical princely states. **Open** 0900-1300 and 1500-1900, daily.

Sardar Vallabhbhai Patel Museum and Planetarium

Housed in a building dating from 1889, the museum displays over 12,000 artifacts, including a collection of porcelain from around the world and 18th c.

wooden furniture. The assortment depicts the rich history and ethnic diversity of Surat. It also stocks literature and maps for travelers. The **planetarium** next door regularly holds a show on the universe in Gujarati. **Open** 1115-1345 and 1445-1745, Wed-Sat; 1445-1745, Sun and Tue. **Closed** Mon.

Chintamani Jain Temple
An outwardly simple temple, its interior is a trove of fine craftsmanship. The wooden pillars display vegetable dye paintings that lead up to carved brackets. Built at the end of the 17th c. during the reign of Emperor Aurangzeb, it testifies to his patronage of art.

Marjan Shami Roza
This tomb of Khwaja Safar Sulemanim, governor of Surat, was built by his son in 1540 and has elements of both Persian and Indian architecture. Be sure to indulge at the small **Saurashtra Bakery** just behind the Roza, where Nanubhai Sayyedwala and his crew bake fresh *nankathai* biscuits in assorted sizes.

The European Tombs
The arresting tombs of the **English Tombs** lie just outside Katargam Gate. The cemetery holds over 400 graves. Notable among them is the shared tomb of Sir George Oxenden and his brother, Christopher.

The **Dutch Tombs**, situated in Gulam Falia on the main road leading to Katargam Gate, is a bit difficult to locate, but the locals will direct you. It has a number of exquisite spired monuments, including the tomb of Baron Adriaan Van Reede, which is composed of fine columns supporting a balcony, surmounted by an enormous double dome. This tomb was once embellished with paintings and wood carvings. The **Armenian Tombs** adjacent to the Dutch burial ground consists mainly of stone slabs inscribed in Armenian. **Photography** is prohibited at all of these sites.

Nankathai

During the 17th c. a combination of European influence and a surplus of wheat led to the local adaptation of the English biscuit using hard dough and ghee. In support of the Swadeshi Movement, many teashops in Gujarat and Bombay added these biscuits to their limited menus. Even today they are displayed in large glass jars at many teashops. Parsi bakers in Surat experimented by baking a local sweet called *dal* and created the *nankathai*. This golden colored biscuit is now made in a range of sizes and flavors and makes a delightful treat, especially when dipped in tea.

Vir Narmad Sarasvati Mandir
This quaint house located on Ambaji Road is the memorial and former residence of the famous poet, Vir Narmad (1833-86). Although there is not much to see there now, he used to hold literary discussions and musical programs in it. Narmad campaigned for a single national language, promoted self-governance and initiated an era of social reform through his literature. Born in Surat, he attended school in Mumbai, and after returning, built this house in 1866.

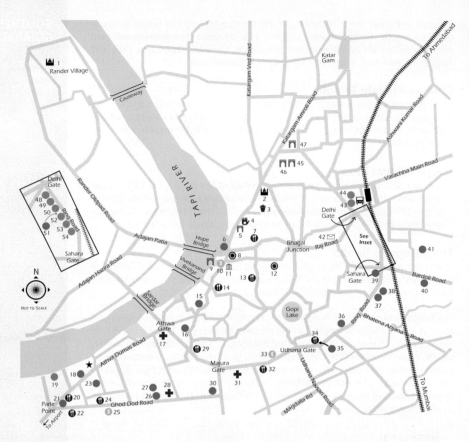

Surat City
Legend

Accommodation
19 Gateway Hotel / Café Riverside / The Haveli Restaurant
43 Hotel Central Excellency
44 Hotel Yuvraj
48 Hotel Stay Inn
49 Hotel Balwas
50 Hotel Samrat
52 Hotel Galaxy
53 Lords Park Inn / Copper Chimney Restaurant
54 Hotel Apex / Sahyog Restaurant

Food & Drink
7   Jamandas Ghariwala
13 Surti Locho
14 Dotivala Bakery
20 Cream n Crust
22 Coffee Culture
24 Silver Nest Restaurant
29 Sasuji Restaurant
32 Sugar n Spice
34 Sankalp Restaurant

Places of Interest
1   Jama Masjid
2   Marjan Shami Roza
3   Parsi Agiari
4   Chintamani Jain Temple
5   Mughalsarai
6   Andrews Library
8   Sir J J Training College
9   Surat Castle
11 Sardar Patel Museum & Planetarium
12 Vir Narmad Sarasvati Mandir
27 Narmad Library
37 Surat Textile Market
38 JJAC Textile Market
39 Sri Ram Textile Market
41 Bombay Market
45 Armenian Tombs
46 Dutch Tombs
47 English Tombs

Nuts & Bolts
10 SBI Bank
15 Gujarat Tourism Office
16 Gandhi Smruti Hall
17 Mission Hospital
18 Reliance World Cybercafé
21 Venus Photo Express
23 Indoor Stadium
25 LKP Forex
26 Food Bazaar
28 New Life Hospital
30 Kodak Express Kauntia Color Lab
31 Civil Hospital
33 ICICI Bank
35 Reliance World Cybercafé
36 Kinnari Cinema
40 Sardar Market
42 General Post Office
51 Belgium Tower
    * Indian Bank
    * Western Union Sangli Bank
    * Cybercafe
    * Pooja Color Lab Digital Studio
    * Blue Dart Express

Narmad Library

This library hosts an extensive collection of more than 15,000 books and a significant library for the blind. **Open** 0830-1300 and 1430-1900, daily.

SOUTHERN GUJARAT

▾ DISTRICT
▸ SURAT
  Surat City
  Bardoli

VALSAD
NAVSARI
THE DANGS
NARMADA
BHARUCH

Diamonds in Surat

Buy diamond jewelry anywhere in the world, and chances are the stones were cut and polished in Surat. Every day, thousands of diamond cutters walk into one of several diamond factories in the city to transform rough crystals into sparkling gems. They cut more than 80 percent of the world's diamonds and earn India about ten billion USD in annual exports.

A Surti entrepreneur returning with a boatload of diamond cutters from East Africa initiated the city's polishing industry in 1901. Business picked up in the 1970s, when India began cutting low-quality gemstones and exporting them to the US.

Although Gujarat dominates the polishing business, it does not produce diamonds. The rough stones come mainly from South Africa and go to Antwerp, Belgium, the nerve center of the international diamond trade, dominated by Hasidic Jews and the Palanpuri Jains of North Gujarat.

The Textile Markets

A flyover passes above the densely packed area between Maan Gate and Sahara Gate where several textile markets are situated. Made up of outdoor kiosks and tall buildings, they sell *saris, salwaar kameez* dress pieces and a host of other cloth in a range of polyester, silk, printed and embroidered materials. The major markets include **Sri Ram Textile Market, JJAC Textile Market** and **Surat Textile Market**. If you rummage through the **Bombay Market** (the best option for *sari* material) you might find an original piece of *jari* work— embroidery done with thin copper wire coated in silver or gold.

Jama Masjid in Rander

The Jama Masjid is situated in Rander, across the causeway. Built in the 16th c., the mosque stands four stories high on the support of wooden carved pillars.

ENTERTAINMENT

Gandhi Smruti Bhavan *Timilyah Rd, Nanpura* hosts regular plays, dramas and musical programs, often in Gujarati.

Indoor Stadium is a newly-built venue for various performances and exhibitions.

ACTIVITIES

Nature Club Surat *9825057678, 81 Sarjan Society, Athwa Lines* organizes numerous nature excursions, hiking, treks and other adventure experiences in the forest-rich areas of southern Gujarat. They welcome non-members to join some of their outings and offer insights into the natural wealth of the region, including places off the beaten track.

NUTS & BOLTS

In and Out
Surat is easily accessible by train on the Mumbai-Vadodara section of the Western Railway's broad gauge main line. ST buses and private coaches connect Surat to various centers in Gujarat, Maharashtra, Madhya Pradesh and Rajasthan. NH 8 also connects the city to Mumbai and Vadodara.

Getting Around
Rickshaws are the best way to travel around the city. ST buses offer services to other destinations in the district.

Tourist Information
Gujarat Tourism Office *2476586, 1/847 Athugar Street, Nanpura.* Another alternative is to visit the **Sardar Vallabhbhai Patel Museum,** which also carries books and tourist maps. Speak to the curator for more information on the city.

Money
ATMs SBI *Opp J J College, Chowk Bazaar;* **ICICI** *Shree Shyam Chambers, Opp Sub-jail, Ring Rd.*
FOREIGN EXCHANGE LKP Forex Foreign Exchange *Rajhans Complex, Ghoddod Rd* and **Indian Bank** *Belgium Towers, Ring Rd.*
MONEY TRANSFER Western Union Sangli Bank *In City Co-Op Bank Building.*

Communication
INTERNET Cybercafe *Belgium Towers, Ring Rd* offers internet use for Rs. 20/hour and Net-2-Phone; **Reliance World** *Ring Rd, Maan Gate, Nxt to Petrol Station; Anjan Shalaka Apt, Athwa Lines.*
COURIER Blue Dart Express *2421130, Belgium Towers, Ring Rd.*

Medical
Mission Hospital *Athwa Lines;* **New Life Hospital** *Ghoddod Rd.*

Photography
Process film at **Venus Photo Express** *Parle Point Place, Ghoddod Rd* and **Kodak Express Kauntia Color Lab** *Bhavik Complex, Ghoddod Rd.* **Pooja Color Lab Digital Studio** *Belgium Tower* also takes care of digital needs.

Markets
Sardar Market *Sara Gate, Puna Gam Rd* is the vegetable and fruit market. **Food Bazaar** *Picnic Building, Ghoddod Rd* carries groceries and everyday products.

ACCOMMODATION

Hotel Samrat *2420447, Opp Linear Bus Stand* is a basic hotel. **Facilities** squat toilet, AC, running hot water, showers, restaurant. **Dorm** 60 **Single** 100-450 **Double** 350-550 **Triple** 500-650 **Extra Bed** 75-100.

Hotel Galaxy *Belgium Tower, Opp Linear Bus Stand* is a cozy hotel. **Facilities** western toilet, AC, running hot water, showers, room service, TV, car rentals. **Single** 375-1000 **Double** 600-1300 **Quadruple** 1600 **Extra Bed** 150.

Hotel Stay Inn *2439455, Opp Delhi Gate* has small rooms and slightly cramped bathrooms. **Facilities** western toilet, AC, running hot water, showers, TV. **Single** 400-550 **Double** 500-650.

Hotel Apex *2432291, Opp Linear Bus Stand* is connected with the Sahyog Restaurant. **Facilities** running hot water, showers, TV, room service, car rental. **Single** 550-950 **Double** 800-1200 **Suite** 1150 **Extra Bed** 200.

Hotel Central Excellency *2425324, Opp Railway Stn, Nxt to Bus Stn* offers a range of rooms and car rentals, which you must request two hours in advance. The Panchvati Restaurant downstairs offers multicuisine fare. **Facilities** western toilet, AC, room service, running hot water, showers. **Single** 575-1400 **Double** 775-1700 **Extra Bed** 200-300.

Hotel Balwas *2425762, Opp Delhi Gate* has moderate sized rooms. **Facilities** western/squat toilet, AC, room service, running hot water, showers, TV. **Single** 550-700 **Double** 700-2000 **Extra Bed** 150.

Hotel Yuvraj *2413001, Opp Railway Stn* is centrally located, with moderate sized rooms. If you take the regency or royal package, rates include a car rental service (7 hrs/70 km). **Facilities** western toilets, AC, running hot water, showers, room service, TV, internet, restaurant. **Single** 990-1650 **Double** 1300-1850 **Extra Bed** 300.

Lords Park Inn *2418300, Nxt to Belgium Square, Nr Japan Market* has several amenities, spacious rooms and houses the Copper Chimney Restaurant. **Facilities** western toilets, running hot water, shower, TV, laundry, room service, swimming pool. **Single** 3500 **Double** 4000 **Extra Bed** 600.

Gateway Hotel *6697000, Ambika Niketan, Athwa Lines* is part of the Taj Group. In addition to all amenities it also has two restaurants, Haveli and Riverside. **Single** 4500-6000 **Double** 5000-7000 **Suites** 8000-10,600.

FOOD & DRINK

Surat is popular around Gujarat for its considerable variety of food preperations. The local cuisine is known for its liberal use of green chili pepper.

The **Haveli Restaurant** *in Gateway Hotel* serves Mughlai food and Gujarati *thalis*. **Sasuji Restaurant** *Ring Rd, at Majura Gate* is frequented by locals for its tasty Gujarati *thali* and also offers open terrace dining. **Sankalp Restaurant** *Ring Rd, Nr Udhana Darwaza, Nr Trade Center* is a popular south Indian chain.

The following are mid-range places that serve the general Indian, Chinese and Continental fare. **Pure Veg Silver Nest Restaurant** *Essen House Cmplex, Ghoddod*

SOUTHERN
GUJARAT

DISTRICT ▾
SURAT ◂
Surat City
Bardoli

Rd and **Lakeview Restaurant** in Piplod, Nr Kargil Chowk, Dumas Rd, an outdoor restaurant. **Sahyog Restaurant** in Apex Hotel serves a variety of options and is best known for its Punjabi food. **Yuvraj** in Hotel Yuvraj, Ring Rd has two sections, one that serves multicuisine dishes and the other, Gujarati thalis.

High-end choices that serve Punjabi, Chinese and Continental are **Copper Chimney** Ring Rd, Nxt to Belgium Square, which has both vegetarian and non-veg dishes, and **Café Riverside** in Gateway Hotel.

For coffee or pastries visit **Coffee Culture** Classic Complex, Ghoddod Rd. **Cream n Crust** Opp Eiffel Tower, Parle Point is a good place for cream pastries.

LOCAL SPECIALTIES Locho, steamed and spiced chick pea flour served with chutney, is popular at **Surti Locho** Gopipura. **Jamandas Ghariwala** Chauta Bazaar is the local favorite for Surat's delicious ghari, a rich, milk-based sweet. In addition to coffee and pastries, **Sugar n Spice** has a small menu of Parsi dishes. **Dotivala Bakery** Ardeshir Kotwal Rd, Makkai Bridge has been in the bakery business for more than two centuries, since the Dutch left their ovens with Faramji Pestonji Dotivala, who continued to supply breads to the remaining colonials. Although they sell a variety of baked goods and confectioneries, the assortment of nankathai and khari biscuits are strongly recommended. An added treat is the Dotivala history they pack with each order.

Every spring, jowar pauk (fresh, roasted millet) is commonly sold at various laris throughout the city. Variations such as pauk bhajiya and dal vada are also found.

EXCURSIONS

Bardoli
30 km from Surat

Bardoli contributed significantly to the Indian freedom struggle. In 1925, the farmers of Bardoli faced a series of floods and famine that affected their crop output and left them in a grave financial condition. The Bombay Presidency also raised the tax rate by 30 percent, and ignored all civic petitions to cancel the increase in sympathy to the natural calamity. The farmers barely had enough property and crops to feed their families, let alone pay the tax. Sardar Vallabhbhai Patel mobilized the farmers to lead a grassroots revolt against the British by refusing to pay the tax. They encountered confiscation of their property and belongings, but remained steadfast. Finally in 1928, the government agreed to restore the seized land and property. It also cancelled the revenue payment and the 30 percent tax raise for the year. It was after the success of the Bardoli Satyagraha that Vallabhbhai Patel received his title Sardar, "leader", from Mahatma Gandhi and achieved national prominence in the country's campaign for independence.

Bardoli Ashram is where Sardar spent most of his life and also where the Bardoli Satyagraha was given shape. The ashram is very well maintained and consists of Sardar's house, the garden to which he personally tended and a sapota orchard. It also supports community initiatives such as Khadi, paper,

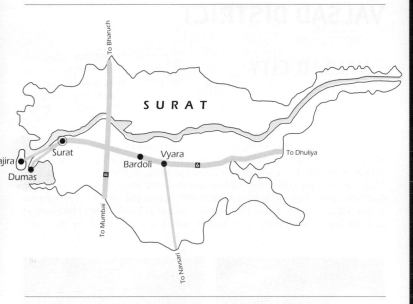

soap and furniture manufacturing units. The ashram also has a hostel and a naturopathy center. Mahatma Gandhi used to spend a month every year here and important Congress Party meetings were also held here. The caretakers show visitors around. To learn more about the processes of handmade paper and organic soap, visit the on-site workshops and interact with the workmen who will gladly explain the procedures. **Open** 0800-1200 and 1400-1800. **Closed** Sun.

On February 1, 1922, Mahatma Gandhi pledged to bring *swaraj* (self-rule) to India and to start the non-cooperation moment against the British under the tree known as **Aitihasik Ambo**, which translates into "historical mango tree".

Sardar Patel National Museum is dedicated to the life and times of Sardar Patel. The pictorial exhibition covers twenty rooms and displays rare historic moments in his life. The curator is helpful and the museum carries a few reference materials on Sardar Patel. **Open** 1030-1730. **Closed** Wed and the 2nd and 4th Sat of every month.

While in Bardoli visit **Jalaram** to purchase some famous export quality dried *patra*, which is otherwise only available abroad.

VALSAD DISTRICT

VALSAD CITY
વલસાડ

POPULATION	145,600
AREA CODE	02632
DISTANCES - AHMEDABAD	345 KM
VADODARA	234 KM
SURAT	77 KM

The city of Valsad, formerly known as Bulsar, is the administrative headquarters of Valsad District, which occupies the southern most part of Gujarat. The tasty Alphonso mango is one of Valsad's claims to fame, and orchards of this fruit bloom across the region just before summer. The district is also intensely cultivated with crops including cotton, millet, pulses and rice. The chief places of interest around the district include the former princely state of Dharampur and the towns of Udwada and Sanjan, which are significant to the Parsi community.

PLACES OF INTEREST

There is not much to see in Valsad, but it makes for a great base to cover the rest of the district.

Panera Dungar

On top of this hill are two temples dedicated to the Goddesses Ambika and Chamunda. Although it is a difficult trek, the climb is rewarded with a great view of the industrial city, Atul. You can also see the railroad tracks associated with Goddess Mahakali, who is said to have thwarted an effort to construct a railway line through the temple area, forcing workers to lay the tracks around the shrine. The hill is about a 20 minute (Rs. 40) ride from Valsad.

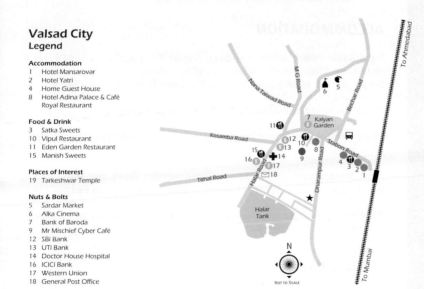

Valsad City
Legend

Accommodation
1   Hotel Mansarovar
2   Hotel Yatri
4   Home Guest House
8   Hotel Adina Palace & Café
    Royal Restaurant

Food & Drink
3   Satka Sweets
10 Vipul Restaurant
11 Eden Garden Restaurant
15 Manish Sweets

Places of Interest
19 Tarkeshwar Temple

Nuts & Bolts
5   Sardar Market
6   Alka Cinema
7   Bank of Baroda
9   Mr Mischief Cyber Café
12 SBI Bank
13 UTI Bank
14 Doctor House Hospital
16 ICICI Bank
17 Western Union
18 General Post Office

NUTS & BOLTS

In and Out

Valsad is well served by trains on the Mumbai-Vadodara section of Western Railway and by road via NH 8.

Getting Around

Rickshaws are the best way to get around. Shuttles also move around the city, and some run the routes between other destinations in the district.

Money

ATMs **Bank of Baroda** *MG Rd*; **SBI** *Opp Avabai High School, Halar Rd*; **UTI Bank** *Doctor House Bldg, Halar Rd;* and **ICICI Bank** *Intersection of Tithal Rd and Halar Rd*, which also encashes traveler's checks and exchanges money.
MONEY TRANSFER Western Union *Opp Manish Sweets, Halar Rd.*

Communication

INTERNET Mr Mischief Cyber Café *Rajput Cplx, Nr Ava Bhai Cmplx* has surfing at Rs. 20/hour and Net-2-Phone.

Markets

Alphonso mangos (also known as *hafus*) and sapotas are available in abundance in the **Sardar Market** on Bechar Road during season.

ACCOMMODATION

Hotel Adina Palace *Adina Chambers, Station Rd* is easily the best hotel in Valsad. **Facilities** western toilet, AC options, shower, running hot water, TV. **Single** 370-600 **Double** 500-850 **Deluxe** 550-950 **Suite** 1600 **Extra Bed** 150.

The following are bare-basic but decent for budget travelers.

Home Guest House *Station Rd.* **Facilities** hot water in the morning. **Single** 75 **Double** 150.

Hotel Maansarovar *Station Rd.* **Facilities** western toilet, hot water in the morning, shower, TV, restaurant. **Dorm** 50-125 **Double** 275 **Extra Bed** 75.

Hotel Yatri *Station Rd* **Facilities** western toilet, shower, hot water, TV. **Single** 165 **Double** 250 **Extra Bed** 70.

FOOD & DRINK

Among *thali* places, **Vipul Restaurant** *Adina Palace* is recommended by locals. **Café Royale** *Adina Palace* serves the best multicuisine fare. **Eden Garden Restaurant** *Opp KB Shopping Mall, Halar Rd* is a lively and colorful place with mid-range prices. It serves sizzlers and hot dogs.

There are plenty of shops selling sweets and snacks. **Jalaram Chaman** *Veg Mkt, Behind Mango Mkt* serves *samosas*, *jalebis* and Valsad's specialty, *chaman*. **Satka Sweets** *Station Rd* and **Manish Sweets** *Nr UTI Bank and Adarsh Hospital, Halar Rd* has a wide selection of sweets, nuts and dry fruits.

EXCURSIONS

SOUTHERN
GUJARAT

▼ DISTRICT

▸ VALSAD

Tithal
Udwada

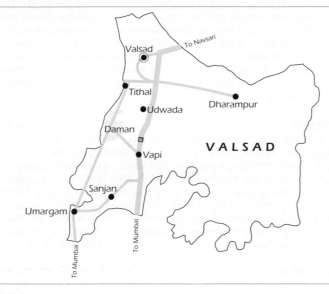

Tithal
6 km from Valsad

A popular hangout for locals, Tithal Beach has clearer waters than the coast further up the Gulf of Khambhat. Although not particularly clean, it is a good place to eat, relax and enjoy the breeze. A rickshaw ride costs about Rs. 35 one way.

Udwada
28 km from Valsad

The most sacred *agiari* of the Parsi community (see **About Gujarat, Religion**) is in Udwada. It is where the Ataash Behram, the eternal fire gifted from heaven, was finally consecrated after a history of trials and tribulations. Only the priest is allowed to approach and feed it with sandalwood logs; non-Parsis are not allowed in the temple. Udwada is connected to the city by slow trains and a roadway.

The Parsis Arrive in Gujarat

The Parsis first came to India from Iran in 698 AD. After staying in Diu for nineteen years, they decided to look for another place to settle, and reached Sanjan, south of Valsad. A popular legend has it that Jadi Rana, the king of Sanjan, offered the newcomers food and one *lota* (pot) filled to the brim with milk, indicating that his kingdom was packed to capacity. The Parsis added some sugar to the milk and returned it. They compared themselves to the milk, which did not spill over, but only got sweeter when they added sugar to it. Similarly, they promised that they would adapt to the local community without causing any disorder and only make it stronger. This won Jadi Rana over and he welcomed them into his kingdom.

SOUTHERN
GUJARAT

DISTRICT ▼

VALSAD ◄

Sanjan
Dharampur
Wilson Hill
Daman

Sanjan

70 km from Valsad

The town of Sanjan is one of the earliest settlements of the Parsis. They settled and prospered here until the end of the 14th c., when it was invaded by Mahmud Tughlaq of the Delhi Sultanate. The sacred Ataash Behram was first sanctified in Sanjan, and then taken to safety in the **Bahrot Caves,** about 12 km away. Priests harbored the holy flame for twelve years before it traveled to other places in south Gujarat. The Bahrot Caves are considered a sacred spot; however, they are heavily deteriorating and the trek to the caves involves a 6 km hike through dense forest area.

Dharampur

32 km by road

Located on the banks of the Swargavahini River, Dharampur is surrounded on three sides by the Sahyadri Mountains, which grace the town with pleasant climate throughout the year. Dharampur, which once belonged to the descendants of the Sisodia Rajputs of Chittod, is the former capital of the princely state of Dharampur. The city was established in 1764 by King Dharamdevji. After the fall of the Delhi Sultanate, the erstwhile state gained a powerful position by controlling seven strategic forts in the area and always fostered cordial relationships with its neighbors, including the Portuguese traders, who even shared a portion of their tax revenues with the state.

The collection at the **Lady Wilson Museum** includes tribal art and artifacts that highlight the local culture. It also displays western musical instruments and Pahari style miniature paintings. **Open** 1015-1715. **Closed** Wed.

The district **Science Centre** has been critical in spreading education among the region's indigenous community. The **Rajyarohan Gate**, which has a strong European influence, marks the city entrance.

Wilson Hill

25 km from Dharampur

This hilltop takes it name from the British Governor Wilson and is crowned with a marble pavilion in his honor. It also affords a great view of the surrounding hills and sea. Wilson Hill belongs to the Pindaval Range, about 2400 feet above sea level, and is home to some 120 villages belonging to tribal communities who speak a language that combines Marathi and Gujarati.

Daman

38 km from Valsad

Situated on the coastline of Valsad, Daman (a union territory) is divided into two areas, **Moti Daman** and **Nani Daman**, split by the Damanganga River. After the Portuguese successfully infiltrated Goa, they searched for a coastal territory in Gujarat to conduct trade. They landed in Daman, and in 1531, the Gujarat Sultan agreed to hand the territory over to the European power in exchange for a share in their customs revenue. The port thrived in trade and ranked more important than Diu for the Portuguese. Daman became part of the Indian Union in 1961.

The town is worth a day trip if you are interested in seeing the lingering influences of Portuguese colonialism, especially in Moti Daman. This enclave is also a popular drinking destination for local tourists from surrounding districts. Of the two former Portuguese territories touching Gujarat, Diu is no doubt the more attractive destination.

The imposing **Moti Daman Fort** was built between 1559-93 over an area once occupied by a small Muslim citadel. It spreads over three hectares (nearly 7.5 acres) in a polygonal layout. Just outside the fort is the **Church of Our Lady of the Remedies**, built at the beginning of the 17th c. The charming **Badrapore District** retains Portuguese influence in its winding lanes and small houses.

The **Chapel of Our Lady of Rosary** was built in the 17th c. Although outwardly simple, the interior is stunning with golden cherubs, rose petals and excellent woodwork.

In **Nani Daman**, the **Fort of St Jerome**, completed in 1627, surrounds an area of about twelve hectares with a striking gateway facing the river. A statue of St Jerome crowns the entrance with two imposing human figures standing guard. You can walk along the ramparts and get a view of the surrounding area. Another prominent building within the stronghold is the **Church of Our Lady of the Sea**. The locals claim that an underground passage connects this fort to the one in Moti Daman.

Though not particularly interesting from the outside, the 17th c. **Church of Bom Jesus**, which is dedicated to baby Jesus, has a beautiful interior crafted by Goan artisans. The walls are embellished with biblical stories and the wooden doors are ornamented with carvings. The church attracts many pilgrims.

To reach Daman take a train to Vapi, from where shared rickshaws will shuttle you the 7 km. ST buses also leave every half hour. Shared taxis charge Rs. 15 and private taxis cost Rs. 100. The bridge between Nani Daman and Moti Daman has collapsed, making road travel between the two impossible, but private boats ferry between. Local taxis and rickshaws are unmetered. Rickshaw costs in Daman vary according to the season.

GETTING INVOLVED

Sanghavi Farm *0260 2563277, 80-82, Inder Sundervan Gate, 5 km from the Umargam Railway Stn, www.savesanghavi.com* was a rural wasteland transformed into an organic farm in 1987 by Bhaskar Save. In 1953, he began his first organic experiment at the Kalpavruksh farm in Dehri Village. Visitors are welcome every Saturday for a tour of Sanghavi farm (1000-1200), followed by lunch and then a tour of Kalpavruksh farm (1400-1600). People may also request to work on the farms. **Contact** Bhaskar Save.

SOUTHERN GUJARAT

▾ DISTRICT
SURAT

▸ VALSAD
Valsad City
Tithal
Udwada
Sanjan
Dharampur
Wilson Hill
Daman
Getting Involved

NAVSARI
THE DANGS
NARMADA
BHARUCH

NAVSARI DISTRICT

NAVSARI CITY
નવસારી

POPULATION	232,400
AREA CODE	02637
DISTANCES - AHMEDABAD	301 KM
VADODARA	190 KM
SURAT	29 KM

From the rows of neatly packed houses, to the lingering Parsi influence and the cool breeze, Navsari exudes a character different from other Gujarat cities. It is also the birthplace of important Parsi figures such as Jamsetji Tata and Dadabhai Naoroji. The city is so small that a rickshaw ride from one end to the other takes no more than fifteen minutes.

The district abounds in sugarcane fields, sapota plantations and mango trees. In summer, the rural roads come alive with bullock carts laden with peak season crops and farmers selling glasses of fresh sugarcane juice from their fields. To the west of Navsari is the coastal town of Dandi, where Mahatma Gandhi held up a fistful of salt as a symbol of the nation's non-violent campaign against British rule.

PLACES OF INTEREST

The city of Navsari does not have any significant tourist sites but deserves a visit for its laid-back ambience. It also makes a good base from which to explore surrounding villages and the historic town of Dandi.

Navsari Parsi Agiari

The Navsari *agiari* (fire temple) once housed the Ataash Behram, or holy fire, of the Sanjana Parsis. It is believed that this was the first holy fire ordained in Gujarat. After many years of peaceful coexistence between the Sanjana Parsis and the Navsari Parsis, tensions rose and the former decided to leave for Udwada, taking the holy fire with them. In 1765, with help from the Parsi community of Surat, a new *agiari* was consecrated in Navsari. Non-Parsis are not allowed into any *agiari*, but the Parsi people are very friendly and would gladly share information about their culture and religion.

The Tata Story

Jamsetji Tata (1839-1904) is considered the father of Indian industry. He was born in Navsari and spent his first fourteen years there. Then his family moved to Mumbai where he attended school and later joined his father's trading company. Eventually Jamsetji founded a cloth mill in Nagpur at a time when most cloth was being imported from England. During his lifetime, he laid the foundation of the Tata business empire and focused on setting up an iron and steel company, a hydroelectric plant and a prestigious institute of science. The legacy of Jamsetji evolved into what is now known as the Tata Group, one of India's most respected corporate conglomerates.

Dastur Meherji-Rana Library

This library in Tarota Bazaar has a picture collection of old Navsari, and one of the oldest religious manuscripts of the Parsi community. In 1572, Akbar annexed Gujarat to the Mughal Empire. A patron of arts and religion, he held a religious discussion at his court. Meherji-Rana represented Zoroastrianism at the forum and so impressed the Emperor Akbar that he ordered the sacred fire to burn day and night in his court, just as it did in the tradition of the ancient Persian kings. He also absolved the Parsis of the tax imposed on all non-Muslims.

ACTIVITIES

Zankar Group

Dipak Rana has been a choreographer of south Gujarat folk dances for the last eighteen years. *For more information contact him at 9879510662 or visit him at Mahalakshmi Cold Drinks, Nr Central Bank.*

NUTS & BOLTS

In and Out

Navsari is a station on the Mumbai-Vadodara section of the Western Railway main line. **Shrinath Travel Agency** *281234, Junathana, Vivekanand Circle* offers private bus service between all major cities in Gujarat and Navsari, including sleeper bus options between several destinations.

Getting Around

Shuttles cost about Rs. 5 to most destinations while private rickshaws cost about Rs. 20 from one end of the city to the other. It is best explored on foot since everything is within a 6 km radius. The walk offers an excuse to quench your thirst at one of the several juice vendors in town.

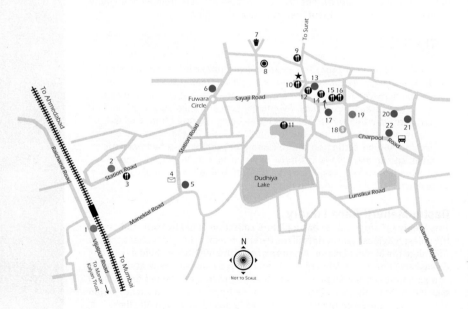

Navsari City
Legend

Accommodation
1   Hotel Anmol
2   Hotel Arunoday / Restaurant
19   Hotel Sauras / Restaurant

Food & Drink
3   Udipi Restaurant
9   The Kolah

10   Mama Patties
11   Ramananda Hotel
12   Vallabh Mitha Sev Khamani
14   Bhikhabhai Bhajiawala
15   Jalaram Dryfruits and Chiki
16   Shrinath Bombay Chowpatty Ice Cream

Places of Interest
7   Navsari Parsi Agiari
8   Dastur Meherji-Rana Library

Nuts & Bolts
4   General Post Office
5   Reliance Supermarket
6   Blue Dart Courier
13   Ishwar Sons Department Store
17   Chit Chat Cyber Café / Forex Moneygram
18   IDBI Bank
20   DHL Courier
21   Shrinath Travel Agency
22   World Links Cyber Café

Money

ATMs IDBI Bank *Chimanbhai Chowk.*
FOREIGN EXCHANGE Forex Moneygram *Central Bank to Library Rd, Nr Shivam Cmplx.*
MONEY TRANSFER Western Union at the General Post Office *Maneklal Rd.*

Communication

INTERNET World Links Cyber Café *Ava Baug Shopping Centre, Opp ST Depot* charges Rs. 20/hour and offers CD writing, printing and webcam services. **Chit Chat Cyber Café and Net-2-Phone** *Central Bank to Library Rd, Opp Shivam Cmplx* costs Rs. 20/hour with facilities for Net-2-Phone and webcam; **Mahalaxmi Cold Drinks** *Nr Vohraji Masjid* also has Net-2-Phone.
COURIERS DHL *232831, Opp DN Mkt, Panch Hatdi*; **Blue Dart** *Nxt to the Fuwara.*

Markets

General stores include **Reliance Supermarket** *Maneklal Rd, Nag Talawadi*; **Ishwar Sons Department Store** *Nr Clock Tower.*

ACCOMMODATION

Hotel Arunoday *250605, Nr Railway Station* is another basic hotel. **Facilities** western and squat toilets, AC. **Single** 150 **Double** 250-400 **Triple** 300-500.

Hotel Anmol *Opp Railway Station,* offers clean and simple rooms and has an attached bakery. **Facilities** AC options, TV. **Dorm** 50 **Single** 150-700 **Double** 200-900.

Hotel Sauras *251365, Central Bank to Library Rd, Nr Sayaji Library* offers clean, basic rooms. **Facilities** western and squat toilets, AC, running hot water, TV, fridge. **Single** 200-400 **Double** 350-900 **Extra Bed** 150.

FOOD & DRINK

Arunoday Restaurant *Nr Railway Station* and **Hotel Sauras Restaurant** *Nr Sayaji Library* both serve multicuisine fares, while the latter also offers Gujarati *thalis.* **Udipi Restaurant** *Station Rd, Nr Civil Hospital* serves a variety of tasty *chaat* items in addition to South Indian, Punjabi, pizza, sandwiches and *pav bhaji.* **Ramananda Hotel** *Dudhia Talav, Nr Shri Pritam Fashion* is reputed for its *pani puri, bhel puri* and *pav bataka,* but it also serves Chinese, Punjabi, Continental, sizzlers and desserts including a delicious assortment of *faloodas,* a milk-based, flavored drink mixed with noodles.

LOCAL SPECIALTIES The Kolah *Tarota Bazaar, Nr Parsi Agiari* has been churning fresh ice cream for more than 60 years. **Shrinath Bombay Chowpatty Ice Cream** *Danagvad Tekro, Nr Library Rd* will satisfy your sweet tooth with *falooda,* milk shakes and ice cream in various flavors. **Vallabh Mitha Sev Khamani** *Opp Tower Rd, Nr Bank of India* makes excellent *sev khamani,* a delicacy made of steamed chickpea batter, grated coconut, mustard seeds and coriander, topped with

SOUTHERN
GUJARAT

DISTRICT ▾

NAVSARI ◄
Navsari City
Ubhrat

sev. **Mama Patties** *Mota Bazaar, Behind Bazaar Gate* is popularly frequented for its patties, boiled potatoes stuffed with coriander and spices, breaded and then fried. **Bhikhabhai Bhajiawala** *Madhumati Jain Derasar, Mota Bazaar, Opp JB House* also serves tasty patties.

Navsari is also famous for its *chana* (boiled and spiced chickpeas) and Alfonso mangos during summer. **Jalaram Dryfruits and Chiki** *Library to Central Bank Rd, Nr Bombay Chowpatty Ice Cream* sells excellent *chana*.

EXCURSIONS

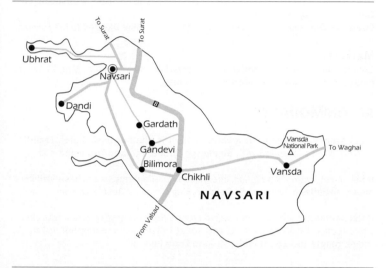

It is worth visiting some of Navsari's surrounding areas, where sugarcane plantations dominate the landscape. In **Gardath** and **Gandevi** (25 km) you can see sugarcane being processed into organic *gol* or jaggery. Gardath also has an interesting **Navagraha Temple**, dedicated to the nine planets.

Ubhrat   20 km from Navsari
Ubhrat has a white sandy beach, where people come to walk and swim. The **Modi Amusement Park**, a resort, is also based here. You can park yourself under a hut made of palm fronds (Rs. 60) or under a cloth shelter (Rs. 30).

Maroli Sugar, en route from Navsari to Maroli, is a sugarcane juice stall with a popular following of locals who travel between Surat and Bombay. Enjoy a glass of juice with a touch of lemon, but the real treat is the chance to see the traditional method of crushing cane with a *kolah*, a bullock-driven rotating press. **Shri Rameshwar Khichadi Centre** *Maroli Char Rasta, Navsari Rd* serves warm plates of *masala khichadi*, a typical Gujarati item made of lentils and rice.

This place spices up the dish with tomatoes, *masala*, peanuts and coriander. *Thalis* also served.

All buses from Navsari to Ubhrat (about 1.5 hrs) go via Maroli. Alternatively, take a shuttle to Maroli Char Rasta and catch a connecting shuttle to Ubhrat.

SOUTHERN GUJARAT

▼ DISTRICT

▶ NAVSARI

Ubhrat
Dandi
Getting Involved

Dandi
16 km from Navsari

On April 6th, 1930 Mahatma Gandhi and his 79 associates reached Dandi after marching 385 km though hundreds of villages over a period of 23 days (see **About Gujarat, In the Footsteps of Gandhiji**). Everyone watched spellbound as Gandhiji picked up a fistful of salt and spun the nation into a non-violent revolution. As news spread across the country people started making their own salt, burning foreign fabrics and challenging laws against publishing treasonous literature. The Salt March (Dandi Yatra) heralded a new intensity in India's struggle for freedom. Other than the open coast, no memorial actually marks the spot of this historic event.

The **Saifee Villa Museum** was established in 1961 to commemorate the Salt March. The museum is located in the former residence of Syedna Taher Saifuddin Saheb, Gandhiji's host on the eve before his trip to the sea to make salt. The museum houses pictures and artifacts from Gandhiji's life. **Open** 1030-1700. **Closed** Sun.

Buses depart from Navsari for Dandi throughout the day, and the ride takes about one hour. Shuttles, which leave from Eru Char Rasta, offer a pleasant view of the fields. Once in Dandi, it is only a ten minute walk from the seashore to the Saifee Villa Museum.

Vansda National Park
71 km from Navsari

The **Vansda National Park** is better accessed through the Dangs (see **The Dangs, Vansda National Park**).

GETTING INVOLVED

The **Manav Kalyan Trust** *02637 283860, www.manavkalyantrust.org* runs two residential schools in the city of Navsari—one for deaf and mute children and another for the mentally challenged. The school houses approximately 400 children. Visitors and volunteers are welcome to teach English and interact with the students. It was founded and is still managed by Mahesh Kothari, who walked with Vinoba Bhave in the Bhoodan Movement (voluntary land sharing) for several years.

The **Gram Seva Trust** *02634 246248, Kharel Village off NH 8, www.gramseva. org* operates a charitable hospital, runs women's self-help groups, mentors adolescent girls and provides pre- and postnatal care to expectant mothers. They work largely with tribal communities of the surrounding areas. **Contact** Dr Ashwin Shah.

SOUTHERN
GUJARAT

DISTRICT ▼
SURAT
VALSAD
NAVSARI

THE DANGS ◄
Saputara
Hatgadh Fort
Waghai
Gira Falls
Vansda National
Park
Ahwa
Shabari Dham
Purna Wildlife
Sanctuary
Girmal Falls
Mahal

NARMADA
BHARUCH

THE DANGS

SAPUTARA
સાપુતારા

POPULATION	187,000
AREA CODE	02631
DISTANCES - AHMEDABAD	420 KM
VADODARA	309 KM

Saputara, "abode of serpents", is a hill resort on a plateau of the Sahyadri Range that offers amazing views and a pleasant climate year round. Although there are only few places of real interest in the town, it offers an excellent base from which to explore the district with its vibrant communities and rich wildlife. Saputara is also a relaxing stopover for people traveling by road from Gujarat to Maharashtra. There is a Rs. 20 tax for entry into town by private vehicle.

The Dangs is distinct from the rest of Gujarat. Dominated by an indigenous tribal population, it is situated on the border of Maharashtra, and the local culture has significant Maratha influences. This is the northern extremity of the Western Ghats, also known as the Sahyadris, which stretch 1600 km from the mouth of the Tapi River to the southern tip of India.

The Western Ghats are among the important biodiversity hotspots of India, and therefore, the Dangs is an important area for conservation. It has many native species, and also hosts the leopard, hyena, jungle cat, cobra, python and chameleon.

Winter is the best time to visit the Dangs, since water is often in short supply in summer. For those particularly interested in the broad spectrum of wildlife in this district, the monsoon is a good time to visit. Although we have highlighted Saputara, Waghai and Ahwa are also good hubs for navigating the district, which is best done by private vehicle.

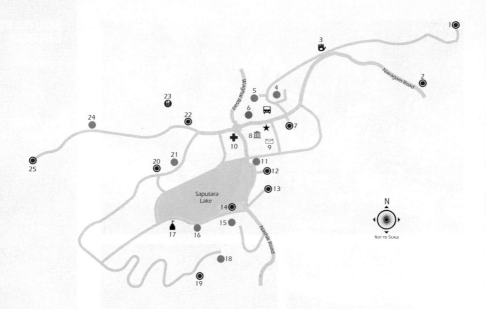

Saputara
Legend

Accommodation
4   Government Rest House
5   Hotel Toran
11 Hotel Lake View
15 Hotel Anando
16 Hotel Savshanti
18 Hotel Vaity
21 Hotel Hare Krishna
24 Mountain View Cottage

Food & Drink
23 Toran Restaurant

Places of Interest
1   Sunrise Point
2   Echo Point
3   Jain Mandir
7   Rose Garden
8   Saputara Museum
12 Artist Village
13 Honey Bee Centre
14 Millenium Garden
17 Nageshwar Mahadev

19 Ropeway
20 Ayurvedic Garden
22 Step Garden
25 Sunset Point

Nuts & Bolts
6   Gujarat Tourism Office
9   General Post Office
10 Hospital

PLACES OF INTEREST

The Saputara Museum

This museum contains interesting information about the topography and anthropology of the Dangs. Although the presentation lacks character, the collection includes stuffed birds, tribal ornaments, jewelry and musical instruments. **ENTRY Students** Re. 1, **Adults** Rs. 2, and **Foreigners** Rs. 50.

By the Lake

The lake is the central feature of Saputara. Here you can hire boats from the boat-house between 0830 and 1830. For half an hour, a pedal boat costs Rs. 20/person and a rowboat Rs. 5. The **Maharashtra border** is a short walk away and just 1.5 km beyond it is a watering hole where you can legally drink beer.

Artist Village

Situated on the main road from Saputara to Nashik, this space displays handicrafts made by the locals. Visitors can pick up pieces of pottery, jewelry, vases, paintings, pen stands and key chains made of bamboo and other local materials. The artisans will also teach their crafts to children who are interested.

Gardens

Saputara has a number of attractive public gardens where you can unwind. Across the bridge on the road to Nashik is the **Millenium Garden,** and a little beyond the bus stop is the **Rose Garden**. Perhaps the most appealing is the **Lakeview Garden**, just below Hotel Anando, which also has a children's playground.

The Ropeway

Suspended above the lake is a cableway that connects Vaity Hotel to **Sunset Point,** situated across the valley. Between 1730 and 1800, jeeps take passengers 2 km from the main roundabout up to the boarding point. The cable circuit takes 15 minutes to cross and offers a majestic view of the city of Saputara and the valley below. A word of caution though—the cable car will not operate without at least twelve passengers. This could sometimes mean an entire day's wait. **Ticket** Rs. 40.

Other Places of Interest

Sunrise Point and **Echo Point** offer breathtaking views of the valley. If you want to learn how bees make honey, visit the **Honey Bees Centre**, where you can also purchase pure honey, although it is a little expensive. Local communities worship the serpent shrine, **Nageshwar Mahadev,** on the southern bank of the Saputara Lake.

NUTS & BOLTS

In and Out

From Ahmedabad, there are four direct ST buses to Ahwa (9 hrs) that stops at major cities along the way. One bus also continues further south to Saputara. It is possible to catch a train to Bilimora, and take a bus from there. The Ahwa bus station is well connected to all major cities in southern Gujarat and in Maharashtra.

Getting Around

Saputara is best seen on foot. Although the Dangs is easier to get around in a private vehicle, it is possible to do the district by public transportation. The roads are fairly good, and ST buses ply along all of them. Another option is to take a shared jeep, which travels the same routes and costs about Rs. 5-15 per journey.

SOUTHERN GUJARAT

▼ DISTRICT

SURAT
VALSAD
NAVSARI

▸ THE DANGS
Saputara

SOUTHERN GUJARAT

DISTRICT ▾

~~SURAT~~
~~VALSAD~~
~~NAVSARI~~

THE DANGS ◂
Saputara

~~Bahaadi Fort~~
~~Waghai~~
~~Gira Falls~~
~~Mahal Forest~~
~~Unai~~

Tourist Information

The **Gujarat Tourism Office** *237226 Btw Bus Stn and Roundabout* is a good place to get oriented to the district.

Communication

INTERNET There are no cyber cafes and hardly any STD/ISD booths in the Dangs. Depending on your service provider, mobile phone connectivity may be difficult, as it is a remote area.

Medical

The medical facilities in Saputara can take care of minor problems, but in case of a major ailment or injury, the nearest centers are Surat (160 km) or Nashik (85 km) in Maharashtra.

ACCOMMODATION

The Government Dormitory *237226* is a very basic lodge that does not provide sheets or towels. Rates include breakfast and a meal. **Dorm** 50-100 **Rooms** 200/person.

Toran Guest House *237226* is a Government Tourism Corporation hotel. Rates include breakfast and one other meal. **Dorm** 50 **Double** 400-500 **Triple** 600-750.

Gokul *237201* is the best among the budget hotels up the road from the bus station. **Facilities** western toilet, shower, TV (Rs. 50 extra). Each room fits up to five people. **Rooms** 100-200/person with a minimum charge of 200-400/room.

Hotel Hare Krishna *237252, Nxt to Chitrakoot Hotel* is a no frills affair but it is situated in an attractive building with a palm-tree garden and rooms full of character. Facilities squat toilets, running hot water, cable TV. **Single** 150-200 **Doubles** 300-400.

Lake View *237315* has attractive cottages with clean interiors and a pleasant outdoor patio. Hidden in a hollow, there is not much of a view. **Rooms** 400.

Vaity Ropeway Resort *237210, On top of the Hill* has the best view and is conveniently located next to the cable cars. There is a pleasant terrace in front of the hotel but no balconies. If you are walking, Vaity means an extra 1 km up and down the hill. **Facilities** western toilet. **Single** 1000 **Doubles** 1790.

Hotel Anando *22660974, Nxt to Roundabout on Rd to Nashik* has beautiful balconies and huge mirrors in the super deluxe rooms. Looking over the lake, it is terraced, making it difficult for the disabled or elderly. **Super Deluxe** 1600.

Hotel Savshanti *237292, Off the Lake* is the most recommended hotel in Saputara and offers beautiful views. **Facilities** activity hall with table tennis, fitness center, swimming pool, party plot. Tariffs include food. **Single** 1050-1250 **Double** 1700-2200 **Extra Bed** 550-650.

SOUTHERN GUJARAT

▼ DISTRICT

SURAT
VALSAD
NAVSARI

▶ **THE DANGS**
Saputara

Hatgadh Fort
Waghai
Gira Falls
Vansda National Park
Ahwa
Shabari Dham
Purna Wildlife Sanctuary
Girmal Falls
Mahal

NARMADA
BHARUCH

Forest Guest Houses

Forest Guest Houses can be found throughout the Dangs, and provide an interesting alternative for accommodation—notably in Waghai, Vansda, Ahwa and Mahal, where running water and simple food are available. Permission to stay in these guesthouses must be sought from the Deputy Conservator of Forests *9426868321*. Prices vary from place to place and must be checked when making reservations.

FOOD & DRINK

There are restaurants offering standard Punjabi and Chinese fare and *thali* options all over Saputara. High quality, low cost Gujarati *thali* is available at the Gujarat Tourism Corporation (Rs. 45 limited/Rs. 60 unlimited). If you want a beer with your dinner, you can skip 1.5 km across the Maharashtra border to **Sai Sharda,** on the road to Nashik. Near the Saputara Museum is a line of *laris* selling various snacks.

EXCURSIONS

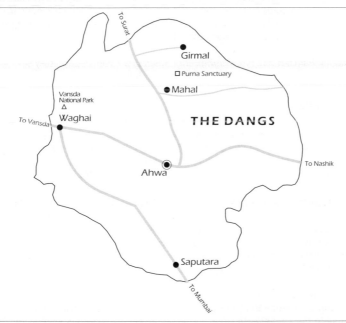

The entire district is a paradise for the adventure traveler since it offers a rich tribal culture and a scenic environment, lush with greenery. Make a trip to

SOUTHERN
GUJARAT

DISTRICT ▾
SURAT
VALSAD
NAVSARI

THE DANGS ◂

Hatgadh Fort
Waghai
Gira Falls
Vansda National
Park

Ahwa
Shabir/LOBAR
Purna Wildlife
Sanctuary
Unimai Falls
Wachal

NARMADA
BHARUCH

surrounding villages such as **Malegoan** or **Ambapada** to experience the depth of the region. **Caution:** leopards and other wild animals roam the area.

Hatgadh Fort   6 km from Saputara

The fort, based on Hatgadh Hill, affords a spectacular view of the surrounding areas. It is said to have been built by the Maratha leader Chhatrapati Shivaji. Hire a guide at the fort, follow his instructions, and walk in line with him to avoid slipping into the valley or marshy land. A stone idol of Ganesh has been carved into the hill at the top. The fort can be reached by bus or jeep for about Rs. 10.

Waghai   60 km from Saputara, 32 km from Ahwa

Although it does not have the infrastructure for tourism, Waghai is near several places of interest and has some accommodation possibilities. It is worth considering as an alternative base to Saputara.

About 2 km from Waghai on the road to Saputara is the 24-hectare **Botanical Garden**, which nurtures a diverse array of native and exotic species. From the coconut used to make *barfi* to the sweet basil believed to cure diarrhea, it is a place that teaches just how much we depend on the forest for our medicinal and culinary needs. Learn to tell your mahogany from your *musafir kell*. The garden also includes a bio-diversity interpretation center, which is open to the public with permission from the superintendent, who you'll find to the right of the entrance. **Open** 0800-1800. **Entry** free.

Waghai Panchat *246339, Waghai Char Rasta* is a cheerful dormitory with four beds per room. **Facilities** squat toilet, bucket bath. **Dorm** 35.

Gira Falls

This site is currently being developed by the Forestry Department. It is marked by a sign, about 3 km from Waghai, on the road to Saputara and is located approximately 1 km down a path from the road. The waterfall is a 30 m natural drop into the Ambica River, and offers a great place to relax. Steps are being built to provide visitors with a comfortable way down to the river.

Vansda National Park   60 km from Saputara, 64 km from Waghai,
                                                             28 km from Ahwa

Spread over 24 sq km, Vansda National Park reaches just over the border into Navsari District. It was the private property of the King of Vansda until 1975, when he handed it over to the state. It is demarcated by the Ambica River in the northeast, and by the Revenue Forest in the southwest.

Once home to the tiger and wild dog, the park still harbors large mammals including the leopard, hyena, Jungle cat, macaques and Barking deer. It is also home to the endangered Great Indian squirrel. With over 115 species of bird, it is a great place for birdwatchers. Visitors are more likely to see birds and plant-life than encounter wild animals, but for those with an interest in natural history, it is a good place to examine animal life through tracks and droppings.

No camping allowed. *You must get permission a few days in advance from the Range Forest Officer 02630 230057.* **ENTRY Indian** free, **Foreigners** Rs. 200.

Kilad Nature Education Campsite This is one of the most exciting and under-valued tourist resources in the Dangs. Located inside the park, on the Ambica, this facility offers travelers the chance to learn about the conservation and bio-diversity issues currently facing the area. You can also enjoy evening campfires under the stars.

An awesome three-story tree house made of bamboo is great for early morning birdwatching. In the morning, a guide will lead you through the park for Rs. 50, revealing the secrets of the forest—tree names and their uses, leopard tracks and bird song. Basic bath and toilet facilities available. **Tent** 200, **Hut** 500. **Food** Rs. 45/dish.

Food is not available at the site. The nearest restaurant, **Sayona**, is a 4 km round trip. *You must get permission a few days in advance from the Range Forest Officer 02630 230057.* **Entry** free.

Ahwa
45 km from Saputara, 32 km from Waghai

Ahwa, the district headquarters, is situated on a plateau that marks the beginning of the ascending terrain from Waghai to Saputara. For arrival by ST bus, Ahwa is frequently the most convenient point in the Dangs.

It is also the site of a forest guesthouse and the comfortable **Hotel R D** *02631 221101.* **Facilities** western toilet, AC options, cable TV. **Rooms** 350.

Tribal Tribulations

Over the last decades, Christian missionaries and Hindu organizations have been active in the tribal belt of Gujarat, especially in the Dangs. Most tribal communities are animists who worship nature, but many have welcomed these religious efforts, less for the faith and more for the attached benefits such as education, water facilities, nutrition and health care. In recent years, there has been a movement of mythologization that affirms the place of the tribal communities within the Hindu fold. Religious leaders have identified various locations in the vicinity as places described in the ancient epics of religious importance. One such example is the recent connection established between the Dangs and Dandakaryana, the forest of Rama's exile.

Shabari Dham

Located on Ahwa Road towards Navapura is this Hindu temple completed in 2006 to commemorate Shabari, a Bhil tribal woman who is narrated in the Ramayana as having fed Rama berries. In 2003, a preacher saint with a huge following said, to the surprise of locals, that Shabari Dham was the site of a stone where Rama, Lakshmana and Shabari had sat together. Pampa Lake, about 6 km from Shabari Dham, is a newly developed water source, which has also been associated with a story of Rama's bathing.

SOUTHERN GUJARAT

▾ DISTRICT
SURAT
VALSAD
NAVSARI

▸ THE DANGS
Saputara
Hatgadh Fort
Waghai
Gira Falls
Vansda National Park
Ahwa
Shabari Dham
Purna Wildlife Sanctuary
Girmal Falls
Mahal

NARMADA
BHARUCH

SOUTHERN
GUJARAT

DISTRICT ▾
SURAT
VALSAD
NAVSARI

THE DANGS ◄
Saputara
Hatgadh Fort
Waghai
Gira Falls
Vansda National
Park
Ahwa
Shabari Dham
**Purna Wildlife
Sanctuary
Girmal Falls
Mahal**

NARMADA-
BHARUCH

Purna Wildlife Sanctuary   40 km from Saputara, 25 km from Waghai, 10 km from Ahwa

This sanctuary has the thickest forest cover in the state and is filled with canopies of teak trees and stands of bamboo among a variety of other flora. The sanctuary covers 160 sq km of rolling hills, plateaus and small valleys, all draining into the river from which it takes its name. The average annual rainfall is 2500 mm, the highest in Gujarat. It is classified as a tropical moist deciduous forest. The communities in the sanctuary comprise the Bhil, Warli, Konkana, Dubla and Kolcha tribes. Their rich cultures are reflected in their housing, clothing, jewelry, musical instruments and folk dances. When the sun sets, the area reverberates with the sounds of tribal music.

Girmal Falls

Possibly the most picturesque sight in the district, these falls, about 1 km off the Mahal-Singana Road that runs along the Gira River, are outstandingly beautiful during the rains. The hill opposite the falls blooms with rich and rare flora. For the adventurous trekker it is a rewarding place to visit.

Mahal   20 km from Ahwa, 50 km from Saputara, 50 km from Waghai

This is the largest village on the fringe of the sanctuary and has a century-old forest bungalow picturesquely located on the bend of the Purna River. You can relax on the elevated bank between the river and the bungalow, which has two spacious suites. The caretaker doubles as a cook, but you may have to bring your own provisions. The forest also offers interesting trekking opportunities. *For more information and possible bookings contact the Deputy Conservator of Forests, Ahwa, 02631 220203.*

NARMADA DISTRICT

RAJPIPLA CITY

રાજપીપળા

POPULATION	35,000	
AREA CODE	02637	
DISTANCES - AHMEDABAD	195 KM	
VADODARA	190 KM	
SURAT	141 KM	

The Narmada is the fifth largest river system in India and the main lifeline of Gujarat. It is also one of the seven sacred rivers revered by Hindus. It originates at Amarkantak in Madhya Pradesh and flows the last one-sixth of its 1300 km course through Gujarat, along the southern border of Vadodara and cutting across Narmada and Bharuch districts, before emptying into the Gulf of Khambhat. Narmada District, which takes its name from the river, was carved out of a larger Bharuch District in 1997. A large part of district is situated in the Shoolpaneshwar Sanctuary, which has teak and bamboo forests and a dominant tribal community. In recent times, the Sardar Sarovar Dam project has been the main source of attention to the area.

Rajpipla is the district headquarters of Narmada and a former princely state. The splendor of its past is evident on the two central roads of the town—Palace Road and Station Road, which are dotted with palaces and regal structures from the 19th and 20th c. Unfortunately the majestic appeal of this city is slowly fading from a lack of proper maintenance. Chokrana, a Parmar Rajput prince of Ujjain (in present day Madhya Pradesh), established Rajpipla in 1470. When he died heirless, his daughter's son ascended the throne, establishing the rule of the Gohil Rajput dynasty in the state. The Gohils fought to protect this territory from the Sultans of Ahmedabad, the Mughal emperors and the Marathas, each time regaining power by joining forces with the hill tribes. Rajpipla's golden period began under Chhatrasinhji, who spearheaded the progressive trend of Rajpipla in the late 19th c. The visionary who built Rajpipla into a modern and affluent state, however, was his son Vijaysinhji, who was crowned in 1915. Among his many feats as an administrator, he introduced primary education, constructed the railway line between Rajpipla and Ankleshwar and introduced pensions for public servants. He also designed a number of elegant new buildings. Vijaysinhji was one of the enlightened rulers who anticipated the changes that would follow the departure of the British. He made appropriate preparations for the transition from a feudal to a democratic order, and urged other princes to do the same.

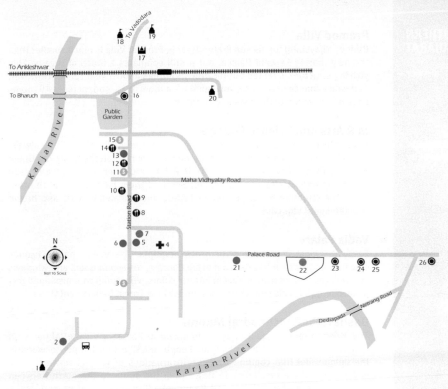

Rajpipla City
Legend

Accommodation
7 Aavkar Guest House
22 Rajwant Palace

Food & Drink
8 Raviraj Cold Drinks
9 Purohit Sweets
10 Neelkamal Farsan Mart
12 Purohit Dining Hall
14 Mohan Bhai na Bhajiya

Places of Interest
1 Vishveshvar Mahadev Temple
2 Champak Niwas & Kishore Niwas
13 White Clock Tower
16 Kala Ghoda
17 Pathan Peer Baba Dargah
18 Dharmeshwar Mandir
19 Veer Vaital Mandir / Hanuman
   Temple
20 Harsiddhi Mata Mandir
23 Pramod Villa
24 M R Arts and Science College
25 Shreeji College of Fine Arts
26 Vadia Palace

Nuts & Bolts
3 Darshaw Mancherji & Sons
4 General Hospital
5 Gayatri Internet Café
6 Maruti Express Courier
11 SBI Bank
15 Bank of Baroda ATM
21 Park Avenue Gift Shop

PLACES OF INTEREST

Rajwant Palace
The key tourist attraction in Rajpipla is Rajwant Palace. Built by Chhatrasinhji for his son Vijaysinhji in 1910, it has recently been converted into a heritage hotel, and is also occupied by the royal descendent Raghuvirsinhji (grandson of Vijaysinhji) and his family. The **Royal Museum** in the palace displays the trophy won by Vijaysinhji at the Irish Derby. A polo enthusiast and ace horseman, he won several races in India and abroad. Part of the palace is occupied by a heritage hotel (see **Accommodation**).

Pramod Villa

Built by Vijaysinhji for his son Pramodsinhji, Pramod Villa is much smaller than the neighboring Rajwant Palace, but it still emanates a touch of royalty. This striking structure is rented out for film shootings almost year round. However, in the rare chance of vacancy, you can have a room at Rs. 500/person. All rooms have AC, attached bathrooms and bathtubs.

M R Arts and Science College

Vijaysinhji divided his time between England and India. When in India he always hosted guests from abroad. To accommodate them he built the European Guest House. This building now houses the M R Arts and Science College and each classroom has an attached bathroom. Some of them have been put to other uses. The structure has an excellent façade and a majestic ivory and brown wooden spiral staircase.

Vadia Palace

Easily the most impressive structure in Rajpipla, this yellow palace exudes elegance and class. It has Italian marble flooring, rosewood doors and windows and walls decorated with murals in natural colors. Vijaysinhji commissioned this palace in 1940 for his son. Currently it houses the Forest Department Office.

Dashavatar Ranchhodrai Mandir

This Krishna temple, built in 1923, is based in Rampara Village, about a 30 minute rickshaw ride from Rajpipla. People flock to this temple to worship the unique idol that combines all ten incarnations of Vishnu. Down the hill is a stretch where the Narmada flows from the south to the north between the confluences of the Maine and Keedimakodi rivers. One of several myths associated with the area is that Bhasmasur, who could turn anyone into ash at will, fell in love with Shiva's consort Parvati and decided to incinerate Shiva. To escape the demon Shiva entered hell at this very place. People consider this area sacred and walk the distance of at least 10 km from one confluence to the other as a pilgrimage.

Harsiddhi Mata Mandir

According to legend, when the king from Ujjain came to Rajpipla to establish the state, Harsiddhi Mata (an embodiment of Goddess Parvati), Veer Vaital (a guardian deity and predecessor to Hanuman), Dharmeshwar (Shiva) and a Pathan soldier accompanied him. Harsiddhi Mata is the guardian deity of the royal family of Rajpipla. It is claimed that the kings would consult the Goddess, veiled by a curtain, about all matters of concern. The temple, located off Station Road, is a colorful structure with an old gate complex that displays intricate wood carvings.

A *dargah* dedicated to the soldier and temples honoring **Veer Vaital** and **Dharmeshwar** all stand in proximity to one another. Next to Veer Vaital Temple is a smaller **Hanuman Temple**, about 300 years old. It has an idol carved out of pulse by Saint Ramdas Maharaj, who renounced the world. The idol remains intact to this day.

Other Places of Interest

Some other buildings symbolic of the bygone era are the **White Clock Tower** on Station Road; **Natwar Niwas, Champak Niwas** and **Kishore Niwas**, all on Rajendra High School Lane off Palace Road. The **General Hospital** was built in 1919 by Vijaysinhji in memory of his father. **Shreeji College of Fine Arts** was once the royal club with sprawling grounds for horse riding and polo. The building has rooms for various indoor games. The **Kala Ghoda**, a statue of Vijaysinhji on his horse, is a tribute to Rajpipla's most popular ruler.

NUTS & BOLTS

In and Out

The best way to get to Rajpipla is by ST bus from Vadodara and Bharuch.

Getting Around

Rickshaws are a good mode of transportation for getting around. Shuttles and shared jeeps are available around Aavkar Guest House and Kala Ghoda. To travel around the district, catch ST buses from the depot at Surya Gate.

Money

ATMs Bank of Baroda Station Rd.
MONEY TRANSFER Darashaw Mancherji & Sons 220074, Opp SBI, Station Rd; **Park Avenue Gift Shop** 221564 Palace Rd.

Communication

INTERNET Gayatri Internet Café 221811, Station Rd.
COURIER Maruti Express Courier 222117, Above Raviraj Cold Drinks, Station Rd.

ACCOMMODATION

Rajwant Palace 9879013118 has rooms with character, defined by a blend of early 20th c. furniture and art work combined with modern facilities. The terraces offer views of the Karjan Dam. A few rooms in the palace have been converted into a museum of trophies, European mirrors, portraits, musical instruments and other artifacts that the family has collected over time. Facilities AC, vegetarian and non-veg restaurant, swimming pool, TV. **Packages** (incl all 3 meals) **couple/night** 5999, **2 nights/3 days** 11,000.

Aavkar Guest House 222333 Nr Jail, Station Rd is very clean and the only decent alternative to Rajwant Palace, but it has no AC options. **Facilities** western toilet, hot running water, shower, laundry. **Single** 150 **Double** 300-400.

FOOD & DRINK

There are a few dhaba style options around the outskirts of town that serve Gujarati and Punjabi fares at budget prices. The following are all located on Station Road.

Purohit Dining Hall offers Gujarati *thali* for Rs. 30. Sweets can be ordered for an additional Rs. 10. **Neelkamal Farsan Mart and Purohit Sweets** sell freshly made Gujarati snacks and Indian sweets. **Raviraj Cold Drinks** serves locally made ice cream. **Mohan Bhai na Bhajiya** has been selling its famous spicy *bhajiya* for the last twelve years.

EXCURSIONS

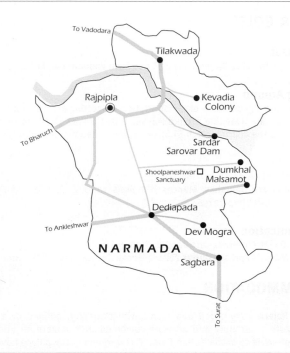

Traveling through any of the areas around Rajpipla is a pleasant experience for the striking landscape consisting of greenery, rugged terrain and the Karjan Dam reservoir.

Nizamshah Dargah

About 450-500 years ago, demons are believed to have inhabited Rajpipla. A saint named Nizamshah Nandodji, popularly known as Dada, miraculously elongated the body of his disciple and gave him the power to destroy the demons. People of all religions come to pay their respect and visit the tomb of Dada and that of his disciple Khijmatali, which is 13.5 m long. Hamid Khan, the keeper of the *dargah*, is a rich source of stories about this site and the town in general.

Kevadia Colony

27 km from Rajpipla

This makeshift town was established to house the workers and officials involved in the Sardar Sarovar Dam project and makes for a budget-friendly center from which to explore the dam site and the Shoolpaneshwar Sanctuary.

The historic **Shoolpaneshwar Temple,** submerged by the Sardar Sarovar Project, was rebuilt on a hill just outside Kevadia, overlooking the Narmada River. Dedicated to Shiva, Shoolpaneshwar means "he who holds a trident." Locals believe that Shiva made the *linga* himself. The sanctum also enshrines a silver snake, allegedly 1000 years old.

It is worth bringing your own vehicle to Kevadia to visit the dam site. Otherwise jeeps can be hired from the Kevadia Market.

The Government Circuit Houses are available to travelers as long as no government official is occupying the premises. Rooms at **Circuit House 1 Pathik Ashram** and **Circuit House 2 Reva Bhavan** must be booked in advance by contacting the **Sardar Sarovar Narmada Nigam** *02640 232208.*

Kevadia offers a handful of budget food options including **Hotel Pratima**, a small setup with outdoor seating that prepares basic but good Punjabi fare. In Kevadia Bazaar, **Jay Annapurna** serves an unlimited *thali* at Rs. 30 while **Mahadev Narmada Lodge** offers Gujarati a-la-carte options.

The Narmada Controversy

The construction of more than 3160 dams of varying sizes to harness the Narmada River has been on the forefront of current controversies in western India. Its supporters say that the project will provide water and electricity to hundreds of villages, and drastically improve the development of the states involved. Opponents believe that the calculated benefits are largely skewed and claim that the project will displace more than 300,000 underprivileged communities with inadequate compensation and affect the livelihoods of thousands of others. They also feel that the project overlooks economically and environmentally viable alternatives. Sardar Sarovar in Gujarat is the largest dam in the project. It is expected to irrigate 1.8 million hectares of land and provide drinking water to 136 urban areas and 45 percent of Gujarat's villages.

Sardar Sarovar Dam

A joint undertaking of the governments of Gujarat, Madhya Pradesh, Maharashtra and Rajasthan, this initiative aims to channel the waters of the Narmada to provide an irrigation network, supply drinking water, generate hydroelectricity and control floods. The Narmada dam, which is 122 m high, took form in 1979. Visit the **Interpretation Centre** at Kevadia Colony to understand the history and logistics of the dam and then obtain an entry pass from the Public Relations Office (PRO), where you can also request a guide, grab a quick bite and use the toilet facilities. **Entry** Rs. 5/person, 20/rickshaw, 10/two-wheeler and 50/four-wheeler.

SOUTHERN GUJARAT

▼ DISTRICT
SURAT
VALSAD
NAVSARI
THE DANGS

▶ NARMADA
Rajpipla City
Nizamshah

Kevadia Colony
Sardar Sarovar Dam

Shoolpaneshwar
Sanctuary
Dediapada

BHARUCH

SOUTHERN GUJARAT

DISTRICT ▾

NARMADA ◄

Sardar
Sarovar Dam
Shoolpaneshwar
Sanctuary
Dediapada

Just outside the PR Office stands a tall idol of the Goddess Narmada offering her blessings to everyone visiting the dam site. **Caution:** Alligators inhabit the river.

Shoolpaneshwar Wildlife Sanctuary

This 600 sq km area of mostly dry deciduous and bamboo forests consists of rolling terrain, verdant canopies, deep valleys, streams, waterfalls and scenic landscapes, all of which culminate at the meeting point of the Vindhya-Saputara hill ranges. The sanctuary harbors leopards, Sloth bears, Four-horned antelope and Barking and Spotted deer. It has some 575 species of flora, and encloses more than 100 villages inhabited by the Vasava and Thadvi Bhil communities, who continue to depend on the forest for their socioeconomic needs. The hilltops are dotted with their teak and bamboo homes, which add to the beauty of the area. The sanctuary is named after the ancient Shoolpaneshwar Temple and is best visited from November to March.

Shoolpaneshwar is full of Mahuda trees, about 200-300 years old, which the Bhils consider sacred. They extract liquor from the flowers and press oil from its seeds. The mango, custard apple, teak and bamboo trees are also found in abundance and the forest has a lot of medicinal plants.

Ninai Dodh, accessible by car, is a natural waterfall. Although you can swim here, there is a heavy undercurrent and diving is not permitted. Just before the small pond, to the right, is a small rock formation with an opening, inside which the temple of **Ninai Mata** is represented by rocks smeared with red vermilion.

Samot, the largest town in the sanctuary, has a six-room boarding house at Rs. 200/night. *For bookings and for permission to trek and camp in the sanctuary, contact the Forest Office in Rajpipla 02649 234271.* The officials at the PRO in Kevadia Colony have compiled information and charted trekking routes. If the group is large enough, they will gladly provide a guide.

Dediapada   35 km from Rajpipla

Dediapada hosts an interesting bazaar, which brims with an assortment of raw materials from the forest area. It is interesting to ramble around town and appreciate innovated versions of traditional mud houses. Dediapada also has a government rest house. About 25 km away from town is the important **Dev Mogra Temple**, recently renovated in concrete. It is dedicated to the Bhil Goddess Pandurimata. During the Mahashivaratri festival (Jan-Feb) people from the neighboring tribal areas line up for several kilometers to offer Mahudi liquor, a chicken and grain to the goddess to pray for a good harvest.

BHARUCH DISTRICT

SOUTHERN
GUJARAT

▾ DISTRICT
SURAT
VALSAD
NAVSARI
THE DANGS
NARMADA

▸ BHARUCH
Bharuch City
Shuklatirth
Kabirvad
Gandhar
Stay Away
Getting Involved

BHARUCH CITY

ભરૂચ

Population		176,400
Area Code		02642
Distances - Ahmedabad		182 km
Vadodara		71 km
Surat		96 km

From crumbling walls of the old fort to a multitude of temples and mosques combined with the Parsi quarters and a lone *gurudwara*, the city of Bharuch is a virtual museum that speaks of the different eras in its history.

Perched on the north bank of the Narmada River, Bharuch, known as Broach during the British Empire, is an ancient port city with 2000 years of history. Legend holds that Rishi Bhrigu founded the city, giving it its original name, Bhrigupur. In the first century AD, it had already developed into a prosperous port. In 1616 the British established a factory, followed by the Dutch in 1617. After the English took possession in 1803, Bharuch started its decline as a trade center.

PLACES OF INTEREST

Bhrigu Rishi Temple

This temple in Dandia Bazaar honors Bhrigu, a son of Brahma and the author of the first Indian astrological work, *Bhrigu-Samhita*. He is said to have documented over five million horoscopes, in which he wrote down the fate of every being in the universe.

Temples swarm the city and each holds its own religious significance. **The Swaminarayan Temple** in Dandia Bazaar is 175 years old and hosts a palette of color on its walls. **Narmadamata Temple**, also in Dandia Bazaar, is 150 years old and dedicated to Goddess Narmada. **The Vaishnav Haveli** enshrines an idol of Balkrishna (the infant Krishna) said to have come from Mathura in 1725. Behind the Old Civil Hospital, the **Khodiyar Mata Temple** overlooks the low lying area of Furja and offers one of the best views of the sunset in the city.

Gurudwara Chadar Saheb

In the 15th c. Nanak Dev, the first Sikh guru, visited Bharuch. It is believed that when a boatman refused to take him across the Narmada, he crossed over on a cloth sheet or *chadar*. The *gurudwara* was later constructed in Kasak, on the site where he landed.

Raichand Deepchand Library

Established in mid-19th c., this library, just opposite the R C Dalal School, has about 200,000 books including some rare manuscripts. Its chairman, Keshavbhai Gohil, is a storehouse of knowledge about the city. The building stands on iron pillars and books are stored in tall wooden cupboards. Make it a point to take a peek at the **Bharucha Hall** above the library, which speaks of another era.

Jama Masjid

This pre-Sultanate mosque from the turn of the 14th c. is one of the earliest examples of an Islamic building in Gujarat that used recycled material from earlier monuments, and yet, conformed to the conventional design of this type of structure. Its interior demonstrates the beginning use of local forms for ornamentation, which evolved to a much higher degree of excellence in the Sultanate period a century later.

Valanda Kothi

This former Dutch factory was taken over by the British and then made into the Union High School. Today it is in a shambles, but an old sundial on the premises is still intact and serves as one of the timekeepers of Bharuch.

The Golden Bridge

In 1881 the British built a bridge across the Narmada River to improve access to traders and administrators in Bombay. The structure was built with rust-resistant iron, and therefore, more expensive than modern steel, lending to the name Golden Bridge.

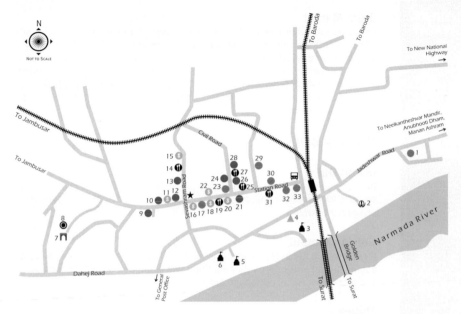

Bharuch City
Legend

Accommodation
1   Gangotri
17 Shalimar Hotel
23 Hotel Plaza Annexe
29 Hotel Palmland
30 Crown Palace
32 Aradhana
33 Anupam

Food & Drink
14 Nyaya Mandir
19 Greenery Restaurant

25 Victoria Restaurant
27 Havmor Ice Cream Parlor
31 Trupti Restaurant

Places of Interest
2   Chadar Saheb Gurudwara
3   Narmadamata Temple
4   Ashoka Ashram
5   Swaminarayan Temple
7   Bharuch Fort
8   Katopar Market
30 Bhrigu Rishi Temple

Nuts & Bolts
9   Global Enterprises /
    Blue Dart Courier

10 Panama Travels
11 UTI Bank
12 Shree Tirupati Courier Service
13 San Cybercafé /
    Mevawala & Sons
15 ICICI Bank
16 Bank of Baroda
18 SBI Bank
21 Kodak Express
22 Chandni Money Exchange
24 Uma Cyber Zone
26 Diamond Supermarket
28 Sify Iway Cybercafé

Narmada River

One of the most important sacred rivers in India, the Narmada is thought to have descended from the sky on demand of Shiva. Many believe that bathing in it releases an individual from all sins, and that her divine sight alone makes one pure. Many temples and ashrams are located along the river. Several ashrams function just to accommodate pilgrims who walk the entire length of the Narmada (1,289 km).

The **Ashoka Ashram,** based in Dholikui, is based around a Shiva temple. Once popular with saints and *rishis*, today it offers a quiet retreat from the hustle of the city. **Anubhooti Dham,** on Neelkantheshwar Mahadev Temple Lane, is run by the Brahmakumaris, an organization that teaches its own technique of meditation. The center holds regular meditation sessions in the morning (0630-0730) and evening (1930-2030).

Sujni Market

Only a handful of atrisans still specialize in **Sujni,** quilts made by a technique of filling cotton in them during the weaving process itself, without using a single stitch. **Bharuch Sujni Stores** *Panchbatti* is an exclusive Sujni store run by the Sujniwala family, who have been in the trade for almost two centuries. The **New Swadesh Sujni Store** *Station Rd* also sells the quilts. **Zardosi** work, embroidery with metal thread, is also crafted in Bharuch and artisans can be found in **Katopar Market.**

NUTS & BOLTS

In and Out

Bharuch is a stop for many of the trains on the Mumbai-Vadodara section of the Western Railway main line. It is also connected by road via NH 8 to important places in the state.

Getting Around

Rickshaws are the best mode of transportation and a trip across the city costs about Rs. 25. Shuttles are also good for travel in the city, while ST buses, jeeps and rental cars are all options to move around the district.

Money

ATMs **Bank of Baroda** *Station Rd,* **SBI** *Station Rd,* **ICICI Bank** *Blue Chip Cmplx, Sevashram Rd,* **UTI Bank** *Jadeshwar Rd, Panchbatti* and **Dena Bank** *Opp HP Petrol Pump, Station Rd.*

FOREIGN EXCHANGE **Chandni Money Exchange** *Opp Shalimar Talkies, Station Rd;* **Panama Travels Services and Money Exchange** *Adarsh Shopping Center, Panchbatti;* **Global Enterprises** *Navdeep Shopping Cmplx, Panchbatti.*

Communication

INTERNET **Shri Sai Communications** *Rang Cmplx, Jadeshwar Rd* charges Rs. 20/ hr; **Uma Cyber Zone** *Opp Relax Cinema, Civil Rd* Rs. 20/hr; **Sify Iway** *Opp Nagar Palika, Civil Rd* costs Rs. 21/hr; **San Cyber Café** *BJ Trade Center, Panchbatti* charges Rs. 15/hr and has Net-2-Phone.

COURIER **Blue Dart** *269540, Navdeep Shopping Cmplx, Panchbatti;* **Tirupati Courier Service** *244170 Ashirwad Cmplx, Panchbatti.*

Photography

Kodak Express *Miranji Complex, Opp Super Mkt, Station Rd.*

Markets

Mevawala & Sons *BG Trade Center, Panchbatti* is a mini-department store. **Diamond Supermarket** *Miranji Mkt, Station Rd* sells groceries and everyday products.

ACCOMMODATION

SOUTHER
GUJARAT

▼ DISTRICT

VALSAD
NAVSARI
THE DANGS
NARMADA

▶ BHARUCH
Bharuch City

All hotels have AC and non-AC options.

Aradhana *Opp ST Depot, Station Rd* is conveniently located near the Railway Station. **Facilities** western toilet, TV in rooms. **Single** 120-430 **Double** 240-550.

Anupam *244089, Opp ST Depot, Station Rd* has rooms with balconies, some with a view of the Golden Bridge. **Facilities** western toilet, hot showers, laundry, TV in most rooms. **Single** 125-350 **Double** 300-500 **Suite** 900 **Extra Bed** 100.

Crown Palace *243316, Opp Bus Depot, Station Rd* has spacious rooms. **Facilities** western toilet, hot shower, laundry, TV. **Single** 200-300 **Double** 300-400 **Deluxe** 500-700 **Extra Bed** 50-100.

Gangotri *229749, Behind Rajeshwar Petroleum, Jadeshwar Rd* is a fairly new hotel overlooking the Narmada. **Facilities** western toilet, hot showers, TV. **Single** 350-700 **Double** 450-900 **Gangotri Glory** 1000.

Hotel Palmland *243618, Falshrutinagar* has the best bathrooms in Bharuch. **Facilities** western toilet, hot showers, TV. **Single** 400-600 **Double** 500-700 **Super Deluxe** 800-900 **Deluxe Suite** 2000.

Hotel Plaza Annexe *244407, Station Rd.* **Facilities** western toilet, TV, refrigerators. **Rooms** 900-1100.

Shalimar Hotel *220803, Station Rd* is one of the most popular and cleanest hotels in Bharuch. Its restaurant is famous for its Gujarati *thali*. **Facilities** western toilets, hot showers, TV, laundry, room service, internet connection for a fee. **Single** 850-950 **Double** 1050-1300 **Suite** 2100-2200.

FOOD & DRINK

Multicuisine restaurants at mid-range prices include **Victoria Restaurant** *Prithvi Trade Centre, Station Rd* and **Hungry Eyes** *Hilton Plaza, Nxt to Railway Station*, which also serves Mughlai food. **Greenery Restaurant** *Rotary Club, Station Rd* has a Gujarati *thali* in addition to a multicuisine menu and **Trupti Restaurant** *Rangoli Cmplx, Station Rd* is considered one of the best restaurants in Bharuch. **Status Plaza** *Hotel Plaza Basement, Station Rd* serves both vegetarian and meat dishes at slightly steep prices.

Trupti Restaurant *Shalimar Shopping Cntr, Station Rd* is a vegetarian fast food place that offers South Indian dishes, pizzas and burgers. **Nyaya Mandir** *off NH 8, Sevashram Rd* is a 24-hour, popular hangout that serves packed foods, ice cream and cheap hot snacks. The onion *bhajiyas* are highly recommended. **New Silver Shabnam** *Opp Nagar Palika, Station Rd* is another local favorite that serves ice cream and other treats. The popular **Havmor Ice Cream Parlor** is in the same complex.

SOUTHERN
GUJARAT

DISTRICT ▾

BHARUCH ◄
Bharuch City
Shuklatirth

US Pizza *Rang Multiplex, Jadeshwar Rd* is a Gujarat-wide chain that serves pizzas, breads, salads and dessert. Try the sizzling brownie.

LOCAL SPECIALTIES Bharuch is known for its *seeng* (peanuts), which are imported into town to be roasted and salted. **Sangam Seeng** *Soneri Mahal* is the most famous peanut shop around.

EXCURSIONS

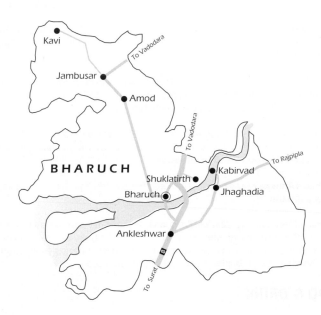

Shuklatirth
18 km from Bharuch

This village is known as Panchtirth, "place of five temples". The most famous of them is **Shukleshwar Mahadev**. Legend says that Shiva was pleased with the devout Chanakya and guided him to salvation. He instructed Chanakya to start his journey in a black boat at the mouth of the Narmada dressed in black and accompanied by a black cow. The place where black would transform into white would mark the location of his liberation. The transformation occurred in Shuklatirth. Shiva stayed with Chanakya at this site in the form of a *linga*. It is believed that this temple houses that same *linga,* and that by praying here all sins are purged and desires fulfilled. The **Omkarnath Bhagwan Mandir** has a tall white idol of Vishnu said to have emerged from the Narmada. ST buses travel between Bharuch and Shuklatirth.

Kabirvad

40 km from Bharuch

An abundance of banyan (*vad*) trees grow on this island in the Narmada. The folktale recounts that a saint told the brothers Jeeva and Tatva, who lived on this island, that they would attain peace of mind only by serving another accomplished saint. So they planted a banyan sapling and nurtured it with water used to wash the feet of saints. For several years the sapling remained dry, but when they washed the feet of Saint Kabir, the plant grew into a healthy tree. This banyan, known as Kabirvad, propagated hundreds of trees that spread across the island. Nobody can identify the original. The entire area has been fenced off and made into a park. There is a fairly new **Kabir Temple** amidst the grove. It is a good idea to carry some food. This place shuts down during the monsoon rains when the river floods the island. Ferries run back and forth from 0800-1830 and a two-way ride costs Rs. 10.

Kadiadungar

This hill in Kadia Village has a **Buddhist cave**, believed to have been briefly occupied by the Pandava brothers. The **Ashram of Gandadas Bapu**, a saint with a considerable following, is at the foot of the hill. Bapu took *samadhi* (liberated his soul from his body) as recently as 1997. Along the hilltop plateau are the ruins of a fort and a small stepwell.

Kavi Village

The *shivalinga* at the **Sthambheshwar Mahdev Temple** sits in the seabed and emerges only when the tide recedes. The stone pillars around this shrine also submerge during high tide. A little idol of Shiva's bull, Nandi, is always found next to the *linga* even though it is not fixed to the ground. **Kamaleshwar Mahadev**, an old Shiva temple, is reached by a path that runs alongside mango and jambun orchards. A narrow staircase in the temple leads up to a platform that offers a view of the Narmada. Take an ST bus from Bharuch to Jambusar, then catch another bus to Kavi.

GETTING INVOLVED

Shantigram Nirman Mandal *02641 238460, Tancha Village, 10 km from Amod* is located on the Jambusar-Bharuch bus route. This organization has joined efforts with Ahmedabad-based Pravaha to provide drinking water and other basic needs to surrounding tribal villages. **Contact** Badribhai Joshi.

Seva Rural *2645 220021, Jhaghadia* operates the 100-bed Kasturba Hospital for rural patients at subsidized rates. They also run an eye care program, organize healthcare training and conduct community healthcare projects to decrease maternal and infant mortality rates. **Contact** Dr Pankaj Shah.

SOUTHERN GUJARAT

▾ DISTRICT

▸ BHARUCH

Kabirvad
Kadiadungar
Kavi Village
Getting Involved

EASTERN
GUJARAT

EASTERN GUJARAT

N

NOT TO SCALE

Poshina

Khedbrahma
Vijaynagar

Idar

Himatnagar
Shamlaji
Roda

SABARKANTHA

AHMEDABAD

Kapadvanj Raioli
PANCHMAHAL **DAHOD**
Balasinor
Sojali **KHEDA**
Bilodra Dakor Ratanmahal **Dahod**
Sanctuary
Nadiad Godhra Bavka
Vaso Vadtal
Vallabh Vidyanagar **Anand** Devgad Baria
Karamsad
ANAND Anklavadi Pavagadh Jambughoda
Champaner Sanctuary
Khambhat
Mahi River **Vadodara** Chhota Udepur
Dabhoi Sankheda
Kayavarohan **VADODARA**
Kawant
Chandod

AT A GLANCE

Vadodara, Gujarat's third largest city, is considered the state's cultural capital. Pavagadh Hill, graced with a combination of Hindu and Jain shrines, towers over Champaner, the 15th c. pre-Mughal Islamic fort. Together they represent the diversity of religious influences that have pervaded Gujarat. Panchmahal District boasts of a distinctive tribal and forest belt that extends through Dahod, a district that shares borders and customs with Madhya Pradesh and Rajasthan. To the west, the neighboring districts of Anand and Kheda share the nickname, Charotar or "the fertile land", with their prosperity rooted in the tobacco and cotton fields that cover the region. Sabarkantha, bordering southern Rajasthan, is a rich tapestry of colorful people, diverse wildlife, fascinating landscapes, places of pilgrimage and nearly forgotten ruins engulfed by the forest.

VADODARA DISTRICT

VADODARA CITY

વડોદરા

POPULATION	1,500,000
AREA CODE	0265
DISTANCES - AHMEDABAD	110 KM
MUMBAI	390 KM

Vadodara is situated on the Vishwamitri River and is the administrative headquarters of Vadodara District. The city is a mixture of many eras and its reputation as "cultural capital" dates largely from the late-19th c, when it was the capital of the princely state of Baroda.

Since the early 9th c. AD this area has witnessed a series of urban settlements, including Vadpatra, named for the abundance of *vad* (banyan) trees in the vicinity. It emerged on the banks of the Vishwamitri, and over time derived its present name, Vadodara. Many places around Vadodara are associated with myth, legend and spiritualism. It is said that sage Vishwamitra's ashram stood on present-day Pavagadh Hill. Kayavarohan, Chandod and Karnali are believed to date from the times of the Mahabharata, about 3500 years ago. The city's recent history begins in 1721 when the Maratha General Pilaji Gaekwad and his clan defeated the Mughals and took control of Vadodara, first as rulers and then as kings, until India's independence.

The ruler Maharaja Sayajirao Gaekwad III (reigned 1875-1939) was a leading reformer of his times, and initiated a series of bold socioeconomic changes. His emphasis on economic development helped start a number of model manufacturing industries, laying the foundation of Vadodara as a modern industrial center. He extensively patronized education and the arts, drawing many talented people to the city, some of whom settled here. Sayajirao III also introduced compulsory primary education (including schooling for girls—a rare phenomenon in India at that time) and a network of libraries, the first of its kind in the country, to support his adult education program. The Maharaja Sayajirao University of Baroda (MSU) boasts of distinguished alumni in many fields and attracts students from all over India and abroad. Modern Vadodara's beauty, educational institutions and masterpieces of architecture are largely accredited to him.

PLACES OF INTEREST

Sayajibaug

The park, also popularly known as Kamatibaug, was named after Sayajirao III, who built it in 1879. It is located opposite the main entrance of the railway station. Spread over 45 hectares of land, the park grounds contain two museums, a zoo, a planetarium and a flower clock among other attractions. There is also an operational toy train. Count on spending at least half a day to really explore the park.

The **Baroda Museum and Art Gallery** is widely recognized for its rich collection of sculptures, antiques, paintings and manuscripts. The museum has galleries focused on specific eras and regions around the world, including one for the State of Baroda. The picture gallery houses a large collection of paintings by European masters, most of them from the private collection of Sayajirao III. Two wings exhibit modern Indian paintings. Sections of the museum display Indian musical instruments and exhibits related to the earth sciences and natural history. A major attraction is the 22 m long, blue-whale skeleton, found in 1972 at the mouth of River Mahi. The whale is believed to have been washed ashore in a storm. The **museum library** has a collection of nearly 23,000 books and periodicals on a range of topics. **Open** 1030-1700. **ENTRY Indians** Rs. 10, **Foreigners** Rs. 200.

The **planetarium** takes you on a half-hour trip across the universe. **Shows** at 1600 (Gujarati,) 1700 (English) and 1800 (Hindi). **ENTRY Adults** Rs. 7, **Children** Rs. 5. An **astronomy park** next door displays ancient Indian astronomical instruments.

One of the most prestigious institutions in western India, the **MS University of Baroda (MSU)** is a leader in fields such as human genome research, social work, technology, fine arts and performing arts. Its main attractions are the **Faculties of Arts, Fine Arts, Performing Arts** and the **Hansa Mehta Library**. The prominent dome of the Faculty of Arts, originally the Baroda College, is a city landmark. Located opposite Sayajibaug is the Faculty of Fine Arts where renowned artists periodically exhibit their works. It also hosts a popular Navratri event with traditional Garba and costumes. If interested, inquire about entry regulations. **The Faculty of Performing Arts**, popularly known as the Music College, has a rich history. When Sayajirao III married a princess from Tanjore, Tamil Nadu, her dowry included a troupe of dancers and musicians, who brought the Bharatanatayam dance form to Vadodara. Today it is still the only South Indian art form in the university's program. No short-term courses are offered. The place is a nucleus of cultural activity with occasional live concerts. It also operates the small theatre **Play Box**.

Hansa Mehta Library is one of the largest university libraries in India with over 700,000 books and an impressive collection of old journals from the Baroda State archives. Outsiders can access it at Rs. 40/day. **Open** 0800-1800.

Tambekar Wada

The former residence of the Baroda State *diwan*, this building has outstanding wall paintings of the 19th-c. Maratha School that illustrate scenes from the

Mahabharata, incidents from Krishna's life, Hindu gods and goddesses and the Anglo-Maratha war. **Open** 1100-1700. **Photography** with permission only.

Sri Aurobindo Niwas

This was once the residence of Aurobindo Ghose, the personal secretary of Sayajirao III, and later, the Vice Principal at Baroda College. He went on to become a social and political thinker, a freedom fighter, a philosopher and a yogi, known to the world as Sri Aurobindo. Some of his personal effects are exhibited here. The Niwas is open to all for meditation. It has a library of Aurobindo literature, a study room and a sales outlet. **Open** 0900-1900, daily.

EME Temple

Built by the Electrical and Mechanical Engineering (EME) Corps, this unusually modern looking temple is dedicated to Dakshinamurti, a form of Shiva as the supreme teacher. The aluminum structure is an interesting piece of army architecture and incorporates the holy symbols of all religions in one place. The Indian army generally does not have separate places of worship for different faiths. The garden around the temple has a collection of 106 ancient statues from the 6th to the 16th c. **Open** 0630–2030. **Photography** prohibited.

Qutbuddin Hajira

The *maqbara,* locally known as Hajira, was built around 1586 over the grave of Qutbuddin Muhammad Khan, a general in the army of the Mughal Emperor Akbar and later the governor of this region. It is the most important Mughal monument in Vadodara. Although not as elegant as either the Gujarat Sultanate architecture of the previous era or its own contemporary Mughal monuments in Delhi and Fatehpur Sikri, the tomb has a quiet dignity and charm. There is an old stepwell nearby.

Laxmi Vilas Palace

This striking palace built between 1878-90 is the private residence of the royal family and permission is required to visit the property. However, the **Darbar Hall** and the **Fatehsinh Museum** inside are open to visitors. The hall was the king's court and a place where musicians performed to entertain the royal family. Today it is a favorite venue for public concerts. The interior is resplendent with chandeliers, glass windows and carved *jharokhas*, a feature that allowed women to look out without being seen. **Entry** Rs. 100. The museum exhibits the private collection of the family, which includes paintings from well-known Indian and European artists, interesting furniture and other artifacts collected by Sayajirao III. It is worth a visit. **Open** 1100-1700. **Closed** Mon. **ENTRY Adult** Rs. 15, **Children** Rs. 10.

Central Library

Another inheritance from the Gaekwads is the Central Library near Mandvi Gate. Revolutionary for its time, it was the hub of library activity across Baroda State, bringing books to people in the interior areas through initiatives such as mobile libraries. Today it carries more than 300,000 books.

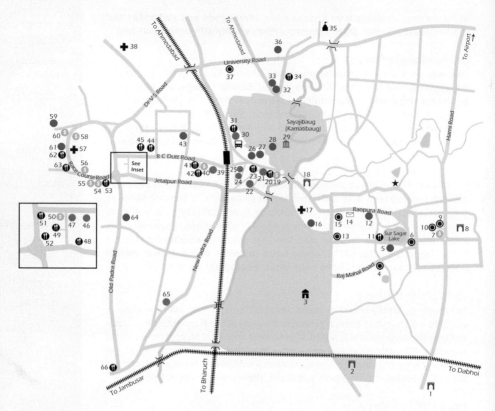

Vadodara City
Legend

Accommodation
21 Apex International
22 Surya Palace
24 Jal Sagar
25 PM Regency
30 Yuvraj
39 Panchsheel
46 Express
47 WelcomHotel
65 Taj Residency

Food & Drink
11 Canara Café
20 Havmor
23 Café Coffee Day
31 Jagdish Farsan
34 Goodies Cafeteria
41 Daawat
42 Amantran
44 Bombay Vada Pav
45 Payal Farsan
48 Anjoy–the Family Restaurant

49 Machu Picchu
51 Rajasthan Kulfi
52 Barista Espresso Bar
53 Mirch Masala
62 Café Coffee Day
63 Goodies Cafeteria
66 Maatel

Places of Interest
1 Qutbuddin Hajira
2 Pratap Vilas Palace / Lalbaug
3 Laxmi Vilas Palace
4 Khanderao Market
5 Faculty of Performing Arts
6 Nyaya Mandir
8 Nazarbaug Palace
9 Central Library
10 Narsinh ni pol, Jagmal ni pol, and
   Dala Patel ni pol
13 Sri Aurobindo Nivas
15 Kothi Kacheri
18 Kirti Mandir
28 Faculty of Fine Arts / Hansa Mehta
   Library
29 Baroda Museum and Art Gallery
35 EME Temple

37 The MS University of Baroda

Nuts & Bolts
7 Bank of Baroda
12 A Roy and Co
14 General Post Office
16 Gujarat Tourism Office
17 Sayaji General Hospital
19 Wall Street Forex
32 Sify Iway Cybercafé
33 Reliance World Cybercafé
36 Maruti Courier
38 Bhailal Amin Hospital
40 Thomas Cook
43 Crossword
50 American Express Foreign
   Exchange
54 ICICI Bank
55 UTI Bank
56 Citibank
57 Unity Hospital
58 HSBC Bank
59 Sify Iway Cybercafé
60 Bharat Overseas Bank
61 Inox Cinema
64 Maruti Courier

Nava Bazaar

This bustling market has everything from household goods to sparkling *chaniya cholis* and Bandhani textiles at rates lower than anywhere in town. The peak seasons of this marketplace are just before Navratri and Diwali.

Khanderao Market

Built in memory of Khanderao II in 1907, this pulsating market is open day and night. People maintain that everything you could possibly need over a lifetime can be found here. The design of the market combines Maratha, Jain, Islamic and Gothic architecture. Part of the building houses Municipal Corporation offices.

Colonial Marketplaces

Many permanent markets were established in major urban centers during the British colonial period. Conceptually modeled after Covent Garden and other European markets, they engage in both wholesale and retail trade. Today these marketplaces continue to be centers of commercial activity. The markets receive vegetables, fruits and flowers from out of town early in the morning, which is also the best time to visit and enjoy the bustling interactions between wholesalers and retailers.

Pols

Like Ahmedabad, Patan and other old cities of Gujarat, Vadodara also has *pols*. Despite modern urban development, about 60 *pols* survive around **Mandvi** and **Raopura Tower,** many of them pre-18th c. They offer a glimpse of the architectural style during that period. Some beautiful *havelis* and old structures still stand in **Narsinh ni pol, Jagmal ni pol** and **Dala Patel ni pol.**

Kirti Mandir

This memorial marks the diamond jubilee of the birth of Sayajirao III. Its spire is adorned with a bronze sun, moon and earth as well as a map of India. Murals inside depict the Mahabharata war and the life of Mirabai.

Other Places of Interest

Sursagar Lake, in the heart of the city, is a popular hangout for locals and a major venue for the ritual immersion of Ganesh idols at the end of Ganesh Chaturthi (see **Fairs and Festivals**). The 20-m tall Shiva statue in the lake is a recent addition. **Pratap Vilas Palace**, also known as Lalbaug, is a royal residence that now houses the Railway State College. **Entry** free, but must get permission. The authorities can arrange a guided tour if you visit during their working hours (0900-1800). **Nazarbaug Palace** was a royal guesthouse for high-ranking visitors. Now in poor condition, it is open to the public. **Kothi Kacheri,** which houses government offices, is a magnificent red building, once used for the offices of the state cabinet. **Nyaya Mandir** or "Temple of Justice", is a notable building that presently accommodates the district sessions court. Four gates mark the borders of old Vadodara, but the city now stretches far beyond them.

ENTERTAINMENT

The Amphitheater

A new attraction at Kamatibaug, the Amphitheater hosts dance performances, drama, poetry readings, recitations and more, mainly in Gujarati. The Tourism cell near the Fatehgunj Circle entrance has advance schedules. The programs generally begin between 1700-1800. **Entry** free.

Abhivyakti

This is an open-air theater near Kirti Mandir that stages plays and displays art work around the year.

Inox

A three-screen multiplex in Ellora Park, the Inox shows English films in addition to Hindi, Malayalam, Telugu and Marathi movies. Tickets Rs. 60-120.

NUTS & BOLTS

In and Out

The city is connected by air to Mumbai and Delhi, and by rail with most of India. Located on NH8, it is also well linked by ST and private buses to places within Gujarat and major cities in neighboring states. Ahmedabad-Vadodara intercity buses (2 hrs) run every 15 minutes. The offices of most private bus companies are on or near Station Road. **National Volvo** *2787373, Opp Natraj Cinema*, **Ashwamegh Travels** *2789951, Nr Railway Godi*, **Tanna Travels** *2793517, Opp Natraj Cinema* and **Laxmi Travels,** *Opp ST Bus Depot* operate several daily buses to Ahmedabad and Mumbai. Ticket prices depend on the type of bus. The average is Rs. 100 to Ahmedabad, Rs. 200 to Mumbai. For short day trips hired cars are a convenient but expensive option. **Express Tours and Travels** *in Express Hotel* rents out cars with driver. Rates range from Rs. 650 without AC to Rs. 2200 for luxury vehicles, for 8 hrs or 80 km per day. Extra mileage costs between Rs. 7-21/km.

Getting Around

Rickshaws are the best way to travel. Before starting, check that the meter is set to zero. Multiply the meter reading by 10 and add one to calculate what you owe.

Tourist Information

Gujarat Tourism Office *2427489, Narmada Bhavan, C Block, Jail Rd.*

Money

ATMs **Bank of Baroda** *Main Office, Mandvi*; **HSBC** *Ellora Park, Race Course Rd, Indraprasth Cmplx*; **ICICI** *Racecourse Rd*; **Citibank** *Gotri Rd.*
FOREIGN EXCHANGE **American Express** *Dwarkesh Cmplx, Alkapuri*; **Thomas Cook** *Opp Circuit House, Alkapuri*; **Wall Street Forex** *Profit Centre, Kala Ghoda*; **Bharat Overseas Bank** *Patriot Cmplx, Race Course Rd.*
MONEY TRANSFER **Western Union** at the General Post Office.

Communication

INTERNET **Sify Iway** *Saffron Cmplx, Fatehgunj; Vrundavan Soc, Race Course;* **Reliance World,** *Nr Saffron Towers, Fatehgunj.* Several cyber cafes are also located around the railway station.

COURIER **Maruti** *3296084, Time Square Bldg, Nr Petrol Pump, Fatehgunj; 2310693, Rajlakshmi Cmplx, Nr Race Course Circle.* **Blue Dart** *23442313, Shri Hari Apt, Alkapuri.*

Medical

HOSPITALS **Sayaji General Hospital** *2424848;* **Unity Hospital** *2354488, Opp Inox Multiplex, Ellora Park;* **Bhailal Amin General Hospital** *2280300, Gorwa Rd.* MEDICAL STORE **A Roy and Co** (24-hours) *2421248, Raopura.*

Bookstores

Crossword *Arunodaya Soc, Alkapuri,* a popular chain with outlets across India, has a large stock of English books, music and computer games.

ACCOMMODATION

Most hotels are clustered within 2 km of the railway station, in Sayajigunj, Alkapuri and on RC Dutt Road.

P M Regency *2361616, Nr Police Station, Sayajigunj* has very clean rooms, some with great views from the balconies. **Facilities** western toilets, AC options, TV, complimentary breakfast. **Single** 295-1600 **Double** 600-2000 **Extra Bed** 200.

Jal Sagar *2361110, Opp BBC Towers, Sayajigunj* is a basic lodging, adequate for sleeping. **Facilities** western toilets, running hot water, AC options, TV restaurant. **Single** 350-650 **Double** 450-800 **Extra Bed** 150.

Panchsheel *233749, Sampatrao Colony, RC Dutt Rd* is a basic but clean option. **Facilities** western toilets, AC options. **Single** 630-1750 **Double** 770-1960 **Extra Bed** 200.

Express *3055000, Alkapuri* is strongly recommended for its friendly service and management. It is good value for the money. **Facilities** AC options, TV, room service, airport courtesy service, wine shop, travel desk, Wi-Fi, complimentary breakfast. **Single** 1275-3500 **Double** 1900-4000 **Extra Bed** 500.

Surya Palace *2363366, Opp Parsi Agiari, Sayajigunj* has spacious rooms and excellent service. **Facilities** western toilets, AC, running hot water, Azure multicuisine restaurant. **Single** 2100-4000 **Double** 2400-4500 **Extra Bed** 500.

Taj Residency *2354545, Akota Garden* is far from the center, but otherwise an excellent luxury hotel. **Facilities** TV, swimming pool, health club. **Single** 2900-7500 (USD 80-200) **Double** 3400-7500 (USD 90-200) **Extra Bed** 500.

EASTERN
GUJARAT

DISTRICT ▾
VADODARA ◂
Vadodara City
Nature Park
Dabhoi
Vadhvana
Wetland
Kayavarohan
Chandod
Gangeshvar
Mahadev
Sankheda
Chhota Udepur
Champaner-
Pavagadh
Jambughoda
Getting Involved

DAHOD
SABARKANTHA
ANAND
KHEDA

WelcomHotel Vadodara *2330033, R C Dutt Rd* is a 5-star luxury hotel with spacious rooms and outstanding service. **Facilities** TV, swimming pool, Wi-Fi, wine shop, health club with sauna, travel desk, Peshwari and Cascade restaurants. **Rooms** 4500 (115 USD)–15000 (375 USD).

FOOD & DRINK

Most good restaurants are in the same stretch of the city as the hotels above, but a few pleasant surprises await those who venture beyond.

Amantran *Sampatrao Colony, Alkapuri* has excellent Gujarati food and *thalis*, but pricier than most places. **Anjoy** *Corner Pt, Alkapuri* is a multicuisine restaurant famous for combos of South Indian and Chinese food. **Kansaar** *Opp Hotel Surya, Sayajigunj* is one of the best places for a Gujarati *thali* and good value for money, with an unlimited *thali* at Rs. 75. **Canara Coffee House** *Nr Dandia Bazaar, Fire Stn* is a small place that serves tasty Marathi and South Indian snacks and good coffee. **Daawat** *Ivory Terrace, Opp Circuit House, Alkapuri*, one of the oldest restaurants in Vadodara, is known for *pav bhaji* and Punjabi dishes. **Maatel** *Ananya Cmplx, Old Padra Rd* is popular for its Punjabi and Jain fare. **Mirch Masala** *Meghdhanu Cmplx, Gotri Rd* has a traditional Punjabi *dhaba* ambience and serves tasty North Indian food and excellent *jalebi*. **Havmor** *Yashkamal Bldg, Sayajigunj* has a multicuisine menu, but is best known for its Punjabi food. Try their famous ice cream, an old brand exclusive to Gujarat.

Goodies Cafeteria *Emperor Bldg, Fatehgunj; Race Course Circle* is a popular hang-out for students and is frequented for its desserts, fast food and snacks. **Machu Picchu** *Nxt to WelcomHotel, RC Dutt Rd* is a cafe lounge with good Chinese fare. The cafe also has Wi-Fi. **Cafe Bistro Melange** *Alkapuri, Nr HDFC Bank* is a one-stop shop for *hookah* lovers at Rs. 150 an hour. It also serves good though pricey food and drinks. **Only Parathas** *Jetalpur Rd* serves more than 105 varieties of *parathas*. **Pizza Inn** *Jetalpur Rd, Nxt to Glaciers Cmplx* makes good pizza. **Express Hotel** *Alkapuri* has three restaurants—**Mandap** for Gujarati *thali*, **24 Carats**, a 24-hour restaurant and coffee shop and **Muffins**, a popular city bakery. For coffee and desserts try **Barista** *Opp Income Tax Office, Race Course Circle* and **Café Coffee Day** *Opp Hotel Apex, Sayajigunj; Nr Inox Cinema, Race Course Rd*.

LOCAL SPECIALTIES **Bombay Vada Pav** *Nr Baroda High School, Alkapuri* is a little stall serving hot *vada-pav* with cheese and garlic chutney. **Rajasthan Kulfi** *Nr Ambedkar Statue, Alkapuri* offers delicious traditional Indian ice cream called *kulfi* in a variety of flavors. **Jagdish Farsan** *Golden Trade Center, Nr Bus Depot* is famous for its snacks—*lilo chevdo* and *bhakharvadi*—made fresh every day. **Payal Farsan** *Opp WelcomHotel* is famous for its *khaman, khandvi, patra*, and for its innovations on traditional snack items using modern technology. Their *patra*, dried crisp in an infrared oven, lasts several days without spoiling. **Bombay Sandwiches** *Alkapuri, Nxt to Raymond Shop* serves *sev puri* and great sandwiches. **Raju Omelettes** *Karelibaug* prepares good omelet. The area opposite MSU at Ellora Park fills with *laris* serving an assortment of street food.

EXCURSIONS

Nature Park   **13 km from Vadodara**

Gujarat Nature Conservation Society has developed a small artificial forest in the ravines of the Mahi River near Sindhrot. Its biodiversity includes rare species of herbs and plants, animals and birds. The floods of 2005 severely damaged the park and swept away many of the animals, but most of it is now restored. It is a good place for short treks. The park office hires out tents at Rs. 200/night. Meals, tea and coffee are available if requested in advance. This is a popular outing for nature lovers.

Dabhoi   **29 km from Vadodara**

A frontier fortress built in the 13th c. during the Solanki period, Dabhoi was occupied successively by the Muslims, Marathas and British. Its four large gates, carved with interesting religious iconography, are respectively called

EASTERN GUJARAT

DISTRICT ▾
VADODARA ◂
Vadodara City
Nature Park
Dabhoi
Vadhvana
Wetland
Kayavarohan
Chandod
Gangeshvar
Mahadev
Sankheda
Chhota Udepur
Champaner-
Pavagadh
Jambughoda
Getting Involved

DAHOD
SABARKANTHA
ANAND
KHEDA

Vadodara Gate (main western entrance into town), **Hira Gate** (east), **Mahudi Gate** (north) and **Nanderi Gate** (south). Hira Gate is relatively well preserved with painstakingly fine carvings. The gate is associated with the legend of Hira, the mason who is said to have been buried alive under the arch adorned with a carved elephant. Dabhoi also has the largest **narrow-gauge railway station** in Asia. Although it is now being phased out, two trains still travel daily from Pratapnagar Station in Vadodara. The town is connected to Vadodara by ST buses.

Vadhvana Wetland

10 km from Dabhoi

Popular for birdwatching, Vadhvana attracts over 110 species and 50,000 birds during its peak season (Nov to Mar). Species include stork, tern, ibis and spoonbill. Built in the early 20th c. as an irrigation reservoir spread over 600 hectares, provides water to 25 surrounding villages. Tourist huts, a watchtower and peripheral roads are being built. There is no bus service, but you can rent a vehicle from Dabhoi. Take the road from Nanderi Gate to reach here.

Kayavarohan

20 km from Dabhoi, 30 km from Vadodara

Locally known as "Karvan", this ancient town is associated with Shiva. It is believed to be the origin of the Pashupati sect, which reveres Shiva as the God of animals. There are several temples including one dedicated to Lakulish, an incarnation of Shiva who is considered the first guru of the Pashupati sect and the creator of yoga. ST buses stop here.

Chandod

50 km from Vadodara, 20 km from Dabhoi

A pilgrimage center known for its *ghats* along the Narmada River, Chandod is a location for post-death rituals and has many temples and ashrams including the renowned **Jeevan Sadhana, Ma Anandmayi** and **Gangeshvar Mahadev** ashrams. The ancient **Shesh Narayana Temple** houses paintings claimed to be 1500 years old that depict episodes from Krishna's life on its ceilings. *Aarti* is performed in the temples in the evening. Boats can be hired for a trip to **Triveni Sangam**, the confluence of the Narmada, Orsang and Gupta Sarasvati rivers, where *asthi visarjan* (immersion of ashes) and rituals are carried out. The only lodging options here are the ashrams. Shared jeeps and ST buses travel between Chandod and Dabhoi.

Gangeshvar Mahadev

3 km from Chandod

This temple is located along a peaceful bank of the Narmada, about 3 km from Chandod. It is a little over a century old and significant because Sri Aurobindo, who later founded the world-renowned Aurobindo Ashram in Pondicherry, meditated here. During the early days of the freedom struggle it was also a den of underground revolutionaries, tacitly supported, and to some extent funded, by the princes and affluent people of the area. The serene environment and the river are the main attractions here.

Sankheda

20 km from Dabhoi, 47 from Vadodara

This town is famous for its lacquer-painted woodwork called Sankheda ware (see **Resource Guide, Craft**) and is worth strolling through just to watch the craftsmen at work. Unlike many other Indian craft traditions, Sankheda has

survived and prospered due to market demand. Finished products include chairs, swings, photo frames and various household objects. The local vendors provide shipping services. ST buses go to Sankheda.

Chhota Udepur

100 km from **Vadodara**

Chhota Udepur is a small but important town in the tribal heartland. Surrounded by forests and mountains, it is known for its indigenous heritage and culture. It shares a history with Devgad Baria and was one of three major princely states in the tribal belt of eastern Gujarat. The town sits on a lakeside and has many structures from the 1920s that give it a distinct character. The **Jain Temple** is a great display of Victorian-influenced plaster art. The impressive **Kusum Vilas Palace** shares a 7-hectare campus with the **Prem Bhavan**. The estate belongs to the local royal family and you need permission to enter.

The colorful *haat* (tribal market) takes place every Saturday and stays open until sunset. Here people from surrounding tribal communities buy and sell a wide range of wares including pottery, tools, tribal jewelry, and bows and arrows. Artisans in and around town craft the bows and arrows, which are technically illegal if sold with sharp tips. There is also a **Tribal Museum** that showcases handicrafts like toys and musical instruments made of wood and clay. Chhota Udepur is a great base to explore the interesting and numerous tribal villages in this area, especially those belonging to the vibrant Rathwa community. This is also an excellent place to visit during the period around Holi (see **Fairs and Festivals**). ST buses frequently travel between Chhota Udepur and Vadodara, but they are usually crowded. A private vehicle is good for exploring the area. For a different experience, try the narrow-gauge train, which returns to Vadodara daily except on Mondays and Fridays.

Kali Niketan is a heritage hotel set in a regal mansion built along the Orsang River over a century ago. It functioned as the summer residence of the royal family. *For more information contact 079 26302019.*

Pithora Painting

The Rathwa community practices ritualistic wall paintings called Pithora, which are an offering to their God, Baba Pithora. The paintings are commissioned to remove ill circumstances and bring peace, prosperity and happiness over the household. They call on the *lakharas* or Pithora painters, who are guided by the narration of the *badwa* or head priest. The central theme is the wedding of Pithora and Pithori, with members of the universe such as the sun and moon, stars, plants and animals attending as guests. Horses, a prominent representation, symbolize a number of forms including family ancestors and visions of God. Other villagers accompany the ritual with singing and drumming. Once the painting is completed, the priest gives life and meaning to each of its elements, linking them to legendary tales. The villagers then sacrifice a goat and end the day with a feast.

The following places are located in Panchmahal District but make sense as excursions from the city of Vadodara. Keep in mind that the eastern belt of Gujarat, which extends from Sabarkantha down to Narmada, shares a geo-cultural and historical continuity. It is worth doing the entire stretch in a single trip. The roads and public transportation are not as good as the rest of Gujarat, so renting a vehicle makes sense. Your reward will be stunning landscapes and a serenity that contrasts dramatically with other parts of the state.

Champaner-Pavagadh 47 km from Vadodara, 90 km from Devgad Baria

These two destinations, located northeast of Vadodara and south of Godhra, are often mentioned separately, but are so closely intertwined in geography (just 4 km apart) and history that it makes sense to treat them together.

Apart from geological reasons, there is a fascinating creation myth that explains the abrupt 800-m Pavagadh Hill that rises from the surrounding plain. Ages ago this was a deep valley situated below the ashram of Rishi Vishwamitra. One day his miraculous cow, blessed with an inexhaustible supply of milk, slipped into the gorge. Unable to climb up the steep slope, she filled the depression with milk and swam to safety. To prevent a repeat episode, the sage prayed for the valley to be leveled. The gods responded by air-freighting a large chunk of the Himalaya with Hanuman. Three quarters of it was adequate for the task. The remaining quarter (*pav* in Gujarati), which juts out of the plain, is Pavagadh.

Pavagadh is an important place of Shakti worship centered around the **Mahakali Temple** that crowns the hill. Rebuilt and renovated several times, the present structure is from the 19th c. An unusual feature of the temple is the shrine built over it dedicated to the Muslim saint, Sadanshah, who is also revered by Hindus. Legend says that Mahakali, in a fit of rage, set out to destroy the world, but Sadanshah pacified her. The shrine honors him for this noble act. The hill also has beautiful Jain temples, most of them in ruins. The oldest standing Hindu temple (10th-11th c.) found here is dedicated to Lakulish, a form of Shiva.

Pavagadh bustles with activity during the Navratri festival. The natural beauty of the area, the breathtaking views from the hill, and the religious importance of the site draw hundreds of visitors daily. A cable car goes up to a point just short of the main temple, reducing the rigors of climbing the long flight of steps. The ride costs Rs. 75 two-way, and the service operates from 0830 to 1730.

Champaner, at the foot of Pavagadh, is believed to have been founded in the 8th c. by King Vanaraj, who ruled Gujarat from Patan, and is named after his governor, Champa. The first known historical reference to Pavagadh and Champaner dates from around the 13th c. AD when it was captured by the Khichi Chauhan Rajputs fleeing from Mewar (the area around Udaipur), which had been invaded by the forces of Alauddin Khilji, the Sultan of Delhi. Descendants of these Chauhans, who built the first fortifications of Champaner, held the place sporadically until 1484, when Sultan Mahmud Begada of Ahmedabad captured it after a long siege. The Khichi Chauhans moved on to set up two small states, Devgad Baria to the northeast and Chhota Udepur to the southeast.

Mahmud shifted his capital from Ahmedabad to Champaner. He improved the fortifications and built most of the grand monuments, water bodies and secular buildings that made the place one of grandest towns of Gujarat. He named it Muhammadabad, after the Prophet Muhammad. His creations include the citadel, the outer fortifications, the town gates, a market, a mint, granaries, warehouses, several mosques, some lakes, gardens, and many other buildings. The total number of monuments in Champaner is well over 100, not all of them notified for protection. Most of them are from the 15th-16th c., and a few from the 10th-14th c. Champaner continued as the capital of the Sultanate after Mahmud's death in 1511, until it was taken by the Mughal Emperor Humayun in 1535. The capital was shifted back to Ahmedabad, marking the end of Champaner's era of glory, and effectively, that of the Gujarat Sultanate.

You could easily spend days rambling around the area to explore the **Hissar-e-khas** (citadel); the town walls and gates; the **Nagina, Kevda, Khajuri** and **Shehari Mosques; Mandvi;** the **Dudhiya, Chasiya** and **Vad lakes**; the **Saat Kamaan** (seven arches); **the helical stepwell;** the **granaries;** the **Amirs' mansions;** and **Patai Rawal's Palace.** The **Jama Masjid** is one of the grandest mosques in Gujarat. It is double-storied, with 30-meter high *minarets* and an ablution tank that resembles an octagonal *kund*. For a detailed listing and photographs of the attractions at Champaner-Pavagadh by the Department of Landscape Architecture at the University of Illinois, Urbana-Champaign, visit http://130.126.206.132:8088/Champaner/index.htm. The Champaner-Pavagadh Archeological Park is listed as a UNESCO World Heritage Site.

ST buses travel up to **Machi Plateau,** where most of the visitors' facilities are located. The only reasonable place to stay is **Hotel Champaner,** run by the Gujarat Tourism Department. There are also a few *dharmashalas* and local guest houses. Local transport includes unmetered rickshaws and shared jeeps.

Jambughoda
70 km from Vadodara, 20 km from Pavagadh

Jambughoda Wildlife Sanctuary is rich with undulating hills, a good forest cover and valleys with small village settlements. It is dominated by teak and bamboo. The top predator is the leopard, which has been able to increase its population in the protected habitat. The Sloth bear, hyena, jackal, Blue bull, wild boar, Four-horned antelope, Barking deer and porcupine are also found here. Reptiles include venomous and non-venomous snakes, pythons and crocodiles. The water reservoirs at **Kada** and **Targol** enrich the aesthetic settings and habitat diversity. Both of these reservoirs have forest rest houses on their banks and Kada also has a picturesque campsite. *For bookings or more information contact the Forest Department Office in Raopura 0265 2428940.* Jambughoda is connected to Pavagadh by ST buses. Hired vehicles are available and are a good option for exploring the forest and to observe the animals at close range.

The **Nature Lover's Retreat** *02676 241258,* is a heritage property inside the sanctuary, run by the royal family. It has beautifully decorated rooms with AC options. Rates vary by season and range between Rs. 1000 and 1500. The food is good, with vegetarian and non-veg options.

GETTING INVOLVED

Shroff Foundation *0265 2680702, Kalali, www.shroffsfoundation.org* works for tribal areas in fields such as health and water sanitation, rural development, awareness and advocacy. **Contact** Girish Pathak.

Muni Seva Ashram *02668 268004, Goraj, Waghodia, www.muniashram.org* works for the upliftment of villagers in Goraj and the surrounding areas. It runs the Kailash Cancer Hospital and Research Centre, equipped with state-of-the-art technology, and promotes productive cultivation, animal husbandry, solar energy, bio-fuel and rural development.

Bhasha Research and Publication Centre *0265 2331968, United Ave, Nr Dinesh Mills, Vadodara, bprc_baroda@sify.com* was started by Ganesh Devy, a renowned social scientist and activist, for the socio-economic empowerment and human rights of tribal and denotified communities. It has an excellent Tribal Academy for the promotion of tribal languages, literature, arts and culture. The center aims to initiate formal education and preserve tribal culture. **The Bhasha Adivasi Academy,** situated at Tejgadh (14 km from Chhota Udepur), includes a library, museum, lodging and boarding. It also puts out research publications.

Heritage Trust *0265 22833415, Golden Apartment, Subhanpura, Vadodara, kga@icenet.net* was established by a group of like-minded architects, artists, art historians, archaeologists, historians, musicologists and writers in 1984 for the conservation of heritage sites in the city of Vadodara. The Trust focuses on creating heritage awareness and related issues. It was responsible for the push to designate Champaner-Pavagadh as a UNESCO World Heritage Site.

V-One Society *0265 2791621, Bhumika Cmplx, Opp Red Church, Fatehgunj, Vadodara, v_one_society@wilnetonline.net* is one of the oldest NGOs in the city and works towards rehabilitating the increasing number of physically challenged people in and around Vadodara. The society trains members in various vocations and crafts and supplies them with tricycles, scooters, hearing aids, walking sticks and other equipment.

Anand Niketan Ashram *02669 273333, Rangpur Village, Kavant via Bodeli* was established by the dedicated Gandhian Harivallabh Parikh to work for the betterment of tribal communities. It is known for its weekly Lok Adalat (People's Court) at which tribals from nearby villages come to settle disputes. The court is held in the open and welcomes observers to its proceedings. More than 71,000 cases have been settled here. **Contact** Nagendra Parikh.

DAHOD DISTRICT

DAHOD CITY
દાહોદ

POPULATION	112,000
AREA CODE	02673
DISTANCES - AHMEDABAD	214 KM
VADODARA	159 KM

Carved out of Panchmahal in 1979, Dahod is the easternmost district of Gujarat and is located where the state's border meets Madhya Pradesh and Rajasthan. The local language, food and lifestyle all reflect this cultural synthesis. The district is part of the larger tribal belt that stretches along most of the length of eastern Gujarat. Up until the 19th c. dense forest covered the entire area, but today, only 16 percent of sparse forestland remains.

The city of Dahod, the district headquarters, is considered the eastern gateway to the state and is said to have taken its name from Saint Dadhichi, who had an ashram on the banks of the nearby Dudhimati River. The town has an interesting ethnic mix of the mercantile Dawoodi Bohras (more than 40 percent of the population), the Bhil tribal community from surrounding areas, and the Hindu communities. Its main industries today include grain and pulse mills, as evident from Dahod's wholesale grain market, the second largest in Gujarat, which buzzes with farmers, mill owners, traders and trucks all playing their role in the business.

EASTERN GUJARAT

DISTRICT ▾
VADODARA

DAHOD ◂
Dahod City
Bavka
Devgad Baria
Ratanmahal
Getting Involved

SABARKANTHA
ANAND
KHEDA

PLACES OF INTEREST

Chhab Talav

This lake is a legacy from the Solanki period, when Siddhraj Jaysinh established Dahod as his base camp to campaign against Malwa (the western part of present-day Madhya Pradesh). According to legend, the lake was built overnight. The army was so large that each soldier had to scoop out just one *chhabadiyo* (a basket) of dirt to create the required depression; hence the name.

Aurangzeb no Killo

Dahod is the birthplace of Aurangzeb, the last of the Great Mughals. When Prince Khurram, who eventually became Emperor Shah Jahan, and his wife were traveling to Delhi, she went into labor and gave birth to their son. The spot is marked by a small memorial, below which Auragzeb's umbilical cord is said to have been buried. Nearby are the remains of a small brick mosque which Aurangzeb later erected. Aurangzeb no Killo was built by Shah Jahan as a resting place for travelers in honor of his son's birth. The Marathas then converted it into a fort. Today it houses government offices and a few *dargahs*.

Dahod City

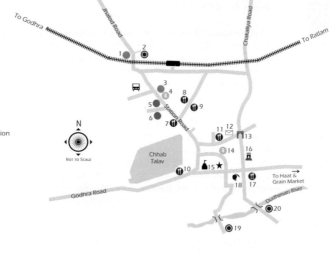

Weekly Haat

A *haat* takes place in Dahod every Wednesday, when people from neighboring tribal areas file into town to buy and sell various items. Next to the array of plastic wares and household goods on sale, you will find terracotta horses, handcrafted bows and arrows, herbs and fruits from the surrounding jungles, and tribal jewelry made of silver mixed with lead.

NUTS & BOLTS

In and Out

Dahod is connected by ST buses to most cities and towns in Gujarat and to important ones in the neighboring states. It is a stop on the Vadodara-Delhi railway line.

Getting Around

Dahod is connected with the rest of the district by ST bus and shared jeeps.

Money

ATMs **UTI Bank** *Opp Bus Stn*; **SBI Bank** *Nr Desai's Petrol Pump*.

ACCOMMODATION

Hotel Rama *220473, Nr Railway Overbridge, Jhalod Rd* is the best option in town, with clean rooms and a friendly staff. **Facilities** western toilets, AC options, TV options. **Dorm** 70-100 **Suite** 600-700.

Vrundavan Hotel and Guest House *221558, Opp the Bus Stn* is reasonably clean, but has stuffy rooms. **Facilities** western toilets. **Dorm** 40 **Single** 115 **Double** 220.

**EASTERN
GUJARAT**

DISTRICT ▼
VADODARA

DAHOD ◄
Dahod City
Bavka
Devgad Baria
Ratanmahal
Getting Involved

SABARKANTHA
ANAND
KHEDA

FOOD & DRINK

Krishna Restaurant serves vegetarian and non-veg Punjabi options. **Vrundavan Lodge** *Opp Krishna Restaurant* offers vegetarian Punjabi fare. **Yaadgar Veg and Non-Veg** is popular for its meat dishes and serves a variety of chicken and mutton preparations, meat stuffed *samosas* and sizzling *seekh kebabs*. It is famous for its *doodh* and *ajmer halwas,* both sweet dishes.

LOCAL SPECIALTIES Across from the Hanuman temple in the main bazaar is a hole-in-the-wall that sells a Madhya Pradesh specialty, *dal pakwaan*—a spicy *dal* served with flaky *puris,* accompanied by onion and green chilies. For less than ten rupees you can eat your fill of this delicious treat. Just on the Chhaab Talav, before the main Shreenathji Temple, is **Jitenbhai's Kachori Stand.** Here you will find *puris* filled with spices and served with a special chickpea flour sauce, curd and onions. **Ratlami Sev Bhandar** *Station Rd* sells a variety of spicy snacks, including Ratlami *sev*, chickpea flour mixed with spices and fried into crisp noodle-like pieces.

EXCURSIONS

Bavka

10 km from Dahod

This town has a 10th c. Shiva temple known mostly for its erotic sculptures. The outer walls and the sanctum door are intricately carved with representations of deities and celestial beings. The spire and the dome over the hall of the temple have collapsed, the fragments of which are displayed around. The temple is located on a knoll near the Hirlav Lake in Chandwada Village. To reach Bavka, take a bus to Chandwada or Dhanpur and get off at Jesawada on the Bavka crossing, or take a shared rickshaw from Dahod to Jesawada. The temple is 2 km from the crossing. A rickshaw from Jesawada village costs about Rs. 35 one-way.

Devgad Baria

46 km from Dahod, 49 km from Chhota Udepur, 120 km from Vadodara

Though not high on the list of travel destinations, Devgad Baria is a charming town with a colorful history, monuments, palaces, hills, forests and a rich tribal culture. Smaller than Dahod and less endowed in infrastructure, it is more central to many of the interesting places in the district, and is recommended as a possible base to explore the surroundings. It has a shared history with Chhota Udepur and the scenic route between them makes it worth combining the two in the same circuit, with a halt at Ratanmahal Wildlife Sanctuary on the way.

Nestled in the foothills of Devgad, "Fortress of Gods", and home to the Baria Koli tribe, Devgad Baria was a princely state founded by the ruler Prithviraj in 1782. Descendants of the Khichi Chauhans (see **Chhota Udepur**), the rulers of Baria, were progressive and started many free educational institutes, hospitals, and veterinary centers.

The town has grown around the Mansarovar Lake and a clock tower welcomes visitors into the main town. Old buildings such as the hospital, Ranjit High School and the court are painted neatly in shades of yellow ochre and red. Other distinctive buildings are the **Rajmahal Palace, Lalmahal, Darbar Hall, Library, Nagarpalika** (with a sample of Pithora painting) along with structures from the British days. The older quarters of the town are lined with *havelis* and houses that share sidewalls and stand on narrow streets. Every Friday a *haat* is held where tribals sell their produce and buy products such as bamboo ware, pottery, wicks, mahuda, dried mangos, bows and arrows, indigenous spices, ropes, plastic bangles and more. There is an old Kali Mata Temple on the hill.

The best accommodation is available at **Royal Farm** 02678 *220466, Nr Avanti Farm,* a property of the local royal family. It has AC suites at Rs. 1000. Food is available upon request. There are two reasonable restaurants, **Meereebha**, which serves North Indian and Chinese food in an open-air setting and **Southland** *foot of TV Relay Tower*, which prepares South Indian snacks for breakfast and dinner only.

Regular direct buses connect Devgad Baria with Ahmedabad and Vadodara. A number of long-distance buses halt at Limkheda, from where local buses and shared rickshaws go to Baria, a scenic 15 km drive through little villages and forests.

EASTERN GUJARAT

DISTRICT ▼
VADODARA

DAHOD ◄
Dahod City
Bavka
Devgad Baria
Ratanmahal
Getting Involved

SABARKANTHA
ANAND
KHEDA

Ratanmahal Sanctuary   **45 km from Devgad Baria, 60 km from Dahod**
Accessed from the village of Kanjeta, the sanctuary spreads over 56 sq km and spills over into Madhya Pradesh. It is best known for its Sloth bear conservation program. Once a game reserve of the Baria royal family, it was declared a sanctuary after the merger of the state. Besides the Sloth bear, Jungle cats, foxes, Honey badgers and porcupines, birds, reptiles and flora all inhabit the sanctuary. Thick vegetation keeps the place cool around the year, and after the rains, the forest canopy is lush and water bodies are full. The **Jaldhara Waterfall** is a scenic spot to relax. There are also great trekking opportunities available here.

Ratanmahal is closed to visitors during the rainy season. The best time to visit is October-February. Accommodation is available in forest department guest houses inside the sanctuary at **Bhindol** (12 tents and 4 log huts with attached baths), **Kanjeta** (2 AC rooms and 4 ordinary rooms), **Pipargota** (2 ordinary rooms) and **Udhal Mahuda** (4 double-bed cottages). **Tents** Rs. 250, **Guest houses** Rs. 500. Camping is permitted and forest officials help locate safe sites and dispatch local guides. Currently a program is being introduced where locals living in the sanctuary provide food on request at Rs. 45. *For more information or to make bookings contact the Deputy Conservator of Forest, Devgad Baria 02678 220425.*

GETTING INVOLVED

Samanvay Resource Center *02678 221025, Devgad Baria, nrpsrc_2000@ yahoo.com* works with youth and HIV/AIDS awareness, rural development, women's empowerment, community based rehabilitation, self-help groups and community empowerment across Dahod and Panchmahal.

Sadguru Water and Development Foundation *02673 238601, Chosalia Village, 10 km from Dahod, www.nmsadguru.org* is a leading organization in the field of water, natural resource management and rural development. The foundation uses these means to work towards the betterment of rural and tribal communities in the surrounding areas.

The Blind Welfare Council *02673 243389, Mission Rd, Nr Railway Overbridge, Dahod, www.bwcdahod.com* runs an integrated learning program for the disabled in and around Dahod and Panchmahal, and focuses on programs related to education, culture, sports and empowerment. It also maintains several residential campuses and a day school for children living in Dahod. **Contact** Yusuf Kapadia.

SABARKANTHA DISTRICT

IDAR
ઈડર

POPULATION	32,800
AREA CODE	02778
DISTANCES - AHMEDABAD	107 KM
VADODARA	218 KM

This district borders Rajasthan to the east and derives its name from the Sabarmati River that separates Sabarkantha from the neighboring districts. The local economy depends heavily on agriculture and dairy farming. Sabarkantha hosts two of Gujarat's main pilgrimage sites, a famous Krishna temple at Shamlaji and ancient temples honoring Brahma and Nana Ambaji at Khedbrahma. It is also home to one of Gujarat's best kept secrets—the enchanting Vijaynagar and Polo Forests that abound with temple ruins.

Idar, a significant town in this district, is a good base for excursions to areas such as Khedbrahma, Vijaynagar and Poshina. It is also en route to Mt Abu and Ambaji. Nestled in the southern base of the Aravali Mountain Range, the town is surrounded on three sides by a hill with towering boulders that dominate the skyline. This natural fortification protected the former princely state from several sieges.

PLACES OF INTEREST

Idar Hill Fort (Idariyo Gadh)

The **clock tower** marks the entrance to the old town of Idar and leads to a road that cuts straight through the market, ending at the base of the **Idar Hll**. From here you can drive around the hill to the top or climb a long flight of steps past the ruins of an early-20th c. palace built by Maharaja Dolatsinhji. The building is falling apart, so it is best admired from a distance.

At the top, perched on a huge protruding rock, is the **Ruthi Rani no Mahal**, or the "Palace of the Sulking Queen". According to legend, when the queen was annoyed with the king, she would sit at this spot until he appeased her. Further ahead is a *kund* with steps leading to the water, along with several prominent temples, shrines and a popular *dargah*. Nearby, the **Ranmal Chowki** stands on a ridge next to a cluster of massive rocks. It houses several beautifully carved deities. The *chowki* offers a panoramic view of Idar and surrounding areas.

Opposite the Mahal are two **Jain temples** belonging to different sects (the Shvetambars and the Digambars) that rise from the top of Idar Fort. Dedicated respectively to Shantinath and Sambhavnath and date back 1200 years, they feature beautiful carvings and idols. **The Shantinath Temple** has exquisite marble panels and colored stone inlay work. Two of these depict the Girnar and Palitana hills, sacred centers for the Jains. At the rear, a natural cave offers a setting for prayers and other rituals. The imposing rocks mark the beginning of the Vindhya Range in Gujarat and are ideal for hiking and climbing.

The **Shrimad Rajchandra Vihar**, situated on the eastern hillock, is especially worth visiting at sunset. This Jain temple complex commemorates Shrimad Rajchandra, one of Mahatma Gandhi's spiritual advisors. In addition to a beautiful idol of Parshvanath, the temple stores a library of religious books. Watching the sunset from this quiet, breezy spot is the perfect way to end a long day of visiting temples and shrines.

NUTS & BOLTS

In and Out

The best way to get to Idar is by ST bus. From Ahmedabad buses leave every half hour for Himatnagar, from where you catch another bus to Idar (half hour). Some buses traveling between Ahmedabad and Mt Abu also stop at Idar.

Getting Around

Rickshaws are unmetered and cost Rs. 10-20 to travel around town. Idar is small enough to explore on foot. ST buses are the best option for traveling around the district and shared jeeps are the most common way to get to smaller, out-of-the -way places.

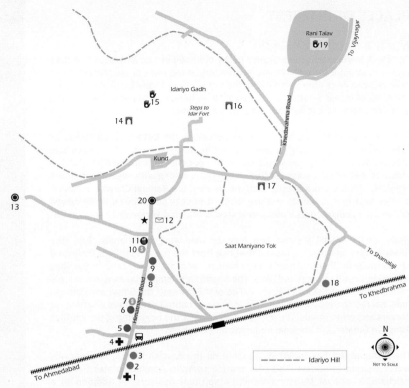

Idar
Legend

Accommodation / Food & Drink
2 Hotel Dreamland / Restaurant
3 City Light Hotel
8 Circuit House
18 Lily Resort / Restaurant
11 Meenaxi Ice Cream

Places of Interest
13 Shrimad Rajchandra Vihar
14 Ranmal Chowki
15 Jain Temples
16 Ruthi Rani no Mahal
17 Gambhirpura Stepwell
19 Jain Temple
20 Clock Tower & Library

Nuts & Bolts
1 Atma Vallabh Hospital
4 Navjivan Hospital
5 Arihant Medicals Store
6 Rajshree Color Lab
7 SBI ATM
9 Sir Pratap School
10 SBI Bank and ATM
12 General Post Office

Money

ATMs **SBI Bank** *Btw Mamlatdar Office and Bus Stn, Nr Petrol Pump; Bank Premises, Nr Apsara Cinema.*
MONEY TRANSFER **Western Union** is available at the General Post Office.

Communication

INTERNET There were no internet facilities available at the time of research.

Markets

There are a plenty of general provision stores near Asha Shopping Centre, across from the bus station.

ACCOMMODATION

Lily Resort *257157, Nr Barela Talav Lake, Ambaji Hwy, about 1 km from Railway Stn* is the best hotel in Idar. It offers clean rooms and good service at affordable rates, but is located on the outskirts of town. Take a rickshaw, about Rs. 20, to get there. **Facilities** western toilet, attached baths, AC options, TV, small gym, restaurant. **Rooms** 200-400.

Hotel Dreamland and **Hotel City Light** are alternative options conveniently located near the railway crossing, but the rooms are much smaller with fewer amenities.

FOOD & DRINK

Hotel Dreamland has a restaurant that serves good North Indian, South Indian, Punjabi and Chinese food. The multicuisine restaurant in **Lily Resort** offers an amiable atmosphere and great food. Gujarati *thali* is available at **Vaibhav Guest House.**

EXCURSIONS

Caution: The stretch of highway from Poshina and Ambaji to Khedbrahma and Idar can be unsafe at night and best avoided after sunset.

EASTERN
GUJARAT

▼ DISTRICT
VADODARA
DAHOD

▸ SABARKANTHA
Idar
Khedbrahma
Poshina
Shamlaji
Vijaynagar
Himatnagar
Roda

ANAND
KHEDA

EASTERN
GUJARAT

DISTRICT ▾
VADODARA
DAHOD

SABARKANTHA ◄
Idar
Khedbrahma
Poshina
Shamlaji
Vijaynagar
Himatnagar
Roda

ANAND
KHEDA

Khedbrahma

27 km from Idar

Khedbrahma attracts thousands of pilgrims each year from Gujarat, Maharashtra and neighboring Rajasthan to its **Brahma** and **Nana Ambaji** temples. Hindu mythology designates this Brahma temple as the place of penance where Brahma dug out a small stream that now flows as part of the Sabarmati River. To commemorate the water flow, there is a stepwell, now in disrepair, with carvings that resemble temple spires and idols of guardian deities. The Brahma Temple is one of only a handful in India, second in importance to the one in Pushkar, Rajasthan. Located nearby is Nana Ambaji, dedicated to the Goddess Amba, which attracts many pilgrims, especially during the full moon when thousands flock here to worship the deities. The temple grounds bustle with people from nearby villages buying and selling trinkets. This pilgrimage site is well connected by buses and taxis along the Ambaji Highway.

Brahma

Brahma, the creator in the Hindu trinity (which also includes Vishnu, the preserver and Shiva, the destroyer), emerged from the lotus stemming out of Vishnu's navel. From Brahma emerged Sarasvati (the Goddess of knowledge), and their union gave birth to space, time and consciousness. Brahma is commonly depicted with four heads, each reciting one of the four Vedas. Unlike most Hindu manifestations, Brahma carries no weapon in any of his four hands. Instead, he holds a scepter in the form of a spoon, a water-pot, the Vedas and a string of rosary beads to help him measure the universe's existence.

According to legend, Brahma and Vishnu set out to tour the universe and discovered a beam of light, which extended further than they could see in either direction. Curious, they decided to separate and search for the source. When they reunited, Vishnu said that he had found nothing, but Brahma claimed he found the beginning. Immediately the pillar of light transformed into Shiva, who cursed Brahma for his lie, sentencing him to an existence without reverence. Another myth relates that the great sage Bhrigu was conducting a *yagna* on earth. He decided that the greatest among all Gods would be made the presiding deity and set out to evaluate the holy trinity. When he approached Brahma, the Creator was so entranced in his wife's music that he did not hear the sage. Insulted, Bhrigu cursed Brahma, saying that no person on earth would ever worship him again. Apparently, the curse still lingers. Only a few temples in India stand in honor of Brahma.

Poshina

70 km from Idar

The northernmost part of Sabarkantha is home to this town famous for tribal shrines, Jain temples, and an old Shiva temple. Originally a part of the Darbargarh Poshina Royal Estate, Poshina retains the charm and simplicity of traditional village life. The huge gates to the palace, now a heritage hotel, welcome visitors into the town. A narrow lane on the right side of the gate winds its way to the old Jain sandstone temples of **Parshvanath** and **Neminath**. A wider street on the right of the palace gate leads to the old **Shiva Temple** and the **royal cenotaphs**. Despite earthquake damage and weathering, the Shiva Temple, with a single spire, is notable for its beautifully carved walls and statues. It is undergoing restoration. Further down the road, across a river bed, is an interesting **tribal shrine** surrounded by trees. Over 2000 terracotta horse offerings to the local

Goddess stand in rows just outside the shrine. Nearby villages have similar regiments of terracotta horses paying homage to a divine form. Communities such as the Garasias, Bhils and the pastoral Rabaris have settled in Poshina. Each tribe retains its distinctive traditions and crafts. The Garasias are known for their colorful attire, the Rabaris for their silver ornaments and the Bhils for arrow making. Poshina is also home to many potters who make the lovely terracotta horses and other earthenware. A few weeks after Holi, Poshina hosts the famous Chitra Vichitra Fair at nearby Gunbhakari (see **Fairs and Festivals**). Buses to Mt Abu or Ambaji through Kheroj go via a junction called Hadad, from where shared jeeps or rickshaws travel to Poshina (12 km).

EASTERN GUJARAT

▾ DISTRICT
VADODARA
DAHOD

▸ SABARKANTHA
Idar
Khedbrahma
Poshina
Shamlaji
Vijaynagar
Himatnagar
Roda

ANAND
KHEDA

Shamlaji

43 km from Idar

The **Shamlaji Temple** stands in honor of Vishnu. The magnificence of the temple is enhanced by exquisite stone carvings, idols of gods, nymphs, musicians and celestial dancers, beautiful domed ceilings and a towering spire. Scenes from the epic stories *Mahabharata* and *Ramayana* grace the walls of this 16th-c. temple.

According to local lore, the temple originated when surrounding tribes began worshipping an idol in a makeshift space at a riverside field. Soon they referred to the idol as Kaliyo Dev or "Dark Divinity". A local merchant built a more permanent structure to house the deity, which was later beautified by the Idar rulers. More recently, a prominent business family further renovated this temple. Located off NH 8, Shamlaji is frequented by ST buses.

Other monuments worth visiting in this town include the **Harishchandra Chori,** a pavilion marking the spot where King Harishchandra wedded his beloved Taramati, and a *toran* that is visible from the highway, on the right, as you go from Himatnagar to Shamlaji. To reach it you must pass through the colorful town bazaar.

About 2 km away, at **Devni Mori**, archeologists unearthed the remains of a Buddhist seminary, *stupas* and *viharas*. The Archeological Department of the MS University of Baroda excavated many idols of Buddha and other relics, such as ancient silver and copper coins from 500 AD, jewelry, earthen pottery and an urn containing ashes. Some objects and plaster replicas are on display in a small museum near the Shamlaji Temple, but most of the artifacts are exhibited at the university.

Vijaynagar

38 km from Idar

Famous for its **Polo Forest** and the ruins of old Hindu and Jain temples, Vijaynagar has both natural beauty and historical significance. Found in a precinct bordering Rajasthan, Vijaynagar was once part of a kingdom ruled by the Rathod Rajputs of Marwar. The best time to visit is after the monsoon rains, between September and December, when the forests radiate with various hues of green and the lakes and rivers are filled to the brim.

EASTERN
GUJARAT

DISTRICT ▾
VADODARA
DAHOD

SABARKANTHA ◄
Idar
Khedbrahma
Poshina
Shamlaji
Vijaynagar
Himatnagar
Roda

ANAND
KHEDA

The Vijaynagar Circuit

This 60 km loop includes a tour of ancient temple ruins, a dam and a palace, all set against a charming landscape. The **Vireshvar Shiva Temple**, near Vijalsan Vasahat, is about 20 km from Idar, just off the Vijaynagar State Highway. The temple, which was recently renovated, stands at the foot of a hill situated in a lush valley. It is surrounded by a thick canopy of forest filled with butterflies and birds and graced with a perennial water spring.

About 10 km down the road is the twin temple complex known as **Ashram** and **Antarsumba**. Several ancient temple ruins are found here with the largest shrine boasting an exquisite *toran* gateway. The temple, with its spire and main dome collapsed, sits on a high platform. Several carved idols and stonework details can be found scattered around. Off the road to Antarsumba are more temple ruins, accessible only on foot; you must use a dam to cross the stream to reach them.

Another 3 km from Antarsumba is the **Saraneshvar Temple**, part of which has collapsed. It was erected in a beautiful courtyard, which has gates on the east and the west sides. The relics of several shrines also lie around the main temple. Further along the road to Vijaynagar, on the left hand side, are memorials of *satis*. About 1 km ahead, nestled between two hills where the road runs parallel to a stream, stands a **sun temple**. Similar to the main temple at Antarsumba, it displays finely carved idols along the outer walls. The roof and the main dome have collapsed and the remains of a fortification are also visible. At this point the natural landscape changes noticeably as the road leads into a scenic forested area.

About 1 km ahead, where the stream runs on the left of the road, are the **temples of Polo,** four structures situated in the serene surroundings of the forest. Three temples are completely damaged but the Jain temple, the largest of the four, has been well preserved. It has a lower level chamber where the idols were concealed safe from aggressors who tried to ransack the premises.

The **Vanaj Dam** is 4 km from the Polo temples, and is surrounded by thick forest inhabited with bears, deer and small reptiles. Several species of water fowl, raptors and passerines also live here. During winter, migratory birds spread out across the forest to enjoy the environs of the dam.

The route ends at **Vijayanagar**, another 11 km down a road that winds through patches of forest and rolling terrain with vistas of little farming villages snuggled in the hillsides. The **royal cenotaphs** welcome visitors into town. Head to the **Hamir Vilas Palace**—a simple but imposing structure with balconies that offer scenic views of the town and the hills beyond. The palace is not open for public viewing without permission from the owner, the Maharao of Vijaynagar.

Traveling the Vijaynagar circuit is easiest by car; the bus system in this area is unreliable and infrequent. With the help of a local guide (see **Kadoli Farm**) you can also trek through any of the numerous tribal villages in the vicinity.

Kadoli Farm *9375523795, Pratapgadh Kampa, Via Kadiyadara, 3 km to the right from Vijlasan Vasahat, Contact H H Harshvardhan Singh, the Maharao of Vijaynagar* is a cozy farm resort in Pratapgadh village, on the State Highway. The farm is located amidst agricultural fields in a grove of trees. Kadoli Farm conducts the Vijaynagar circuit tour and treks and also organizes safaris to the tribal villages. They serve both vegetarian and non-veg North Indian food. **Single** 350 **Double** 500.

Himatnagar
28 km from Idar, 79 km from Ahmedabad

This small trading town and home of the Sabar Dairy is also the district headquarters of Sabarkantha. The **market** area is fun to saunter through, after which you can enjoy a spicy treat at **Charbhuja Kachoriwala** *Station Rd, Nr Durgaji Fatak*. The **Sir Pratapsinh Palace** is more than a century old and worth a visit. It houses portraits of English royalty, hunting scenes, trophies and more. The king had a harem of 16 wives, so he expanded the palace to more more than 4.5 hectares to accommodate his growing family and their unusual collection of cars, elephants and even aircraft. You must seek permission from the caretaker to visit the premises. Frequent buses connect the city with Ahmedabad (1.5 hrs).

Roda
18 km from Himatnagar

This town has **five temples** dating from the 7th to the 8th c. that comprise some of the earliest Hindu monuments in the state. The **Pakshi Mandir** ("Bird Temple") is 1 km from the main road. This little shrine, dedicated to birds, has no idol or deity. The neighboring temple features a lotus motif on the ceiling of the sanctum, the two columns that support the roof and the doorframe of the main chamber. About 500 m away, along the dry bed of a stream, are two temples dedicated to Shiva, overlooking the **Ladushah Kund**. Small shrines at each corner of this rectangular pond pay homage to Vishnu and Ladushah among other deities. All of these temples were damaged in varying degrees during the 2001 earthquake. There are two more temples on the far side of the stream bed. The **Navagraha Temple** is dedicated to the nine planets, whose images appear on the door frame of the sanctum, which has no idol. Elaborate images of *apsaras*, *dwarpalas* and other celestial beings are placed around the temple. The last and largest temple has beautiful images of Ganesh and other deities on its walls.

Roda is a bit out of the way and best reached with a private vehicle from Himatnagar. It lies to the right of the Himatnagar-Hathrol Road. A narrow dirt road, marked with a metal signboard (in Gujarati), leads to the temple cluster. Ask local people for directions.

EASTERN GUJARAT

▾ DISTRICT
VADODARA
DAHOD

▸ SABARKANTHA
Idar
Khedbrahma
Poshina
Shamlaji
Vijaynagar
Himatnagar
Roda

ANAND
KHEDA

ANAND DISTRICT

ANAND CITY
આંણદ

POPULATION	218,500
AREA CODE	02692
DISTANCES - AHMEDABAD	73 KM
VADODARA	39 KM

The city of Anand was established in the 9th c. by a cowherd named Anandgar. Today, it is the district headquarters and is celebrated for the revolutionary Amul Dairy Cooperative. The city is surrounded by tobacco and wheat fields. Its neighboring town, Vallabh Vidyanagar (V V Nagar), hosts the Sardar Patel University, an institute founded with the vision to spread education in rural areas. Karamsad is associated with Sardar Patel, India's "Iron Man" and a key figure in the country's freedom struggle. Further southwest is the historically significant port city of Khambhat, where artisans still make agate crafts.

EASTERN GUJARAT

▼ **DISTRICT**
VADODARA
DAHOD
SABARKANTHA

▶ **ANAND**
Anand City
Karamsad
Navali
Vadtal
Khambhat
Anklavadi
Getting Involved

KHEDA

PLACES OF INTEREST

Amul Dairy Cooperative Museum

Take a guided tour of the Amul plant to understand the advanced pasteurization process of milk collected through the co-op and watch as it is transformed into Amul's famous butter and cream. Follow the tour with a 15 minute walk through the Amul museum, previously the garage residence of Dr Verghese Kurien, where a guide will explain the timeline of Amul's history. Afterwards enjoy any of Amul's products at the on-site canteen or the small Amul store just outside the dairy gates. This factory deserves a visit as it highlights a successful cooperative model and the technological capabilities of the country. **Open** 1500-1700, daily. **Entry** free.

The Amul Story

Sardar Patel, a leading light of India's Freedom Movement, envisioned setting up cooperatives to bring financial security to farmers in Kaira (Anand and Kheda districts) and spur local development. This vision materialized as the Kaira District Cooperative Milk Producers' Union Limited (KDCMPUL) in 1946, with Tribhuvandas Patel as the chairman.

During this time, Dr Verghese Kurien, after earning his masters degree in the USA, returned to India and was assigned the post of dairy engineer at the government creamery in Anand. In May 1949, bored with his government job, young Kurien volunteered to help Tribhuvandas Patel establish a processing plant at the cooperative, marking the birth of Amul. Today Dr Kurien is known as the "Milkman of India" and the "Father of the White Revolution" because of the success of the Amul model and his engineering of Operation Flood, the largest dairy development program in the world.

Amul derives its name from the Sanskrit word "amoolya", which means priceless. Lal Bahadur Shastri, Prime Minister of India at the time, founded the National Dairy Development Board (NDDB) in 1965 to replicate Amul's success across the country. Dr Kurien was elected chairman.

In 1970, NDDB launched Operation Flood to create a flood of milk nationwide by linking rural farmers and their milk supplies to India's metropolitan cities. The movement led to increased milk production, removed dependency on milk imports and stabilized consumer prices for dairy products. It also improved dairy infrastructure and technology across the nation. This White Revolution has made India one of the largest milk producers in the world and has helped alleviate poverty.

Dr Kurien also set up Gujarat Cooperative Milk Marketing Federation (GCMMF) in 1973 to sell the products manufactured by the dairies. Previously middlemen controlled the marketing and distribution of milk. Since milk is perishable, farmers would sell it for any price offered. The farmers realized that exploitation would stop only if they marketed the milk themselves. Today GCMMF is jointly owned by 2.41 million milk producers across Gujarat and sells Amul products in India and overseas.

Since 1967, Amul's mascot has been the Amul Baby, a chubby girl in a frock, who appears on billboards and product wrappers with the tagline "Utterly Butterly Delicious Amul". Amul advertising uses witty sketches with the Amul baby commenting innocently on the latest news. This is one of the longest running campaigns ever.

Today, Amul is the largest food brand in India, with an annual turnover of 850 million USD in 2005-06. The average milk collection in 2005-06 was 6.3 million liters a day. Amul Parlors across Gujarat offer flavored milk, *chaas* and ice cream treats along with other Amul goodies.

D N High School

During the Salt March in 1930, this school served as a night halt for Mahatma Gandhi and other pilgrims. Built in 1916, the 16-hectare campus was named after Dadabhai Naoroji, an eminent scholar and statesman. The school supported India's struggle for independence and even allowed its students to

Anand City
Legend

Accommodation
4   Surabhi Regency / Udupi Restaurant
9   Hotel Pooja International
16   Hotel Aaram
17   Hotel Relax
18   Hotel Kavita

Food & Drink
8   Dwaraka Restaurant
11   3 Musketeers Restaurant
14   Sahyog Restaurant

19   Yogesh Khaman House
25   Café Coffee Day
26   Sankalp
27   Icy-Spicy
28   Flavours Restaurant
30   Sahyog Restaurant

Places of Interest
1   Tribhuvandas Foundation
2   Institute of Rural
3   Anand Agriculture University
12   Amul Dairy
22   D N High School Agriculture (IRMA)
     Management and

Nuts & Bolts
5   Granary Grocery Store
6   HDFC
7   Cyberworld
10   FedEx
13   Dena Bank / Yahoo Internet Café
15   C N Church
20   Reliance World Cybercafé
21   HDFC Bank
23   Ramkrishna Homeopathic Hospital
24   Town Hall
29   ICICI Bank
31   Sify Iway Cybercafé

abandon academic activity when the country called upon them. Consequently, the British suspended grants to the institution, but local citizens and the Gujarati Diaspora raised funds. It is also believed that the idea for V V Nagar originated from this school.

**EASTERN
GUJARAT**

DISTRICT ▾
VADODARA
DAHOD
SABARKANTHA

ANAND ◂
Anand City
Karamsad
Navali
Vadtal
Khambhat
Anklavadi
Getting Involved

KHEDA

Institute of Rural Management, Anand (IRMA)

The Central Government, Gujarat State Government, NDDB and IDC collectively established IRMA in 1979 to develop managers with skills necessary to steer rural enterprises in the cooperative and public sectors to help sustain the rural economy. The lush 26-hectare campus, 4 km south of Anand, has a bell tower that, through digital design, chimes any music fed into its system. Rickshaws charge Rs. 15-20 from the train and bus stations to reach IRMA.

Vallabh Vidyanagar (V V Nagar)

Sardar Vallabhbhai Patel inspired the establishment of the Charotar Vidya Mandal, Sardar Patel University (SPU) and the township of V V Nagar in 1945 to foster rural resurgence through education in a post-independent India. V V Nagar, 6 km south of Anand, offers a charming combination of greenery, metropolitan amenities and small town feel. The township has evolved into a suburb of Anand. A shuttle to V V Nagar will cost about Rs. 5 while a rickshaw can be hired for Rs. 20.

Flo Art

This 60-year-old homestead was converted into a gallery and workshop 15 years ago. Spread over two floors and 1000 sq m, Flo Art combines cottage industry talent with quality and style, resulting in an eclectic mix of contemporary and traditional designs. It produces unique handmade crafts including miniature deities, custom made murals and a variety of household accessories. Kalpa Amin, who uses only natural materials and traditional techniques, encourages sustainable livelihoods for rural artists and formed Flo Art for this purpose. **Open** 1000-2100, Mon-Sat and 7 days a week from Oct-Mar.

NUTS & BOLTS

In and Out

Anand falls on the railway line between Ahmedabad and Vadodara and is also accessible by ST bus from both destinations.

Getting Around

Rickshaws are unmetered and mostly cost between Rs. 10-20 across town. The city has an extensive shared rickshaw system, which collects passengers from all major destinations, including the bus stations, train station and stops along Amul Dairy Road. Most trips around town cost about Rs. 7. The shuttles also travel across the district to other towns and cities. Buses also connect most places in the district.

Money

ATMs **Dena Bank** *Amul Dairy Rd, Nxt to Kataria Automobiles*; **HDFC Bank** *Amul Dairy Rd*; *Mayfair Rd;* **ICICI Bank** *Anand-V V Nagar Rd, Nxt to Subway*. MONEY TRANSFER **Western Union** is located at the General Post Office.

Communication

INTERNET **Cyberworld** *Shri Hari Cmplx, Amul Dairy Rd* has Net-2-Phone; **Yahoo Internet Café** *Below Dena Bank, Opp Amul Dairy Cmplx*; **Sify Iway** *Anand-V V Nagar Rd* costs Rs. 25/hr and offers Net-2-Phone; **Reliance World** *Mayfair Rd.* COURIER **FedEx** *Zilla Panchayat Shopping Center, Opp Amul Dairy Cmplx* offers domestic and international courier services.

Markets

Granary Grocery Store *Amul Dairy Rd, Nr Hotel Surabhi* carries a wide selection of fruits, groceries and toiletries.

ACCOMMODATION

Anand does not offer much choice in accommodation and mid-range options are modest at best. Hotels are clustered along Amul Dairy Road, while cheaper ones are on Bus Station Road, closer to the heart of the city.

Hotel Aaram *253351, 1st Flr, DK Shopping Centre, Bus Station Rd* is a walking distance from the old bus station and situated above a noisy shopping complex. It offers basic but stuffy rooms with clean bathrooms. **Facilities** squat and western toilets, TV, hot water, AC options, room service, laundry, credit cards accepted. **Single** 180-500 **Double** 200-600 **Triple** 350-400 **Extra Bed** 105.

Hotel Pooja International *254253, Amul Dairy Rd, Opp Aryanagar* is a basic hotel. **Facilities** western toilets, cable TV, hot showers. **Single** 199-450 **Double** 275-1200 **Extra Bed** 75.

Hotel Relax *242429, 3rd Floor, Hariba Vyapar Bhavan, Bus Station Rd* is one of the best options in town with nicely furnished rooms, clean bathrooms and pleasant ambience. It is a walking distance from the railway station and the old bus station. **Facilities** western toilet, cable TV, hot showers, AC options, laundry. **Single** 300-650 **Double** 400-725 **Extra Bed** 100–150.

Surabhi Regency *242018, Amul Dairy Rd, Jay Tower* is centrally located and has a helpful staff and decent suites. **Facilities** western toilets, cable TV, AC options, room service. **Single** 425-2000 **Double** 500-2000 **Extra Bed** 200.

FOOD & DRINK

Amul Dairy Road has a few family restaurants with the usual Indian, Chinese and Continental spread, while Anand-V V Nagar Road offers more dining options, with a few catering to the university population.

Several multicuisine, mid-range restaurants are found along Amul Dairy Road including **Udupi Restaurant** *Below Surabhi Regency, Amul Dairy Rd*, **Dwaraka Restaurant** *Amul Dairy Rd* and **Sahyog Restaurant**. A different **Sahyog Restaurant** *1st Flr, Sterling Arcade, Nr ICICI Bank* is situated along Anand-V V Nagar Road and, in addition to multicuisine choices, it offers a Punjabi *thali*.

**EASTERN
GUJARAT**

DISTRICT ▼
VADODARA
DAHOD
SABARKANTHA

ANAND ◄
Anand City
Karamsad
Navali
Vadtal
Khambhat
Anklavadi
Getting Involved

KHEDA

3 Musketeers Restaurant *Amul Dairy Rd, Nr Amul Dairy Coop* is a budget eatery and one of the few places in town that offers non-veg options.

Flavours Restaurant *Anand-V V Nagar Rd, Bhaikaka Char Rasta, Nr ICICI Bank* serves good Continental, Chinese and Punjabi dishes at mid-range prices. **Icy-Spicy** *Anand-V V Nagar Rd, Suketu Cmplx* is a popular hangout that serves a selection of Gujarati fast food, milk shakes, sandwiches and pizzas.

For some coffee and basic snacks visit **Café Coffee Day** *Citadel Cmplx, Anand-V V Nagar Rd.* **Mongini Bakery** *Anand-V V Nagar Rd* is part of an Italian bakery chain that sells cakes and quick snacks like pizza bread and stuffed rolls.

LOCAL SPECIALTIES **Yogesh Khaman House** *Mayfair Rd* is a snack joint that offers three varieties of Anand's famous *khaman*, a chickpea and rice flour batter, fermented with curd, then steamed and garnished with cilantro and coconut.

EXCURSIONS

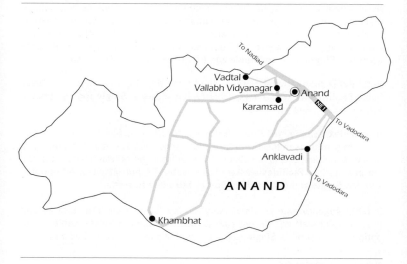

Karamsad

5 km from Anand

This is the hometown of Sardar Patel. Patel, along with Gandhiji and Nehru, was a key national figure in the first half of the 20th c. during India's freedom struggle. He firmly integrated 600-odd princely states into the Republic of India and was also India's first home minister. Karamsad is also one of the six main centers of the enterprising Patidar community.

The house that Sardar Patel grew up in has floors still coated in *lipan* and a charming little garden outside. It is locally known as **Navagruh**. The house hosts a picture exhibition of various moments in Sardar Patel's life, while the outer

wall features a traditional mural, once common in this region, consisting of two elephants painted with natural colors. Across the road from the house are two busts of Sardar Patel and his brother, Vithalbhai Patel. **Open House** 1100-1230 and 1430-1800 **Closed** Sun. **Garden** 0500-0730 and 1730 -1930 **Closed** Sun.

The Sardar Vallabhbhai Patel and Veer Vithalbhai Patel Memorial is enclosed by a beautiful garden with several walking paths and contains a picture and quote exhibition commemorating Sardar Patel and Vithalbhai Patel. It also has a library with books about the two brothers, India's Freedom Movement, great leaders and some reference material. They also sell the biography of Sardar Patel. **Open Memorial** 0930-1230 and 1430-1800; **Closed** Sun. **Garden** 0500-0730 and 1630-1900; **Closed** Sun. **Entry** Rs. 5.

Catch a shuttle to Karamsad (20 min) from Sardarbaug, across from the New Bus Station in Anand. Private rickshaws will cost about Rs. 25 while the bus charges Rs. 6.

Navali
5 km from Anand

Navali is one of hundreds of milk cooperative collection points set up by Amul Dairy. By decentralizing and computerizing milk collection, Amul Dairy transformed the time-intensive process of taking milk to the market, selling it and receiving payments into a five-minute collection and payment transaction. A computerized machine tests milk quality and makes the collection process transparent and fair to farmers. This operation can be seen in action at the Navali Cooperative, which was launched in 1950 (the computerization came much later) and consists of 975 members. After passing through the gateway of Navali, across from the bus stand, travel straight along the road until you come to the town center. The collection center operates every day from 0530-0730 and 1800-2000 and purchases milk from producers of surrounding areas. The cooperative also runs a small scale dairy—fresh buffalo milk out of a bucket —which is very popular locally.

Catch a shuttle from Borsad Chowkdi to Navali for Rs. 5. To come back to town (25 min), catch a shuttle, bus or private rickshaw (Rs. 30) at the bus stand near the town's main gate entrance.

Vadtal
15 km from Anand

Although the farmers of Vadtal and surrounding areas once gained prosperity by cultivating tobacco, the presence of the Swaminarayan sect has influenced them to decrease investments in the cash crop and move to other agricultural options. They have also taken an initiative to develop the area with their own resources to cater to the growing popularity of Vadtal as a pilgrimage site.

A direct bus to Vadtal leaves from the New Anand Bus Station in the late morning. Shuttles from Sardarbaug travel to Bakrol Chowkdi for Rs. 5, from where you can catch a shuttle to Vadtal. A private rickshaw between Anand and Vadtal costs about Rs. 20.

EASTERN GUJARAT

▾ DISTRICT
 VADODARA
 DAHOD
 SABARKANTHA

▸ ANAND
 Anand City
 Karamsad
 Navali
 Vadtal
 Khambhat
 Anklavadi
 Getting Involved

 KHEDA

EASTERN
GUJARAT

DISTRICT ▾
VADODARA
DAHOD
SABARKANTHA

ANAND ◄
Anand City
Karamsad
Navali
Vadtal
Khambhat
Anklavadi
Getting Involved

KHEDA

Vadtal Dham is built in honor of Swami Sahajanand (1731-1830), who spread the doctrine of the Swaminarayan sect to the masses and established Vadtal as one of the two main seats for his following, known as the Uddhava Sampradaya. This temple has colorful wood carvings on its pillars and has a *dharmashala*. Follow the dirt road outside the town gate to the northwest to find the **Gnanbaug**. This garden commemorates the time Swami Sahajanand spent in Vadtal, and contains four memorials in his honor. The museum exhibits Swami Sahajanand's life through paintings and the **Darbar Ghat**, an exact replica of his original house displays an interesting array of handicrafts and antiques, are worth visiting. **Open** 0800-1200 and 1330-1800, daily. The garden is accessible all day. **Photography** not permitted in Gnanbaug.

Khambhat

60 km from Anand

Despite peeling paint and crumbling buildings Khambhat retains its charm with winding roads, stone houses and colonial remnants that reveal its colorful past as one of medieval India's richest cities. Until the 17th c. it was a thriving sea port. Muslim writers referred to Khambhat as the first city of "Hind", or India.

Also known as Cambay, Khambhat manufactured silk and chintz and supplied textiles across the world. The trade temporarily declined in the early 16th c. It was revived when Emperor Akbar ascended the throne in 1573. The English and Dutch established factories here in the early 17th c. The final decline commenced with the arrival of the Portuguese. Over time, silt from the Sabarmati and Mahi rivers filled up the harbor, making navigation difficult. Competition from European companies, the shift of maritime trade to other ports and the coming of the railway in 1863 all led to the city's eclipse. It reentered the limelight in 1958 with the discovery of oil in the Gulf.

Khambhat can be reached by bus from most of the major cities and towns in the region, or by train from Anand. ST buses leave roughly every fifteen minutes for Ahmedabad, Vadodara, Surat and Nadiad. Rental cars are available near the railway station and bus depot and are convenient if you want to travel outside the city.

A 6 km stretch of bricks is all that remains of the **fort wall** that once protected the city. The **Jama Masjid**, built in 1325 AD, is largely assembled with recycled material from earlier monuments. This mosque is important because it marks a stage in the evolution of Islamic architecture in Gujarat. The absence of *minars* and the presence of a *toran* inside the central arch anticipate the Gujarat Sultanate architecture.

Stambhan Parshvanath Jinalaya, southeast of the city, is an 11th-c. Jain temple in ruins and partially submerged in sand. The Jain temple, one of 73 in Khambhat, contains a deep blue colored idol. The principal deity, according to the inscription, is of Parshvanath, which was carved during the reign of Emperor Akbar. Some parts of the temple are coated in gold.

BD Rao College Museum is located on the campus of the Bhagavatilal Dahyabhai Rao College. The main attraction in this very basic museum is the

Hindu mythological sculptures ranging from the 3rd to the 19th c. The collection also includes coins from the 3rd c.

Khambhat's **agate** artisans were renowned for cutting and polishing the beautifully striped gemstone into ornaments and beads for export to foreign markets, including China and Europe. Akik is the local name for agate. Recently a local demand for agate jewelry has emerged because it offers an affordable substitute for silver and gold ornaments. You can purchase agate items in stores located in the **Jhanda Chowk Market. Nazami Akik Store** *Parekh Plaza Basement, Opp Bus Stand* and the **Cambay Agate Stones and Jewellery Trading Corporation** *Krishna Pol* sell a variety of agate products.

The local specialties of this town include the sweet dishes, *sutarapheni* and *halavasan,* and a range of **salty snacks** that originated as durable food items for seafarers to carry on their journeys. **Shree Krishna Sweet 'n Snacks** *Station Rd* carries a good variety of these eatables.

Anklavadi   **42 km from Anand**
The **Shree Shree Ravi Shankar Ashram,** just outside of Anklavadi, is perched on a cliff overlooking the Mahi River. Everyone is welcome to stay at the ashram so long as they have completed the three-day Art of Living course. The stay costs Rs. 200 per day, and includes food and accommodation. *For more information call 0265 250067 or visit www.artofliving.org.*

Buses traveling from Anand to Vadodara stop at Vasad (1 hr), from where buses and shuttles depart frequently for Anklavadi (10 min). The ashram is 3 km from the Anklavadi bus stop. Although locals insist that shuttles pass through frequently, count on hiking along picturesque tobacco and wheat fields if you have not arranged for transportation in advance.

GETTING INVOLVED

Tribhuvandas Foundation *251166, Rajodipura, Nr Chikhodra Rlwy Crossing* was established in 1975 by Tribhuvandas Patel, a farmer from Kaira, to help cater to the health and development needs of 65 villages in the area. The foundation runs programs in maternal and child healthcare, income generation, women's development, model daycare centers, smokeless *chulahs* (wood fueled stoves), low-cost latrines and bio-gas plants. Villagers pay Rs. 10 a year to join the trust. Call in advance for permission to tour the campus.

EASTERN GUJARAT

▾ **DISTRICT**
VADODARA
DAHOD
SABARKANTHA

▸ **ANAND**
Anand City
Karamsad
Navali
Vadtal
Khambhat
Anklavadi
Getting Involved

KHEDA

EASTERN
GUJARAT

DISTRICT ▾
VADODARA
DAHOD
SABARKANTHA
ANAND

KHEDA ◄
Nadiad
Vaso
Dakor
Bilodra
Balasinor
Raioli
Kapadvanj
Sojali

KHEDA DISTRICT

NADIAD
નડિયાદ

POPULATION	196,800
AREA CODE	0268
DISTANCES - AHMEDABAD	52 KM
VADODARA	59 KM

Kheda District was once part of the Balasinor princely state. It has a strong agricultural base in cotton and tobacco and also hosts some major pilgrimage and heritage sites. The administrative headquarters, Nadiad, is a nodal market for neighboring districts.

Nadiad developed amid a cluster of nine ponds and has since grown into a major market center. In modern times it has been at the forefront of economy and politics in Gujarat, producing leaders like Sardar Vallabhbhai Patel, the chief architect of the unified India that emerged after the British left, and Indulal Yagnik, who led the Mahagujarat Movement, which resulted in the formation of Gujarat as a separate state from Bombay. Nadiad was also the headquarters for Mahatma Gandhi's Kheda Satyagraha (1917-1918), a revolt led by the local farmers against unjust taxes imposed by the British. The enterprising Patidar community, well-known abroad by its most common surname "Patel", contributed greatly to the Independence Movement, and also make up the majority in the town. They blocked a British military train and dismantled railway fishplates to stop the British army from proceeding to Ahmedabad. The group was detained and put on trial in what is known as the "Patta Case", but they were all acquitted. Around the turn of the 20th c., Nadiad was home to eminent Gujarati literary figures such as Govardhanram Tripathi, who wrote the famous Gujarati novel *Sarasvatichandra*.

Kheda is also home to Dakor, a temple town that attracts thousands of pilgrims every year. The town of Balasinor has one of the world's largest dinosaur fossil collections and Vaso boasts of beautiful carved mansions called *havelis*.

EASTERN GUJARAT

▼ **DISTRICT**
VADODARA
DAHOD
SABARKANTHA
ANAND

▸ **KHEDA**
Nadiad
Vaso
Dakor
Bilodra
Balasinor
Raioli
Kapadvanj
Sojali

PLACES OF INTEREST

Santaram Temple

A popular pilgrimage site in Gujarat, this temple is dedicated to Saint Santram Maharaj, who is believed to be an incarnation of Dattatreya—a deity combining the Hindu trinity of Brahma, Vishnu and Shiva, depicted with three heads and six hands and accompanied by a cow and dogs. The temple commemorates the place of *samadhi* of the saint. Built as a memorial by one of his disciples, it has an exhibition on his life. The temple trust conducts socio-religious activities such as free medical camps and clinics that offer Ayurvedic and homeopathic treatment among many other philanthropic deeds.

NUTS & BOLTS

In and Out

Nadiad is well connected by road and rail. ST buses run every 20 minutes between Ahmedabad and Nadiad. Local and express trains between Ahmedabad and Mumbai halt in Nadiad.

Getting Around

The best way to get around Nadiad is on foot since everything, including the hotels, is in close proximity. Rickshaws are unmetered and cost about Rs. 15- 25 for a one way journey. **New York Travels** *Opp Bus Station, Below Akshar Motel* assists in booking tickets for all modes of travel.

Money

ATMs **SBI Bank** *Opp Santaram Temple; Opp Town Hall, Nr Railway Stn*; **UTI** *Opp Bus Stn, Below Akshar Motel*; **Bank of Baroda** and **ICICI** *Piplag Rd, Opp Reliance Supermarket*; **HDFC** *Btw Santaram Temple and Woodlands Restaurant*.
MONEY TRANSFER **Western Union** at the General Post Office.

Nadiad
Legend

Accommodation
5   Hotel Palace
6   Akshar Motel
8   Motel Shivashray
10 Hotel Blueroom/Restaurant

Food & Drink
16 Woodlands Restaurant

Places of Interest
14 Santaram Temple

Nuts & Bolts
1   Bank of India
2   SBI ATM
3   Town Hall
4   Asian Courier Services
7   UTI ATM
9   PC Clinic Cyber Café

11 Vegetable Market
12 SBI Bank
13 General Post Office
15 Bank of India
17 Mahagujarat Hospital
18 Log In Cyber Café
19 ICICI ATM
20 Reliance Supermarket

Communication
INTERNET **PC Clinic Cyber Café** *Behind Motel Shivashray* has Internet and Net-2-Phone facilities; **Log In Cyber Café** *Piplag Rd Junction.*
COURIER **Asian International Couriers** *Trimurti Cmplx, Nr Bus Station.*

Medical
HOSPITAL **The Mahagujarat Hospital** *Nadiad-Anand Rd, Nr Woodlands Restaurant* is the best option in town.

Markets
Fruit and vegetable market *Btw Bus Stn and Santaram Temple.* The **Reliance Supermarket** *Piplag Rd* is a full service supermarket for general provisions.

ACCOMMODATION

Hotel Palace *2563029, 3rd Flr, Trimurti Cmplx, Opp Bus Stn* is the cleanest option in town. **Facilities** western toilets, running hot water, AC options. **Single** 200 **Double** 300-500.

Hotel Blue Room *2566071, Pij Rd, Nr Bus Stn* has stuffy but clean rooms. The surroundings can be noisy. **Facilities** western toilets, AC options, multicuisine restaurant. **Single** 150-500 **Double** 200-600 **Extra Bed** 50-100.

FOOD & DRINK

Although Nadiad does not have many restaurants, the **Woodlands Restaurant** *Opp Kheta Talav* serves good multicuisine vegetarian food in a plush interior with prices to match. **Hotel Blue Room** offers a similar menu in a basic setting and at lower prices.

EXCURSIONS

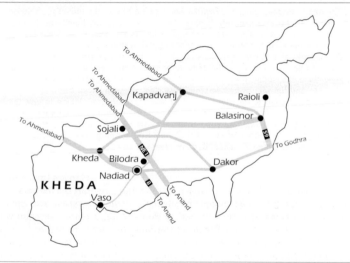

Vaso
14 km from Nadiad

Vaso is famous for the beautifully carved *havelis* of **Gopaldasji Desai** and **Vithaldas Amin**. The former, privately owned by the Prince of Rajkot, is in good condition and has some of the finest examples of woodwork in Gujarat. Traditional paintings of hunting scenes, elephants and wild cats adorn the walls on the second floor, and elaborate carvings embellish every column, rafter, beam and door. Unfortunately, indifferent maintenance and paint over the carvings along the exterior have diminished the fine craftsmanship of the

EASTERN GUJARAT

▼ DISTRICT
VADODARA
DAHOD
SABARKANTHA
ANAND

▶ KHEDA
Nadiad
Vaso
Dakor
Bilodra
Balasinor
Raioli
Kapadvanj
Sojali

EASTERN GUJARAT

DISTRICT ▾
VADODARA
DAHOD
SABARKANTHA
ANAND

KHEDA ◀
Nadiad
Vaso
Dakor
Bilodra
Balasinor
Raioli
Kapadvanj
Sojali

Vithaldas Haveli, which is closed to visitors. Vaso is accessible by shuttles from Shreyas Cinema (about Rs. 20) and by ST buses from Nadiad.

Dakor
33 km from Nadiad

Dakor borrows its name from the ancient **Dankanath Mahadev Temple** dedicated to Shiva. The **Gomti Tank**, a small lake spreading over an area of 230 hectares opposite the temple, is said to have been carved out by Bhima, the legendary Mahabharata hero.

Krishna devotees regularly flock to Dakor, walking long distances to the **Ranchhodrai Temple**, which dates back to 1772. Its architectural style, unusual in Gujarat, belongs to neighboring Maharashtra since the temple was built by a Maratha noble. It has eight domes and 24 turrets covered with gold leaf. The main hall features paintings depicting events in Krishna's life. Its dome, fitted with small mirrors and silver, sits on eight arches. The black stone idol is in a richly carved, gold and silver alcove.

The Legend of Dakor

The devout Bodana walked to Dwarka every month to visit the idol of his beloved Krishna at the Dwarkadeesh Temple. As he grew old, he found the journey increasingly difficult. On what he thought was his last visit, tears welled up in his eyes, but Krishna promised to return to Dakor with his devotee. Miraculously, Bodana was able to carry Krishna's idol back to Dakor, but the priests of Dwarka tracked him, and demanded the deity. After some time they insisted that Bodana give them the statue's weight in gold instead. The only gold possession the devotee and his wife owned was her nose ring. They balanced the idol against it, and astonishingly, the statue weighed less than the ring. Willing to give the greedy priests reprieve, Krishna promised that a second idol would appear in a well at Dwarka. The original stayed on in Dakor. On every full moon day, this event is commemorated with a fair at Dakor. People from far-off places attend, walking the distance as a reenactment of Bodana's feat.

Bilodra
10 km from Nadiad

For those seeking solitude and a space for reflection, the **Hari Om Ashram**, also known as Maun Mandir or "Temple of Silence", provides a serene atmosphere and simple accommodation. Founded by Pujya Mota, a renowned saint who dedicated his life to the upliftment of Harijans, the ashram runs entirely on donations. Once you enroll, you must stay for at least seven days. The ashram also operates schools in many remote villages of Gujarat. It is a one-kilometer walk from the ST bus stop. *Contact the manager at 0268 2567794.*

Balasinor
65 km from Nadiad

The **Garden Palace Heritage Hotel**, though not a lavish heritage property, offers a first-hand glimpse of royal life. Located on Sudarshan Lake, Garden Palace is maintained and partly occupied by the royal family, the Babis.

The true character of this place lies in the impeccable hospitality of the queen, Begum Farhat Sultana, who personally attends to every guest. The hotel offers

day excursions including a guided Dinosaur Safari to nearby Raioli, tours of Balasinor, boating on the lake and sunset views from the Hanuman Mandir hillock. You can opt for the spiritual healing packages, or participate in the Begum's Bounty, where she teaches Balasinor Mughlai cuisine in her own kitchen. At the palace craft shop guests can buy articles made by a women's self-help group supported by the Begum. *For advance bookings call 02690 266786.* **Packages** (incl three meals) **Single** 1800 **Double** 2500. **Begum's Bounty** 500/person; **Dino Safari** 200/person; **Bonfire dinner with folk artists** 250.

Raioli
15 km from Balasinor, 80 km from Nadiad

Raioli is a treasure of fossils and fossilized eggs of the 10-meter dinosaur known as *Rajasaurus narmadensis.* According to carbon dating, these fossils are about 65 million years old. The heavy reptiles, related to their counterparts in continental Africa, Madagascar and South America, walked on two legs and preyed on long-necked herbivorous dinosaurs.

The Gujarat government has attempted to create a Dinosaur Park, but most of the unearthed material is actually at museums and universities around the world. The park has some basic plaster models and information about the dinosaur. It is a 2 km trek from the village to the plateau where the fossils were found. Many more still lie buried at the site. **Note:** Locals may offer to sell you fossils, but this is illegal. Please do not support such activity.

To get to Raioli, hop into a shared jeep or rickshaw from Balasinor. Buses are infrequent.

Kapadvanj
44 km from Nadiad

Kapadvanj has two beautiful subterranean water structures—a **kund** and the **Battris Kotha ni Vav**, both built by King Siddhraj Jaysinh. The *kund* is a large, square tank with steps on all four sides leading down to the water. One of the finest examples of a *toran* in Gujarat stands on one side while elegant *chhatardi*s frame the other three sides. The *vav* descends five stories. The columns that support the pavilion roofs have carvings of *yakshas* and *kichakas*.

Sojali
22 km from Nadiad, 38 km from Ahmedabad

This town is important for the **Roza Rozi**, a charming stone mausoleum built in the 15th c. by Sultan Mahmud Begada in tribute to his mentor, Hazrat Mubarak. It is a pavilion with numerous arches and domes. The columns, capitals and base are decorated with geometrical patterns. Stone grilles enclose the main chamber. Alongside are two other memorials dedicated to Hazrat's parakeet and cat. Sojali is 8 km from Khatrej Junction.

NORTHERN GUJARAT

NORTHERN GUJARAT

AT A GLANCE

Patan and Mahesana, replete with architectural excellence, represent the height of Gujarat's cultural achievements during the Golden Period of Solanki rule. Patan is home to the Ranki Vav, Patola weavers and the Bohra *havelis* at Siddhpur. Mahesana has the famous Sun Temple at Modhera and the *torans* of Vadnagar. Banaskantha, at the northeastern periphery of Gujarat, is characterized by undulating hills and forests from the Aravali Range. It is a mosaic that brings together elements of all the surrounding areas—rich tribal culture, pilgrimage destinations, wildlife and a Nawabi heritage.

NORTHERN GUJARAT

DISTRICT ▾
PATAN ◀
Patan City
Siddhpur

MAHESANA
BANASKANTHA

PATAN DISTRICT

PATAN CITY

પાટણ

POPULATION	113,750
AREA CODE	02766
DISTANCES - AHMEDABAD	125 KM
VADODARA	238 KM
MAHESANA	52 KM

This historic town, formerly known as Anahilvada-Patan, was Gujarat's thriving capital city for more than 600 years. It was founded in 746 by Vanaraj, the first of the Chavda rulers, followed by the Solankis and then the Vaghelas. Under Solanki rule (942-1244) Patan flourished as a center of trade and learning. It demonstrated new heights of achievement in the realm of architecture. Towards the end of the 13th c. Ulugh Khan, commander of Alauddin Khilji, looted and destroyed Patan completely, stripping the city of its former glory. In 1411 Gujarat's capital shifted to the newly founded Ahmedabad, and Patan gradually sunk into oblivion. This quaint town is still famous for its entrancing Ranki Vav, Patola *saris*, and Sahasralinga Talav. The nearby town of Siddhpur, situated on the Sarasvati River, is famous for its Bohra *havelis* and Rudra Mahalaya ruins.

NORTHERN GUJARAT

▼ DISTRICT
▶ PATAN
   Patan City
   Siddhpur

   MAHESANA
   BANASKANTHA

PLACES OF INTEREST

Ranki Vav

The ancient city of Anahilvada once stood about 2 km northwest of present-day Patan. One of its legacies, Ranki Vav, literally "Queen's stepwell", was commissioned in 1063 by Rani Udayamati, wife of King Bhimdev I of the Solanki Dynasty. Probably the finest stepwell in India, it is a subterranean treasure of more than 800 elaborately sculpted images including a majestic center panel of *sheshashayi*, Vishnu sleeping on the coil of a cobra with its hood serving as a canopy. At some point in its history, the *vav* was flooded by

NORTHERN
GUJARAT

DISTRICT ▾
PATAN ◄
Patan City
Siddhpur

MAHESANA
BANASKANTHA

the neighboring Sarasvati River and buried in mud. It was excavated in the late 1980s by the Archeological Survey of India, revealing its carved images in pristine condition. The carvings are different from other stepwells in that each image conveys an interesting tale of its own, but collectively they form a narrative. The ten incarnations of Vishnu form a central theme, enhanced with depictions of *sadhus*, *brahmins*, *apsaras* and more. The voluptuous figures of the *apsaras* are shown applying make-up and fixing their jewelry among other daily activities, offering an interesting glimpse into the society of that time. As a tribute to the thriving textile culture of the period, several blocks along the entrance on the left side depict embroidered, appliquéd and mirrored textiles including a design of Patan's famous Patola. **Open** 0800-1800. **ENTRY Indian** Rs. 5, **Foreigner** 2 USD.

Sahasralinga Talav

Just north of Ranki Vav is a reservoir built by Siddhraj Jaysinh in 1084 on what was once the bank of the Sarasvati River. The lake had 1008 Shiva shrines dotting the embankment, hence the name Sahasralinga—"lake of a thousand *lingas*". Estimated to spread over seven hectares (17 acres), the *talav* ruins include a Shiva temple with 48 pillars. Towards the west end is the finely carved, three-ringed sluice gate that channeled water from the Sarasvati into the reservoir. Only 20 percent of the lake has been unearthed. It is said that it had an inbuilt natural filtration system and served as the water source of the royal family. On the way to Sahasralinga stands the **Kali Temple**, which Siddhraj built 1000 years ago in honor of Goddess Kali, the *kuldevi* (family goddess) of the Solankis. The temple guards over the town.

Patan Fort Wall and Gates

The city's fort wall and several of its gates are largely intact. Within the fortified walls is a charismatic town perfect for exploring at a leisurely pace. You are likely to come across people occupied in livelihood activities such as rope and *bidi* making. The old residential areas are divided into *pols* with narrow lanes supporting beautiful Hindu and Muslim *havelis* that have elaborate wooden facades and brackets. Areas worth exploring include **Nagarvada, Kapur Mehta no Pado, Shantinath ni Pol** and **Dave no Pado**. The bustling bazaar is also a great place to wander around.

Panchasara Parshvanath Jain Derasar

During the Solanki era, Patan was a center for Jainism and even today the town has more than 100 Jain temples, including the **Panchasara Parshvanath Jain Derasar**. It is one of Patan's largest temples with the sophisticated stone carvings and white marble floors that characterize Jain architecture. Nearby is the **Hemachandracharya Jain Gnan Mandir**, an ancient library built by the renowned Jain scholar and poet Hemachandracharya, who is credited with formulating Gujarati grammar. The collection includes a number of ancient palm-leaf Jain manuscripts and literature written by the poet. **Open** 1000-1700.

Patola and Mashru Weavers

According to a legend, King Kumarpal (12th c.) wore a new Patola robe, woven in Jalna (South Maharashtra), every day before offering *puja*. On learning that

SARASVATI RIVER

To Dees

Pitambar
Lake

27

'1

2

Aghara Gate
Chindiya Gate

26

3

Fatipal Gate

16

25
23 22
24

28

Rajmahal Road

To Vagdod

4

17
Bagvada Gate

19 20

Station Road

29

Siddhpur Road

15
14
13

21
18

30

Bazaar Road

11 12

Sardar Road

5

6
7

10
9

Gungdi
Lake

Gayatri Temple Road

8

34

Canal

To Mahesana

Khansarovar
Gate

N
Not to Scale

To Harij

Siddhi
Sarovar

To Chanasma

To Lanava

Patan City
Legend

Accommodation
24 Hotel Gokul
25 Hotel Yuvaraj
28 Hotel Surya Palace

Food & Drink
18 Gurjari Restaurant
19 Nirav Restaurant
29 Hotel Siddharaj
34 Garden Restaurant

Places of Interest
1   Sahasralinga Talav
2   Ranki Vav
3   Kali Temple
4   Patolawala Farmhouse
5   Patan Patola Heritage House
8   Mashru Weavers
9   Nagarvada
10 Kapur Mehta no Pado
14 Hemchandracharya Jain Gnan Mandir
15 Panchasara Parshvanath Jain Derasar
17 Panchamukhi Hanuman Temple

Nuts & Bolts
6   Maa Hospital
7   Municipal Office
11 Bank of Baroda ATM
12 Civil Hospital
13 SBI Bank ATM
16 Vegetable and Fruit Market
20 UTI Bank ATM
21 Janata Hospital
22 General Post Office
23 City Point Shopping Centre & Cinema
26 Reliance World
27 North Gujarat University
30 ICICI Bank ATM

NORTHERN GUJARAT

DISTRICT ▾
PATAN ◄
Patan City
Siddhpur

MAHESANA
BANASKANTHA

the King of Jalna was actually sending him used clothes, Kumarpal declared war and defeated the southern ruler. He relocated 700 Patola weaver families to Patan. Today only two Salvi families practice the dexterous craft. A single Patola *sari* generally takes 4-6 months to complete and involves a laborious process of dyeing the threads according to a preplanned design and then weaving it accordingly (see **Resource Guide, Craft**). You can visit **Vinayak** and **Bharat Salvi** at **Patan Patola Heritage** *231369, Patolawala Salvivado, Patolawala St* or **Ashok Salvi** at **Patolawala Farm House** *232172, Outside Phatipal Gate* and watch master craftsmen at work or order your own Patola, which starts at Rs. 90,000. They keep a stock of smaller Patola scarves beginning at Rs. 5000.

Mashru, a vibrant fabric woven with a combination of silk and cotton (see **Resource Guide, Craft**) is also traditionally produced in Patan. A revival project is underway in **Tankwada ni Pol**, where a group of Mashru weavers are returning to traditional designs and quality. You can visit the neighborhood to watch the weavers at work and purchase material. *For more information on the project contact* ***Janakbhai Khatri*** *9979775705.*

NUTS & BOLTS

In and Out
Several intercity and local trains travel from Ahmedabad to Patan (4.5 hrs). ST buses are available from Ahmedabad (3 hrs) and Mahesana (1 hr). Shared jeeps are slightly quicker but crowded and uncomfortable.

Getting Around
Rickshaws are the best way to get around town. Shuttles move across town for about Rs. 5-10. Walking is a good way to explore the market and *pol* areas.

Money
ATMs **Bank of Baroda** *ST Rd, Hingalachchar* and **UTI Bank** *Shreedev Cmplx, Opp Post Office, Station Rd.*
MONEY TRANSFER **Western Union** is available at the General Post Office.

Communication
INTERNET **Reliance World** *College Rd*; **AMPM Cyber Café** *University Plaza*; **Campus Cyber Café** *in the University Campus*; **Sun Infotech** *Devdarshan Cmplx, Opp Santokba Hall, Rajmahal Rd.*

ACCOMMODATION

Hotel Surya Palace *232544, Yash Plaza, Nr Rly Crossing* is a new hotel with simple, but clean rooms, located on the outskirts of town. **Facilities** western toilets, AC options, restaurant. **Single** 250-700 **Double** 350-1000 **Triple** 500-800 **Extra Bed** 75.

Hotel Gokul *2645133, 2nd Flr, Bhagat Cmplx, Bus Stn Rd.* **Facilities** AC options, restaurant. **Single** 150-500 **Double** 200-500 **Extra Bed** 50-100.

FOOD & DRINK

Surya Palace Restaurant *in Hotel Surya Palace* opens at 0900 and offers a vegetarian selection of Chinese, Indian and Punjabi food. **Hotel Siddhraj** *Nr Siddhpur Char Rasta* and **Hotel Gurjari** *Nr Sardar Road* have a decent selection of Punjabi, Chinese and South Indian dishes. **Hotel Nirav** *Nr Kohinoor Theatre* and **Hotel Garden** *Opp GEB* serve Gujarati *thalis* and Punjabi food.

EXCURSIONS

NORTHERN GUJARAT

▾ DISTRICT
▸ PATAN
Patan City
Siddhpur

MAHESANA
BANASKANTHA

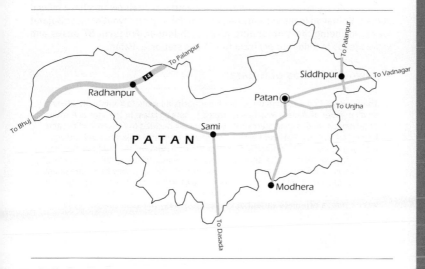

Siddhpur

28 km from Patan

This town is on the banks of the holy Sarasvati just where it veers eastward. For this reason, Siddhpur is considered pious by Hindus. It has many ashrams and the sacred Bindu Lake, where people perform rites to invoke peace upon their departed mothers' souls. The town is also an important settlement for the Dawoodi Bohra community.

The temple ruins of **Rudra Mahalaya** honor Rudra, an earlier form of Shiva associated with wind, storm, hunting and death. King Mulraj first ordered its construction in 983 AD but only one story was built during his lifetime. The incomplete structure lay untouched for three generations until Siddhraj Jaysinh resumed its construction. The temple was finished only after 175 years. According to ancient documents, Rudra Mahalaya had a three-storied *shikhara*, 1600 pillars and 12 entrance doors. Surrounding the structure were eleven shrines of Rudra and a *toran* at the eastern entrance. After the Solanki period, Ulugh Khan and Ahmed Shah destroyed parts of the temple and used them to build a mosque. Today the structure is an interesting amalgam of both

**NORTHERN
GUJARAT**

DISTRICT ▾
PATAN ◄
Patan City
Siddhpur

MAHESANA
BANASKANTHA

religions; part of the mosque has been excavated, revealing the temple. A typical Muslim *vazu* (used for the ritual washing before *namaz*) also exists in the entrance courtyard. Images of deities lie scattered around. Although closed to the public, the security guard may allow you to walk around as long as you do not touch anything.

Bohravad is a neighborhood of the Dawoodi Bohras and consists of spacious row houses painted in pastel colors with facades that share architectural features. Built about a century ago by the affluent community, many of whom have been conducting trade abroad for years, these mansions infuse European elements. Today some 500-700 *havelis* are empty as their owners have moved abroad. Bohravad looks surreal compared to the organic layout of most Gujarat towns, including the surrounding areas of Siddhpur. Frequent ST buses and shared jeeps to Siddhpur ply from the ST bus station at Patan.

Dawoodi Bohras of Gujarat

The Dawoodi Bohra community of Siddhpur traces its roots to Khambhat, where a small number of Yemeni Muslims migrated to spread Islam in the 11th c. A group of privileged Hindus from mercantile communities decided to convert and became known as Bohras. The word Bohra is derived from the Gujarati word *vehvaar*, meaning "trade". The conversion helped them circumvent the traditional Hindu taboo against crossing the seas and served to enhance their trading activities. Mainly based in Siddhpur and in Kapadvanj (Kheda District), they have spread out to various towns around Gujarat and abroad to establish their businesses. The men typically wear *topis*, white crocheted caps with golden embroidery. The women wear a *rida*, a two-piece variant of the *burqa*, usually in pastel colors. The face is generally not veiled.

MAHESANA DISTRICT

MAHESANA CITY
મહેસાણા

POPULATION		141,450
AREA CODE		2762
DISTANCES - AHMEDABAD		74 KM
VADODARA		185 KM
PATAN		52 KM

One of the most affluent cities in Gujarat, Mahesana does not offer much to the tourist beyond huge commercial complexes and multiplexes along the highway. The colossal Simandhar Jain Temple, also on the highway, is hard to miss. The old city skyline is dominated by the domes of a palace, which now houses government offices. The city's prosperity is largely linked to the Dudhsagar Dairy Cooperative and the cash-crop based economy of the surrounding areas. Mahesana, with decent accommodation and restaurants, makes for a good station to explore the region, including Patan District.

Mahesana District is a repository of Solanki period architecture, such as the stunning Modhera Temple, the hill-top Jain temples of Taranga and the famous *toran* of Vadnagar, which has become a symbol of Gujarat.

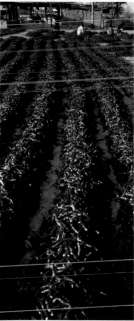

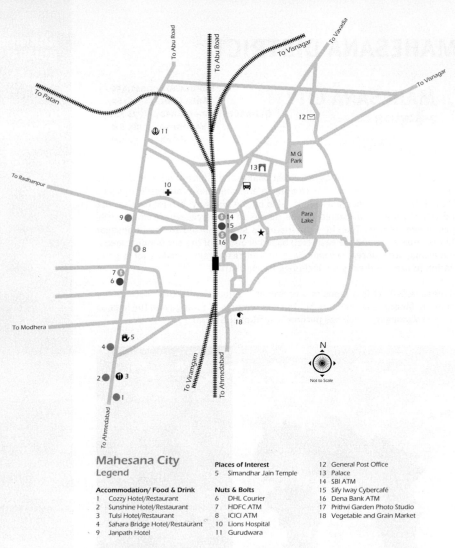

Mahesana City
Legend

Accommodation/ Food & Drink
1   Cozzy Hotel/Restaurant
2   Sunshine Hotel/Restaurant
3   Tulsi Hotel/Restaurant
4   Sahara Bridge Hotel/Restaurant
9   Janpath Hotel

Places of Interest
5   Simandhar Jain Temple

Nuts & Bolts
6   DHL Courier
7   HDFC ATM
8   ICICI ATM
10 Lions Hospital
11 Gurudwara

12 General Post Office
13 Palace
14 SBI ATM
15 Sify Iway Cybercafé
16 Dena Bank ATM
17 Prithvi Garden Photo Studio
18 Vegetable and Grain Market

NUTS & BOLTS

In and Out
ST buses travel between Ahmedabad and Mahesana (3 hrs), while several trains (2 hrs) also pass through.

Getting Around
The best way to get around the city is by rickshaw.

NORTHERN GUJARAT

▾ DISTRICT
PATAN

▸ MAHESANA
Mahesana City
Modhera
Thol Lake
Tirupati
Nature Park
Vadnagar
Shanku's
Nature Health
Taranga

BANASKANTHA

Money

ATMs **SBI Bank** *Nr Gopinala Underbridge, Nxt to Mahiti Bhavan;* **HDFC** *Nr Circuit House;* **ICICI** *Opp Circuit House;* **DENA Bank** *Nr Mahiti Bhavan.*

Communication

INTERNET **Sify Iway** *Nxt to Mahiti Bhavan.*
COURIER **DHL** *State Hwy, Nr Circuit House.*

ACCOMMODATION

Cozzy Hotel *Wide Angle Cmplx* is a new hotel, with clean, moderate sized rooms. It is the best value-for-money option. **Facilities** western toilet, AC options, TV, multicuisine restaurant. **Single** 200-400 **Double** 300-475.

Hotel Tulsi *233491, Opp Nagalpur Bus Stand,* is most popular for its multicuisine restaurant. The rooms are simple and well-kept. **Facilities** AC options, restaurant, running hot water, room service, TV, car rentals. **Single** 300-500 **Double** 400-600 **Extra Bed** 50.

Sunshine Hotel *246293 Nr Jyoti Petrol Pump, Nagalpur* is another good alternative. **Facilities** western toilets, AC options, TV, laundry, courtesy airport transfer. **Single** 390-1890 **Double** 490-1890 **Extra Bed** 200.

Hotel Sahara Bridge *230823 Apollo Enclave, Opp Simandhar Jain Temple* is the town's most upscale hotel and has a staff that is eager to please. **Facilities** western toilets, AC rooms, restaurant, laundry, room service. **Single** 800-1600 **Double** 1000-1750 **Extra Bed** 150.

FOOD & DRINK

Sahara *in Hotel Sahara* has an excellent multicuisine restaurant for relatively high-end prices. **Tulsi** *in Hotel Tulsi* and **Cozzy** *in Hotel Cozzy* have cheaper menus offering the same variety—Punjabi, Chinese, Indian and snack dishes.

NORTHERN
GUJARAT

DISTRICT ▾
PATAN

MAHESANA ◂
Mahesana City
Modhera
Thol Lake
Tirupati
Nature Park
Vadnagar
Shanku's
Nature Health
Taranga

BANASKANTHA

EXCURSIONS

Modhera   **25 km from Mahesana, 34 km from Patan**

About 2 km west of the town towards Pushpavati River stands the striking **Surya Temple**, dedicated to the sun. Like most structures built during the Solanki period, the stone blocks were fit without mortar. Commissioned in 1027 AD by Bhimdev I, the temple consists of three parts: the *Suryakund,* the pavilion and the temple. Traditionally, pilgrims would bathe in the *kund* before entering the temple. Along the *kund* steps are 108 shrines. Steps ascending to the pavilion lead to two beautifully carved pillars which belong to a *toran* that once stood here. Along the wall of the pavilion are twelve images that depict the sun. Take note that the sun idol is shown wearing boots. The main temple stands past the pavilion. It is believed that the central area was once crowned by a dome. Many claim that it was damaged during a natural calamity or destroyed by the hands of iconoclasts. The temple was built facing the east so that at the equinox, the first rays of the sun would penetrate the sanctum. There is no longer an idol in the sanctum, possibly because sun worship had gone out of fashion by the time the deity vanished and was not considered worth replacing. The temple's exterior is clad in carvings of the Sun and Agni in addition to several erotic images. **Open** 0800-1800. **ENTRY Indians** Rs. 5, **Foreigners** 5 USD. There is a **Toran Restaurant** nearby that serves snacks and *thalis*. Take a bus to Mahesana, and then catch another bus or shared jeep to Modhera (40 min).

Thol Lake

70 km from Mahesana, 40 km from Ahmedabad

This small but scenic lake, measuring 7 sq km, has several manmade islands and attracts more than 75 types of birds, including the Blue-winged teal, Pintail, Redhead pochard, flamingo, Grey-leg goose and Sarus crane. It is a great excursion from Ahmedabad as well. *For more information contact the Assistant Conservator of Forests, Sanand 02717 223500.*

Tirupati Natural Park

20 km from Mahesana, 5 km from Visnagar

Spread over 20 hectares, Tirupati is a community initiative led by locals who cultivated the barren land and turned it into a park as an effort to protect the natural environs and create a space that expresses the importance of nature. You can visit the park for boating, children's rides, a herbal garden and the mini zoo. **ENTRY Adult** Rs.10, **Child** Rs. 5.

The park also has 15 cottages set next to a reservoir and some gardens. The accommodation is conveniently located for excursions to Taranga, Banaskantha and northern Sabarkantha. **Rooms** 550-1000. A restaurant serves snacks and Chinese and Indian dishes (0800-2100). *Contact 02765 264110, Visnagar-Unjha Rd, Iyasara.* Take a bus from Mahesana to Visnagar. Here you change buses or take a jeep traveling to Unjha and get off at Tirupati.

Vadnagar

30 km from Mahesana

Vadnagar, one of Gujarat's ancient cities, predates history. This pleasant city is built on an elevation fortified with well-preserved gates and surrounded by rolling terrain.

Located just outside town, the 500-year-old **Hatkeshvar Temple** is dedicated to Hatkeshvar, the deity of the Nagar Brahmins, who were once a prominent community in Vadnagar. The temple walls come to life with the elaborately carved musicians and evocative dancing *apsaras* who share the space with depictions of the Ramayana and Mahabharata. It is believed that this temple and Sharmishtha Lake, now on the outskirts, once stood in the center of town, testifying just how vast Vadnagar was at one point.

Two *torans* about 40 feet tall, built in red and yellow sandstone, stand just north of the walled town. Perhaps erected after a war victory, the structures are cloaked in carvings of battle and hunting scenes. The one to the east is in better condition and has become a symbol of Gujarat. The *torans* might have belonged to a large temple complex, but there are no remains.

The **Tana and Riri Samadhi,** south of town, honors the feat of two sisters, Tana and Riri. The story narrates that Tansen, the greatest musician in Akbar's court, was ordered by the emperor to sing the Deepak *raga*. Despite knowing that it would generate excessive heat and cause him to suffer an extreme fever, Tansen followed the Emperor's orders. Afterwards, the musician set out in search of somebody who could sing the Megh Malhar *raga*, which would produce rain and cure his fever. He found his saviors in a village near Vadnagar. The sisters Tana and Riri sang the *raga* and cured Tansen. When Akbar heard about the incident,

NORTHERN GUJARAT

DISTRICT ▼
PATAN

MAHESANA ◄
Mahesana City
Modhera
Thol Lake
Tirupati
Nature Park
Vadnagar
Shanku's
Nature Health
Taranga

BANASKANTHA

he sent for the girls and asked them to perform in his court. As Brahmins, it was against their customs to do so, and they refused. When Akbar sent his forces to Vadnagar to convince them to sing, the sisters committed suicide to avert any hardship to their town or the emperor.

On the outskirts of Vadnagar is the rundown seven-story **Pancham Mehta ni Vav** built in the 16th c. The **Gaurikund**, a square-shaped pond with a pavilion, continues be visited by people for post-death rituals. The steps leading to the pond have inscriptions from the Hindu scriptures.

Shanku's Nature Health Centre   55 km from Ahmedabad

This is a great place for rejuvenation through the traditional practices of naturopathy and yoga. The center offers a large range of therapies in addition to yoga sessions, meditation and oil massages. It is well equipped and has a panel of trained and experienced doctors. The importance of a balanced diet is stressed, and organic food is grown on the premises. Packages range from three to ten days. *For rates contact 2762 282351, Amipura, Ahmedabad-Mahesana Hwy, www.shankusnaturalhealth.org.* The location is right next to Shanku's Water Park and Luxury Resort.

Taranga   56 km from Mahesana

The Solanki King Kumarpal (12th c.) converted to Jainism under the guidance of Hemachandracharya. Afterwards, he built the imposing **Ajitanath Temple** at Taranga. Despite later additions, it is one of the best preserved Solanki structures and a masterpiece in its own right. The temple exterior is covered with stone images of dancing maidens along with gods and goddesses. The figures are depicted in life-like poses, with scrupulous detailing in their faces and costumes. The large temple spire is supported by eight pillars, and the structure resembles a Hindu temple. Inside is an alabaster idol of the second *tirthankar*, Ajitanath. In addition to regular buses, three slow trains travel daily between Mahesana and Taranga (2 hrs). Take a bus or jeep to Timba from Mahesana, and then catch a shared (Rs. 5) or private (Rs. 50) jeep for the 8 km to Taranga.

BANASKANTHA DISTRICT

PALANPUR CITY
પાલનપુર

POPULATION	122,300
AREA CODE	02742
DISTANCES - AHMEDABAD	147 KM
VADODARA	257 KM
MAHESANA	72 KM

Banaskantha, the northernmost district of Gujarat, shares a border with Rajasthan. Its headquarters, Palanpur, dates from the 8th c. It was ruled by several dynasties before the Nawabs of Afghan descent took over in the late 14th c. Taley Muhammad Khan, the last of the Nawabs, ascended the throne in 1917 and ruled until the state merged with the Indian Republic. Today, Palanpur is home to a Jain community that is at the forefront of the diamond cutting and polishing industry.

The district is dominated by the colorful Garasia and Rabari communities. It also has a number of pilgrimage destinations such as the Ambaji Temple and the Jain shrines at Kumbharia. The Jessore Sanctuary in the northeast protects the endangered Sloth bear.

NORTHERN GUJARAT

DISTRICT ▾
PATAN
MAHESANA

BANASKANTHA ◀
Palanpur City
Danta
Balaram
Chitrasani
Virampur
Balundra
Iqbalgadh
Balaram-Ambaji
Sanctuary
Ambaji
Kumbharia
Jessore
Sanctuary
Getting Involved

PLACES OF INTEREST

Mithi Vav

This 18th c. four-storied stepwell, though in disrepair, is one of the main sites of Palanpur. It is built with sandstone probably borrowed from the remains of another monument. The carvings along the inside walls include a four-armed Ganesh, a dancing Bhairav, and a variety of dancers and *apsaras*.

Pataleshwar Mandir

Local legend claims that Siddhraj Jaysinh was born in Palanpur. His mother, Minaldevi, ordered the construction of a stepwell to commemorate his birth. While digging, a *Shivalinga* was found buried in the ground, and so, it was decided to build a temple instead. In its antiquity, this place is believed to have been a kingdom of serpents, whose impressions were found on stones discovered during excavations for the temple.

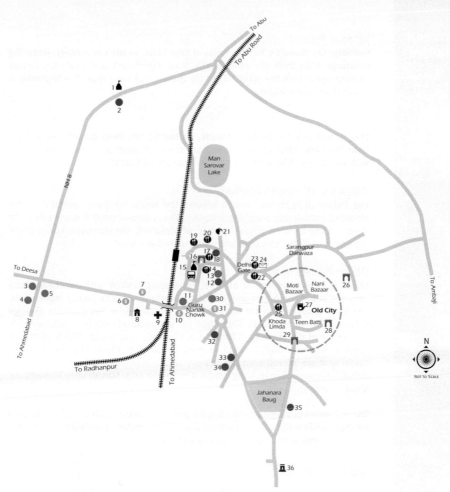

Palanpur City
Legend

Accommodation
3   Hotel Lajwanti
4   Hotel Way Wait
5   Hotel Cappal
11 Hotel Banas
13 Hotel Bilipatra
30 City Light Hotel / Web Planet

Food & Drink
14 Jain Ice Cream
19 Guptaji's / Sher-e-Punjab
20 Jitendra Dinning Hall
22 Jayanti Fafda House
23 Alpahar Sweets
25 Janata Kachori House

Places of Interest
1   Gayatri Mandir
2   Sur Mandir Multiplex
8   Joravar Palace
15 Pataleshwar Mandir
16 Kirtistambh
26 Shahi Roza
27 Motu Derasar
28 Mithi Vav
29 Meera Gate
35 George V Club

Nuts & Bolts
6   SBI Bank
7   HDFC Bank
9   Doctor's House
10 Bank of Baroda
12 Maruti Courier

17 Central Studio
18 City Food Corner
21 Vegetable Market
24 General Post Office
31 SBI Bank
32 Neelam Super Market
33 Treasure Book Stall
34 UTI ATM
36 Forest Office

NORTHERN GUJARAT

DISTRICT ▾
PATAN
MAHESANA

BANASKANTHA ◀
Palanpur City
Danta
Balaram
Chitrasani
Virampur
Balundra
Iqbalgadh
Balaram-Ambaji
Sanctuary
Ambaji
Kumbharia
Jessore
Sanctuary
Getting Involved

Joravar Palace

Formerly the Nawab's Palace, today it functions as the town court. Beautiful paintings hang from the walls of the main courtroom and fine sandalwood carvings embellish the stairs. **Open** (to the public) 1100-1700. **Photography** is allowed with permission.

Old City

Take a walk around the **Moti Bazaar, Pathar Sadak, Nani Bazaar, Jhaverivad, Teen Batti** and **Khoda Limda** to explore the traditional *pols*. Each has *havelis* with wood carved facades and profusely adorned brackets.

Palanpur Diamond Market

The Palanpuri Jains are famous around the world for their control over the diamond cutting and polishing industry. The diamond market along City Light Road is home to about 30-40 diamond wholesalers. Get permission from any of the shops to watch how diamonds are cut and polished.

Other Places of Interest

Shahi Roza is a collection of royal cenotaphs crafted with excellent stone carvings along the pillars and domes. Unfortunately it is poorly maintained. **The Motu Derasar** is an ancient Jain temple dedicated to Parshvanath. **George V Club** was built by Nawab Sher Khan to commemorate the royal visit and the coronation of King George V. Today it is a private sports club. The four-storied **Kirtistambha** was built in 1936 in memory of Sher Khan. The marble slabs covering it are carved with the history of the Nawab's rule and information about Palanpur. **Jahanarabaug** is a garden named after Nawab Taley Muhammad Khan's Australian wife.

The renowned photographer A L Syed (1904-1991) was the official photographer for the royal families of the Palanpur State. *If interested in seeing his collection, contact his son Azmat Syed 02742 254480.*

NUTS & BOLTS

In and Out

The city is well connected with ST buses to all major cities in Gujarat. Buses of most private companies such as **Patel, Eagle** and **Shrinath** depart from Guru Nanak Chowk. Express trains traveling north from Ahmedabad, 3 hrs away, halt at Palanpur. Travel agencies, all located at Guru Nanak Chowk, include **New Pooja Travels** *265041, Nr Banas Hotel;* **Kalpna Travels** *251544 Nr Banas Hotel,* **Sona Travels** *257792.*

Getting Around

Rickshaws are the best option for moving around in the city. Shared jeeps are good for traveling around the district.

Money

ATMs **SBI Bank** *Nr Jorawar Palace*; **HDFC** *Opp Jorawar Palace*; **Bank of Baroda**, *Nr White House, Guru Nanak Chowk.*
FOREIGN EXCHANGE SBI Bank *Nr Sardar Patel Gunj.*

Communication

INTERNET Web Planet *City Light Cmplx.*
COURIERS Maruti *First Ln, Panchratna Cmplx, Amir Rd.*

Photography

Video Photography Central Studio *253947, Simla Gate, City Light Cmplx.*

ACCOMMODATION

There are plenty of low cost hotels and guest houses opposite the railway station and near the ST bus station.

Bilipatra *261267, 2nd Flr, Above Dena Bank, Amir Rd* is another good option. **Facilities** AC options, western toilets, TV, room service, restaurant. **Single** 200 **Double** 350-500 **Extra Bed** 100.

City Light *394900, Main Circle, NH 14* is located above a noisy commercial complex, but otherwise a good place. **Facilities** western toilets, AC options, shower, restaurant. **Single** 350-550 **Double** 400-700 **Extra Bed** 100.

Hotel Cappal *250777, Ahmedabad-Palanpur Hwy.* **Facilities** AC options, TV, room service. **Single** 300-1600 **Double** 300-1600 **Extra Bed** 100.

Hotel Lajwanti *257200, Main Circle, NH 14,* recently renovated, is one of the best options in the city. **Facilities** western toilets, AC options, laundry, room service, running hot water, restaurant. **Single** 220-900 **Double** 280-1200 **Extra Bed** 100.

Hotel Way Wait *253753, Main Circle, NH 14,* the choicest option in town, is also conveniently located. **Facilities** western toilets, AC options, shower, TV, room service, restaurant. **Single** 810 **Double** 910-2100 **Extra Bed** 100.

FOOD & DRINK

Suruchi *in Cappal* is a dining hall that serves pure Gujarati *thalis.* **Way Wait Restaurant** is reputed for its Punjabi cuisine. **Millenium** is a popular and often congested restaurant that offers really good Punjabi, Chinese and South Indian. **Guptajis'** *Opp Railway Stn* cooks tasty and affordable Punjabi food. **Banas** serves delicious *dahiwada* and **Lajwanti** is the place for *masala dosa,* although it also prepares a range of various dishes. **City Food Corner** *Nr Ambaji Temple* has good pizzas, sandwiches, *pav bhaji* and other snack items. **Ram-Jhupdi** *Abu Rd Hwy* is a popular *dhaba* that serves traditional village fare.

NORTHERN GUJARAT

DISTRICT ▾
PATAN
MAHESANA

BANASKANTHA ◄
Palanpur City
Danta
Balaram
Chitrasani
Virampur
Balundra
Iqbalgadh
Balaram-Ambaji
Sanctuary
Ambaji
Kumbharia
Jessore
Sanctuary
Getting Involved

LOCAL SPECIALTIES Station Road is the place to go for good non-veg options—**Hotel Sher-e-Punjab** *Opp Railway Stn* is the most popular. **Jayanti Fafda House** *Nr Delhi Gate* is a local favorite for *fafda* and *jalebi*. **Janta Kachori House** *Nr Moti Bazaar* is famous for its *kachori*. **Guru Nanak Chowk** fills with street food vendors after 1800.

EXCURSIONS

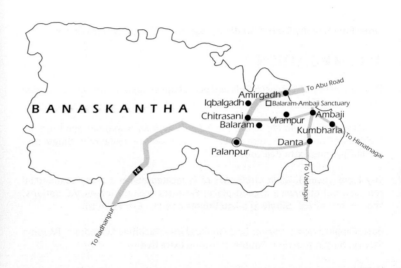

Danta
38 km from Palanpur

Danta, a former princely state under the Parmars, has ties with royal families in Gujarat and Rajasthan; both cultures have influenced the local architecture. Located at the base of the Aravali Hills, the town is set amidst forest cover and boulders and is home to the Bhil community.

Bhavani Villa *02749 278705* is the royal residential complex of Maharana Mahipendrasinh, a gracious host who personally tends to each of his guests. The residence is a colonial villa with a regal Rajput ambience. All five guest rooms include most modern amenities except a TV set. The kitchen, solely reserved for hotel guests, prepares traditional Rajput cuisine according to the preferences of those dining. Meat dishes can also be made. Guests can enjoy a folk concert while dining at the stud farm in the garden. The Villa offers horse safaris, treks and jeep rides through the Balaram-Ambaji Sanctuary. You can interact with the local Bhil and Garasia communities, who live in little hamlets in the hills.

Balaram
15 km from Palanpur

Balaram Palace Resort was built in the 1920-30s by Nawab Taley Muhammad Khan as a hunting lodge and country refuge. Neo-classical columns and European arches with terrace views of the Aravali Hills adorn the palace. The swimming pool, between the palace and the river, is fed by a natural stream. The resort is surrounded by a riverbed, patches of scrubland, agricultural land, forest area and tribal villages. **Facilities** room service, laundry, car rental, sightseeing on request, in-house restaurant with an extensive menu. Ask about bicycle rentals, camel/horse riding, jeep safaris, jungle treks, indoor games, badminton, football, cricket and volleyball. **Single** 1900-2300 **Double** 2500-3500 **Extra Bed** 500. *Contact 079 26582191 for more information.* The resort is 2 km off the Ahmedabad–Abu Highway. There are three daily buses from Palanpur to Balaram: 1000, 1130 and 1345.

Tribal Villages

The area surrounding Balaram is home to several interesting communities. **Chitrasani** *15 km from Palanpur* is largely inhabited by the Rabari Marwaris, known for their colorful dress and silver ornaments. Their traditional trade includes animal husbandry and farming. **Virampur** *25 km from Palanpur* hosts a market that buzzes with activity as locals come here to purchase traditional clothing, ornaments and daily commodities. **Balundra** *31 km from Palanpur* is another village belonging to the Marwari Rabaris. This is a great place to see potters sculpt the terracotta horses that locals offer to Mamadev, a god of the Garasia tribe. **Iqbalgadh** *26 km from Palanpur* is famous for the making of traditional silver ornaments worn by the Garasia and Rabari communities. One of the oldest shops in the village is **Jawanmal Ganeshji** *02742 235466*—it has been around for 85 years and has an interesting collection of antique and traditional tribal jewelry. Located on Abu Highway, Iqbalgadh takes about 30 minutes to reach from Lakshman Tekri in Palanpur by shared jeep (Rs. 10).

The Garasia Community

Concentrated along the Aravali Range, the traditions of the Garasia have a strong Rajasthani influence, as does the language, which combines Marwari, the Bhil dialect and Gujarati. They are mostly agriculturalists but also depend on the surrounding forest, selling its produce for income. The men work in the field while the women take care of the home. The community believes in ancestral worship, and erects memorial stones called *suras* over the buried bones of their dead. During the Chitra Vichitra Fair, they mourn and wish peace for departed souls. The Garasia believe in Bhakar Bhavsingh, the supreme deity. Bakhar is the name of a hill range in Garasia territory while Bavsingh is a mountain god whose mount is a horse. This ties in with their tradition of offering terracotta figures, usually horses, when they want to communicate with the divine. Once the offering is made and prayers are given, they believe that the spirit inside the horse is absorbed by the deity and all that remains is the terracotta figure, which is left to disintegrate.

Balaram-Ambaji Sanctuary
22 km from Palanpur

Situated in the picturesque Aravali Hills, the sanctuary covers about 540 sq km along the Gujarat and Rajasthan border. The scenic landscape of Danta, Ambaji and Amirgadh is combined with vegetation and rocky terrain, creating an ideal environment for trekking and hiking. This sanctuary harbors more than 480 species of flora including a variety of rare medicinal plants. Wildlife species found here include panther, hyena, jungle cat, jackal, Indian fox, Nilgai, Langur, bat and porcupine. It is also a good place for birdwatching. **Entry** free. Camping is permitted. *For more information contact the Forest Division Office in Palanpur 02742 257084. The sanctuary is connected to Palanpur by jeep and bus.*

Ambaji
60 km from Palanpur

Situated on Arasur Hill, towards the southwestern end of the Aravali Range, the **Ambaji Temple** is flocked by millions of pilgrims every year, especially on the full moon night of Bhadarva (see **Fairs and Festivals**). *Padyatris*, pilgrims on foot, carry colorful buntings and banners while others push along replicas of the shrine on wheelbarrows accompanied with loudspeakers blaring *bhajans*. Some devotees form a *mandali* and dance on the road to the rhythm of cymbals and *dhols* while others trudge along shouting chants. Camps are set up along the route to provide pilgrims with food, drinks and healthcare. The Ambaji Temple marks one of 51 *Shakti peethas* (see box below) in the country. The shrine, built of marble, has no idol but a niche with a matrix of geometric shapes, called the *vishvo yantra*. Nearby is the ancient Gabbar Temple where Krishna had his tonsure ceremony. Ambaji Town is known for its marble quarries, and artisans chiseling away meticulously at the stone can be seen everywhere. Locals sell fresh honey, wax and other forest products. Buses traveling between Ahmedabad and Mt Abu stop at Ambaji.

Shakti Peethas

As legend narrates, Sati married Shiva against the wishes of her father, King Daksha. To take revenge, Daksha organized a huge *yagna* and invited all the gods and deities, barring his new son-in law. Although Shiva tried to dissuade her, Sati decided to attend the *yagna* anyway. Upon arrival, the King ignored his daughter and insulted Shiva in front of all the guests. Unable to bear her father's insults towards her husband, Sati committed suicide by jumping into the pyre of the *yagna*. When Shiva learned what had happened, he grew furious. He broke into his dance of destruction, obliterating everything around the *yagna* site. Then distraught with wild grief, he carried Sati's burning body and flew wildly across the skies. The gods appealed to Vishnu to calm Shiva. With his *sudarshan chakra*, Vishnu severed Sati's body into 51 pieces to bring Shiva back to sanity. The places where the various parts of Sati's body fell are known as *Shakti peethas*. Her heart is believed to have fallen where the Ambaji Temple stands today.

Kumbharia
67 km from Palanpur, 7 km from Ambaji

Located ten minutes away from Ambaji, Kumbharia was one of the Jain religious centers during the Solanki period. Five Jain temples of varying sizes and styles built between the 11th and 12th c. stand here. They are similar in general layout, but each one has its own character and varying images carved into it. Everything from gods and goddesses, *apsaras*, dancers, musicians and horsemen cover the wall. The main temple is dedicated to the *tirthankar* Neminath. To reach Kumbharia catch a private or shared jeep from Ambaji on the Khedbrahma Highway. **Open** 0630-1930. **Photography** Rs. 40 and **Videography** Rs. 150 for the interiors.

Jessore Wildlife Sanctuary
32 km from Palanpur

Jessore offers excellent trekking options through its hilly terrain and dense forest. Along the way there are places of interest such as the ancient **Kedarnath Mahadev Temple,** which is surrounded by lots of monkeys, and the **Muniji Ki Kutia.**

The forest sanctuary covers about 180 sq km and encompasses a natural lake. It is a habitat of the endangered Sloth bear, which can be sighted on occasion. In addition to a variety of birds, other animal species include the Indian civet cat, Indian porcupine, Striped hyena, fox, jackal, Blue boar, hare, Nilgai, Langur and wolf. The sanctuary acts as a buffer between the desert and the forest ecosystems. A number of agricultural, pastoral and tribal communities live in surrounding villages and depend on the resources of the forest for sustenance.

The climb up to Kedarnath takes about 30 minutes and is best to start in the morning to avoid the afternoon heat. Be sure to carry a water bottle and food with you. **Entry** free. Camping is not allowed. *For more information contact the Forest Division Office in Palanpur 02742 257084.* From Palanpur local buses and shared jeeps travel to Balundra and Iqbalgadh. From these villages catch a shared jeep to Jessore (Rs. 6-10).

GETTING INVOLVED

Sarvodaya Kendra *02742 249751, Btw Virampur Mkt and Iqbalgadh* works with tribal communities across 70 villages in areas such as education, women's empowerment and handicraft development. **Contact** Hasmukh Patel.

SAURASHTRA

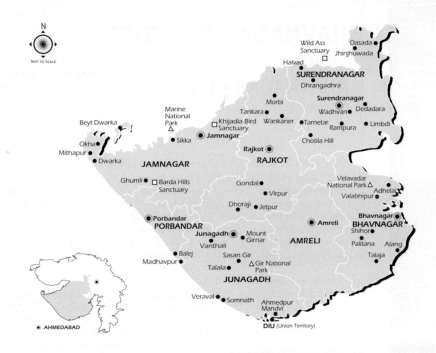

AT A GLANCE

Saurashtra, "land of one hundred kingdoms", was divided among some 220 princely states before becoming a part of Gujarat. It was popularly known as Kathiawad for the Kathi tribe that migrated to Gujarat around the 7th-8th c. AD. The different theories about their geographic roots unanimously point north of Saurashtra. Most places in the peninsula retain a small town feel, local cadences of Gujarati called Kathiawadi, and a tradition of a daily siesta when everything shuts down. The region abounds in religious shrines, wildlife sanctuaries, palaces and relics of royal legacies. From the Asiatic Lions of Gir and the Jain temples of Palitana to ancient ruins scattered in the Barda Hills and the laid-back Portuguese-influenced enclave of Diu, the region offers a wide spectrum of fascinating places to visit.

BHAVNAGAR DISTRICT

BHAVNAGAR CITY
ભાવનગર

POPULATION	517,700
AREA CODE	0278
DISTANCES - AHMEDABAD	200 KM
VADODARA	280 KM
RAJKOT	178 KM

Bhavnagar District, on the southeastern coast of the Saurashtra peninsula, was a princely state under the rule of the Gohil Rajputs in the 13th c. It emerged as one of the most affluent states in the region with a flourishing maritime trade through its busy port at Gogha. As sea trade prospered and ships became larger, navigation in the heavily silted Gulf of Khambhat decreased. This combined with the rise of Bombay and the advent of railways, diminished the fortunes of the port, the state and of eastern Saurashtra. Today the district's main link to its maritime past is Asia's largest ship breaking yard at Alang.

The Gohils, over six centuries, shifted their seat several times. Finally, in 1723 Bhavsinhji established the city of Bhavnagar as his capital. His successor made it a center of economic activity, culture and learning and his grandson Takhatsinhji, who came to power in 1878, set up a modern system of civil and criminal justice, a reformed revenue department, civic amenities and schools. Takhatsinh's son, Bhavsinhji II, commissioned relief efforts during the famine of 1900. His successor, Krishnakumarsinhji, was closely involved in the Independence Movement and was one of the first rulers to accede to the Indian Republic.

PLACES OF INTEREST

Gandhi Smriti

Bhavnagar's association with Gandhiji, who briefly attended Samaldas College in the city in 1888, is celebrated at the Gandhi Smriti. The collection includes photographs depicting Gandhiji's life with captions in Hindi. Gujarati and English translation booklets are available at the office. **Entry** free.

Both the **Khadi Mandir** in Gandhi Smriti and the shop next door sell products associated with Gandhiji's economic and industrial philosophy, such as Khadi, dry foodstuffs and Ahimsa *chappals* (made from the hide of cows only after their natural death). There is also a good library next to the museum.

Ganga Chhatardi

This late 19th-c. memorial honors Takhatsinhji's wife and is one of the finest monuments in the city. The delicate stone grilles inset with the state emblem of Bhavnagar are impressive.

Takhteshwar Temple

Another legacy of Takhatsinhji, this Shiva temple is mainly recommended for its hilltop location, which offers views of the sea and the city, making it one of the most pleasant places in Bhavnagar.

Pill Garden

Near the lake and next to Samaldas College, Pill Garden is a lively spot where groups of retired men gather to play traditional games like *chowpat*. Similar to Ludo, *chowpat is* played on a four arm game board with seven shells used as dice. For each shell that lands with the smooth side up, the player gets two moves; for each of the other shells, he gets one. The objective of the game, played by two to four people at a time, is to be the first to get your four pawns "home", marked in the center of the board.

Bhavnagar Station

This is perhaps the only railway station in India where you will see women porters. The Bhavnagar State Railway was built in the late 19th c. under a royal initiative. The line originally extended to Nilambagh Palace.

Gaurishankar Lake

Located at the north end of the city, it is usually dry except when the rains have been kind. Now often used as a cricket field, it was built by the kings as a source of water supply for the town.

NUTS & BOLTS

In and Out

Jet Airways *2433371, Surat House, Opp Madhav Hill, Waghawadi Rd* has a daily morning flight to Mumbai. A rickshaw to the airport costs about Rs. 80. There is a bus service to/from the airport that stops just behind High Court Road. A direct express train travels from Bhavnagar to Mumbai, with a few halts en route. There is one daily train to and from Mumbai via Ahmedabad (6 hrs). Major places in Saurashtra, and most places within the district, are conveniently reached by ST bus. **Tanna Travels** *2425218, Waghawadi Rd* and **Shrinath Travels** *2427755, Nr Rubber Factory* offer frequent private bus services to Ahmedabad (4 hrs) and Vadodara (7 hrs) and a daily bus to Mumbai (14 hrs).

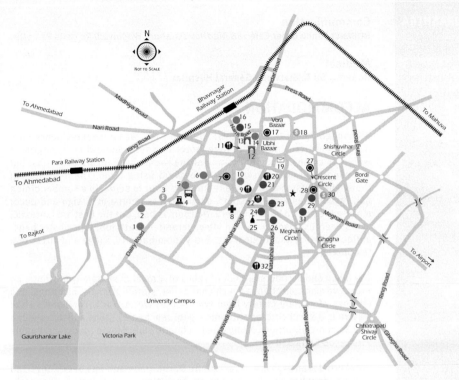

Bhavnagar City

Legend

Accommodation
1. Narayani Heritage Hotel
2. Nilambagh Palace Hotel
5. Hotel Apollo
6. Hotel Sun Shine
10. Bluehill Hotel
14. Hotel Vrindavan

Food & Drink
9. Tulsi
11. Vrindavan
16. Hotel Mini

Places of Interest
7. Pill Garden (Sardar Baug)
12. Ganga Chhatardi
13. Old Darbargadh
25. Takhteshwar Temple
28. Gandhi Smriti
29. Khadi Mandir

Nuts & Bolts
3. State Bank of Saurashtra
4. Forest Office
8. Takhtasinhji Hospital

20. Rasoi
22. Das Aatithiya
32. Bageecha

15. Bike Rentals
17. Market
18. SBI Bank
19. General Post Office
21. Galaxy Cinema
23. Yahoo Cyber Café
24. Tanna Travels
26. Jet Airways
27. Clock Tower
30. HDFC ATM
31. Shrinath Travel Agency

Getting Around

Rickshaws and city buses are the main means of getting around the city. The city bus stand and a taxi stand are situated at Talav Circle. You can also rent bikes off Station Road just near the Mini Hotel.

Money

ATMs **HDFC** *Nr Gandhi Smriti Museum.*
FOREIGN EXCHANGE **SBI Bank** *Nr Darbargadh.*

SAURASHTRA

DISTRICT ▾
BHAVNAGAR ◂
Bhavnagar City
Velavadar
National Park
Palitana
Shihor
Talaja
Alang
Getting Involved

JUNAGADH
PORBANDAR
JAMNAGAR
RAJKOT
SURENDRANAGAR

Communication

INTERNET **Yahoo Cyber Café** *188 Madhav Darshan, Wagawadi Rd* costs Rs 25/hr.

Medical

HOSPITAL **Sir Takhatsinhji General Hospital.**

ACCOMMODATION

Nilambagh Palace Hotel *2424241,* built in 1859, was a royal residence until it was converted into a heritage hotel in 1984. Somewhat incongruous within its colonial grandeur, many of the rooms have luxury bath tubs, but a conservation notice asks guests to avoid using them. The food, decent though not outstanding, can take up to an hour to serve, in a somber dining hall. While rates are consistent, each room is unique in design and décor making the hotel a bit of a lottery. No room is bad, but the best are fantastic, with generous space, a garden view, verandah, bath tub, four-poster beds, antique mirrors, and original art. Every room has a TV, fridge and direct-dial telephone.

The lobby and corridors are full of relics of a royal past—family portraits, an extensive map collection, a Czech chandelier, stuffed animals, paintings, and etchings of military history from Waterloo to World War I. The hotel's chief feature is a small circular swimming pool reached by steps and surrounded by a Roman-style atrium. Alongside is a health club. **Single** 1500-2500 **Double** 2100-3500 **Extra Bed** 500.

Hotel Vrindavan *2519149* is part of the Darbargadh and has been converted into a budget hotel with basic rooms. **Facilities** squat toilets, bucket bath, attached bathrooms available, TV. **Single** 100-150 **Double** 200- 250 **Extra Bed** 50.

Hotel Apollo *2425250, Opp Central Bus Stn* is comfortable and spacious. **Facilities** western toilet, AC options, running hot water, TV, complimentary breakfast. **Single** 500-1000 **Double** 700-1200 **Extra Bed** 300.

Narayani Heritage Hotel *Nxt to Nilambagh* is perfect for those keen to experience the colonial heritage on a shoe-string budget, since it has access to the Nilambagh facilities. **Single** 690-805 **Double** 920-1090 **Extra Bed** 230.

Bluehill Hotel *2426951, Opp Pill Garden, Talav Circle* rivals Nilambagh for comfort, minus the royal frills. **Facilities** western toilet, AC options. **Single** 900-1950 **Double** 1350-2400 **Extra Bed** 200.

Hotel Sunshine *2516131, Panwadi, ST Rd* has well kept rooms and is good value for the money. **Facilities** western toilets, AC, internet, restaurants. **Single** 1100 **Double** 1400-2250 **Extra Bed** 200.

FOOD & DRINK

Das Aatithiya *Kalanala* and **Rasoi** *Opp Collector Office* have great Gujarati *thalis*. **Vrindavan** *Amba Chowk*, **Hotel Mini** and **Restaurant Murli** *In Sunshine Hotel* also serve good *thalis*. **Tulsi** *Kalanala* is a no-frill, good-quality place that serves Gujarati food. **Bageecha** *Waghawadi Rd, Opp Dakshinamurti School* is set in a pleasant garden and provides a welcome change from monolithic AC halls. The food selection is excellent and includes Punjabi, Chinese and Continental.

EXCURSIONS

Velavadar National Park   40 km from Bhavnagar

The Velavadar National Park (34 sq km) was formerly private grassland of the Maharaja of Bhavnagar. It extends to the high tidal zone of the Gulf of Khambhat in the south and floods periodically. The rest of the park is surrounded by wastelands and agriculture fields. Its main species, the Blackbuck, is found mainly at the northern end, in grassland that lies between the Parvalia and Alang rivers, which drain into the Gulf. Conservation of Blackbuck in Velavadar has been a remarkable success story. An exclusively South Asian antelope, it was once abundant in grasslands throughout India, but today its largest

SAURASHTRA

DISTRICT ▼
BHAVNAGAR ◄
Bhavnagar City
Velavadar
National Park
Palitana
Shihor
Talaja
Alang
Getting Involved

JUNAGADH
PORBANDAR
JAMNAGAR
RAJKOT
SURENDRANAGAR

population is found here. The Blackbuck has sharply pointed ringed horns, up to 70 cm long, that spiral through three or four turns. Its movements are visible from long distances and most striking as it jumps over stands of grass. The chances of spotting Blackbuck in the sanctuary are high. Courtship among these animals is quite ferocious. The males fight each other to win females, sometimes leading to the death of the weaker animal. Other species found here are Nilgai, wolf, jackal, Jungle cat and fox.

A small wetland next to the gulf attracts birds such as pelicans, flamingoes, White storks, Painted storks and Sarus cranes. The park is a haven for Demoiselle cranes, Common cranes and a variety of raptors. It provides one of the world's best roosting sites to thousands of harriers that arrive here from Central Europe for wintering. With luck, you may sight the courtship display of the Lesser florican, one of the 50 rarest birds of the world.

Contact the Conservator of Forests 0278 2426425, Bahumali Bhavan, Bhavnagar for permission to stay overnight. To arrange for a meal contact the **Velavadar Rest House** *0278 2880222*. **Rooms Indian** Rs. 500-1000 **Foreigner** 50-75 USD. **Meals** Rs. 70. You can enter the park from Adhelai on the new Bhavnagar-Ahmedabad Highway or near Valabhipur on the old highway. **Closed** from mid-Jun to mid-Oct.

Palitana
55 km from Bhavnagar

Bhavnagar District, which has a significant Jain community, is also home to the Jain temple complexes at Palitana, associated with the first *tirthankar* Adinath, who is believed to have attained enlightenment here. Some of the temples date from the 11th c., but with frequent renovations, hardly anything you see today is older than the 16th c. This is the principal pilgrimage center for Jains, who come in thousands every month. It has accumulated about 900 temples in about the same number of years. New temples continue to be built.

Palitana was a princely state until independence. Its location on Shetrunjaya Hill has protected it from repeated invasions by Muslims and Rajputs alike. Pilgrims and tourists must climb more than 3000 steps to the top, where the nine most important *toonk*s (clusters of shrines) are located. At the base be ready for people aggressively offering to carry you up in a *doli* (a rope chair slung on a pole supported by two porters). They charge about Rs. 800-1000 and zip up to the top in less than an hour and return when you are done. The entire hill is considered sacred. You may not carry or wear any leather goods (footwear, belts) and should be dressed in appropriate clothing.

A few hundred meters short of the entrance to the main *toonk* the path splits. Most people take the left fork, the shorter route, but the right trail goes past the little-visited **Angar Pir**, a citadel with a green flag. This is the tomb of a Muslim saint reputed to have protected the place against invasion by other Muslims. It is now associated with fertility miracles, and many childless couples visit it.

The **Adinath Temple** has an idol more than 2 m tall. Stairs at the sides of the quadrangle lead to a balcony that looks down into the center of the temple.

In order to beat the heat, climb at dawn. This is also when the largest number of devotees congregate in the main *toonk* at the top. Catch rituals like the bathing of idols at about 0930 and the *puja* around 1200. Give yourself at least a couple of hours to explore and carry plenty of water. Start your descent before dusk. No one is allowed to spend the night in the temples. The views are seductive, with sights of surrounding valleys, rivers and temples on the way to the top. **Photography** Rs. 40. Seek permission to shoot inside the shrines.

For in-depth information, visit the **Shri Vishal Jain Museum** at the foot of the hill before you climb. It exhibits ancient palm-leaf manuscripts, excavated idols, history of Jainism and important incidents in the life of Mahavira. Some of the documentation is in English. **Open** 1100-1500 and 1600-1800. **Entry** Rs. 6.

The nearby **Jambudweep Temple** presents the Jain cosmic view. It explains that the earth is not round, that Apollo never went to the moon and that the sun, moon and stars revolve around the earth. The so-called "Jain mathematics" used for arriving at these conclusions can be interesting even to a skeptic. It employs unusual units to measure distance, height, weight and time and explains how the Jain cosmos is divided into seven parts: the earth, three spheres above and three below—respectively corresponding to heaven and hell. A free show on the subject is held at the temple every evening at 1800.

Palitana has more than 120 *dharmashalas* reserved for Jain pilgrims. There are hotels near the bus stand. Food and water is available at the bottom of the hill.

Vijay Vilas Palace *022 24042211, 4 km from Palitana in Adipur,* formerly a country retreat for the king of Palitana, has been converted into a heritage hotel. It has six rooms with great views of the hill. **Single** 1200 **Double** 2400 **Extra Bed** 250.

Many private and ST buses connect Palitana with Bhavnagar and Talaja. Private luxury and ST buses ply between Palitana and various cities in Gujarat, including Ahmedabad. Some even travel all the way from Mumbai. There are also a few fast passenger trains from Bhavnagar that come here. Within and around Palitana, autorickshaws and *chhakadas* are the common mode of transportation.

Shihor   30 km from Bhavnagar

The town's impressive skyline is dominated by a rocky hill. The place is of considerable antiquity and has some prehistoric associations. It was the capital of the Gohils before they shifted to Bhavnagar in the early 18th c. Remains of the old city wall can be seen at the outskirts and near the bus stand.

Apart from relics of the past, Shihor is famous for its *pendas* and its bronze and copper work, which includes an assortment of pots, vessels, religious idols and decorative pieces. The metal market, known as **Pittal Bazaar**, is close to the main market. If interested, the craftsmen will be happy to demonstrate their

SAURASHTRA

DISTRICT ▼
BHAVNAGAR ◄
Bhavnagar City
Velavadar
National Park
Palitana
Shihor
Talaja
Alang
Getting Involved

JUNAGADH
PORBANDAR
JAMNAGAR
RAJKOT
SURENDRANAGAR

processes, right from melting down the metal to the final polishing. **Satsheri** is the hilltop monument erected by the Gohils to repent for the scores of Brahmins they killed in the Battle of 1570. It is said that the weight of the Brahmins' sacred threads alone was the equivalent of 35 kg. The climb is difficult, but it is rewarded with the view of the town from the top.

A visit to the **Shihor Darbargadh,** the royal residence of the Gohil Rajputs between 1570 and 1723, is highly recommended for the colorful Kamangari murals depicting the historic Battle of Chital, preserved in pristine condition on every floor. In natural blues, reds and browns, the paintings portray the attire of the period, the weapons used, and the expressions on the warriors' faces. Though more than 300 years old, the colors are relatively unaffected by the passage of time. The main figure in the paintings is Vakhatsinhji, the then ruler of Bhavnagar. Clan bards and historians documented the events on the battlefield itself, accompanied by a traditional Kamangari painter from Kachchh and impressionists to execute sketches. The priest of the adjoining temple knows quite a bit about the *darbargadh* and may show you around. The visit also provides an opportunity to walk through Shihor's atmospheric old town.

The **Brahmakund,** a half-hour walk out of town, near the Hanuman Temple, is said to have been built by an ancient king who was cured of a skin infection by a bath he took here. The monument, though poorly maintained, is worth a visit for the tiers of steps and landings that descend to the pool at the center. At each tier are niches housing idols of various divinities from the Hindu Pantheon. Some of them are unusual, such as a horse with a parasol and no rider. The arcaded pavilions above the *kund*, which were built more recently, make pleasant places for repose.

Shihor is located on the Bhavnagar-Rajkot Highway with ST buses and shared rickshaws traveling there from the Gangajalia Lake in Bhavnagar (Rs. 12). If you intend to visit more remote locations like Brahmakund, rent a vehicle from Bhavnagar.

Talaja   54 km from Bhavnagar, 32 km from Palitana

A picturesque and serene town, Talaja sits on the Shetrunji River, 10 km inland from the small port of Sartanpur. On the hill alongside the town is a **Jain temple.** Further down the slopes, 30 or so ancient **Buddhist caves** are cut into the rocks. Although these are great for exploring, the climb is difficult. For those interested in Gujarati culture, Talaja is also the birthplace of the medieval saint and poet **Narsinh Mehta,** whose famous hymn *Vaishnav Jana To* is a favorite around Gujarat. His house still stands in the old part of town. Other than sentimental appeal, however, it has nothing that will interest the casual visitor.

Alang
54 km from Bhavnagar, 22 km from Talaja

As an offbeat excursion to get acquainted with the underbelly of liberalization and globalization in a rapidly developing country, a visit to Alang, reputedly Asia's biggest ship breaking yard, can be insightful. The environmentally hazardous business of dismantling condemned ships and salvaging scrap from them for recycling or direct resale was once a highly profitable business, with up to 90 percent of the scrap processed for reuse as high quality steel. In the 80s, developed countries began to squeeze margins by tightening environmental laws, and this industry was one of the first to be off-loaded to the developing world.

In 1982, the Gujarat government introduced some Mumbai-based ship breakers to Alang. A new ship breaking yard with ten plots was built in 1983. Business quickly boomed, generating employment for desperately poor, unskilled and semiskilled workers from all over India, who flocked to this rural backwater. Apart from often exploitative work conditions and occupational health hazards, they were also subjected to subhuman living conditions. Their presence led to major disruption of the local environmental and social fabric, with issues such as pollution, public health and the flesh trade (some of it involving local women) coming to the fore.

By 1988 there were 182 plots, which scrap merchants would take on lease from the Gujarat Maritime Board. Their activities spawned hundreds of re-rolling mills that supplied 12-15 percent of the demand from the building industry. By the end of 2004, Alang had recycled more than 30 million metric tons of ship materials. The industry also gave rise to ancillary activities such as oxygen plants, maintenance and service workshops and scrap shops known as *khadas*. In the 90s it became fashionable to own used furniture, fridges, air-conditioners and even crockery and cutlery stripped off ships at Alang. These are sold at about 450 *khadas* in Alang and Manar, and a score of "Alang Shops" in the big cities of Gujarat.

Since 2003, owing to alarm bells sounded by Greenpeace and other environmental NGOs, and restrictions on the international movement of hazardous wastes by the International Maritime Organization, India has enacted tough environmental laws, to the detriment of the industry at Alang. From a peak of 40,000, the workforce was down to less than 10,000 by the end of 2005. Ironically, the workers have come to resent the whistle-blowers as a threat to their much-needed jobs. While conditions have improved somewhat, the situation illustrates the paradox of positive intervention being shunned due to desperate poverty.

If you want to see the huge infrastructure and the process, you need to know an insider (a ship-breaker from the city). Without prior permission, you will not be entertained, especially as ship-breakers have become wary of journalists. Private buses and shared *chhakadas* travel from Bhavnagar and Talaja to Alang.

GETTING INVOLVED

Parsanben Narandas Ramji (PNR) Society *0278 2420836, 51 Vidyanagar, Bhavnagar, www.pnrsociety.org* has a highly specialized team committed to serving the needs of children affected by cerebral palsy and other disabilities to help them become self-reliant. On average they treat 1500 people every day at their various centers. **Contact** Anant Shah.

SAURASHTRA

DISTRICT ▾
BHAVNAGAR

JUNAGADH ◂
Junagadh City
Gir National
Park
Kankai
Vanthali
Kutiyana
Talala
Veraval
Somnath
Ahmedpur
Mandvi
Diu

PORBANDAR
JAMNAGAR
RAJKOT
SURENDRANAGAR

JUNAGADH DISTRICT

JUNAGADH CITY

જૂનાગઢ

POPULATION	252,100
AREA CODE	0285
DISTANCES - AHMEDABAD	327 KM
VADODARA	396 KM
RAJKOT	102 KM

Steeped in history, culture, spirituality and religion, Junagadh is the soul of Saurashtra. In just 60 km the terrain descends from Mt Girnar, Gujarat's highest point at 1000 m, to the Veraval coast. The Gir National Park and Wildlife Sanctuary is the only remaining habitat of the pure Asiatic Lion. The countryside has much to offer but calls for a determined effort to explore. At the very least, a concentration of places in Veraval-Patan and Junagadh City are a must on the itinerary of the traveler in Saurashtra.

Junagadh, nestled at the foot of Mt Girnar, is an amazing amalgam of the old and new. It is a relatively small place, where bustling bazaars and winding narrow streets alternate with monuments that span two millennia and civic spaces that must have been gracious before they suffered crowding and encroachment. The people are generally friendly and hospitable. From here pilgrims to Mt Girnar and visitors to the Gir Lion Sanctuary set out on their journeys. In the city, most tourist attractions are within a radius of 5 km. Some of the monuments are not well-maintained, but are nonetheless fascinating.

In popular lore, Junagadh and the sacred precincts of Mt Girnar pre-date history. Some incidents in Krishna's life are associated with the mountain. In early history the city was important as a regional capital under successive dynasties centered in North India from 4th c. BC to 5th c. AD. Afterwards its importance declined as Saurashtra came under the control of Rajput dynasties that moved the capital to Valabhi (near Bhavnagar). Under the Solankis (10th-13th c.) the center of power moved to Patan in north Gujarat. By the end of the 13th c. authority had again shifted northward, and Saurashtra, together with Gujarat, became a province under governors appointed from Delhi who ruled from Patan. For the next two centuries Gujarat was an independent Sultanate ruled mainly from Ahmedabad until the Mughals took over, once again reducing it to a province. In the mid-18th c. when Mughal power weakened, an Afghan soldier of fortune named Sher Khan Babi established Junagadh State, which his successors ruled until India's independence.

Archaeological and historical records bear evidence that the elevated northeastern quarter, called Uparkot, has been continuously settled since around the 3rd c. BC. Today, the old town is a reflection of Babi rule.

PLACES OF INTEREST

Uparkot

The oldest part of the city, Uparkot, which means "upper fort", can be covered on foot. The local guides narrate many stories about the citadel, all very fascinating though not always plausible. If history, archaeology or architecture interest you, this place is bound to turn you on. **Open** 0700-1900, daily. **Entry** Rs. 2. **Vehicle Entry** Rs. 10.

At the entrance to Uparkot is the insignia of a former ruling dynasty, followed by temples of Ganesh, Hanuman and Shakti. The first major attraction is a pair of cannons, named **Neelam and Manek**. They were cast in Cairo and brought by the Turkish flotilla that came in 1538 to the aid of Sultan Bahadur Shah against the Portuguese in Diu. The Gujarat forces were defeated, and the Turks retreated leaving the guns behind. It is unclear when and why they were brought from Diu to Uparkot. The larger gun has an Arabic inscription stating that it was cast in AH 937 (around 1530 AD).

A third cannon known as **Kadanal** is placed on a bastion in the wall in another part of Uparkot. The name of Ali bin Sarja, possibly the gunsmith who cast it, is inscribed in elegant Arabic script.

The 15th c. **Jama Masjid** resembles a fort due to the merlons, crenels and loopholes along the roofline. It is interesting for its covered courtyard, a feature uncommon in Indian mosque architecture. The roof has three octagonal openings, probably crowned by domes raised on pillars at one time. The entry is one floor lower than the main areas of worship. Some scholars suggest that the building was originally a palace, later converted into a mosque.

Buddhist Caves, about 2000 years old, are among the oldest monuments at Uparkot. They are carved out of monolithic rock formations, and although in no way comparable to the marvels at Ajanta and Ellora (in neighboring Maharashtra), they are interesting examples of architectural response to monastic life. The caves are adorned with decorated pillars and entrances, water cisterns, horseshoe shaped *chaitya* windows, an assembly hall and cells for meditation. **ENTRY Indian** Rs. 5, **Foreigner** Rs. 100.

The simple **Adi Kadi Vav** differs from other well known stepwells of Gujarat. It was not built, but carved out of virgin rock. The rock strata along the side walls are amazing. Legend narrates that when Uparkot was built, the king decided to make a stepwell, but while digging through the hard stones, no water source could be found. The royal priest informed the king that water would flow only if two unmarried women were sacrificed. The sisters Adi and Kadi were chosen and the prophecy was fulfilled. Even today colorful cloth and bangles are hung on a tree at the *vav* in memory of the girls.

Navghan Kuvo, partly hewn in rock and partly built, is named after Rao Navghan (11th c.), and was built during his reign. A small arched doorway leads down a flight of steps into a magnificent forecourt. At the far end is the actual well, with steps winding around a square light shaft. In ancient times it provided enough water to withstand long sieges.

The last important destination in the fort is the reservoir built by Mahabat Khan Babi. Even today this **artificial lake** supplies water to the city. Interested travelers can also take a walk on the **Uparkot ramparts,** which offer vistas across the city, views of the higher reaches of Girnar, the Kadanal gun, and places such as the **Dhakkabari**, from where criminals sentenced to death were given the final push.

Ashokan Rock Edicts

Ashoka's Edicts, located on the way to **Girnar Taleti** (the mountain base) date from the 3rd c. BC when Emperor Ashoka had adopted Buddhism. There are fourteen edicts inscribed in the Pali language about the sixteen attributes of a virtuous life and about the construction of Sudarshan Lake for the welfare of society. A later ruler, Rudradaman, added Sanskrit edicts about the canals bordering the lake. The location of the lake itself is an archaeological mystery. There is also an edict by Skandagupta from the 5th c. AD. **Open** 0800-1800, daily. **ENTRY Indian** Rs. 5, **Foreigner** Rs. 100.

Mount Girnar

The highest point of elevation in Gujarat, this mountain was a former volcano. It has 866 Hindu and Jain temples and hermitages scattered on the five peaks, named Amba Mata, Gorakhnath, Oghad Shikhar, Dattatreya Shikhar and Kalka. A stone-paved path connects them. There are 9,999 steps from the Taleti to the last temple on the highest peak. On a clear winter day, just before sunset, the western horizon transforms into a glow of spectacular orange light reflected from the sea. Also, every year thousands participate in the **Lili Parikrama**, a spiritual trek around the mountain (see **Fairs and Festivals**).

The steps start at **Damodar Kund,** where the **Damodar** and **Baldevji temples** stand. Narsinh Mehta used to come here daily for his bath. It is where he composed most of his famous *prabhatiya* or morning hymns. Further up is the famous **Bhavnath Temple** dedicated to Shiva. During the Shivaratri festival a large number of *naga bawas* (nude sadhus) come here to bathe in the **Mrugi Kund** (see **Fairs and Festivals**).

The first hill along the way hosts a group of sixteen Jain temples, which form a temple city adorned with courtyards, walkways and shrines. The **Neminath** and **Mallinath** temples were built by Vastupal and Tejpal, the architects known for the famous Jain temples of Mt Abu and Palitana.

The final 2000 steps to the summit, though rigorous, are worth the effort for the breathtaking views at the top. The total climb takes five to eight hours,

SAURASHTRA

DISTRICT ▼
BHAVNAGAR

JUNAGADH ◄
Junagadh City
Gir National
Park
Kankai
Vanthali
Kutiyana
Talala
Veraval
Somnath
Ahmedpur
Mandvi
Diu

PORBANDAR
JAMNAGAR
RAJKOT
SURENDRANAGAR

and other than some Jain *dharmashalas* there are no resting places for long stretches. Although *chai* and *bhajiya* are available along the route, carry adequate food and water. There are masseurs at the Taleti who will rub your feet with oil to refresh you.

The **Amba Mata Temple** at the top attracts both Hindu and Jain pilgrims, particularly newlyweds seeking the blessings of the Mother Goddess for a happy marriage. Steps lead down from this temple and then up again along a narrow ridge towards **Gorakhnath Peak**. At the furthest point of the ridge is a shrine dedicated to the fierce Hindu Goddess Kali. This is a haunt for near-naked Aghora ascetics who express their absolute renunciation from the world by ritually enacting their own funerals, living among corpses on burial grounds, and smearing themselves with ash from funeral pyres. Just beyond this last point is a temple where you can have a quick and satisfying meal.

Willingdon Dam and Datar Hill
On top of the adjoining Datar Hill is a shrine dedicated to **Saint Jamial Sha Datar** that is revered by Muslims and Hindus alike. His blessings are invoked for curing leprosy. The climb is around 2500 steps. This is also the route to **Willingdon Dam**, which is a water source for the city and a popular excursion for locals. There are lots of monkeys here, generally harmless, but do not offer them food or they will mob you.

THE OLD CITY

Narsinh Mehta no Choro
This is where the renowned medieval Gujarati poet and saint, Narsinh Mehta, is believed to have sung his *bhajans*. Nearby is the small **Madhavraiji Temple**, marking the spot where his house probably stood. He was born in Talaja near Bhavnagar, but spent most of his active life in Junagadh.

Tombs of the Babi Kings
About a dozen mausoleums belonging to the Babi Dynasty are enclosed in one area. These include the founder of the dynasty, Sher Salabat Khan, who took advantage of the weakening hold of the Mughals and proclaimed Junagadh an independent state in 1748. He ruled it until his death ten years later. His successor Mahabat Khan I (1758-75) and the wife of a later Nawab, Bahadur Khan I are also buried here. Although weeds cover the area and the monuments are poorly maintained, the tombs are worth visiting. Some of the stone grille work is among the best you will see in Junagadh.

Mahabat Maqbara
Probably the best preserved monument from the Babi period, the *maqbara* is built over the grave of Nawab Mahabat Khan II (1851-82). Its architecture is an interesting mix of Moorish, Hindu and European influences (pronounced in the French windows and the Gothic columns), which are common in late-19th

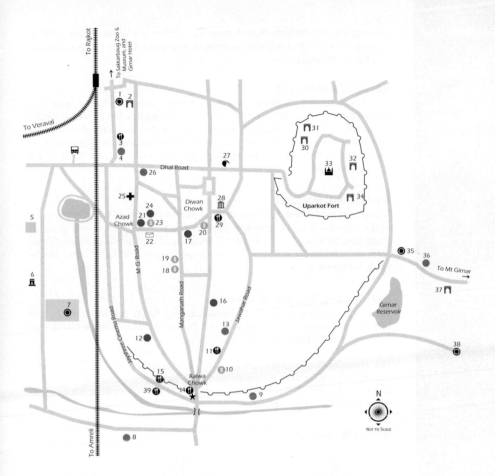

Junagadh City
Legend

Accommodation
4   Hotel Somnath
8   Circuit House
9   Hotel National
13 Hotel Paramount
26 Relief Hotel
36 Leo Resorts

Food & Drink
3   Geeta Lodge
11 Raj Restaurant
14 Modern
15 Swati
17 Sagar Restaurant
29 Jai Ambe Juice

Places of Interest
1   Narsinh Mehta no Choro
2   Mahabat Maqbara
7   Coconut Plantation
28 Darbar Hall Museum
30 Adi Kadi Vav
31 Buddhist Caves
32 Navghan Kuvo
33 Jama Masjid
34 Mahabat Khan Reservoir
35 Kesar Mango Orchard
37 Ashokan Edicts
38 Datar Mountain & Willingdon Dam

Nuts & Bolts
5   Sardarbaug
6   Forest Department
10 SBI Bank
12 Sify Iway Cybercafé

39 Reliance World
18 UCO Bank
19 Bank Of Baroda
20 SBI ATM
21 City Bus Stand
22 General Post Office
23 Bank of Baroda ATM
24 Junagadh Library
25 Civil Hospital
27 Vegetable Market

c. Junagadh architecture. The minarets have external stairways that spiral in opposite directions to maintain symmetry. Alongside stands the **Jama Masjid** and **Vazir's Maqbara.**

Najubibi's Maqbara

This mausoleum of Mahabat Khan II's mother has five domes with four entrances and is decorated with floral images. Alongside are graves of twelve noblemen from five centuries earlier, referred to as the **Bara Saiyad** (probably a corruption of *shaheed*, meaning "martyr"). During the invasion of Junagadh by Zafar, Governor of Gujarat under the Tughlaqs, the local ruler took these twelve warriors hostage and killed them.

Darbar Hall Museum

Also known as **Kacheri Hall,** this was the court of the Nawabs. It is in the heart of the city near Diwan Chowk and consists of a palanquin room and galleries displaying pictures, textiles and arms. **Open** 0900-1215 and 1445-1800. **Closed** Wed, the 2nd and 4th Sat of the month and public holidays. **ENTRY Indian** Rs. 2, **Foreigner** Rs. 50.

Sakkarbaug Zoo and Museum

The oldest zoo in Gujarat, Sakkarbaug is known for its captive breeding and conservation program for the Asiatic Lion. **Open** 0900-1830. **Closed** Wed. **ENTRY Indian** Rs. 10, **Foreigner** Rs. 50.

The **museum** has a collection of silver art, archaeology, furniture, coins, inscriptions, sculptures, carpets, paintings, porcelain, woodcraft, costumes and stuffed animals. It also has a library facility for researchers. **Open** 0900-1800. **Entry** Rs. 5. **Photography** Rs. 2.

NUTS & BOLTS

In and Out

Junagadh is well connected by ST and private buses to other cities of Gujarat, mainly via Veraval and Rajkot. The best way to get here is by road. By train, Junagadh is a halt on the Rajkot-Veraval section of the Western Railway. Rajkot is 2.5 hours and Veraval is just under 2 hours by slow train. Two daily express trains between Ahmedabad and Veraval also stop here, one overnight (arrives from Ahmedabad at the inconvenient hour of 0430 and from Veraval at 2145), and one during the day. The journey from Ahmedabad takes 7.5 hours. Many private bus companies operate services from Junagadh to cities all over Gujarat and neighboring states. **Mahasagar Travels** *2624313 Jayshree Talkies Rd, Kalwa Chowk* travels to most places and also arranges taxis.

Getting Around

In the city area, unmetered rickshaws are the principal means of transport and cost about Rs. 15-30 depending on distance. The average fare for shuttles is

Rs. 5-20, but rates are higher to go to the Taleti or the forest area. Junagadh has a city bus service, but may not be convenient for new visitors. You can rent a bicycle or motorbike from Chittakhana Chowk or from Hotel Relief. This is a good way to move around the city if you are comfortable with the traffic.

Money
ATMs Most of the banks and ATMs are in Kalwa Chowk, on Mahatma Gandhi Road and in the Jayshree Cinema area.
FOREIGN EXCHANGE SBI Bank *Diwan Chowk*; **Bank of Baroda** *Station Rd.*
MONEY TRANSFER **Western Union** at **Bank of Baroda** and **UCO Bank** *Azad Chowk, MG Rd.*

Communication
INTERNET **Reliance World** *Jayshree Cinema Rd*; **Sify Iway** *Puneet Shopping Centre, MG Rd*; **Online Cyber Cafe** *Jayshree Cinema Rd.*

Medical
HOSPITALS **Hatkesh Hospital** *2653652, Opp Bhutnath Temple.*
MEDICAL STORES **Shree Medical,** *ST Rd*; **Ashirwad Medical Stores,** *Zanzarda Rd*; and **Universal Medical,** *MG Rd.*

Photography
Boss Digital Color Lab *Vanthali Rd*, **Sky Color Lab** *Vanthali Rd,* and **Rajkamal Studios** *MG Rd, Nr Kalwa Chowk* are all good for film processing.

ACCOMMODATION

Girnar Hotel *2621201, Nr Majevadi Gate* is a Gujarat Tourism property. Ordinary rooms have bucket baths and squat toilets while deluxe rooms offer running water. Dorm rooms are for drivers only. Food can be prepared if told in advance. **Facilities** AC options. **Double** 150-650.

Relief Hotel *2620280 Chitta Khana Chowk* is popular with tourists and is the place to find Mr Sorathia, who is a wealth of local information. Book a few days in advance. **Facilities** western toilets, bicycle and motorbike rentals, restaurant. **Single** 200 **Double** 400 **Quadruple** 600.

Hotel Paramount *2623983 Kalwa Chowk, Nr Indian Oil Petrol Pump* is in a shopping complex on a noisy main road. It is a good option for single occupants. Rooms are easily available off-season. **Facilities** western toilet, AC options. **Single** 300-800 **Double** 400-1050 **Extra Bed** 75-150.

Leo Resorts *2652844 Taleti Rd, Nr Ashokan Edicts* is a lavish new resort with a refreshing ambience, located at the base of Mt Girnar. **Facilities** AC rooms, swimming pool, gym, laundry, lockers, health spa. **Single** 2010 **Double** 2150 **Extra Bed** 250.

SAURASHTRA

▼ DISTRICT
BHAVNAGAR

▶ JUNAGADH
Junagadh City
Gir National Park
Kankai
Vanthali
Kutiyana
Talala
Veraval
Somnath
Ahmedpur Mandvi
Diu

PORBANDAR
JAMNAGAR
RAJKOT
SURENDRANAGAR

FOOD & DRINK

DISTRICT ▾
BHAVNAGAR

JUNAGADH ◄
Junagadh City
Gir National
Park
Kankai
Vanthali
Kutiyana
Talala
Veraval
Somnath
Ahmedpur
Mandvi
Diu

PORBANDAR
JAMNAGAR
RAJKOT
SURENDRANAGAR

Junagadh is a great place for Kathiawadi cuisine, which is served in addition to the standard Gujarati thali at many of its restaurants.

Sagar Restaurant *Jayshree Cinema Rd, Nr Kalwa Chowk* is a new, dimly lit AC place that serves delicious, but somewhat overpriced, Punjabi and Continental food. It specializes in *paneer* items and sizzlers. **Geeta Lodge** *Stn Rd, Opp Forest Office* is one of the best *thali* places in town with fixed Gujarati *thalis* at Rs. 50. Sweets are extra; the mango pulp and *shrikhand* are recommended. **Raj Dining Hall** *Kalwa Chowk, Nr Statue* also serves Gujarati *thali* for Rs. 40. **Swati Restaurant** *Jayshree Cinema Rd, Nr Kalwa Chowk* serves tasty South Indian dishes.

LOCAL SPECIALTIES **Modern Lassi and Patties House** *MG Rd, Kalwa Chowk* is popular for its thick *lassis* and potato patties, which are stuffed with filling and lightly fried. **Jai Ambe Juice Centre** *Diwan Chowk, Nr Kacheri* is centrally located and serves excellent fresh juices.

EXCURSIONS

Junagadh District is strewn with interesting sites. It makes sense to rent a vehicle to visit some of the places located deep in the interior that have limited or non-existent bus connections. Chhakadas and shared jeeps generally charge Rs. 5-25 depending on the distance, but they can be crowded and uncomfortable for longer journeys.

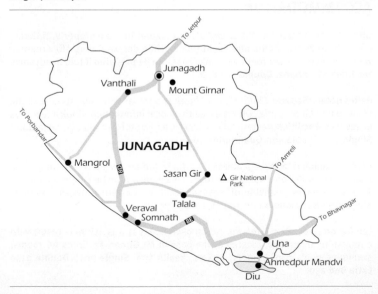

Gir National Park

65 km from Junagadh, 40 km from Veraval

The Asiatic Lion is the major attraction for most visitors to Junagadh, and the Gir Forest is its abode. As a result of excessive hunting, poaching and forest depletion, the lion population was on a dramatic decline before 1965, when the government set up the sanctuary across 1153 sq km to protect it. A decade later 258 sq km inside the sanctuary was declared a national park. Currently the lion population is at about 359.

The Maldhari Community

About a century ago, the nomadic Maldhari community moved into Gir to provide pastures for its livestock to graze on. They sell milk and its byproducts to sustain their livelihood. Although the Maldharis live in harmony with the king of the jungle, they are aware of the dangers they face by settling in the lion territory. They choose to do so for lack of a better alternative. Approximately 25 percent of the lions' food comes in the form of livestock. Even though the government offers compensation for these losses, many Maldharis do not accept the money because they are grateful to the lion for sharing its forest and consider the loss an offering of *prasad* in this exchange. On the flip side, the Maldharis also pose a concern to the sanctuary by slowly depleting its resources to both sustain themselves and supplement their income, leading to a deficiency in the ecosystem that could threaten the habitat of the lions. The challenge lies in finding a balance between Gir's trichotomy—the lions, the Maldharis and their livestock.

Sasan Gir is the entry point to the sanctuary. The forest has extremely rugged and hilly terrain, which is of volcanic origin. It is considered the largest dry-deciduous forest in western India. In addition to the lion there is the Jungle cat, hyena, jackal and some 500 leopards. With luck it is possible to sight jackals and leopards in their natural habitat. There are also Nilgai, Spotted deer, Sambar, Blackbuck, porcupine, hare and the rarely seen Pangolin. The forest has about 300 species of birds including King vulture, Crested serpent eagle, Great horned owl, Bush quail, woodpecker and hornbill. The area around the Hiran River is great for birdwatching.

Although a knowledgeable guide may help, the chances of spotting many of the wildlife species, especially the lion, are low. To orientate the floods of visitors, the forest department has set up a special **Gir Interpretation Zone (GIZ)** at Devalia, 12km west of Sasan Gir. To ensure that your trip does not go entirely in vain, four to five lions are always kept on a sizeable precinct. It is not exactly the same as the real forest. **Entry** Indian Rs. 75 (Mon-Fri), Rs. 95 (Sat-Sun), Rs. 115 (Holiday); **Foreigner** 20 USD. **Open** 0800-1100 and 1500-1700. **Closed** Wed.

You can obtain your permit for entry into the sanctuary at the **Sinh Sadan Orientation Centre,** where they also screen a slightly outdated film on lions every night at 1900. A 35-40 km route (2.5-3 hrs) has been designated for visitors to follow. Gir is accessible from mid-Oct to mid-Jun. **Open** 0700-1100 and 1500-1730. The timings change according to sunrise and sunset. **Entry Private Vehicle** (for up to 6 people): **Indian** Rs. 400 (Mon-Fri), 500 (Sat-Sun),

SAURASHTRA

DISTRICT ▼
BHAVNAGAR

JUNAGADH ◄
Junagadh City
Gir National
Park
Kankai
Vanthali
Kutiyana
Talala
Veraval
Somnath
Ahmedpur
Mandvi
Diu

PORBANDAR
JAMNAGAR
RAJKOT
SURENDRANAGAR

600 (Holiday Season), **Additional Person** Rs. 50; **Foreigner** 40 USD. **Guide** Rs. 50. Although prices are quoted in dollars, you must pay in rupees. *For more information contact the Forest Department in Sasan Gir at 02877 285541.*

Gir also hosts the largest population of marsh crocodiles in India. A crocodile rearing center is just near the entrance of the Sinh Sadan complex where eggs of the reptiles are collected and then sent to Junagadh for hatching under supervision. Although everything is written in Gujarati, it is a fascinating process to observe. **Open** 0800-1200 and 1500-1800. **Entry** free.

ACCOMMODATION

These prices vary in the tourist season.

Government Guest House *Opp Sasan Railway Stn* has a museum and shows a film on the sanctuary. It provides lunch for Rs. 70. **Rooms** 500-1500 (30-50 USD).

Amidhara Resort *02877 285950, Sasan-Gir* provides a good range of amenities for those interested in staying near the sanctuary. **Facilities** AC options, restaurant with vegetarian and non-veg dishes, indoor and outdoor game facilities, swimming pool. **Rooms** 3000-5000.

Maneland Jungle Lodge *02877 285555, Gir National Park and Sanctuary, Junagadh Hwy* is located on a small hillock. It is built with local materials and technology, aiming to create an ambience similar to the natural surroundings. **Facilities** restaurant serving vegetarian and non-veg, courtesy transfer to/from Keshod, Rajkot and Junagadh, vehicles for sanctuary with drivers and guides, provide information about flora and fauna of the jungle, swimming pool, library. **Rooms** (incl all meals and taxes) 3500/person.

Kankai   50 km from Sasan Gir
A shrine dedicated to **Kankai Mata**, the benefactor of the shepherds of Gir, is based in the heart of the jungle. It is a great place to experience the wild. You can hear the roar of lions and calls of other animals that come at night to drink water at the neighboring lake. The lofty temple walls and sound doors ensure safety. Most of the light and heat requirements are met by solar energy. They also use biogas. As an experiment in off-the-grid, self-sufficient, environment-friendly living it is worth checking out. The single daily bus leaves Junagadh at 0800, arrives at Kankai around 0945 and returns to Junagadh after an hour's halt—adequate for a rushed visit. But to really enjoy the place, a private vehicle or an overnight stay is recommended. The temple gates close by 1930. Then it is just you and the jungle around.

Vanthali   30 km from Junagadh
This town is close to a 14th c. stepwell called **Ra' Khengar Vav,** which has some unusual features. Along the sides of the first landing are walkways that lead past balconies, which project over the steps, to a passage that goes around the main well shaft. A tiled building, probably an addition from the Babi period, sits on top and

despite its different architectural style, it has merged fluidly with the original *vav*. The little town of Vanthali also has a number of vintage 1945 Ford Super Deluxes that have been converted into shared taxis to shuttle people between neighbouring villages. According to the locals, these cars were previously owned by the former Nawab of Junagadh and his officials. When they fled for Pakistan, many of them sold or gifted the vehicles to loyal friends and supporters. They were eventually sold for nice sums to local garages and businessmen, who converted the cars into 15-passenger taxis. It is not uncommon to see the occasional vintage-car taxi in other parts of Saurashtra and southern Gujarat, areas formerly dominated by princely states. There are frequent ST buses to Vanthali.

Kutiyana
68 km from Junagadh

A large number of Muslim pilgrims flock to this town during the **Pir Miskinsha Urs**, held from the 13th through 15th day in the Muslim month of Sabaan. On this occasion lamps are burnt, not with oil, but with water from the local stepwell. People believe that the blessings of the Pir enable this miracle.

Talala
75 km from Junagadh, 25 km from Veraval

Talala and surrounding areas are famous for their **Kesar mangos**, one of the few Indian varieties known around the world. If horticulture interests you, it is worth visiting a *wadi* (orchard) before the harvesting season at the beginning of summer.

Close to Talala is the large, ancient **Bhimdeval Sun Temple**. The scale and spaciousness of the *mandap* are cathedral-like. Two interesting images flank the entrance to the sanctum. A small shrine in the spire is reached by a stairway added to the outside of the temple.

The Siddi Community

Originally from Abyssinia (present-day Ethiopia) in East Africa, the Siddis came to India in several waves during the second millennium AD as slaves, sailors, mercenaries and merchants. They settled in pockets of the west coast, mainly in Gujarat and Maharashtra, and over time merged into the ethnic mosaic of India while retaining some of their cultural distinctiveness.

In many places they rose to high military and administrative positions. Some even established their own kingdoms, such as Jaffrabad in Saurashtra. In Junagadh City a small group of Siddis live around the shrine of Bava Gor, a Sufi saint of the same descent. There is also a community settled in the Ratanpor area in Bharuch District.

The Siddis of Jambur and Jamvala, towns based in Gir, belong to the more deprived segments of this community. Largely poor and relegated to the status of a "tribe", they no longer remember their original African languages and lack the knowledge of where their ancestors came from or why they settled in India. Siddi culture and traditions are strikingly different from those of other tribes nearby or anywhere else in India. They have retained their music and dance heritage and perform a kind of music called Goma, which has African origins. The Siddis also use a string instrument known as the *gangal*, an open ended cylindrical base attached to a piece of wood to which they tie strings made of dried goat intestines. The instrument accompanies rituals and is used during Dhamaal, a dance form that migrated with them from Africa.

SAURASHTRA

DISTRICT ▼
BHAVNAGAR

JUNAGADH ◄
Junagadh City
Gir National
Park
Kankai
Vanthali
Kutiyana
Talala
Veraval
Somnath
Ahmedpur
Mandvi
Diu

PORBANDAR
JAMNAGAR
RAJKOT
SURENDRANAGAR

Veraval

94 km from Junagadh, 100 km from Diu

Veraval is a major fishing port with the smell of fish hanging heavily over the town. Along the coastline, dhows and fishing boats are still built and repaired by traditional methods. Before the rise of Surat, a major portion of the pilgrim traffic to Mecca passed through this port. Veraval is conveniently close to the famous Somnath Temple, the historical town of Prabhas Patan, and other nearby pilgrimage centers. It is also a great place for seafood aficionados. It is easily accessible by road from all over Saurashtra and by railway from Ahmedabad via Surendranagar, Rajkot and Junagadh.

On the way from Veraval to Somnath, you will pass the Maipuri Mosque, next to which is a *dargah*. The blue and white tiles that cover its exterior can be decieving, but inside, over the Pir's grave, is an outstanding domed ceiling. It is 6 m in diameter, exquisitely embellished and probably taken from an early 12th c. monument. A relatively recent artificial ceiling eclipses it, but there is a trapdoor, a ladder and an electric lamp to aid you in viewing this architectural delight.

Somnath (Prabhas Patan)

6 km from Veraval

Apart from Gir, this famous temple by the sea is another major center for tourists and pilgrims. It is one of India's twelve *jyotirlingas* (spontaneously formed *Shivalingas)*. In 1026 Somnath's prosperity drew Mahmud of Ghazni, on the last of his 17 expeditions to India. He ransacked the town, plundered and destroyed the temple and carried away camel loads of gold and precious stones. However, this was just one of the half a dozen times that the temple was destroyed through its history, dating from the pre-Christian era. Each time it was rebuilt.

The present temple, built in 1947-95, is the seventh reconstruction on the original site. It is illuminated every evening and the **sound and light show,** *Jay Somnath*, is presented every night from 2000 to 2100 with the temple as the backdrop. The sea at Somnath is often rough and not safe for swimming.

Veraval Gate, with its archway, is part of the old fort wall of Prabhas Patan and dates from the 11th-12th c. The outer face has a *jharokha* and images of dueling elephants. The pillars are adorned with *kichakas* and the niches with a lotus-and-chain motif.

A little-known architectural gem worth searching for is a **Jain temple** from the 13th c. Though poorly maintained, it has very unusual features. Inside the sanctum is a *toran*, which is normally found outdoors to represent the transition from a temple to a *kund* or another distinct precinct. It has a high ceiling and arches at the upper level to let in light through stone grilles—the only source of light for the interior. Lost among nondescript houses that obscure it from view, the temple is no longer in use. Even after you ask for directions from several people, you may still end up at another, better-known Jain temple that has been converted into a museum.

Another pleasant surprise is the 14th c. **Sun Temple** situated next to the Sitala Mata Temple. It is a little difficult to locate. Follow the imposing entrance porch across an elaborate threshold to reach the outer wall of the sanctum, which has alcoves installed with images of the Sun God and his attendants.

Ahmedpur Mandvi
147 km from Junagadh, 98 km from Veraval

The Ahmedpur Mandvi Beach is one of Gujarat's best coastal stretches. It faces the island of Diu across a creek and, with its continuation as Ghogla Beach into the adjoining part of mainland Diu, it measures about 6 km long. The beach is excellent for swimming and water sports and is dotted with several vibrant fishing hamlets.

If you want direct access to the beach from your hotel, the best accommodation, even compared to options in Diu, is **Magico do Mar Beach Resort**. It has hammocks slung between shady trees and cottages that offer a view of the beach and the sea beyond, with the picturesque fort completing the frame. Part of the resort includes a three-storied building called Haveli, that is located closer to the beach and has spacious though sparsely furnished, sea-facing rooms. The views are best from the top floor or the east wing of the second floor; avoid the ground floor. Rates vary by season and the length of your stay. **Double** (incl breakfast and dinner) 2800 to 7500.

For alcohol, walk across to the Suzlon Resort next door in Diu territory, where drinking is legal. If you expect to take a lot of excursions to Diu (3 km by road), check out bus timings or be prepared to travel by *chhakada*. Rickshaws are few and far between.

DIU

DIU TOWN દીવ		
POPULATION	44,100
AREA CODE	02875
DISTANCES - AHMEDABAD	495 KM
VADODARA	595 KM
VERAVAL	90 KM

Diu, with its pleasant beaches and generally few tourist crowds, offers a great change of pace from Gujarat and Goa. Made up of five villages and a town, the territory is dominantly occupied by fishing communities. The creek on the north side of the island has salt pans and marshes that attract large flocks of birds, while the south coast, facing the open sea, has limestone cliffs and palm-fringed sandy and rocky beaches.

The island's documented history begins with the Parsis who landed here briefly in the 12th c. before moving east to southern Gujarat. After passing through a number of rulers, Diu came into the hands of the Ottoman Turks between the 14th and 16th c., during which time it flourished as a prosperous

SAURASHTRA

▼ DISTRICT
BHAVNAGAR

▶ JUNAGADH
Junagadh City
Gir National Park
Kankai
Vanthali
Kutiyana
Talala
Veraval
Somnath
Ahmedpur Mandvi
Diu

PORBANDAR
JAMNAGAR
RAJKOT
SURENDRANAGAR

trading port and ship building center. The Portuguese failed at a number of attempts to conquer Diu. Finally Nuno da Cunha convinced Sultan Bahadur Shah of Gujarat to sign a peace treaty, while actually conspiring and eventually succeeding to assassinate him and take over Diu. It became a Portuguese enclave administered from Goa. Then in 1961, the Indian army took over the Portuguese-occupied pockets of India, and created the Union Territory of Goa, Daman and Diu. Later, Goa became a state, and Daman and Diu were jointly made into a Union Territory administered from Delhi.

Although Roman Catholicism and the Portuguese language are both on the decline, the Portuguese influence survives in the buildings, churches and the narrow winding streets that converge at piazzas. Its carefree people and colorful fishing villages give Diu a unique flavor. However, it can get a bit noisy on weekends and holidays when boisterous groups (largely male) from the surrounding areas of "dry" Gujarat flock here to legally enjoy alcohol. Nonetheless, this laid-back island is the perfect place to enjoy chilled beer, clean beaches and a peaceful ambience.

SAURASHTRA

▼ DISTRICT
BHAVNAGAR

▸ JUNAGADH
Junagadh City
Gir National
Park
Kankai
Vanthali
Kutiyana
Talala
Veraval
Somnath
Ahmedpur
Mandvi
Diu

PORBANDAR
JAMNAGAR
RAJKOT
SURENDRANAGAR

PLACES OF INTEREST

Diu Fort

The town's central landmark is the Diu Fort built by the Portuguese during the late 1530s. It is perched on cliffs that break the waters at the southeastern coast and commands a seductive view of the sea. The **Panikota Forte do Mar**, which stands unperturbed in the middle of the sea, is also visible. This sentinel, skirted by the sea on three sides and by a moat on the fourth, encloses an area of about 56,700 sq m. Cannons and cannon balls litter the place. A functional jail, chapel ruins and the Cavalier lighthouse, once the highest point in Diu, exist within the fort walls. In winter, a veil of fog cloaks the island and creates a mysterious ambience. **Open** 0700-1800. **Entry** free.

Diu Museum

The **St Thomas Church** has been converted into a museum, which contains antique statues, various stone inscriptions of the earlier rulers, wooden carvings, Hindu idols and relics of Jain temples. **Open** 0800-2200, daily.

St Paul's Church

This early-17th c. church decorated with shell-like motifs is dedicated to Our Lady of Immaculate Conception. Built in Gothic style, it has an imposing three-storied façade. The fantastic wood carved panels are crafted by Goan artisans. A local Catholic school functions upstairs and services are held on Sundays. The entire structure is floodlit at night.

Makata Lane

This street near Zampa Gate is lined by striking mansions that belonged to affluent Portuguese and Indian merchants. They represent everything from European-influenced architecture to local style bungalows. The three-storied **Nagarsheth Haveli,** with carved balconies and entrances, is an interesting blend of European and Indian designs.

Beaches

Jalandhar Beach, facing the open sea to the south, is the closest to Diu town, just 1 km from the fort. However, this rocky beach is probably not the place to sun bathe or swim. On a hilltop nearby stands the domed **Jalandhar shrine** dedicated to the demon king who was killed by Vishnu. The king's face is carved in a niche.

A 20 minute drive through palm tree plantations, past the airport towards Bucharwada Village, will take you to the island's best beach at **Nagoa**. This is a great place to relax and enjoy the coastline enhanced by the surrounding hoka palm trees. The crowds of day trippers tend to concentrate around the arrival point, where the hotels are clustered, but are easy to escape by walking a little further out. The western end of the beach is particularly recommended for swimming. Nagoa also has paragliding, boating and water skiing. Though a little pricey, there are some good restaurants and bars. **Bucharwada** is a vibrant fishing village where you can walk through the **fish market** early in the morning and watch craftsmen build large wooden **dhows.**

Adjacent to Diu town, **Chakratirth** is a quaint beach surrounded by hills. It is a great place to catch the sunset and enjoy a serene ambience.

Ghoghla Beach and its continuation into Gujarat, **Ahmedpur Mandvi**, offer great panoramic views of the island. It is good for swimming, but beware of the strong current a few meters out. **Jyoti Water Sports** and **Magico do Mar** rent out parasailing, speed boating and water skiing equipment.

Entertainment

The night market next to the post office is popular for a late stroll. Most bars are open until around 2130. Evening cruises with music leave from the jetty at Bandar Chowk.

NUTS & BOLTS

In and Out

The airport is 6 km out of Diu, near Nagoa Beach. A rickshaw into town costs about Rs. 50. A daily flight connects the island with Mumbai. From Gujarat, the best way into Diu is by ST or private bus. They leave from every major city and arrive in Una (14 km away), although some travel directly to Diu. From the Clock Tower at Una, catch a bus to Diu. You can also get a *chhakada* or shared rickshaw up to the border check-post at Ghogla, where you walk across and take another shared vehicle for the last 3 km into Diu. A "special" (private) rickshaw from Una will cost Rs. 150, which includes a Rs. 50 entry fee for Diu that does not apply if you are not entering the territory.

Getting Around

Diu can be seen by foot within and around the fort, but the beaches outside town are far and require a rickshaw ride. Rickshaws (Rs. 50) and buses (Rs. 5) travel to Nagoa, but buses are few and far between.

Diu

Legend

Accommodation
2 Hare Krishna Guest House
9 Uma Shakti/ Restaurant
13 Sanmaan Palace /
   Restaurant
14 Samrat / Restaurant
15 Hotel Super Silver
17 Hotel Sao Tome Retiro /
   Diu Museum / St. Thomas
   Church
19 Jay Shankar Guest House

Food & Drink
8 Ram Vijay
11 Alishan
12 Apana
16 Ashiyana

Places of Interest
18 Nagar Sheth Haveli
20 St Francis of Assisi Church
   Hospital
21 St Paul's Church
22 Diu Fort

Nuts & Bolts
1 Fish Market
3 Jivabhai Super Market
4 State Bank of Saurashtra
5 A-Z Forex
6 General Post Office / DP
   Cyber Café
7 Diu Tourism Office
10 Vegetable / Fruit Market

If you intend to extensively explore the island, hiring a moped or motor bike is a sensible option. You must have a valid driver's license, make a refundable deposit (Rs. 1000 for a 150-250 cc bike) and generally have to fill your own gas. Rentals can be taken on an hourly or daily basis. There are a couple of rental places within a short distance of the main bus stand on the road leading to the fort. Be sure to check your vehicle carefully, so that you do not risk getting stranded. Bicycle rentals are another option to explore this flat island, especially on cooler days. You can pick up a bicycle from **Chandani Bike Hire** *Main Square* for Rs. 40-50/day. **Hotel Super Silver** also rents bicycles (Rs. 25/day) and mopeds (Rs. 150/day).

Tourist Information
The Diu Tourism Office *02875 252653, Bandar Rd* carries maps and information about the island.

Money
ATMs **State Bank of Saurashtra** *Nr Gold Moon Bar, Bandar Chowk.*
FOREIGN EXCHANGE **A-Z Forex** *Bandar Chowk* changes money for decent rates, but you get better options on the mainland.
MONEY TRANSFER **Western Union** is readily available around town.

SAURASHTRA

DISTRICT ▾
BHAVNAGAR

JUNAGADH ◂
Junagadh City
Gir National
Park
Kankai
Vanthali
Kutiyana
Talala
Veraval
Somnath
Ahmedpur
Mandvi
Diu

PORBANDAR
JAMNAGAR
RAJKOT
SURENDRANAGAR

Communication

INTERNET **DP Cyber Café** *Bandar Chowk, Post Office Bldg* charges Rs. 25/hr.

Markets

Most of the general stores are situated at Bandar Chowk. **Jivabhai Super Market** carries a variety of everyday products.

ACCOMMODATION

Diu has a surplus of hotel accommodation except during peak seasons (Mar-Jun); 3-4 days around Janmashtami (Aug-Sep); two weeks around Diwali (Oct-Nov); and three weeks around Christmas and New Year. There are considerable mark-ups during the peak periods and heavy discounts during the off-season. Discounts of 25-50 percent are not uncommon. At many hotels, the longer you stay the lower the rates. Some hotels, even at the high end, do not accept credit cards.

DIU TOWN

Most of the mid and low-end hotels are on or just off the road along the creek front leading to the fort.

Hare Krishna Guest House *252213* is a great option for the budget traveler with simple and clean rooms. **Facilities** squat toilets. **Double** 200.

Hotel Sao Tome Retiro *253137, upstairs in St Thomas Church* is an airy place with spacious rooms and a friendly hostess. **Double** 300-350 **Extra Bed** 50-100.

Jay Shankar Guest House *252424, Jalandhar Beach* is good value for your money and some rooms offer sea views. **Facilities** squat toilets. **Rooms** 250 **Extra Bed** 50.

Uma Shakti *252150, Nxt to Super Silver* has a great restaurant. **Facilities** AC options, rooftop terrace and bar. **Double** 300-500 **Extra Bed** 150-100.

Hotel Super Silver *252020, Nr Samrat* is another good low-budget place with really clean rooms. **Facilities** western toilets, AC options, Internet. **Double** 350-800 **Quadruple** 800-1300 **Extra Bed** 100.

Samrat *252354, Opp Veg Mkt* offers comfortable rooms. **Facilities** western toilets, AC options, running hot water, TV. **Double** 500-1000 **Extra Bed** 100-150.

Sanmaan Palace *253031, Fort Rd* formerly the municipal guest house known as Pensao do Mar, is now a high-end hotel under private management. It has recently been renovated and expanded to include a dozen cottages, which are basic from the outside but clean and spacious inside. **Facilities** attached toilets, TV, laundry, help with rail and air bookings, rooftop restaurant with excellent cuisine and view. The following are peak season rates, which include breakfast. **Double** 2250-3450.

Resort Hoka *253036, Nagoa Beach* has about a dozen small but pleasant rooms, a nice ambience, courteous staff and personal supervision of every detail by the owner-manager. The beach is a short walk away, though out of sight. **Facilities** western toilet, hot water, swimming pool, bar, a small library. The patio restaurant serves excellent food that claims no ethnic or cultural origins. **Double** 1250-1450 **Extra Bed** 250.

Suzlon Resort, *Ghogla Beach*, and the adjoining **Magico do Mar** (see **Ahmedpur Mandvi**) in Gujarat territory, are the best options for high-end hotels with a pleasant view and easy access to the beach. Suzlons rates include breakfast and dinner. **Facilities** western toilets, laundry, TV, outdoor space to lounge. **Double** 1400-7500.

FOOD & DRINK

Most hotels in Diu have their own restaurants. The island serves excellent sea food, especially prawns. Restaurants open early for breakfast here, and vegetarian-only is the exception rather than the norm.

Alishan *Fort Rd* offers vegetarian dishes and good meat and fish varieties. **Apana** *Fort Rd* serves large platters of seafood that include shark, lobster and kingfish crab for about Rs. 300. Portions are large enough to split between five people. **Ram Vijay** *Nr State Bank of Saurashtra* has excellent fresh ice cream, shakes and sodas. **Ashiyana** *Old Portuguese District* serves good Gujarati *thalis*. **Sanmaan** *Fort Rd* has a charming rooftop restaurant with a multicuisine menu; the chicken and fish dishes are recommended. **Samrat** *Collectorate Rd* has excellent Punjabi food. **Uma Shakti** *Opp Veg Mkt* is another nice rooftop hotel that serves an assortment of tasty food.

SAURASHTRA

DISTRICT ▾
BHAVNAGAR
JUNAGADH

PORBANDAR ◂
Porbandar City
Barda Hills
Sanctuary
Madhavpur
Balej
Bhansara

JAMNAGAR
RAJKOT
SURENDRANAGAR

PORBANDAR DISTRICT

PORBANDAR CITY
પોરબંદર

POPULATION	197,300
AREA CODE	0286
DISTANCES - AHMEDABAD	412 KM
VADODARA	481 KM
RAJKOT	187 KM

Once known as Sudamapuri for its association with Krishna's childhood friend, Sudama, the city of Porbandar is best known as the birthplace of Mohandas Karamchand Gandhi. The Jethwa Rajputs named it their capital and ruled from it for 1200 years. Its central position between Veraval and Mandvi allowed the port to flourish in trade, mainly with Arabia and Africa. It continued to thrive during the Mughal rule, so much so that the Portuguese attacked it in 1531, burning boats and looting civilians to establish their power along the Saurashtra coast. This charming coastal town, with planned roads and a lovely seafront, is often called the "White City" for the white local stone used in many of the buildings.

PLACES OF INTEREST

Sudamapuri Temple

Although the temple structure is not extraordinary, it is associated with a popular tale of Krishna and his dear friend Sudama (see **Krishna in Gujarat**). The shrine marks where Sudama's hut once stood and is the only temple dedicated to him in India. You can walk here from the city bus stand or hire a rickshaw for Rs. 2-5.

Kirti Mandir

The main attraction for most visitors to this city is the three story house where Gandhiji was born in 1869. The spot where his mother gave birth is marked with a *swastika*. A narrow stairway leads up to his study. Adjacent to the 165-year-old residence is the 24 m high Kirti Mandir with 79 lamps on its peak—one for each year of Gandhiji's life. Inside are pictures of the Mahatma and his wife, Kasturba. Twenty-six marble pillars surround the central area and are inscribed with messages from Gandhiji's writings, the *Bhagvad Gita* and other inspiring texts. There is also a pictorial biography including photos from South Africa, the Indian National Movement, England and various political events, a library and a prayer hall. The office sells Gandhian literature in several languages. Just behind Kirti Mandir is **Navi Khadki**, the family house of Kasturba. She married Gandhiji when she was 13 years old. In addition to being one of Gandhiji's supportive forces, she was deeply involved in the Freedom Movement. **Open** 0800-1330 and 1500-1800, daily. **Entry** free.

Bharat Mandir and Nehru Planetarium

The Bharat Mandir is a permanent exhibition that highlights the natural features and prominent spiritual and historical figures of India. Upstairs is the Nehru Planetarium, also known as Tara Mandir, with slightly outdated technology. Nearby are mud flats popular with migratory birds. It is a great spot for birdwatching.

Underworld of Porbandar

The birthplace of Gandhiji, India's Apostle of Peace, is also a city that was once associated with a notorious underworld. Formerly reputed as the "Chicago of Gujarat", Porbandar and surrounding areas were under the grips of some ten crime syndicates that harassed civilians, extorted money and flaunted power. All of this changed in 1993 when Neeraja Gotru, a new chief of police, took the reigns. She initiated a campaign to clean up the streets and used public humiliation to demoralize the gangsters. Gotru also encouraged civilians to start lodging complaints and ensured that corruption did not exist among her own officers. Her efforts brought the crime world to its knees and sent into hiding most of these gangsters, including Sankotaben Jadeja, better known as the Godmother, who was the inspiration of a Hindi film by the same name.

SAURASHTRA

DISTRICT ▾
BHAVNAGAR
JUNAGADH

PORBANDAR ◄
Porbandar City
Barda Hills
Sanctuary
Madhavpur
Balej
Bhansara

JAMNAGAR
RAJKOT
SURENDRANAGAR

Sartanji no Choro

King Sartanji (1757-1813) commissioned this pavilion as a venue for music concerts. The ceiling is made of wooden panels with floral images. Statues of musicians and doorkeepers adorn the columns and outside corners. A water tank inside keeps the place cool.

Beachfront

The **dhow building yard** and **fishing ports** stir with activity. You can watch fish being dried or observe craftsmen assembling boats with wooden planks. The beachfront offers a view of charming villa façades.

NUTS & BOLTS

In and Out

A daily flight connects Porbandar and Mumbai. A rickshaw ride from the airport (4 km) costs around Rs. 40. The two cities are also connected by train

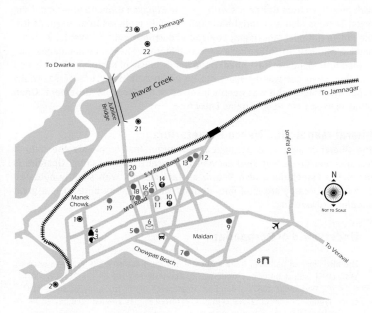

Porbandar City
Legend

Accommodation
5   Hotel Sheetal
7   Hotel Toran
12 Kandhli Krupa Guest House
15 Flamingo Hotel
17 Hotel Moon Palace
19 Hotel Kuber

Food & Drink
10 Bombay Dining Hall
14 Swagat

Places of Interest
1   Kirti Mandir
2   Dhow Building
4   Sudama Mandir
8   Hazur Palace
21 Mud Flats
22 Nehru Planetarium

23 Bharat Mandir

Nuts & Bolts
3   Vegetable Market
6   General Post Office
9   Paradise Cinema
11 SBI ATM
13 Sify Iway Cybercafé
16 State Bank of Saurashtra ATM
18 Skyline Cyber Café
20 Divyaraj Foreign Exchange

via Ahmedabad and Jamnagar. ST and private buses ply to major destinations across Saurashtra and Gujarat. The NH 8B makes car travel a convenient option. **Bhagat Taxi** *2245927, Ashapura Soc, Chhaya Rd* rents out cars.

Getting Around
Rickshaws are the best way to get around. You can also rent bicycles from near the ST bus stand.

Tourist Information
Gujarat Tourism has prepared a map charting a **heritage walk** starting from Kirti Mandir that covers nine places over a 2 km stretch. Most hotels carry these maps.

Money
ATMs **State Bank of Saurashtra** *MG Rd;* **SBI Bank,** *MG Rd.*
FOREIGN EXCHANGE **Divyaraj** *Limda Chowk.*

Communication
INTERNET **Skyline Cyber Café** *ST Rd, Opp Swaminarayan Temple* costs Rs. 20/hr; **Sify Iway** *MG Rd, basement of Sheel Cmplx.*

ACCOMMODATION

Kandhli Krupa Guest House *SV Patel Rd* is a great option and conveniently located near the railway station. **Facilities** AC options. **Rooms** 200-500.

Hotel Toran *2245476, Chowpati* is run by the Gujarat government. It offers a great sea view but is slightly rundown. **Facilities** western toilet, running hot water, AC options (AC rooms have TV and phone connections). Gujarati food is available but you must inform the reception in advance. **Dorm** 75 **Rooms** 300-700 **Extra Bed** 75.

Hotel Kuber *2241289, On ST Rd, Nr Swaminarayan Temple* has a free airport and railway pickup service. **Facilities** western toilet, AC options, running hot water, TV, laundry. **Single** 350-2000 **Double** 450-2000 **Extra Bed** 100-150.

Hotel Sheetal *2247596, Opp GPO* has interesting interiors especially in the more fancy rooms, which are decorated in retro green. **Facilities** western toilets, AC options. **Single** 350-1450 **Double** 500-1500.

Hotel Silver Palace *2252591, Silver Cmplx, ST Rd* is centrally located and offers comfortable rooms. **Facilities** western toilet, AC options, running hot water, TV, laundry, room service. **Single** 700-1200 **Double** 400- 850 **Suites** 1400.

FOOD & DRINK

Swagat *MG Rd* is a popular place with excellent *thalis* and good Punjabi and Chinese dishes, all at low prices. **Kadambari Restaurant** serves Gujarati,

SAURASHTRA

▼ DISTRICT
BHAVNAGAR
JUNAGADH

▶ PORBANDAR
Porbandar City
Barda Hills
Sanctuary
Madhavpur
Balej
Bhansara

JAMNAGAR
RAJKOT
SURENDRANAGAR

Punjabi and fast food at mid-range prices and also has good *thalis*. **Bombay Dining Hall**, best known for its *thali,* also prepares *pav bhaji* in the evenings. **Hotel Flamingo** *MG Rd* serves South Indian, Chinese and Punjabi cuisine.

Devang Parotha House makes delicious *parothas* and offers full meals for affordable prices. **Modern** has a few sea food dishes on its menu and is probably the best option in town for non-veg selection.

EXCURSIONS

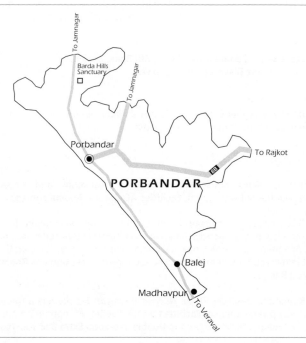

The district's coastline is scattered with temple ruins in picturesque settings, perfect for a traveler longing to explore. A few of these are listed below.

Barda Hills Sanctuary   30 km from Porbandar

The Barda Hills are a trekker's delight. After the rains and in the early winter, the area abounds with greenery, cascading streams and migratory birds. Due to the undulating terrain, local wildlife is difficult to spot. Abhapara is the highest summit in Barda, measuring about 617 m. The sanctuary has a forest cover of 192 sq km, which is relatively small but abundant in floral diversity, with more than 650 flowering plants, a number of medicinal plants and a high percentage of rare and endangered species. Wildlife species include leopard, hyena, wild boar, wolf, jackal and Blue bull, in addition to bird species such as the rare

and endangered Spotted and Crested Hawk eagles. The Maldhari, Bharvad, Rabari and Gadhvi communities live in these areas. Barda is earmarked as an alternative territory for the Asiatic Lions of Gir if the main sanctuary is ever affected by an epidemic or natural calamity.

The sanctuary spreads between Porbandar and Jamnagar. The main entry point is about 3 km from Ranavav in Porbandar. An alternative is to enter from Jamnagar District. One option is to access the reserve from Kapudi Naka and take a car up to Kileshwar Temple, from where you trek down into the valley and to the forest. Another option is to begin at Abhapara Hill, located on the route between Ghumli and Bhanvad. It is recommended to take a private vehicle to each of these starting points. Mornings are the best time to start. Wear sturdy shoes and take along a walking stick to help you along the difficult stretches.

No lodging facilities are available. Camping is allowed with permission. *Contact the Conservator of Forests Office, Porbandar, 0286 2242551.*

Madhavpur
60 km from Porbandar

A scenic town, Madhavpur is situated on a sandy coastline and is endowed with coconut trees and fertile agricultural land. It hosts the beautiful **Madhavraiji Haveli Temple** in addition to the **Rukmini no Choro,** which marks the place where Krishna supposedly married Rukmini (see **Krishna in Gujarat**). This event is celebrated with an annual fair held by the Mer community. Nearby are the ruins of a Shiva temple, probably from the 12th c. The beach is not safe for swimming, but perfect for taking in the sea breeze.

South of town, a signed road leads to an ashram whose resident enlightened guru gives daily talks (0800 and 2000) on the philosophy of Osho and Gurdjieff. It is a peaceful place with spaces to meditate. You can also help tend to the Aran trees in the surrounding wilderness.

Balej and Bhansara
45 km from Porbandar

These places are worth visiting if you have your own vehicle. Balej is home to four 7th c. Hindu temples and a rudimentary *toran*. **The Kotha Temple,** the oldest of the group, is named for its use as a *kotho* or watchtower in medieval times. The interior has been considerably altered. Other shrines include the **Pithad Mata Temple,** the **Shakti Temple,** which has an interesting band of gorgon heads, and the **Shiva Temple.** The village of Bhansara, just 2 km south of Balej, has a cluster of seven temples from the same period.

SAURASHTRA

▼ DISTRICT
BHAVNAGAR
JUNAGADH

▸ PORBANDAR
Porbandar City
Barda Hills
Sanctuary
Madhavpur
Balej
Bhansara

JAMNAGAR
RAJKOT
SURENDRANAGAR

JAMNAGAR DISTRICT

JAMNAGAR CITY
જામનગર

POPULATION	557,000
AREA CODE	0288
DISTANCES - AHMEDABAD	313 KM
VADODARA	382 KM
RAJKOT	88 KM

Until its merger with the Indian Union after independence, Nawanagar was one of the more important princely states of Saurashtra. It was established by Jam Raval in the 16th c. and ruled by his descendants. The capital was Jamnagar, which now gives the district its name. Legend associates the area with Krishna, who migrated from Mathura and established his kingdom at Dwarka. The Jams trace their ancestry to Krishna's Yadav clan.

During his reign, Jam Ranjitsinhji (1907-33) laid the city out on a western model. He was one of the greatest cricket players in the history of the game, even though he played mainly for England, and drew inspiration from his exposure to Europe.

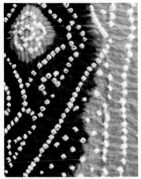

PLACES OF INTEREST

Solarium

Built in 1920, this medical facility was ahead of its time and is possibly still the only one of its kind. The top floor rotates slowly to provide daylong sunlight for the treatment of skin ailments. It was closed in 1996, when the last physician who knew how to operate the elaborate system retired. Today it stands as a memorial to Ranjitsinhji's rule. It is officially closed to visitors, but the small government engineering office next door has friendly staff that will show you around the facilities if you ask.

Lakhota Lake

Located in the center of town, the lake is busy in the evenings, when people come to the surrounding promenade to enjoy the breeze and to shop at the impromptu stalls. You can take a 15-minute motor-boat ride around the lake or rent a paddle boat. Parks and gardens, a night market for vegetables, *chaat* vendors, and a small zoo surround the lake. In the middle is a fort-like structure called **Lakhota Tower**, connected to the bank by two causeways. Built in the 19th c. as a drought-relief project, the tower now contains the **Lakhota Museum**.

Lakhota Museum

The collection includes a number of 18th c. artifacts and some stunning specimens salvaged from medieval monuments. A photograph collection from the 1930s highlights the city's major monuments, putting its faded splendor into perspective. Also on display are coins from various eras that circulated in Jamnagar and Jam Vibhaji's elaborate turban. **Open** 1030-1750. **Closed** Wed, 2nd and 4th Sat of every month and public holidays. **Entry Indian** Rs. 2, **Foreigner** Rs.50.

Bhujiyo Kotho

This fort-like building to the south of the lake once served as an arsenal. After damage during the 2001 earthquake, access was restricted but repairs have been underway and parts of it may be possible to visit. Look for the caretaker, who will guide you around the safer parts. The top of the Kotho offers an excellent view across the lake. The **Khambhalia Gate,** just a short walk from the Kotho, is one of the five gates built as part of the fortification of the city. It is named after the town to which it leads.

Khijada Mandir

This is the founding temple of the Pranami sect in Gujarat. The Pranami faith is rooted in Hinduism, but propounds the unity of all religions. Followers greet each other with *pranam* (folded hands and acknowledgement of the divine in one another). The temple depicts scenes from the life of Krishna. It is built around two 400-year-old sacred trees. *Aarti* is performed five times a day. The priest of this temple is very active in social service, including HIV/AIDS prevention. If you are interested in a detailed history or want to participate in the work, meet Navinbhai Parikh or Shri Surendraji, a monk in residence.

Swaminarayan Temple

A tiny doorway across the street from Supermarket leads to the courtyard of the Swaminarayan Temple, which belongs to the Vadtal sect. The dome of the sanctum contains beautifully crafted scenes from the life of Swami Sahajanand. The exquisite floor and ceiling of this temple are worth examining. The *aarti* is at 1900.

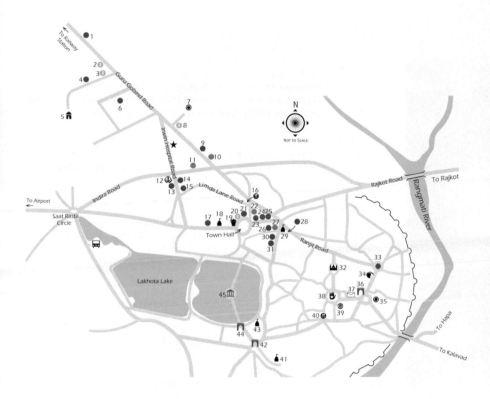

Jamnagar City
Legend

Accommodation
10 Hotel Royal Stay
11 Hotel Celebration
22 Hotel President
27 Hotel Ashiana

Food & Drink
16 Ram Dairy
24 Fresh Point Restaurant
40 H J Vyas

Places of Interest
5 Pratap Vilas Palace
6 Gujarat Ayurved University
7 Solarium
18 Bhidbhanjan Temple
19 Parsi Agiari
29 Swaminaryan Temple
32 Ratan Bai Mosque
35 Willingdon Crescent
36 Darbargadh
38 Jain Temples
39 Chandi Bazaar
41 Khijada Temple
42 Khambhalia Gate
43 Bala Hanuman Temple

44 Bhujiyo Kotho
45 Lakhota Museum

Nuts & Bolts
1 Reliance World
2 UTI ATM
3 HDFC Bank ATM
4 Sify Iway Cybercafé
8 ICICI Bank ATM
9 Amber Cinema
12 Gurudwara
13 Vasudev Foods
14 Reliance Supermarket
15 Sify Iway Cybercafé
17 Indian Airlines

20 UTI Bank ATM
21 LKP Forex
23 Save Time Travel
25 Plezer Color Lab
26 Supermarket
28 The West India Agency
30 Sify Iway Cybercafé
31 Indraprasth
33 Subash Market
34 Vegetable and Fruit Market
37 General Post Office

Bhidbhanjan Temple

This temple was erected in the early 20th c. on land gifted to a Brahmin by Ranjitsinhji. It is one of the few structures built in a local style during a period largely associated with western influences. The paintings on the ceiling depict mythology related to Shiva. Intricate moldings on the doors reflect the fine silver craftsmanship that is still practiced in Jamnagar.

Jain Temples

In the center of the city is a triad of large Jain temples with intriguing interiors. **Raisi Shah's Temple**, dedicated to Shantinath, is divided into several chambers that demand at least a few hours of exploration. The marble floor has elaborate geometric designs and many of the rooms have mirrored ceilings, best viewed in the morning. The sanctum dome is ringed with gold inlay work. Next to it stands the **Vardhaman Shah Temple**, dedicated to the first *tirthankar,* Adinath. It is simpler in layout, but more colorful. The third adjoining Jain temple is much smaller, but just as interesting. **Open** 0530-1300 and 1530-2100.

Ratan Bai Mosque

It is hard to miss the Ratan Bai Mosque in the town center, with its two towering green and white minarets. The mosque has its own rainwater harvesting system, which provides water to the tank used for the ritual washing before *namaz*.

Chandi Bazaar

The area around the Jain temples and Ratan Bai Mosque is known as the **Chandi Bazaar** or silver market. Its winding streets are still filled with silver artisans practicing their ancestral trade, though it is now possible to see other metal workers sharing the space. The area is best explored on foot.

Willingdon Crescent

Jam Ranjitsinhji built this curved arcade in an attempt to remove Jamnagar's worst slum area. It is more popularly know as Darbargadh. The ground floor of the arcade is full of shops selling everything from Bandhani to suitcases. At the center of the crescent is an equestrian statue of Digvijaysinhji.

Bala Hanuman Temple

This famous temple complex on the periphery of Jamnagar's central lake has resonated for 40 years to the nonstop chant of "Sri Ram, Jai Ram, Jai Jai Ram" performed in relays by priests and by the devout. The depth of faith and religiosity are very moving. The temple is open through the night for those who feel the need to verify or contribute to the good work.

Gujarat Ayurved University

Wedged between Hospital Road and GG Road is the campus of the largest Ayurvedic teaching center in Gujarat. It has two hospitals that give free medicines and consultations. Several of the doctors and residents at the post-graduate hospital speak English. The campus grows many of its own herbs. The Director of the International Center can help organize a campus tour, and also provide information about short and long courses offered. Foreign students can expect to pay about 1000 USD for a basic 12-week introductory course on Ayurvedic medicine. If you plan to seriously pursue studies in this field, you can apply to the 5.5 year Bachelor of Ayurvedic Medicine and Surgery (BAMS) program. *For more information check www.ayurveduniversity.com.*

NUTS & BOLTS

In and Out
Indian Airlines *2552911* has a daily flight between Mumbai and Jamnagar. The airport is about 10 km from town (rickshaw Rs. 25, taxi Rs. 50). **Save Time Travel** *Town Hall Rd* can help book domestic tickets. There are a few daily trains from Mumbai, including the Saurashtra Express and the Saurashtra Mail, which arrive at 0950 and 1215 respectively. The intercity train from Ahmedabad leaves in the early morning and takes about seven hours. The Surat-Jamnagar Intercity comes in a little after midnight. If you are traveling from within Saurashtra, the best choice is bus, either ST or private coaches. ST buses leave hourly to/ from Rajkot and every half hour to/from Junagadh. For private buses contact **Shrinath Travel** *2662215, KD Cmplx, Nr Guru Dwara Circle, Indira Rd.*

Getting Around
Rickshaws are the best means for getting around town. Most places in the city take about ten minutes travel time. You can rent cars near the ST bus stand to travel outside the city, and be sure to fix the rate in advance.

Money
ATMs **HDFC** *Nr DKV College, GG Rd*; **ICICI** *Nr Income Tax, GG Rd*; **UTI** *Nr DKV College, GG Rd; Nr Town Hall.*
FOREIGN EXCHANGE **LKP Forex** *Nr President Hotel.*

Communication
INTERNET **Sify Iway** *GG Rd, Btw Bedi Gate and Hospital Rd*; **Reliance World** *GG Road, Nr Patel Colony.*

Medical
HOSPITAL **Guru Gobind Singh Hospital** *Pandit Nehru Rd*; **Samarpan Hospital** *Airport Rd.*

Photography
Plezer Color Lab *Nr Fresh Point* handles most film and digital needs.

Bookstores
The **West India Agency** is Jamnagar's best book store. Its aisles are full of English and Indian language titles. The helpful staff seems to know the entire inventory offhand. **Anand Book Stand** *Nr Madras Hotel* carries a wide range of English titles and magazines. A good selection of western and Ayurvedic textbooks can be found at GG Road, between the GAU and Amber Cinema.

SAURASHTRA

DISTRICT ▼
BHAVNAGAR
JUNAGADH
PORBANDAR

JAMNAGAR ◄
Jamnagar City
Khijadia
Bird Sanctuary
Dwarka
Beyt Dwarka
Nageshwar
Mahadev
Gop
Ghumli
Marine
National Park

RAJKOT
SURENDRANAGAR

Markets

Subhash Market, housed in a colliseum-style building with an old-world charm, is Jamnagar's best fruit and vegetable market. **Vasudev Foods** *Nr Gurudwara, Hospital Rd* is the place to stock up on the few products, like peanut butter and soy sauce, that you may miss from home. Also try the **Reliance Supermarket** across the road.

Shopping

Jamnagar produces some of the best Bandhani, a type of tie and dye fabric (see **Resource Guide, Craft**), which is available at **Supermarket** and the **Indraprastha Shopping Centre.**

ACCOMMODATION

Hotel Ashiana *2559110, in Supermarket* has small but clean and well-maintained rooms. **Facilities** western toilets, AC options, showers with hot water (0600-1200), room service, laundry service, travel counter. **Single** 200-600 **Double** 300-700 **Extra Bed** 60-100.

Hotel Royal Stay *2555444, Nr Amber Cinema* has been recently renovated. The rooms are spartan, but a decent mid-range value. **Facilities** AC options, 24-hour room service, TV, hot water (0600-1200), laundry. **Single** 500-950 **Double** 650-1150 **Extra Bed** 150.

Hotel President *2557491, Teen Batti* is centrally located. It has luxurious rooms with private balconies, but a lot of street noise. The owner/manager, Mustak, is a veritable mine of information about the city. **Facilities** western toilets, AC options, TV, room service, foreign exchange, laundry, restaurant, internet. **Rooms** 500-1600 **Extra Bed** 220.

Hotel Celebration *2555523, Indira Rd, Nr Gurudwara*, is a new establishment with comfortable rooms and modern decor. **Facilities** AC options, TV, 24-hour room service, forex, restaurant, travel counter, laundry. **Single** 800-1700 **Double** 950-1900 **Extra Bed** 150.

FOOD & DRINK

Aram Hotel serves one of the best *thalis* in town for Rs. 80. **Fresh Point Restaurant** *Nxt to Save Time Travel,* known for its Chinese dishes, **Madras Hotel,** one of Jamnagar's best budget options, and **Hotel Swati,** which does excellent *idli-sambar*, all serve the popular Chinese, Punjabi and South Indian fare.

Pragray *Nr Hotel Swati* is one of the few non-veg eateries in town. **Seven Seas** *in President Hotel* is a nautical-themed restaurant that serves the best seafood in Jamnagar. Specialties include soups and *chicken tikka masala*.

H J Vyas, where the dry fruit *kachori* was invented, is a sweets and snack shop whose owner will make you try everything and convince you to buy just

as much. Be sure to try the extraordinary ginger *kulfi*. Several places nearby also sell *kachori*, but the main difference is the "export quality" packaging. **Ram Dairy** *GG Road, Nr Kalpana* is the best ice cream shop in town, offering 40 flavors made in-house. It has a second shop across from Amber Cinema. **Ummaji** *Nxt to Supermarket* is the place for *bhajiya*.

EXCURSIONS

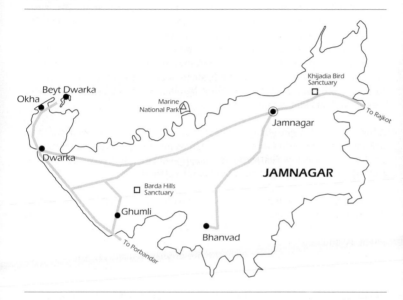

Khijadia Bird Sanctuary   15 km from Jamnagar

This sanctuary and its adjoining areas protect remarkably diverse ecosystems that include marine and fresh water habitats, marshy lands, mangroves, Prosopis areas, salt pans, mudflats, creeks, forest scrub, sandy beaches and adjoining farmlands. Owing to this variety, the sanctuary is inhabited by more than 220 species of resident and migratory birds across a relatively small area of 6 sq km. Khijadia is important for its conservation value and fosters several globally threatened species such as the Dalmatian pelican, Darter, Asian open bill stork, Black-necked stork, Black-headed ibis, Eurasian spoonbill, Pallas's fish eagle, Pallid harrier, Indian skimmer and Osprey. It offers the opportunity to sight rare birds in large numbers. The sanctuary is the outcome of two man-made dykes placed in a natural environment to keep fresh water separate from sea water. As a result you can simultaneously observe the species that belong to each habitat and those that share both. Watchtowers, trails and paddleboats are available to help the visitor get a closer look at the biodiversity. There are no overnight lodges. Rickshaws and private vehicles can be hired, but ST buses do not frequent the destination.

Dwarka

131 km from Jamnagar

Considered one of the four most sacred Hindu pilgrimage sites in India, Dwarka is also the ancient kingdom of Krishna and is believed to have been the first capital of Gujarat. It sits at the mouth of the Gomti River on the Arabian Sea and is famous for the Dwarkadeesh (Krishna) Temple among other significant historical and religious sites in the area.

Jagat Mandir or "Temple of the World" marks the place where the great-grandson of Krishna supposedly built a temple more than 2500 years ago. The present temple dates from the 15th-16th c. and contains a group of several smaller temples. The spire is 78 m high, topped with a banner decorated with symbols of the sun and the moon. The *Moksha Dwara* (Gate to Salvation) is the main entrance, while *Swarga Dwara* (Gate to Heaven) is the south gate leading to the Gomti River. It is believed that Mirabai, Krishna's devoted follower, merged with his idol in this temple.

A friendly priest might offer you a free tour around the temple, but may also ask for a little donation in exchange. Janmashtami, the birth anniversary of Krishna (see **Fairs and Festivals**), is a major event and thousands of devotees from all over India and abroad come here to celebrate.

Sharada Peeth is the first among four *peeths* (religious seats) established by Adi Shankaracharya (686-718 AD), who spent his life reforming Hindu beliefs and unifying different schools of Vedic philosophy around India. Sharada Peeth is situated in the premises of the Dwarkadeesh Temple. The wall paintings illustrate incidents from the life of Shankaracharya, while carvings on the inner surface of the dome depict Shiva in various stances.

Gomti Ghat is situated at the mouth of the river. A bath in these waters is believed to purge the soul. The solemnity of this belief contrasts with the lively atmosphere of boys jumping into the waves and turning somersaults as people photograph them. Decorated camels, tea stands, and bearded men selling seashell jewelry by the water add to the ambience. The banks are dotted with innumerable shrines dedicated to Sarasvati, Lakshmi and Samudra (God of the Sea). **Caution:** The water in this area has a strong undercurrent.

There are plenty of places to stay around town, including a number of *dharmashalas*. A number of reasonable accommodations ranging from dorm beds (Rs. 50) to high-end hotels (Rs. 1200) are concentrated around the Teen Batti Chowk and the fountain area. The **Toran Tourist Bungalow** near the Government Guest House has decent rooms and a helpful manager with travel information.

Dwarka is well connected by railway and by bus. Private vehicles are available from Okha, Porbandar, Jamnagar and major towns in the district.

Beyt Dwarka
1.75 nautical miles from Okha

Beyt Dwarka is considered the original abode of Krishna. The island was a full-fledged port before Okha developed nearby. The main temple was built about 500 years ago by Sri Vallabhacharya, a prominent guru of the Pushtimarg Sampradaya, and has an idol believed to have been made by Rukmini. The traditional donation of rice to Brahmins has special importance here as it is believed to be the place where Krishna's friend Sudama presented him with rice. The main temple complex includes several smaller temples dedicated to Shiva, Vishnu, Hanuman and Devi. Watch out for the *pandas* (priests), who are more interested in money and food than knowledge.

The beautiful **Hanuman Dandi Temple** is about 6 km away (Rs. 10-12 by rickshaw). It has many idols of Hanuman and his son Makaradhwaja. In case you wonder how the celibate Hanuman had a son, legend has an explanation. A drop of his perspiration impregnated a fish, which conceived and bore a son as strong and brilliant as Hanuman.

With luck you may see dolphins from the island. There are long stretches of coastline for picnicking and wading. Carry your own drinking water. Electric boats and ferries charge Rs. 5 from Okha to Beyt.

Nageshwar Mahadev
15 km from Dwarka

Situated towards Okha, this temple enshrines one of the 12 *jyotirlingas* in India. The legend relates that centuries ago the jungle (*vana*) that covered this area was inhabited by a demon couple named Daruka and Daruki and so it was called Daruka Vana, which later became Dwarka. Daruki was a devotee of Parvati and blessed with the power to transpose anywhere with the jungle and its population. This boon made the couple very powerful and they tyrannized people in the vicinity. One day they captured a boatload of pilgrims, including a trader named Supriya, who prayed to Shiva to protect them. Shiva emerged from the soil as a *linga*. He could not kill Daruki as she was blessed by his own wife, but he assured Supriya that he would remain with him in the form of a *linga* so that the demoness could not harm any being in its proximity. The *linga* thus came to be worshipped. One of Nageshwar's attractions is the 26 m statue of a sitting Shiva outside, which can be seen from a distance. The temple is relatively modern compared against the antiquity of the *linga*.

Gop
60 km from Jamnagar, 60 km from Porbandar, 20 km from Bhanvad

Now popularly known as Gopnath Mahadev, this 6th c. shrine in Nani Gop Village is one of the earliest built temples in Gujarat. Opinion is divided on whether it was originally dedicated to the Sun or to Shiva. It has a two-layered pyramid-shaped roof. The high platform and the open space around the sanctum gives the temple an appearance of enhanced height.

ST buses take you to the entrance of the village, from where the temple is 7 km away. To access it you must climb 600 steps. Alternatively, you can drive most of the way up in your own vehicle.

Ghumli   75 km from Jamnagar, 40 km from Porbandar

Ghumli, nestled in the Barda Hills, is a picturesque place, especially after the rains. It is home to some outstanding monuments. The **Navlakha Temple (**12th-13th c. AD) is a masterpiece of Solanki architecture, magnificent even in its present damaged condition. Look out for the sculptures of dueling elephants with their trunks entwined. The temple has an unusual two-storied pavilion preceding the sanctum and exquisite carvings of humans, animals and mythical beasts on the sides of the high platform on which the temple stands. Next to this huge temple is a small **Ganesh Temple** from the 10th c.

You can climb up a gravelly 2-km track to the older **Sonkansari temples** (9th-10th c.). These are smaller and less ornate than the Navlakha, but beautifully proportioned and spectacular in their own way. The views from the hill can be breathtaking. Carry enough drinking water to last you four to six hours.

There are a number of interesting monuments down the hill, in and around the village. The 13th c. **Vikia Vav** is said to be among the largest stepwells in Gujarat. There are also some ruined temples worth a visit for the beautiful sculptures scattered in the remains of the old town gate. Although very little of the gate stands, it is an exquisite example of its period.

Opposite the Navlakha and Ganesh temple enclosure are steps leading up to Ghumli's other famous temple dedicated to **Goddess Ashapura**. According to folklore, Jam Udanji from Sindh marched up to Ghumli in the 14th c., but could not conquer it. His son, Bamaniyaji, returned with a large army and seized Ghumli. That night Goddess Amba appeared in his dream and instructed him to build a temple in her name since she had fulfilled his father's desire (asha) to conquer Ghumli. Bamaniyaji built the temple on the hill and named it Ashapura, "the one who fulfills desires". It has idols of Amba, Samudra Devi and Sarasvati in the main building. The views from the hill are stunning. The nearest town is Bhanwad, linked by road to Porbandar and Jamnagar.

Marine National Park and Wildlife Sanctuary

Created in 1980, the Marine National Park and Sanctuary lies in the intertidal zone (the area between the lowest and highest tide levels) along the northern coast of Jamnagar District and the islands in the Gulf of Kachchh. Its coral reefs, mangroves and archipelago of 42 islands among other habitats form a unique, though fragile, eco-system. The coral reefs and mangroves are important to conservation efforts and form the richest concentration of marine biodiversity anywhere in the country. Flooded by the sea twice a day, the park is like an underwater forest and a treasure trove of coral reef and sponges, giant sea anemone, jelly fish, octopus and starfish to name just a few species. On occasion you might spot a dolphin. The whale shark also inhabits the surrounding sea. Considered the largest fish in the world (an average of up to 13 m long), it feeds off plankton. Killed for its flesh, liver, cartilage and oil, the shark is now on the endangered list. **Narara** and **Pirotan Island** are two of the park's popular tourist destinations for viewing marine invertebrates.

Mangroves

Mangroves are a salt-tolerant plant species that grow in coastal and estuarine areas. Crucial to protecting, nurturing and conserving marine life and coral reefs, they can also withstand periodic submergence in sea water, low oxygen and nutrients, heavy winds and waves. Fringe mangroves stabilize sediment and protect the shore from erosion.

Boats can cover the distance of 20 nautical miles to the island only at high tide, twice a day with a 12-hour gap between. Give yourself adequate time and remember that tide timings change daily. Inquire locally about the particular day you intend to make the trip and arrive at the boarding point (**Bedi Bandar** or **Nava Bandar** near Jamnagar) an hour before high tide. A ferry costs Rs. 2500 return and can take 25-30 passengers. **ENTRY Indian** Rs. 20, **Foreigners** 5 USD; **Car Parking** Rs. 1750. **Photography** Rs. 150, **Video** Rs. 2500.

There are no lodging facilities or amenities on the islands; carry your own food and drinking water. Unfortunately, only a few guides are available. *For permission to visit the sanctuary or for more information contact the Conservator of Forests Office 0288 2679357 Nagnath Gate, Van Sankul, Ganjiwada, Jamnagar.* Despite the hassles of getting permission, it is a breathtaking place that any nature lover should visit.

Beaches

While the locally popular **Balachadi** is the closest beach to the city, the district has a number of good beaches, including **Shivrajpur,** located 12 km from Dwarka heading towards Okha.

Jamnagar also has some unspoiled coastline, especially around the edges of the 42 islands in the Gulf. The following beaches require permission from the Conservator of Forests Office. **Positra** is the best option. It stretches along a lagoon where the water is calm and the sand is soft, though there are a few rocky patches. Climb the rocks for a vista of the surrounding area and the distant islands. **Dabdaba** is an island just off the coast of Bhadu. You can get there by boat and swim to your heart's content. **Tiny Sandy Island** in Bhadu Lagoon is a mix of sandy and rocky beach. It provides excellent swimming during high tide. **Pirotan Island** has some beautiful clean beaches, but check the tide timings before you set sail. If you are a birder, you will find huge flocks along all of these shorelines.

SAURASHTRA

▾ **DISTRICT**
BHAVNAGAR
JUNAGADH
PORBANDAR

▸ **JAMNAGAR**
Jamnagar City
Khijadia
Bird Sanctuary
Dwarka
Beyt Dwarka
Nageshwar
Mahadev
Gop
Ghumli
**Marine
National Park**

RAJKOT
SURENDRANAGAR

RAJKOT DISTRICT

RAJKOT CITY

રાજકોટ

POPULATION	1,003,000
AREA CODE	0281
DISTANCES - AHMEDABAD	225 KM
VADODARA	294 KM

The former capital of the princely state of Saurashtra, Rajkot was founded in the 16th c. by the Jadeja Rajputs, who ruled until independence. During the colonial period, the city was the administrative headquarters of the Saurashtra region, and today it is the district headquarters. The city is situated on the Aji River and sprawls with regal architecture. It is also an industrial center and an important hub for the body building of vehicles. The city proudly boasts of its association with Gandhiji, who spent his early years in Rajkot while his father was a Diwan to the local ruler. The house where he lived is now a museum. The district is also a handicrafts and textile center known for its fine silverwork, Bandhani, Patola *saris* and beadwork. The towns of Wankaner and Morbi host beautiful royal estates, some of which have been converted into heritage hotels.

SAURASHTRA

▼ **DISTRICT**
BHAVNAGAR
JUNAGADH
PORBANDAR
JAMNAGAR

▶ **RAJKOT**
Rajkot City
Wankaner
Morbi
Gondal
Khambhalida
Virpur
Jetpur
Tankara
Dhoraji

SURENDRANAGAR

PLACES OF INTEREST

Watson Museum and Lang Library

Located in the Jubilee Gardens, the Watson Museum is named after a former British political agent of Kathiawad. Its collection includes early Indus Valley artifacts, textiles, paintings and colonial memorabilia. The neighboring **Lang Library** houses a special Kathiawad history collection and a set of old English books from the British rule in India. **Museum: Open** 0900-1300 and 1400-1800. **Closed** Sun, every 2nd and 4th Sat and public holidays. **Library: Open** 0800-1630. **ENTRY Indian** Rs. 2; **Foreigner** Rs. 50.

Kaba Gandhi no Delo

The former residence of Gandhiji, Kaba Gandhi no Delo is located in a small lane off Gheekanta Road. It offers a pictorial tour of his life with captions in Hindi and Gujarati. It also houses sewing classes run by a non-profit organization for local girls. **Open** 0900-1200 and 1500-1700. **Closed** Sun.

Rashtriya School

The institute was founded in 1921 to impart Gandhian values and encourage participation in the nation's development. The **Bapu Upavas Khand Memorial** is where Gandhiji fasted as part of a civil disobedience campaign. The institute supports small industries such as Khadi, spinning and oil pressing as prescribed by the concept of *swaraj* or self-rule. It also has a unique Patola *sari* weaving unit to help preserve this disappearing craft form. **Open** for visitors 0900-1200.

SAURASHTRA

DISTRICT ▼
BHAVNAGAR
JUNAGADH
PORBANDAR
JAMNAGAR

RAJKOT ◄
Rajkot City
Wankaner
Morbi
Gondal
Khambhalida
Virpur
Jetpur
Tankara
Dhoraji

SURENDRANAGAR

Bangdi Bazaar

Located along Kanak Road in the old city, this market is a labyrinth of shops nestled in small lanes. You can find beadwork, tie-dye *saris* and other handicrafts in addition to the colorful *bangdi* or bangles after which the market is named. Close by is the **Soni Bazaar**, where you can purchase Rajkot's reputed gold and silver ornaments.

Shri Ramakrishna Mission

Set up to teach the Vedic principles of Ramakrishna Paramahansa (1836-86), a yogi with a large following across India, this campus has a guest house, Ayurvedic dispensary, public library, value education center and an exhibition of Ramakrishna's life. *Aarti* is at 0500 and 1930.

Rajkumar College

Also known as RKC, this college was built in 1868 to educate the children of Kathiawad royalty and aristocracy. RKC later became the first exclusive school of its kind to open its doors to the public and is now a co-ed school for grades K-12. The Gothic structure occupies an 11-hectare campus in the heart of the city.

NUTS & BOLTS

In and Out

A couple of daily flights connect Rajkot and Mumbai. A rickshaw ride into the city costs about Rs. 25. The city is well connected to other major cities of Gujarat and to Mumbai by rail and ST bus. Many private agencies have frequent buses to Ahmedabad, Vadodara and other parts of Saurashtra. Mostly located at Limda Chowk, some of these include **Shrinath Travels** *2241185, Apurva Bldg;* **Paavan Travels** *3043132, Apurva Bldg;* **Ashwamegh Travels** *2228403, Aakar Cmplx;* **Ekal Travels** *Limda Chowk,* **Holiday Travels** *2458255, Nr Garvi Handloom* handles domestic and international ticketing and other services. **Joshi Travels** *2233006, 14 Millpara, Nr Gujarati Samaj* rents out cars.

Getting Around

Some parts of Rajkot, such as the old city and main areas like Yagnik Road, can be covered on foot. You will need a rickshaw to navigate out to Ring Road and Kalawad Road. Rickshaws are unmetered. Most places within the city can be reached in Rs. 15 or less. Shuttles run along all major thoroughfares and cost between Rs. 2-5, while *chhakadas* generally run between the city and other destinations in the district.

Tourist Information

Gujarat Tourism Office *2234507, Jawarhar Rd, North of Sanganwa Chowk, Behind State Bank of Saurashtra.*

Money

ATMs There are plenty of ATMs and banks along Yagnik Road and Kalawad Road.

Rajkot City
Legend

Accommodation
1 Reeyo Motel
2 Hotel KK
4 Hotel Capital
10 Hotel Kuber Classic
12 The Imperial Palace
20 Hotel Suryakant
24 Hotel Kavery
25 Hotel Nildeep
26 Rainbow Hotel
39 Hotel Savera Palace
42 Hotel Bhabha
44 The Galaxy

Food & Drink
6 Cream Fresh
7 Café Coffee Day
11 Jai Siyaram Pendawala

23 Sadguru Alpahaar
27 Labela Ganthiya House
32 Temptations
33 Lord's Banquet Cuisine
37 Roshani Pani Puri
40 Jalaram Chiki
43 Adingo Temple Of Taste
50 Havmor Restaurant

Places of Interest
15 Rotary Doll Museum
19 Rashtriya School
28 Bangdi Bazaar
29 Kaba Gandhi No Delo
30 Watson Museum & Lang Library

Nuts & Bolts
3 Yahoo Online Cyber Village
5 Blue Dart Courier
8 Reliance World
9 Kotak Mahindra Bank

13 Raspberry Dept. Store
14 Western Union
16 Dev Forex
17 Sify Iway Cybercafé
21 Holiday Travels
22 Garvi Handloom Store
31 Vegetable Market
34 Eagle Tourism and Forex
35 Sanjivani Hospital
36 Maruti Courier
38 Shrinath Travels/ Ekal Travels
41 Paavan Travels
42 Ashwamegh Travels
45 Satnam Cybercafé
46 State Bank of Saurashtra
47 Gujarat Tourism Office
49 UTI ATM
51 General Post Office
52 Ranchhoddasji Bapu Charitable Trust Hospital

SAURASHTRA

DISTRICT ▼
BHAVNAGAR
JUNAGADH
PORBANDAR
JAMNAGAR

RAJKOT ◄
Rajkot City
Wankaner
Morbi
Gondal
Khambhalida
Virpur
Jetpur
Tankara
Dhoraji

SURENDRANAGAR

FOREIGN EXCHANGE **Eagle Tourism and Forex** *Yagnik Rd*; **Dev Forex** *City Plaza, Yagnik Rd.*
MONEY TRANSFER **Western Union** *Yagnik Rd.*

Communication

INTERNET **Reliance World** *Kalawad Rd , Nr Racecourse*; **Sify Iway** *Yagnik Rd, Opp DH College;* **Satnam Cyber Café** *Nr Galaxy Hotel, Jawarhar Rd* charges Rs. 15/hr; **Yahoo Online Cyber Village** *Kalawad Rd, Nr Hotel KK* costs Rs. 10/hr and has Net-2-Phone.
COURIERS **Blue Dart** *Nr Racecourse and Café Coffee Day;* **Maruti Courier**, *Moti Tanki, Nr the bus booking offices.*

Medical

HOSPITALS **Sanjivani Hospital** *2481811, Chitralekha Chowk, Moti Tanki Rd;* **Shri Ranchhoddasji Bapu Charitable Trust** *2457003, Kuwadawa Rd.*

Photography

There are a number of photo labs on Sardarnagar Main Road and a few on Yagnik Road.

Markets

Raspberry Department Store *Yagnik Rd, Nr Kanya Chhatralay.*

Shopping

Garvi Handloom *Yagnik Rd, Pramukhswami Arcade, Nr Malaviya Chowk* sells a variety of Gujarati handicrafts and a few items from around India.

ACCOMMODATION

Hotel Bhabha *2220861, Panchnath Rd, Nr M G Vidyalaya*, is fairly new with clean basic rooms and a friendly staff. It houses a popular *thali* place. **Facilities** western toilets, AC options, running hot water. **Single** 200-450 **Double** 395-650 **Triple** 475-850 **Quadruple** 500 **Extra Bed** 100.

Hotel Capital *2453234, Kishanpura Chowk, Race Course Rd* is a great bargain and conveniently located. **Facilities** western toilets, AC options. **Single** 325-550 **Double** 500-750 **Extra Bed** 100-150.

Hotel Savera Palace *2474798, Limda Chowk, Opp Shastri Maidan* is a good alternative to the Galaxy. **Facilities** western toilets, AC options, running hot water, TV. **Single** 390-625 **Double** 500-825 **Extra Bed** 150.

The Galaxy *2222905, Jawahar Rd, Nr M G Vidyalay* is recommended for those seeking more comfort. **Facilities** western toilets, AC options, running hot water, carpet and fridge options. **Single** 440-1760 **Double** 660-2640 **Triple** 1380-3090 **Extra Bed** 160-210.

Hotel KK *2454433, Kalawad Main Rd* is a reputed hotel in the city. The basic suites are a nice option at Rs. 1380. **Facilities** foreign exchange, airport courtesy transfer, mini-bar, travel desk, room service. **Rooms** 1200-5000.

The Imperial Palace *2480000, Yagnik Rd* is Rajkot's choice option. **Facilities** flat screen TV, mini-bar, direct access to internet, 24-hour coffee shop, boutique. **Single** 1900-3400 (43-76 USD) **Double** 2400-3900 (53-87 USD) **Suites** 5500-8500 (122-189 USD).

FOOD & DRINK

Rainbow Hotel *Lakhaji Raj Rd, Sanganva Chowk* is a local favorite for its cheap but good South Indian dishes and ice cream. **Hotel Suryakant** *Lodhawad Chowk, Gondal Rd* is Rajkot's famous 24-hour restaurant that serves simple Gujarati food, tea and snacks. It is always packed, mostly with men.

The **Adingo Temple of Taste** *Toran Apt, Limda Chowk* is a Kathiawadi restaurant with great *thalis* during the day and a-la-carte options at night. **Havmor Restaurant** *Jawahar Rd, Opp M G High School* has the usual suspects of Punjabi, Chinese, pizza and more. **Hotel Bhabha** *Panchnath Rd* serves a great *thali* for Rs. 60, and makes good *chaat*. **Kavery Hotel** *Kanak Rd, Nr GEB* is popular for its *thalis* and also offers sizzlers, Punjabi, pizza and more. The high power AC can be a bit much though. **US Pizza** *Kalawad Rd, in Hotel KK* has an all-you-can-eat buffet including salad, soup, garlic bread and pizza. **Temptations** *Kasturba Rd, Nr Mohanbhai Hall, Race Course* serves the regular multicuisine fare. They have interesting mocktails.

For a splurge try **Reeyo Motel, the Village Resort** *Kalawad Rd, Nr Drive-in Cinema.* It is a long haul, but worth the drive if you want a village setting, traditional Kathiawadi food and entertainment. **Lord's Banquet Cuisine** *Kasturba Rd, Nr Mohanbhai Hall, Race Course* is a Rajkot staple known for its Punjabi dishes.

Cream Fresh 27 *Race Course Rd* makes great homemade ice cream in flavors like carrot and cookie. **Senso - the Coffee Shop** *Imperial Palace, Dr Yagnik Rd* serves coffee and snacks in a swanky setting, open round the clock.

LOCAL SPECIALTIES Rajkot is known for its *jalebi, fafda* and *penda*. **Jai Siyaram Pendawala** *Yagnik Rd* is famous for *pendas* in various flavors. **Jalaram Chiki** *Limda Chowk* sells a variety of *chiki* (brittle) and sugar-free sweets made of figs and dates. **Labela Ganthiya House** *Dhebar Chowk* serves fresh *ganthiya and fafda* with hot *jalebi* and a tasty chutney called *sambharo* – a mix of carrots, cucumbers and other vegetables, with a dash of lime. **Roshani Pani Puri** *Limda Chowk* has do-it-yourself *pani puri* by the plate. You mix the ingredients and chutneys you want and fill your own *puri*.

SAURASHTRA

▼ DISTRICT
BHAVNAGAR
JUNAGADH
PORBANDAR
JAMNAGAR

▶ RAJKOT
Rajkot City
Wankaner
Morbi
Gondal
Khambhalida
Virpur
Jetpur
Tankara
Dhoraji

SURENDRANAGAR

EXCURSIONS

Wankaner   53 km from Rajkot

This town on the Gandhio Hilltop is known for its heritage properties. The **Ranjit Vilas Palace** built by Maharana Raj Shri Amarsinhji is still occupied by the royal family, but a few rooms have been converted into a museum displaying royal heirlooms and trophies. The two guest houses, **Royal Residency** and **Royal Oasis**, have been made into heritage hotels. The former was under renovation at the time of research.

The **Royal Oasis**, on the bank of the Machhu Lake, was completed in 1940. It has 12 grand rooms for tourists. The area is covered by leafy trees and the atmosphere is calm and pleasant. A beautiful garden, an early 20th c. three-storied stepwell and a spacious indoor Art Deco pool add to the grandeur. It has a multicuisine restaurant. **Deluxe Room** 2500 **Super Deluxe** 2800 **Suite** 3500. *For reservations contact 02828 220000.* Wankaner is easy to reach by ST bus.

Morbi   67 km from Rajkot, 53 km from Wankaner

The town welcomes the visitor with larger than life statues of Maharaja Lakhdev Bahadur and his horses at the entrance. Morbi was the capital of a state ruled by the Jadeja clan. Located on the Machhu River, this beautifully planned town reflects the progressive thinking of its former rulers. When Morbi was taken over by the British in the early 20th c., many of the royal properties acquired foreign names. A walk through the main bazaar gives a glimpse into its past splendor. The **Green Chowk** (the town square) is surrounded by **Nehru Gate** and **Lloyd's Gate,** which demonstrate contrasting styles. This square is also ideal to wander around and observe Morbi's reputed **clockmakers** at work. **Mani Mandir** was earlier used as the queen's residence and converted into the **Willingdon Secretariat** in 1936. After independence the building was taken over by administrative offices. It is an exquisite structure laden with fine carvings on the doors, walls and ceilings. The building demonstrates exquisite Rajput craftsmanship fused with European gothic influences and Islamic domes. The **suspension bridge** was built at the turn of the 19th c., and at one time connected Mani Mandir with the **Art Deco New Palace**, which has a simple two-story outward appearance that disguises its quirky, art nouveau interiors. The courtyards of Mani Mandir are open to the public, but permission must be taken from the caretaker to visit the palace. Morbi is well connected by ST bus.

Gondal

35 km from Rajkot

Gondal was a princely state ruled by the Jadeja Rajputs. Its main attractions are its palaces and buildings. **Riverside Palace** was built in 1875 by Bhagwatsinhji for his son. It is now a heritage hotel with balconies overlooking vistas of the manicured garden and rooms equipped with modern facilities. **Orchard Palace**, built as a guest house in the 19th c., is also now a heritage hotel, with part of it still housing the royal family. The personal train carriage of the king is also on exhibition, displaying a western kitchen, sitting room, bathroom and bedroom. Both hotels charge Rs. 2500/person, including three meals. *For bookings contact Kanaksinh Jadeja at 02825 224550 or 9824831541.*

The classic and vintage car museum (Rs. 100 for a tour) is interesting for car lovers. Its collection includes a 1910 New Engine, 1935 Mercedes and several vintage Cadillacs. Most cars are restored to original. **Open** 0900-1200 and 1500-1700, daily. **Entry** Rs. 10. **Navlakha Palace** (Darbargadh) was built around the 17th c., allegedly for nine *lakh* rupees (*nav lakh*—900,000). This building is a composition of delicate arches, splendid balconies, stone carvings and a unique spiral staircase. Now a private museum, it is open to guests of the Orchard Palace and showcases, among other items, the silver and gold caskets that held messages for the Silver and Golden Jubilees of Bhagwatsinhji and the scales on which he was weighed in silver and gold on his respective birthdays. The Darbar Hall is lit with chandeliers and decorated with stuffed panthers and Belgian mirrors.

Shri Bhuvaneshvari Peeth is dedicated to Goddess Bhuvaneshvari and supported by a trust, which also administers a charitable Ayurvedic hospital, a Kathiawadi horse breeding farm and a cattle farm. There is also the old Swaminarayan Temple resplendent with brightly painted wood carvings. A walk around Gondal is a pleasant experience. **Mandvi Chowk** is famous for its

SAURASHTRA

▼ DISTRICT
BHAVNAGAR
JUNAGADH
PORBANDAR
JAMNAGAR

▶ RAJKOT
Rajkot City
Wankaner
Morbi
Gondal
Khambhalida
Virpur
Jetpur
Tankara
Dhoraji

SURENDRANAGAR

handloom stores and street hawkers who sell items like beads, handmade toys and fresh farm produce in the evenings. Pick up some *dudhi tel*, hair oil made from green squash that cools the head. Gondal is accessible by road and rail.

Khambhalida   28 km from Gondal

Rock-cut caves flanked with two impressive carvings of Bodhisatvas at the entrance are situated in Khambhalida village. Buddhist monks hewed the caves in the 4th c. out of an isolated cliff. In the background you can you can hear the cry of peacocks. You will need your own transportation to reach this site.

Virpur   18 km from Gondal

The **Jalaram Temple** is a popular pilgrimage site and the former residence of the worshipped saint and social reformer, Jalaram Bapa (1800-78). He dedicated his life to selfless service and practiced the ancient Indian tradition of treating the guest as God. At 18, together with his wife, he started a *sadavrat*, a 24-hour kitchen, and fed anyone who came. This noble deed found many supporters and continues even today. P*rasad* is served twice a day. *Aarti* takes place at 1930.

Minal Vav nearby honors Minaldevi, mother of Siddhraj Jaysinh. Besides an image of the Queen, the stepwell depicts various deities. Women who want to have children come here for blessings. Frequent buses connect Virpur with Rajkot and Gondal.

Jetpur   69 km from Rajkot, 30 km from Gondal

As you approach Jetpur, known for its blockprints and Bandhani, you can catch a view of bright *saris* spread out under the sun for drying. Several showrooms near the ST stand offer live demonstrations of these textile processes.

Tankara   44 km from Rajkot

This is the birthplace of Swami Dayanand (1824-83), a saint and social reformer who founded the Arya Samaj, a Hindu reform movement based on Vedic principles. Dayanand's house now doubles as a memorial that displays a pictorial story of his life with Hindi captions. There are frequent buses from Rajkot to Tankara, but it is difficult to find return buses; jeeps are a good alternative (Rs. 20).

Dhoraji   88 km from Rajkot, 49 km from Gondal, 23 km from Junagadh

During the Islamic month of Rajab, a 6-day fair in memory of Khwaja Garib Nawaz Laal Shah Pir attracts thousands to the saint's *dargah* near Mandvi Chowk. The festivities include Mujra dance performances, not commonly associated with such observances. The town also has an old two-storied *darbargadh* with beautiful *jharokhas* and stone façades carved with animal figures.

SURENDRANAGAR DISTRICT

SURENDRANAGAR CITY
सुरेन्द्रनगर

POPULATION	156,200
AREA CODE	02752
DISTANCES - AHMEDABAD	116 KM
VADODARA	200 KM
RAJKOT	111 KM

Both geographically and culturally, Surendranagar is the interface between Gujarat and Saurashtra. To its north and east is the Little Rann of Kachchh, home of the Indian Wild Ass. The eastern boundary of the district roughly coincides with what several thousand years ago may have been a sea channel connecting the Gulf of Khambhat with the Rann, when it was an extension of the Gulf of Kachchh. Even today, the narrow strip of land between the two gulfs is flat and barely a few meters above sea level.

Few people visit Surendranagar for its own sake, but the district is brimming with attractions such as the Wild Ass Sanctuary near Dasada, the 11th c. gates of Jhinjhuwada and, if you go at the right time, the colorful Tarnetar Fair. For the more determined explorer there are medieval towns, capitals of erstwhile princely states, such as Wadhvan, Dhrangadhra, Halvad and Limbdi with their forts, palaces, gates, stepwells and temples. The countryside is practically littered with stepwells and the ruins of ancient temples.

Not too many decades ago Surendranagar was a rich grassland. Many of the animal species associated with that ecosystem, now adapted to fields of food crops, can still be seen in the wild. Prominent among these are the Nilgai.

Cotton plantations comprise a major part of Surendranagar's income and a significant share of the state's cotton production. Thangadh, near Tarnetar, is a major center for ceramics production. The district's northern edge along the Little Rann is lined with salt pans in which brine is accumulated and evaporated in the sun, leaving behind salt that is then collected and purified in factories.

Surendranagar town, on the Bhogavo River, is not very old by Indian standards. It was established by the British in the 19th c., during the reign of Maharaja Surendrasinhji, as an extension of the much older Wadhvan. Today the city is mainly important as a railway junction and a center of trade and agro-based industries. It offers a wider choice of hotels and restaurants than other places in the district, and is a convenient base from which to explore the surrounding areas.

NUTS & BOLTS

In and Out
About five trains that run daily between Ahmedabad and Rajkot stop at Surendranagar. From Ahmedabad the travel time by express train is about 2.5 hours; the frequent daytime ST buses take 3 hours. Private luxury buses are available to and from all major cities.

Getting Around
Rickshaws are the best mode for traveling in the city. ST buses and private minibuses, though crowded, are a good and cheap way to travel within the city and to nearby locations. The best way of getting to remote areas is by *chhakadas*, which charge between Rs. 5-20 depending on the distance. Shared rickshaws are also available within the city and to Wadhvan.

Money
ATMs **State Bank of Saurashtra** *Nagarpalika Office;* **UTI** *Bus Stand Rd;* **HDFC Bank** *Nr Milan Cinema;* **Dena Bank** *Main Rd.*

Communication
INTERNET **Ash InfoTech** *Main Rd;* **Labh Cyber** *Wadhvan Rd ;* **Net-2-Phone Cyber Café** *Wadhvan Rd* also offers Net-2-Phone facilities.

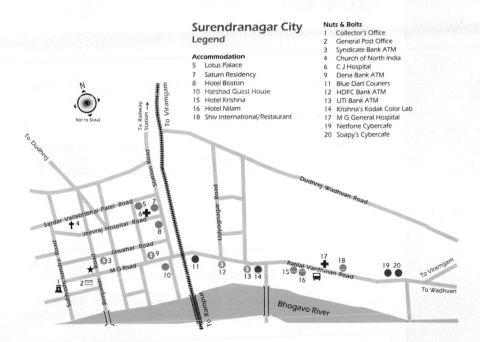

Surendranagar City

Legend

Accommodation
5   Lotus Palace
7   Saturn Residency
8   Hotel Boston
10 Harshad Guest House
15 Hotel Krishna
16 Hotel Nilam
18 Shiv International/Restaurant

Nuts & Bolts
1   Collector's Office
2   General Post Office
3   Syndicate Bank ATM
4   Church of North India
6   C J Hospital
9   Dena Bank ATM
11 Blue Dart Couriers
12 HDFC Bank ATM
13 UTI Bank ATM
14 Krishna's Kodak Color Lab
17 M G General Hospital
19 Netfone Cybercafe
20 Soapy's Cybercafe

Markets

The **main market** on MG Road has everything from shampoo to sandals.

ACCOMMODATION

Hotel Boston *224193, Station Rd* has basic dormitory accommodation with four beds in each room. **Dorm Bed** 50.

Harshad Guest House *222183, Station Rd* offers private rooms and dormitories. **Facilities** attached bathroom options. **Dorm** 55 **Single** 75-100 **Double** 150.

Hotel Nilam *224788, Bus Stand Rd* has small affordable rooms. **Facilities** western toilet, AC options. **Single** 100 **Double** 150-500 **Extra Bed** 50.

Hotel Krishna *222882, Bus Stand* has basic but clean accommodation at reasonable rates. **Facilities** western toilet, AC options. **Single** 125 **Double** 250-500 **Extra Bed** 50.

Shiv International *221762, Wadhvan Rd* is the only upscale hotel in town. **Facilities** western toilets, AC options, breakfast included, restaurant. **Single** 425-750 **Double** 490-850 **Suite** 1550 **Extra Bed** 125.

FOOD & DRINK

Shiv International is the best option in town, with tasty Punjabi and Chinese food at moderate prices. **Vrindavan Garden** also serves the same fare at similar rates, but it is set in a pleasant garden.

LOCAL SPECIALTY The city is famous for **Sikander Seeng**, a 40-year old peanut shop.

EXCURSIONS

Wadhvan   5 km from Surendranagar

Wadhvan is one of the finest examples of a lived-in fort town in Gujarat. Founded on the banks of the Bhogavo, it dates from at least the 12th c. Its rulers were of the Rajput Jhala clan, different branches of which reigned over neighboring principalities such as Dhrangadhra, Limbdi and Wankaner, collectively known as Jhalawad. The town fort has **six gates**, each leading in from different directions.

The ambience of the **old bazaar** is charming. People clad in traditional dress bustle away under low wooden buildings that house shops on the ground floor and residences above. Balconies jutting over the street add the final touch.

Wadhvan is famous for Bandhani (see **Resource Guide, Craft**). **Khandi Pol**, a major market for the craft, sells material at reasonable prices. Other local craft

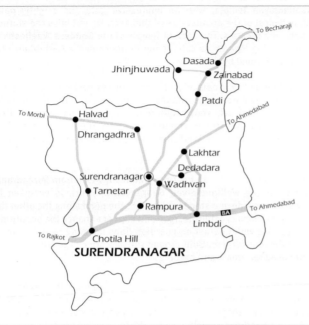

SAURASHTRA

▼ DISTRICT
BHAVNAGAR
JUNAGADH
PORBANDAR
JAMNAGAR
RAJKOT

specialties include brass, metal ware and wooden toys. The local food delights include *ganthiya* and *penda*.

The **Madha Vav,** from the late 13th c., is an exquisite stepwell in town. **Ganga Vav,** dating from the 12th c., is unfortunately poorly preserved but still worth a visit. The 19th c. **Raj Mahal** has sprawling grounds that include cricket pitches, tennis courts, gardens, fountains and lily ponds. The palace is designed around a central pillared courtyard with marble fountains, statues and furniture. Its **Darbar Hall** houses the royal throne and life-size paintings of past rulers. The **Shish Mahal** (Palace of Mirrors) is decorated with Belgian mirrors. The later rulers of Wadhvan were great automobile enthusiasts. Their passion is reflected in their collection of vintage, classic and sports cars in addition to a well-stocked library of automobile books. Raj Mahal is being converted into a ten-room heritage hotel.

The **Ranakdevi Temple** stands on the cremation ground at the southern edge of Wadhvan, alongside royal cenotaphs and *paliyas*. The story claims that Solanki King Siddhraj Jaysinh fell in love with Ranakdevi and pursued her. He killed her husband Rao Khengar to improve his chances, but Ranakdevi committed *sati* to protect her honor. Before she died she cursed the Bhogavo River, a mute witness to the injustice, to go dry forever. In medieval Hindu tradition a *sati's* curse is highly dreaded.

The **Swaminarayan Temple,** with an impressive gate and brightly painted interiors, is typical of the architecture of this sect. Do not miss the statues of gatekeepers with firearms. The ancient **Temple of the Goddess Wagheshvari** is worth a visit during Navratri to catch a performance of the Garbi dance form, traditionally performed by men only.

Hawa Mahal, literally "wind palace", is an ambitious project that was abandoned midway. The incomplete structure stands outside the fort and is worth studying for its architecture, which shows different stages of construction. Nearby Sompura artisans carve stones commissioned for Hindu and Jain temples in India and abroad. To reach Wadhvan take a local bus or shared auto from Surendranagar.

Dedadara
12 km from **Wadhvan**, 19 km from **Surendranagar**

This town hosts the well-preserved **Ganga Kund,** which is enclosed by a straight wall on one side and steps leading into the pond along the other three. Stones with sensual hues of purple, rose and copper enhance the beauty of this structure. A shrine with interesting guardian lions hovering over the entrance trim each of the four corners. Built around the late 9th c., the *kund* still stores clean water used for rituals and bathing.

Rampura
20 km from **Surendranagar**

This is the home of **Rataba Vav,** a stepwell in excellent condition that has remarkable pyramid shaped roofs crowning every tower visible above the ground. The surroundings, which include a lawn, are kept very clean.

Pratappur
25 km from **Surendranagar**

Here you will find the 17th c. **Chandrisar Talav,** an octagonal lake nearby Rajsitapur Village right off the Surendranagar-Dhrangadhra Road. The lake can be entered by any of the three side ramps. A sluice, a three-ring gate traditionally opened to let in water, stands at the far end.

Limbdi
35 km from **Surendranagar**

The capital of a princely state in Jhalawad, Limbdi was a prosperous cotton trading center between Saurashtra and the rest of mainland Gujarat. The arcaded bazaar, a conscious attempt in urban design, terminates at a handsome palace that has now been converted into the **Vivekanand Memorial. The Green Chowk, Gandhi Smriti Mandir, Tower Bungalow, Jagdish Ashram** and **Fulnath Mahadev Temple** are also worth visiting.

Chotila Hill
60 km from **Surendranagar**, 160 km from **Ahmedabad**

Chotila Hill on the Rajkot Highway is a pilgrimage site for devotees of Goddess Chamunda. She represents old age and death and is the most terrifying of the seven Mother Goddesses, all forms of Shakti. The **Chamunda Temple** stands at the summit reached only after climbing 700 steps. On both sides of the highway, at the foot of the hill, are shops and street vendors selling food, clothes, toys, and religious paraphernalia. Devotees often come here after walking long distances, sometimes even barefoot. Chotila can be reached by ST bus.

Dhrangadhra

35 km from Surendranagar

A former capital of the Jhala Kingdom, Dhrangadhra has colorful carved houses, hidden temples and two palaces. Despite devastation by the 2001 earthquake, the town has preserved much of its charm, in the quaint houses around **Green Chowk** and in the vibrant, often rowdy, vegetable market. For centuries, it has been a center of excellent stone carving. The Sompuras, traditional stone masons, of this town are still engaged in the trade and have kept the ancient architectural tradition of Hindu and Jain temples alive through their work in India and abroad (see **Resource Guide, Craft**). Outstanding examples of their craft can be seen in public and royal buildings such as **Suraj Mahal, Man Mahal**, the **bazaars** and the **towers** in town. The **Raj Mahal** palace sits on a hill just outside the town, and the **Old City Palace**, now partly converted into government offices and a school, is in the heart of town. These palaces are not open to visitors, but you can ask permission to visit them at the Raj Mahal Gate. The office of the Deputy Conservator of Forests is located here, making it a convenient strike-off point for the Wild Ass Sanctuary.

Halvad

27 km from Dhrangadhra, 62 km from Surendranagar

An otherwise ordinary town, Halvad's treasure is found at its cremation grounds where some 50 *paliyas* or memorial stones stand in and around a composition of *chhatardis*. These stones commemorate various members of the Jhala clan who gave their lives in battles fought between 1600 and 1800 AD. The women who sacrificed their lives to protect their honor are also memorialized by *sati* stones. Halvad also has a **palace** decorated with fine wood work and a 16th c. **stepwell** near Saraneshvar Temple.

Paliyas

Made out of sandstone, these memorial tablets are erected throughout Gujarat in memory of soldiers and warriors who sacrificed their lives in war or other brave feats. The face of the stone depicts images representing the celebrated individual or group while the sides are often adorned with symbols associated with their religious beliefs. Depending on the region, the details of the carvings change. Horsemen are common in Saurashtra while camel riders and seafarers are more likely in Kachchh. Images of a single hand or a female symbolize a *sati* or a woman who immolated herself on her husband's funeral pyre to protect her family's honor.

Tarnetar

90 km from Surendranagar, 200 km from Ahmedabad

During the famous Tarnetar Fair (see **Fairs and Festivals**) the town comes to life with magicians, snake charmers, puppet artists, traditional acrobats, dancers and tattoo artists. Sadus set up camps called *ravtis*, where they gather and sing devotional songs. Additionally, the fair hosts a **Rural Olympics,** complete with horse-cart, bullock-cart and camel races. The celebration takes place around the **Trineteshwar Mahadev Temple**, which is flanked by a pond on three sides. The temple is one of the rare examples of an ancient monument in Gujarat actually restored according to its original design. The town is connected by ST buses.

SAURASHTRA

▼ DISTRICT
BHAVNAGAR
JUNAGADH
PORBANDAR
JAMNAGAR
RAJKOT

▸ SURENDRANAGAR
Surendranagar City
Wadhvan
Dedadara
Rampura
Pratappur
Limbdi
Chotila Hill
Dhrangadhra
Halvad
Tarnetar
Wild Ass Sanctuary
Dasada
Zainabad
Jhinjhuwada

Wild Ass Sanctuary
130 km from Ahmedabad

The Wild Ass Sanctuary virtually encircles the Little Rann of Kachchh in a narrow band that covers nearly 3600 sq km in the four districts bordering on the Little Rann, and another 1400 sq km in Banaskantha, along the eastern edge of the Great Rann. The sanctuary was established in 1973 to protect the Indian Wild Ass (locally known as Ghudkhar). Ghudkhars are slightly bigger than donkeys and share many features, such as speed and physical strength, with horses. The sanctuary is home to approximately 4000 Wild Asses.

The sanctuary can be entered from three different places: **Dhrangadhra, Range Bajana** and **Range Aadeshwar**. Range Bajana is the best if you are visiting during winter because it is close to wetlands where a variety of migratory birds nest. Range Aadeshwar is at the confluence of the Little and the Great Ranns.

Classified as an endangered species, the Indian Wild Ass is found only in this part of Gujarat. The sanctuary also protects a host of other animals such as Blue bull, Blackbuck, wolf, Desert fox, jackal and a few species of snakes. The Wild Ass and the Nilgai are the most abundant species. It is not always easy to spot wildlife since the animals are wary of human contact. In winter, besides indigenous species of quails and sparrows, birds such as flamingoes, pelicans, falcons, and eagles nest at the sanctuary. The migratory birds stay for up to six months, laying eggs and hatching their young.

Transportation and accommodation are most easily available in Dhrangadhra. Buses or private vehicles going to Patadi can be used to reach the Range Bajana Gate. It is strongly recommended that you hire a knowledgeable guide and visit the sanctuary in the early hours to maximize your chances for spotting animals. Carry ample drinking water, food and other necessities with you on the trip. Private jeeps can be hired from Dhrangadhra and Patadi or from the Rann Riders Resort at Rs. 800-1500/day (6 people only). The sanctuary is open from November to March. *For more information contact Range Bajana 02757 226281.*

Dasada
67 km, Ahmedabad 90 km

Dasada was an independent state until it merged with India in 1947. While there are few notable remnants from its past, a key attraction of the place today is **Rann Riders,** a resort that has cottages, a swimming pool, a restaurant and offers jeep and camel safaris, horse riding, fishing and other recreational activities. It also organizes safaris to the Wild Ass Sanctuary. In winter Rann Riders offers exciting birdwatching trips. **One-night packages** (incl meals, safaris, sightseeing and mineral water) **Indian** Rs. 3600/couple (with one safari a day), **Foreign** Rs. 5600/couple (with two safaris a day). *For more information contact Mr Muzahid Malik 9879786006.* Buses are available from both Ahmedabad and Surendranagar.

Zainabad
100 km from Surendranagar

Desert Coursers is a resort that captures a traditional eco-friendly rural ambience combined with a few modern comforts. It offers warm hospitality with

an out-of-the-ordinary travel experience. The owners treat visitors as personal guests, and conduct 1-3 day excursions into the Little Rann to introduce people to local wildlife and the distinct pastoral culture. Tours are offered only when the sanctuary is open. The resort was started in 1984 by a local hunter-turned-conservationist. A significant part of its earnings fund basic education, health and water projects in surrounding areas.

The camp includes 16 traditional *kooba* houses arranged around a courtyard and embellished with patterned mud walls and mirrors. *Kooba* houses are the traditional dwellings of the Bajania community. **One-night packages** (incl three meals and a safari) **Indian** Rs. 1100/night, **Foreigner** Rs. 1900/night. *For more information contact Mr Dhanraj Malik 9426372113.* The management can also organize village stays for those interested in learning about rural life and culture. Buses and *chhakadas* will take you to Zainabad from most neighboring towns. You can also make arrangements from the train station at Viramgam.

Jhinjhuwada   80 km from Surendranagar, 115 km from Ahmedabad

Jhinjhuwada, about 10 km beyond Zainabad, stands on the eastern edge of the Little Rann of Kachchh. It is associated with the birth of the Solanki ruler, Siddhraj Jaysinh. Legend says that Minaldevi conceived him by the blessing of a saint who lived nearby. The town was a frontier fort of the Solankis and inscriptions on its walls testify to its antiquity. The **fort** was built in the 11th c. with huge stone blocks. It is one of the fine examples of pre-Islamic fortification in India, similar to that at Dabhoi in Vadodara District. The soul of this town exists in the **four gateways** that face the cardinal points. They boast of intricately carved brackets resting on massive piers with large statues of guardian deities flanking the gateways on both sides. Finely carved *jharokhas* project from above. There is also an old, man-made **lake** with side walls that have images of the ten incarnations of Vishnu and symbolic representations of the nine planets as deities.

Other interesting structures in the town include a **stepwell** and the remains of what may have been an **inner citadel,** with two minor arched gates more recently constructed. Although Jhinjhuwada is located in Surendranagar, it is in a remote corner of the district and is more easily accessed from Ahmedabad.

Navagraha (Nine Planets)

In traditional Hindu astrology the nine planets refer to the sun, moon, Venus, Mercury, Jupiter and Saturn. The remaining two, known as Rahu and Ketu are the points where the orbit of the earth around the sun intersects with the tilted orbit of the moon around the earth, also known as ascending and descending nodes. Rahu is always depicted as a bust and Ketu has a spiral coiled tail.

KACHCHH

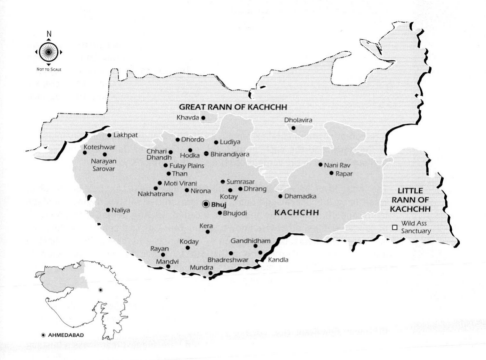

GREAT RANN OF KACHCHH

Khavda ●

Dholavira ●

● Lakhpat

Koteshwar

Narayan
Sarovar

Chhari ●
Dhandh

● Dhordo

Hodka ●

● Ludiya

● Bhirandiyara

● Fulay Plains

● Than

● Moti Virani

Nakhatrana

● Nirona

● Sumrasar

● Dhrang

Kotay

● Bhuj

● Bhujodi

KACHCHH

● Naliya

Kera
●

Koday
●

Rayan

Mandvi ●

Bhadreshwar ●

Mundra ●

Gandhidham
●

Kandla

● Nani Rav

● Rapar

● Dhamadka

LITTLE
RANN OF
KACHCHH

□ Wild Ass
Sanctuary

● AHMEDABAD

AT A GLANCE

With its notable mud architecture, a medley
of craft traditions and exquisite apparel, this
eminently colorful and culturally rich land has
a wonderful handcrafted feel. Each community
has its own oral traditions, dance, craft and
dress. Stretching along the Tropic of Cancer,
from Rajasthan to the edge of Pakistan and
the Arabian Sea, Kachchh covers a little over
45,000 sq km and is geographically one of
India's largest and most distinctive districts.

KACHCHH DISTRICT

BHUJ
ભુજ

POPULATION	136,500
AREA CODE	02832
DISTANCES - AHMEDABAD	395 KM
VADODARA	465 KM
RAJKOT	220 KM

A region of environmental extremes, Kachchh extends from the salty marshes in the north and the east through the grasslands of Banni and the central highlands down to the verdant coast along the Gulf of Kachchh.

The Indus River once flowed into the Great Rann near Lakhpat, but in 1819, when an earthquake raised a bank, the course shifted westward and altered the landscape of the area. The seawaters receded, leaving behind a broad swath of saline swamps, otherwise known as the Ranns of Kachchh. When the rains submerge the Ranns, the land becomes a virtual island resembling the back of a turtle, which is called *kutcho* in the local language and gives the region its name. The coast and the marshlands host many migratory and domestic birds, including giant flocks of flamingoes.

From the Great Rann rise sporadic outcrops of firm land known locally as *beyt* (island). Recent excavations on one such *beyt* known as Khadir have unearthed the most significant city, outside Pakistan, of the 5000-year-old Indus Valley Civilization. The seals and pottery discovered here suggest that it was a bustling port, with links to places as far as Zanzibar and Mesopotamia. Throughout its history, until the advent of railways, Kachchh was an important node on the trade routes of this part of Asia. This mercantile tradition has endowed Kachchhis with an inclusive worldview that long preceded colonization and globalization. Extensive contact with the world has fostered a rich ethnic mix in Kachchh while the contact with Sindh, a neighboring region in Pakistan, has been particularly important in shaping its cultural contours, especially language, cuisine and crafts.

The history of Kachchh as a kingdom begins in the 13th c. with the rule of the Samma Rajputs, who originated in Sindh. Their descendant Lakho Jadeja established the clan of the Jadeja Rajputs, who reigned until the region merged with the Indian Union. In 1549 Khengarji I (1548-85) consolidated independent territories and shifted the capital from Anjar to Bhuj. Under Bharmal I (1586-1631) Kachchh came under Mughal rule. The king impressed Emperor Jahangir with several lavish gifts and free passage for pilgrims to Mecca. In exchange the Emperor pardoned the region from paying tribute and granted permission to mint an independent Kachchhi currency, the *kori*. King Lakhpatji (1741-60) discovered Ramsang Malam, the legendary sailor turned master craftsman, and commissioned him to construct the Aina Mahal (glass palace) among other splendid works. The king was also pivotal to the development of Kachchhi painting. Desal II (1834-60) campaigned against *sati*, female infanticide and the slave trade. Administrative and social reforms were introduced by Pragmalji II (1860-75), who also initiated the construction of Pragmahal Palace. Protected forest areas called *rakhals* were introduced by Khengarji III (1875-1942), who also spread education and encouraged trade and industry. The British arrived at the turn of the 19th c. Although there was no revenue to be collected in this kingdom, they wanted to secure the Sindh border and control piracy along the Kachchh coastline. The growth of Mumbai also led to the decline of Kachchh's major port towns—Mandvi, Mundra, Lakhpat, Jakhau and Koteshwar—and it was in this same period that almost half of the district's population migrated to Mumbai and abroad.

In addition to frequent droughts, Kachchh has faced many natural disasters. The most destructive in living memory was the violent earthquake in January 2001 that devastated lives and property as far as Ahmedabad. While scars of the seismic tragedy still linger, the Kachchhi spirit remains indomitable. Walking around Bhuj today, set against the dramatic backdrop of the Bhujio Hill, you can see the vitality and resilience of its people.

PLACES OF INTEREST

The 2001 earthquake caused varying levels of damage in many places around Bhuj and around Kachchh. The sights we have listed still retain their charm despite the destruction, and many of them are under restoration.

The Aina Mahal Museum

The Aina Mahal, also known as the Palace of Mirrors, was built in 1761 under Maharao Lakhpatji, a great patron of art and culture. He envisioned the mahal as a pleasure retreat. Decorated with resplendent chandeliers, fountains, and doors inlaid with ivory and gold, the palace cost eight million *kori* to build. Lakhpatji's protégé, Ramsang Malam, spent seventeen years in Holland learning skills and crafts before returning to Kachchh and adapting European technology and techniques to local crafts. In addition to the palace, Lakhpatji commissioned Ramsang to create masterpieces, which are also on display at the museum. These include a pendulum clock coordinated with the Hindu

calendar, a sword and shield adorned with precious stones and shoes that spray perfume with each step. An Edison phonograph and century-old glass photo negatives are also exhibited. **Open** 0900-1200 and 1500-1800. **Closed** Sat. **Entry** Rs. 10. **Photography** Rs. 30.

The Pragmahal Palace

In the same complex as the Aina Mahal stands the impressive Pragmahal Palace, built by Maharao Pragmalji II in 1865. On the first floor is the large Darbar Hall, ornate with carved columns and statues. The palace's 45 m tower stands tall over the Bhuj skyline. While the structure is an architectural marvel, currently only three halls and a balcony are open to visitors. **Open** 0900-1145 and 1500-1745, daily. **Entry** Rs. 10. **Photography** Rs. 30, **Video** Rs. 100.

The Vegetable Market

Based in the **Shroff Bazaar**, the British built this fruit and vegetable market, which is still in use today.

The Kutch Museum

This museum, one of Gujarat's oldest, dates back to 1884. It features a wide collection of exhibits covering traditional textiles, metal artifacts, pottery, woodwork, sculpture, archeological objects, inscriptions and more. The Kutch Museum was constructed during the reign of Khengarji and facilitated by the Governor of Bombay, Sir James Fergusson. It is currently under renovation, so check the status before visiting.

Swaminarayan Temple

Coated in vibrant colors, this temple displays fine wood carvings and beautiful statues of Krishna and his beloved Radha. It also marks the spot where Swaminarayan sat with several holy men when he passed through Bhuj. The original idol has been shifted to a new marble temple on College Road.

Hamirsar Lake

The majestic Hamirsar Lake with a small park jutting into the middle of it lies in the center of Bhuj. A road circles the lake connecting **Alfred High School**, the Kutch Museum, and other historic sites. Next to the lake is a grove of trees that provides refuge from the mid-day heat.

Ramkund

Ramkund is a traditional square tank with short flights of steps waltzing down to the water. It is tucked away inside a narrow alley opposite the Kutch Museum, behind the **Ram Dhun Temple**. The walls of the *kund* have a narrow band of beautifully carved miniature idols depicting the ten incarnations of Vishnu along with other deities of the Hindu Pantheon.

Rao Lakhpat's Chhatardi

To the south of Hamirsar Lake are the *chhatardis*, or cenotaphs, of the royal family. A memorial stone commemorates the spot where the body was cremated,

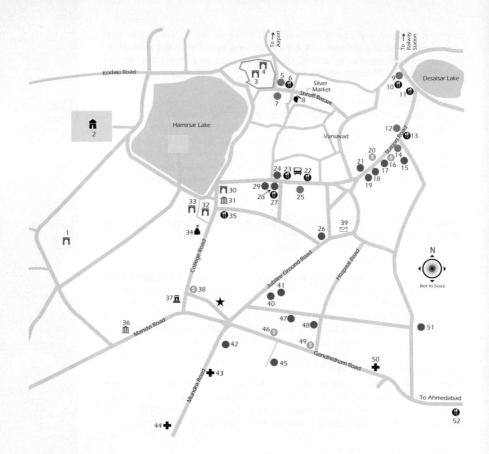

Bhuj
Legend

Accommodation
5 Hotel Gangaram &
   Guest House
7 City Guest House
9 Annapurna Hotel/ Restaurant
12 Hotel Prince (Jesal & Toral
   Restaurant)
14 Hotel KBN
25 Hotel Sahara Palace

Food & Drink
6 Green House
10 Sher e Punjab
11 Noorani Mahal
13 Nilam Restaurant
22 Joker
23 Gopi's Juice & Gola
27 Green Rock
35 Anando Restaurant
52 Hotel Hill View

Places of Interest
1 Chhatardi
2 Sharadbaug Palace
3 Pragmahal Palace
4 Aina Mahal
8 Vegetable Market
31 Kutch Museum
32 Temple Ruins
33 Ramkund
34 Swaminarayan Temple
36 Bharatiya Sanskriti
   Darshan Museum
41 Khamir
40 Qasab
45 KMVS
51 Kutch Navnirman Abhiyan

Nuts & Bolts
15 Ravi Cinema
16 Legend Forex
17 Reliance World Cybercafé
18 Jet Airways
19 Metro Travels

20 SBI ATM
21 Indian Airlines
24 Patel Travels
26 Abhay Digital Photo Lab
28 Sahajanand Travels
29 M K Auto Bike Rentals
30 Alfred High School
37 Collector's Office
38 ICICI ATM
39 Dty Superintendent of Police
42 Reliance Supermarket
43 Accord Hospital
44 MMJM Leva Patel Hospital
46 HDFC ATM
47 Orbit Cyber Café
48 www.cyber.com
49 UTI ATM
50 G K General Hospital

KACHCHH

▼ DISTRICT
▶ KACHCHH
   Bhuj
   Bhujodi
   Dhamadka
   Rudramata
   Kotay
   Kera
   Dhrang
   Sumrasar
   Bhirandiyara
   Ludiya
   Navavas
   Khavda
   Kalo Dungar
   Hodka
   Dhordo
   Jura
   Nirona
   Dinodhar Hill
   Chavda Rakhal
   Bohter Yaksh
   Moti Virani
   Fulay Plains
   Chhari Dhandh
   Lakhpat
   Narayan Sarovar
   Koteshwar
   Nani Rav
   Dholavira
   Mandvi
   Koday
   Bada
   Navjivan Nature
   Cure
   Rayan
   Mundra
   Bhadreshwar
   Getting Involved

with a pavilion built around it. The *chhatardis* of Lakhpatji, Rayadhanji II and Desarji are still partially intact and have elaborate arches and columns. The memorial of Lakhpatji also hosts a series of dancing girls along the capitals. Although several of the other tombs lie in ruins, the tranquil location of these memorials makes them one of Bhuj's most interesting attractions.

Bharatiya Sanskriti Darshan Museum

Founded by a forest service officer, Ramsinhji Rathod, who had a passion for Kachchhi folk art and handicrafts, the museum features an array of artifacts from remote regions of Kachchh collected while Rathod traveled the district on official duty. It has grown into an institution that is dedicated to the promotion and preservation of local crafts and culture. The displays include reconstructed models of rural architecture, paintings, archeological collections, ethnological arts and crafts. The museum's collection of textile art is excellent. **Open** 1000-1315 and 1400-1700, daily. **Closed** Mon. **ENTRY Indian** Rs. 10, **Foreign** Rs. 50. **Photography** is not permitted.

Sharadbagh Palace

Sharadbagh Palace remained the King's residence until Madansingh, the last ruler of Kachchh, died in 1991. Upon his demise, the palace became a museum. Surrounded by gardens of flowering and medicinal plants, it gives a glimpse into the past grandeur of Kachchh. Although the palace is off limits, the royal collection of china, game beasts, ivory and coins is on display in a small cottage museum. **Entry** Rs. 25. **Photography** requires special permission from the Palace Trust and a fee of Rs. 25. **Open** 0900-1200 and 1500-1800. **Closed** Fri.

NUTS & BOLTS

In and Out

Depending on the season, there is one or more daily flight between Mumbai and Bhuj. Check current status with a travel agent. There are two daily express trains connecting with Mumbai (16 hrs) via Ahmedabad (8 hrs), but their schedules are designed for the convenience of Mumbai passengers. ST and private buses ply regularly between Bhuj and major towns and cities in Gujarat. One option from Gandhinagar, Ahmedabad and Bhavnagar is the sleeper bus, which leaves between 2100-2300 and arrives in Bhuj between 0600-0800. These fill up quickly, so book in advance with a travel agent. Private buses (sitting only) with and without AC are also available.

Getting Around

Bhuj is centrally located and serves as a convenient hub from which to explore the district, either by ST bus or private vehicle. If you are traveling light, shared jeeps and shuttles are a good alternative to the ST buses for travel between Bhuj and major towns such as Mandvi and Mundra. Outside the larger towns, *chhakadas* are often the only public transport available between destinations.

Rickshaws are convenient for getting around Bhuj and should cost about Rs. 15-25 to most places. You can rent a motorcycle from **M K Auto** *222243, Nxt to Sahajanand*

Tours and Travels. Motorcycle rentals cost approximately Rs. 300 for 24 hours. Although there are various transportation options, Bhuj is best enjoyed on foot.

Rent a private vehicle to explore the villages in Banni and Pachchham, the Kalo Dungar and the Ranns. Most hotels can arrange car rentals (with driver). Alternatively you can approach any of the parked cars across the bus station and negotiate a rate with the driver.

Tourist Information

Visit the privately run tourist information center at the Aina Mahal, where the curator Pramodbhai Jethi *9374235379, 220004* offers extensive firsthand knowledge and literature on the history, crafts, culture and people of Kachchh. His books on Kachchh, among other good resources, are available at the museum reception desk; he can also help arrange guide services. Another great source of information is Dalpatbhai Danidharia with the **Kachchh Eco-Education Tourism Cell** *221379 Kachchh Nav Nirman Abhiyan, Dr Rajaram Campus, Nr St Xavier's School*, who has been developing an ecotourism circuit in Kachchh.

Travel Agencies

Most tour and travel operators are located on Bus Station Road. **Sahajanand Tours and Travels** *222236* and **Patel Tours** *221499* book private bus tickets for travel to Ahmedabad and other major destinations in Gujarat. To book a flight or make hotel reservations, contact **Metro Travels** *229751, Opp SBI, Bus Station Rd* or **Smriti Travels** *Nxt to Sahajanand Travels*.

Money

ATMs **SBI** *Bus Station Rd*; **ICICI Bank** *Collector's Office, College Rd*; **HDFC Bank** *Gandhidham Rd, Nr General Hospital*; and **UTI Bank** *Gandhidham Rd*.
FOREIGN EXCHANGE **Legend Forex Changer** *225576, Arihant Chamber, Station Rd*.
MONEY TRANSFER **Western Union** is available at the General Post Office.

Communication

INTERNET **Reliance World** Bus Station Rd, Nr Metro Travels; **www.cyber.com** *Jay Somnath Apt, Hospital Rd* has broadband internet service, image downloading, burning facilities, a digital camera card reader, scanners and web cameras; **Orbit Cyber Cafe** *Ashutosh Apt, Ganshyam Nagar Rd, Opp PPC*.
COURIER **Nisu Couriers** *229751, Opp SBI*.

Medical

HOSPITALS Rebuilt and upgraded after the 2001 earthquake, Bhuj has several outstanding hospitals including **GK General Hospital, Accord Hospital**, and the **MMJM Leva Patel Hospital** all equipped with the latest technology and 24-hour service. There are plenty of medical stores along Hospital Road.

Photography

Abhay Digital Studio *Nxt to Temple Ruins at Jubilee Ground Rd and Bus Station Rd Intersection*, is a good place for procuring and processing still and digital photography.

Bookstores

The book stalls in the **Hotel Prince lobby** and **Aina Mahal** stock a variety of books, especially related to travel and Kachchh.

Markets

Reliance Supermarket *Mundra Rd, Nr Jubilee Ground*, the **Shroff Bazaar**, and the **Vaniavad** area are good places to pick up basic commodities.

Shopping

Bhuj is a great place to purchase traditional handcrafted products from around the region (see **Resource Guide, Craft**). For textile products such as traditional Bandhani (tie-dyed cloth) or embroidery, shop at one of the Shroff Market outlets or at the **Kachchh Kutir Udhyog** *Ashirvad Cmplx, Opp Apna Bazaar, Vaniavad*, which stocks beautiful embroidery and block printed textiles.

Several non-profit organizations work directly with artisans and help with the design, marketing and quality assurance of their crafts. **Qasab**, *Nutan Colony, Behind the Santoshi Mata Temple, Jubilee Ground Rd*, run by **Kutch Mahila Vikas Sangathan (KMVS)**, sells fine embroidered products stitched by rural women. The **Khamir Craft Resource Centre** *Nxt to KMVS* carries a unique collection of lacquer crafts, leather work, copper bells, earthen pottery, wood crafts, tie-dye garments, block print work, woven shawls and stoles. Khamir assists local artisans to develop products for today's market without abandoning traditional knowledge and techniques. For more information about these non-profits see **Getting Involved** at the end of this section.

ACCOMMODATION

Annapurna Hotel *220831, Opp Bhid Gate* is a family run operation with simple and clean accommodation. Owner-manager, Jyotindra Gor interacts with guests, and personally oversees the hotel's management. He has a great collection of books on Kachchh and is well-versed on the region. The hotel is strongly recommended for the budget traveler and it has two good restaurants on the ground floor. **Dorm** 40 **Single** 150 **Double** 100-200.

City Guest House *221067, Langa St, Nr Shroff Mkt* has plenty of rooms. **Facilities** western toilets available. **Single** 70 **Double** 150-180.

Jay Guest House *221389, Nr Meera Market, Bus Stand, Vaniya Vad* is a good budget option. **Single** 120-170 **Double** 180-260.

Hotel Gangaram and Guest House *224231, Nr Aina Mahal, Darbargarh Chowk, Mallsheri* is another good option for budget travelers. Although there is a restaurant on the premises, it is a better idea to walk to **Green Restaurant** nearby. **Facilities** attached baths, western toilets, on-site travel bookings, foreign exchange, car rentals, steam and sun baths, email, ISD. **Single** 300 **Double** 400.

Hotel Sahara Palace *220970, Opp Bus Stn* is easily accessible from the ST bus station and offers clean rooms and good service. It also houses a good multicuisine restaurant. **Facilities** AC options, accepts all major credit cards. **Single** 350-850 **Double** 500-1000.

Hotel KBN *227251, Station Rd* offers clean rooms and a friendly staff. It also has an attached restaurant that serves good continental fare. **Facilities** running hot water, laundry, AC, taxi and guide service, accepts all major credit cards. **Single** 600-3000 **Double** 1300-3500 **Extra Bed** 400.

Hotel Prince *220370, Station Rd* is one of the best hotels in Bhuj. It has two restaurants, **Toral** and **Jesal** and offers a wide variety of amenities. **Facilities** western toilets, running hot water, AC, laundry, room service, airport courtesy transfer, money exchange, wine shop, taxi and guide service, safety deposit boxes, accepts all major credit cards. **Single** 700-2500 **Double** 900-2800.

OUTSIDE OF BHUJ

The Garha Safari Lodge *9825013392, Rudramata Dam (14 km out of Bhuj)* is a resort consisting of 17 *bhungas* equipped with modern facilities and attached bathrooms overlooking the Rudramata Dam. It offers special theme dinners with folk performances and organizes safaris into the Banni villages. **Facilities** western toilets, running hot water, room services. Contact for rates.

Shaam E Sarhad, Hodka *02832 221379, www.hodka.in* is an eco-friendly option. This resort, built entirely of local materials, integrates indigenous design, promotes village development, and helps sustain local artisans. Accommodation is offered in traditional *bhungas* or family tents. Packages include all meals except lunch (separately arranged on request) and folk performances. The resort operates Sep-Mar. **Facilities** western toilets, attached bathrooms, running hot water. **Individual Tents** 1600 -1800 **Family Tents** 2400-3000 **Bhunga** 2600-2800 **Extra Bed** 500.

FOOD & DRINK

Hotel Nilam *Station Rd*, **Green Rock** *Nr the Bus Stn, Above Sahajanand Travels*, **Anando** *Ganshyam Rd, Nr the Kutch Museum*, **Green Restaurant** *Opp Veg Mkt, in Shroff Mkt*, **Joker** *Bus Station Rd*, **Hill View Hotel** *Katira Complex at RTO Relocation Area* and **Hotel KBN** *Station Rd* are all good vegetarian restaurants that serve Gujarati, Punjabi, South Indian and Chinese fare.

Toral *in Prince Hotel, Station Rd* offers an extensive Gujarati *thali* worth the higher price. **Annapurna** *in Hotel Annapurna* serves Gujarati *thalis* and Indian vegetarian food in a simple ambience.

Jesal *in Prince Hotel, Station Rd* is a more upscale restaurant that offers poached or scrambled eggs and cornflakes for breakfast. They prepare fish flambé, fish florentine and a variety of vegetarian and meat options throughout the day. **Hotel Delhi Darbar** *Opp the Bus Stn* and **Hotel Noorani Mahel** *Station Rd* serve good meat dishes. **Sher e Punjab** *Bhid Gate Behind Annapurna Hotel* also has non-veg food, but tends to be crowded at times.

Station Road and the area around **Vijaynagar Complex** on **Kalpataru Road** come alive in the evenings with *laris* selling assorted eatables ranging from *pani puris*, *dabelis*, ice cream and more. **Gopi's Juice and Gola Parlor** is recommended for ice cream and *golas* (crushed ice, flavored with fruit syrups).

LOCAL SPECIALTIES Kachchhi *dabeli*, a bun stuffed with a spicy filling and peanuts, is a local specialty worth trying. The district is also renowned for a variety of delicious sweets. Be sure to try *mesuk*, made with chickpea flour, sugar and ghee, and *gulab paak*, a sweet made of milk, sugar and rose petals. If you are around in winter, *adadiya* (a pulse-based sweet, rich in ghee, jaggery, and nutmeg) is worth sampling. Bhuj has several **Khavda Sweet Shops** but **Khavda Mesuk Bhandar**, a modern looking shop in the narrow back-lane leading from the ST bus station to Vaniavad Gate, is strongly recommended.

EXCURSIONS

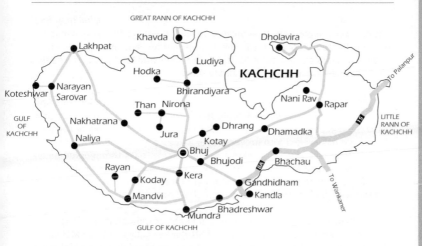

Note: Since Kachchh is a border area, it is important for visitors to take permission from the **Deputy Collector's Office** or the **Deputy Superintendent of Police** in Bhuj before visiting certain areas. Please inquire before heading out of Bhuj.

Bhujodi
8 km from Bhuj

Nestled away in Bhujodi is a community of master artisans versed in traditional weaving, tie-dyeing and block printing. You can see live demonstrations and buy directly from the artisans. **Vankar Shyamji Vishram**, nationally awarded for his hand weaving, has an excellent collection of shawls, stoles and sheets. About a kilometer behind Bhujodi is the **Ashapura Crafts Park**, a non-profit venture by the Ashapura Group of Companies that works with artisans across Kachchh to display their skills and sell their products. On weekends the Park also organizes music and dance performances.

KACHCHH

▾ DISTRICT
▸ KACHCHH
Bhuj
Bhujodi
Dhamadka
Rudramata
Kotay
Kera
Dhrang
Sumrasar
Bhirandiyara
Ludiya
Navavas
Khavda
Kalo Dungar
Hodka
Dhordo
Jura
Nirona
Dinodhar Hill
Chavda Rakhal
Bohter Yaksh
Moti Virani
Fulay Plains
Chhari Dhandh
Lakhpat
Narayan Sarovar
Koteshwar
Nani Rav
Dholavira
Mandvi
Koday
Bada
Navjivan Nature Cure
Rayan
Mundra
Bhadreshwar
Getting Involved

Shrujan, situated past Bhujodi on Gandhidham Road, is a non-profit organization that was established in 1968 after a serious drought. It works to supplement the income of rural women through their embroidery skills and by marketing their products (see **Getting Involved**). In addition to a store, **Shrujan** also houses a design center, manufacturing unit and a fine collection of embroidery. Take a tour of the campus, which uses local traditional environmentally conscious architecture.

Dhamadka   50 km from Bhuj

In this village you will find artisans who still print Ajrakh (block printed cotton cloth used traditionally by local herdsmen) with natural dyes. The geometrical and abstract motifs often emulate those found in Islamic-influenced Indian architecture. Visit **Ismail Khatri**, a national award winner for his Ajrakh prints, and his family to learn more about this craft. After the earthquake, part of the printers' community has been rehabilitated in a new settlement, closer to Bhuj, called Ajrakhpur.

Rudramata   14 km from Bhuj

The **Rudrani Temple** here is dedicated to four Hindu goddesses—Ashapura, Rudrani, Ravechi and Momaya. The temple garden and nearby nursery of medicinal plants stand in stark contrast against the arid landscape. The garden draws water from the nearby **Rudramata Dam**.

Kotay   18 km from Bhuj

The exquisitely worked **Kotay Temple** has recently been restored. It belongs to the Solanki period (10th-14th c.) and is covered with outstanding carvings. The temple has evoked a controversy over whether it is dedicated to Shiva or the Sun. Veer off the road heading towards Khavda, pass through Rudramata and follow the right fork in the road towards Dhori. The dirt path leading to the temple is also wide enough for a motorbike. There is no signage, but the local villagers will gladly point you in the right direction.

Mekran Dada (1719-52), also known as Saint Kabir of Gujarat, is associated with the popular legend that with the help of his donkey Laliya and dog Motiya, he rescued and cared for travelers who lost their way or fell ill in the Great Rann. He was also a mystic, credited with composing progressive poems called *duha*, directed against social ills and superstitions prevalent in society. The **Mekran Dada Temple**, which has been reconstructed with cement, is built at the place where his soul attained liberation from his body.

Kera   22 km from Bhuj

Kera village is home to a **Shiva Temple** from the Solanki period. The only prominent features that remain are part of the sanctum walls and half of the spire, which was split vertically by the 1819 earthquake. It has some classic sculptures and simple but elegant stone grilles. For a closer view of the details on the spire and the sanctum walls, you can climb the mound alongside the temple. Next to the temple stands the poorly-maintained **Fort of Kapilkot**. Part of its wall was realigned to make space for the temple.

Banni and Pachchham

Banni consisted of grasslands that once covered more than 4000 sq km and supported a rich livestock culture in about 30 villages. Over the last couple of decades, these grasslands have been disappearing at an alarming rate, and of the 40 endogenous species of grass that once existed, only ten to fifteen remain.

Crazy Weed

The land is plagued by the invasive exotic species of a thorny shrub, *Prosopis juliflora*, locally known as **Gando Baawal** (crazy weed). Introduced in 1960 by the Forest Department to combat desertification, the Gando Baawal has rebounded by ousting many local species of flora and drastically lowering the water table. Locals, however, have learned how to extract gum and make charcoal from these shrubs as a source of income generation.

Besides their traditional occupations, the Banni communities also excel in woodcarving, a variety of embroidery styles, patchwork, quilting and leather work. The people are extremely hospitable. If you are lucky you might get to hear the local Sufi music. The men gather late into the night to sing spiritual hymns accompanied by local instruments. If the opportunity arises while in Banni or Pachchham, do not miss sleeping under the glittering night sky, infinitely filled with constellations.

Banni and Pachchham together host a variety of colorful villages and exquisite crafts (see **Resource Guide, Craft**). Below the names of the respective villages, we have listed the names of master artisans of various skills who can offer a keener insight in their area of expertise. It is usually possible to purchase directly from the artisan. Please pay what you honestly feel each piece is worth, keeping in mind the dexterity and time put into the craft. It is worth hiring a vehicle to explore this vast area.

Dhrang

This village hosts the **Dhrang Mela** (see **Fairs and Festivals**).

Sumrasar
25 km from Bhuj

On the way to Banni from Bhuj take a detour to Sumrasar to visit **Kala Raksha**, the non-profit organization that works with a number of communities, mainly the Rabaris, in developing unique handicraft designs (mostly embroidery) and marketing them to help sustain the communities. There is a shop located on the campus that sells a variety of these products. There is also a small museum that showcases the culture of local communities.

Bhirandiyara
60 km from Bhuj

A stop along the road between Bhuj and Khavda, this town is most famous for its fresh *maavo*, milk reduced to a thick fudge-like consistency and sweetened with sugar—best when eaten hot. You can purchase it from a few of the roadside stalls clustered around the Bhirandiyara bus stop and maybe even catch one of the men stirring a pot of this delicacy over an open fire. The local Meghwal community is

known for its fine embroidery and colorful mud *bhungas*. To see samples of their leatherwork, meet with craftsman **Arjan Vela**. From the rains, shallow lakes form along the road to Bhirindiyara, attracting flocks of flamingoes in the winter.

Bhunga

These circular mud huts with thatched roofs are visually striking against the desert landscape and were the only housing structures to withstand the 2001 earthquake. The mud, dung and twig (*lipan*) combination used to plaster the huts make them wind resistant, while the conical roof overlaid with a layer of dung, topped with another layer of grass, provides water resistance. A household may consist of two or more *bhungas* in an enclosure, each used for a different purpose. Women paint the outside of the huts every year around Diwali with colorful geometric designs using clay and mineral rock colors. The interiors are exquisitely embellished with designs made of mirrorwork set in lime and mud plaster, which they also use to make in-built shelves and cupboards. They showcase their vessels and other belongings on these as decorations and as a display of their wealth.

Ludiya   63 km from Bhuj

Located about 1 km off the main road to Khavda, Ludiya is divided into several hamlets. **Gandhi nu Gam**, inhabited by the Meghwal community, boasts of beautifully painted circular huts organized around the temple. Between the vibrant *kanjari* blouses of the women and the men hunched over in various corners carving wood, the village is an aesthetic delight. In the effort to curb exploitation and experiment with community marketing, the hamlet has set up an *otlo* or a roofed platform next to the temple, where each household brings its embroidered goods for selling. Please respect this effort and avoid browsing through items in individual households. The remaining hamlets belong to the Samma community, who are primarily herdsmen and slightly more conservative towards tourists.

Navavas   63 km from Bhuj

Situated just before Ludiya, the village of Navavas also comprises the Meghwal community and is another great place to find beautifully crafted embroidery and woodwork. Meet with **Hirabhai**, who heads the village work shed, to see interesting experiments with wood designs.

Khavda   66 km from Bhuj

The main town of the Pachchham region, Khavda is a good stopover for picking up bottled water and some fruits. There are also a few rustic lodges that serve Kachchhi food. Opposite the main bus stand is the home of **Ibrahim Kaka**, whose family of potters create amazing earthenware. Visit **Khatrivas** for artisans printing and selling Ajrakh; there are also skilled leather craftsmen in town. Off the main road towards the Public Health Center is a new women's hospital built by KMVS. The organization has trained traditional midwives in modern and locally appropriate healthcare practices. The **KMVS office** in Khavda, on the other side of the road heading to Bhuj, is run almost entirely by local women and has a small retail outlet selling beautiful embroidered products and handmade dolls.

Kalo Dungar (The Black Hill)   **90 km from Bhuj**

The highest hill in Kachchh, Kalo Dungar rises 462 m above sea level and lies near the India-Pakistan border. At the top you can enjoy a cool breeze and a panorama of the Great Rann of Kachchh. There is also a temple dedicated to the Hindu deity Dattatreya, the trinity of Brahma, Vishnu and Shiva in one body with three heads and six hands that is accompanied by a cow and four dogs. Every day, following the afternoon and evening *aarti*, jackals emerge from the rocky terrain to eat *prasad* from the temple. If possible, you should visit the hilltop around sunrise or sunset for a breathtaking view. Buses travel from Khavda to Kalo Dungar only on weekends around 1700 and leave early the next morning around 0500. From Khavda you can also hire a vehicle, preferably a jeep because the roads are steep. The hill also makes for some great trekking. For a night stay, the *dharmashala* is an option. Carry an extra supply of food and water.

Hodka   **35 km from Bhuj**

Cattle-rearing is the main occupation of this village that is largely inhabited by the Meghwals and the Halepotras, who migrated from Sindh in the 18th c. These lively and hospitable craft communities live in *bhungas* and offer a striking variety of embroidery and leather craft. Visit master craftsman **Bhasar Bhura**, who won a national award for his leatherwork.

Dhordo   **80 km from Bhuj**

Full of Banni hospitality and rich culture, Dhordo is mostly occupied by the Mutwa community, who hail from Sindh. The women are ingenious with thread and needle and do an extremely fine style of embroidery called Mutwa that is patterned around tiny mirrors. The village also has a few talented mud artisans whose work is seen on several of the local *bhungas*.

Traditional Water Systems

Extreme weather conditions and frequent droughts in this area have led the local people to evolve innovative ways to capture and manage rain water. They dig shallow pits called *virdas* in almost invisible depressions in the ground, just over the layer of salty groundwater. When it rains, the *virdas* collect water flowing across the surface. The people scoop it out when needed. Even if it seeps down to the body of saline water, the fresh water remains on top because of its lower density. Since it cannot be readily agitated underground, the two do not easily mix. As the fresh water diminishes, the saline water gradually rises through the soil and collects at the bottom of the *virda*, but does not immediately contaminate the potable water above. Just 25 cm of rain is enough to provide fresh water for a few months.

Jura and Nirona

On the way back to Bhuj try to stop by Jura and Nirona. Meet master craftsman **Ilyas Lohar** or **Haji Vali Mohammad** to learn about the skill-intensive process of tuning the famous copper bells of Jura. Nirona, about 6 km from Jura, is home to about half a dozen distinct craft forms. Visit **Abdul Gafur Khatri,** who belongs to the last remaining family of Rogan artisans, and watch him use a metal stick and some castor-oil based colors to create a masterpiece. Observe **Sugar Saya** or **Mala Khamisa** in **Vadavas** as they transform wood with bright lacquer colors.

Than Monastery and Dinodhar Hill 60 km from Bhuj

The Dinodhar Hill, 386 meters high, stands near Aral village. On its summit is a temple dedicated to **Dhoramnath**, who is said to have performed rigorous penances here for 12 years. This is a good trekking spot with ample wildlife and flora. At the foot of Dinodhar is the **Than Monastery** with another **Dhoramnath Temple** and several other shrines. On the first floor of the building are some beautiful Kamangari paintings of Hindu deities, floral patterns and the story of the Rajasthani Romeo and Juliet, Dhola and Maru. A bus leaves every evening for Than from Bhuj and remains there overnight to leave early next morning. Arrange your own transport unless you plan to stay 36 hours.

Chavda Rakhal

The former rulers of Kachchh declared protected forest reserves called *rakhal,* which were not commercially exploited, although grazing cattle were allowed in some. Kachchh has about 45 *rakhals*. Chavda Rakhal, near Samtra on Nakhatrana Road, is one of the best preserved and makes for a good place to relax.

Bohter Yaksh 34 km from Bhuj

The **Bohter Yaksh Temple** is associated with the legend of Jam Punvaro, a tyrant king. He married the King of Sindh's daughter, who was a devotee of Shiva. She brought a deity with her to Sanyana village, her new home, where she installed the idol in a temple. The temple is known as **Puanreshwar Temple** and exemplifies Solanki period stone architecture. Punvaro continued to oppress his subjects, especially the Sanghar people in the neighboring village. To deliver them from his tyranny, 72 (*bohter*) warriors or *yakshas* (*jakhs* in Kachchhi), believed to be of Assyrian origin, and their sister Sayari, settled on a nearby hilltop, named Kakkad Bhit after the eldest of the *yakshas*. They killed the king. The Sanghars made the *yakshas* their patron deities and erected the Bohter Yaksh Temple in memory of this event.

Moti Virani 57 km from Bhuj

Shantidas Tulsidas Solanki and family are among the few artists who still handcraft silver jewelry with indigenous designs for various communities.

Centre for Desert and Ocean (CEDO) was founded and is run by the enthusiastic ecologist, **Jugal Tiwari**, who is also a keen birdwatcher and passionate environmentalist. Wildlifers, geologists and ornithologists from all over visit this place for research and fieldwork. Tiwari takes his guests on safaris and birding trips in the Fulay Plains. Accommodation (with food) is available at CEDO at Rs. 600 for a 24 hours stay. Desert safari, birdwatching and handicraft excursions in an AC Jeep cost about Rs. 1200. Special ornithology expertise is Rs. 1000. Pick-up or drop-off at the Bhuj airport or railway station costs another Rs. 1200. The best time to visit is from September to March. *Contact 02835 200025, cedoindia@yahoo.com in advance to book a trip.*

Fulay Plains and Kiro Dungar

Kiro Dungar is an extinct volcano in the Fulay Plains, about 20 km from Moti Virani village and 5 km from the town of Nakhatrana. This place abounds in

65-million-year-old fossils of snails, conches and other marine organisms. It is also a birdwatcher's paradise.

Chhari Dhandh
75 km from Bhuj

A *dhandh* is a large, shallow pond of collected rainwater. Kachchh has 34 *dhandhs*. Chhari, which covers about 10 sq km, is the largest of them and lies between Banni and Dhinodhar Hill. It attracts over 50 species of waterfowl, including the endangered Indian Skimmer and Dalmatian pelican.

Lakhpat
140 km from Bhuj

Lakhpat Fort sits at the point where **Kori Creek** meets the Great Rann of Kachchh. It was once a thriving port with daily revenue believed to exceed one hundred thousand (one lakh) *koris*, hence the name Lakhpat. Jamadar Fateh Muhammed erected the first fortifications in 1801 and enclosed the entire town within a 7 km long fort wall, most of which still stands. The walkway along the northern battlement offers stunning views of the creek merging into the Rann, and has watchtowers at regular intervals.

After the displacement of the Indus River in 1819 the busy port was abandoned and the town that once brimmed with 10,000 people stands almost completely uninhabited today.

Guru Nanak, the first Guru of the Sikhs, is believed to have camped in Lakhpat on his way to and from Mecca. The house where he stayed was later sanctified as a *gurudwara* (a Sikh temple). Some of his personal belongings were later brought and displayed here. Recently renovated, the *gurudwara* has a 34-m tall **Nishan Saheb** (a flagpole robed in saffron cloth and topped with a banner bearing the **Khanda Saheb**, the symbol of Guru Nanak). However, this *gurudwara* is not particularly significant for the Sikh community.

The **Ghaus Mohammed no Kubo** is the mausoleum of the mystic **Pir Ghaus Mohammed**, who became a fakir at the early age of twelve. The Kubo is an admirable example of stone architecture with very intricate carvings and took thirteen years to build. The body of the Pir rests here along with other members of his family. Nearby is a small water tank that is believed to possess therapeutic properties, which can cure skin diseases.

Sayyed Pir no Kubo is a beautiful mausoleum dedicated to Sayyed Pir Shah. It has nine domes with the largest dominating the center while eight smaller domes surround it. The entire mausoleum is built in stone with exquisite carvings and fine details along the doors and windows. The latticed *jalis* are especially outstanding. Due to its distance, Lakhpat does not attract many visitors. However, it is a very breezy place and an overnight stay promises a memorable experience. The sunrise and sunset seen from the northern ramparts of the fort are spectacular, and the night sky can be absolutely breathtaking on and around the new moon. On request the caretaker will provide accommodation with good wash facilities. The *gurudwara* has a *langar* that serves food in the afternoon and evening, after prayer, but be sure to pack extra supplies.

Narayan Sarovar
145 km from Bhuj and 50 km from Lakhpat

The famous temple complex of **Narayan Sarovar** and the lake (which is mostly dry) is one of five sacred Hindu lakes of India, including Mansarovar, Pushkar Sarovar, Bindu Sarovar and Pampa Sarovar. It is believed that in the Puranic era, when this area was drought stricken, many great sages congregated and performed penance. Narayan, a representation of Vishnu, appeared in response. He touched the soil with his right toe and water sprang out to fill a whole lake. The gods bathed in the consecrated waters, which led to the belief that bathing in this lake has special religious importance. The main temples and the fortified complex were built by the wife of Desalji. It is only worth visiting as a detour en route to Koteshwar from Lakhpat. **Note:** Bathing in the water is not recommended.

Koteshwar
165 km from Bhuj

Perched on the western Land's End of the Indian mainland, this Shiva temple is close to Narayan Sarovar. According to a legend, the powerful King Ravana of Lanka performed rigorous penance for which Shiva presented him with an *amarlinga*, the immortal phallic symbol of Shiva, with the condition that he would not place it on the ground until he reached his kingdom. The gods, worried that this would make Ravan invincible, tricked him into placing the *amarlinga* on the ground. When he tried to pick it up again, Ravana saw ten million (*koti* in Kachchhi) *amarlingas*, hence the name Koteshwar. He carried the wrong *linga* home, while the original remained in Koteshwar. The marks of Ravana's fingers are said to still be visible on it. The temple is built on a breezy headland looking out over the sea and the Kori Creek and has a beautiful view of the beach close by. On a clear, dark night you can see the glow of the lights of Karachi (Pakistan) on the western horizon.

Nani Rav
150 km from Bhuj

Celebrated by several communities from the surrounding areas, **Ravechi Mela** (see **Fairs and Festivals**) is held in Nani Rav.

Dholavira
250 km from Bhuj

Part of the Harappan Civilization, Dholavira dates back to about 3000 BC. It is on the island of **Khadir** in the Great Rann and is reached via Bhachau and Rapar. The site was unearthed by the Archeological Survey of India in 1967. According to archeologists the residents of this formidable city were prosperous and known to trade by sea with places as far as Mesopotamia. The ruins are spread over an area of 100 hectares and represent an excellent example of ancient town planning, striking architecture and elaborately designed water and drainage management system. The construction used both sun dried bricks and stone masonry. The central part of the town has an imposing citadel with well laid out lanes leading to the middle town and further to the lower town. Huge reservoirs at the periphery of the city demonstrate the water management skills of builders, especially considering the area's sparse rainfall. A number of artifacts were excavated, including terracotta pottery, colorful beads and ornaments of gold and copper, seals, animal figurines, tools, urns and some vessels from western Asia that indicate trade links with distant lands. One of the seals was engraved with an ancient script, one of the oldest in the world, but has yet to be deciphered.

A bus leaves for Dholavira (known as Kotada locally) from Bhuj at 1400 and arrives at 2030. It departs at 0500 the next morning, reaching Bhuj by 1130. One-way fare is about Rs. 80. It is more comfortable and convenient to rent a vehicle to visit Dholavira, and allocate one full day to account for the roundtrip travel time. Accommodation is available at the government-run **Dholavira Toran Resort and Restaurant**. Be sure to carry your own food and sufficient drinking water. **SAATH** is a non-profit organization based at Dholavira that operates a small campus where you can get accommodation upon request. **The Susheel Trust**, which runs a residential school, also has a guest house.

MANDVI માંડવી	POPULATION	42,400
	AREA CODE	02834
	DISTANCE - BHUJ	60 KM

Mandvi, famous for its ship building industry and clean beaches, is a quaint port town that also makes for a good base to explore the southern stretch of Kachchh. A seafarer's destination since ancient times, Mandvi attracted ships from as far as East Africa and southeast Asia. Local traders and merchants had created a niche by trading precious stones and fine textiles. It also attracted many artisan families who settled near the port.

PLACES OF INTEREST

Beaches

Mandvi has a nice stretch of blue waters. **Mandvi Beach** is the closest to town, located across the bridge over the **Rukmavati River** and along the road beyond Salaya near the Kashi Vishvanath Temple. The beach is within walking distance of the temple. Towards the west of town is the **Wind Farm Beach**, named after the windmills that line it and generate power. It is about 7 km from town and a rickshaw will cost between Rs. 50-70 depending on how long the driver has to wait.

Vijay Vilas Palace

This royal summer retreat was built about 8 km from Mandvi in 1929 by Vijayrajji. Constructed of red sandstone in the Rajput style, its rooftop balconies offer a striking view of the surrounding area, the tomb of Vijayrajji's wife and the sea beyond. There is a large collection of stuffed game, portraits and furniture on display. The popular Bollywood film, *Hum Dil De Chuke Sanam*, was partly filmed here. **Open** 0900-1300 and 1500-1800, daily. **Entry** Rs. 20, **Vehicle Entry** Rs. 10. **Photography** Rs. 50.

The Main Town

The street façades of Mandvi are worth exploring. The properties of wealthy merchants depict various foreign details such as angels, the faces of kings and colorful stained glass windows. These also indicate the former European influence that resulted from extensive trade. Amble through the bustling market and its narrow lanes.

Shipbuilding

Mandvi is famous for a 400-year-old shipbuilding industry and craftsmen who still use traditional techniques to build ships for domestic and international clients. Along the Rukmavati River you can watch these vessels being assembled plank by plank. A large timber market in Mandvi thrives on this industry.

NUTS & BOLTS

In and Out

The best way to Mandvi from Bhuj is by ST buses or shared jeeps. They leave for Mandvi every 30 minutes. Shuttles also frequent this route.

Getting Around
Mandvi is best explored on foot. Rickshaws are good for further distances. Bicycles can be rented from **Bharat Bicycle Shop** *Jain Dharmashala Rd* at Rs. 30/day.

Money
ATMs **SBI** *Lakda Bazaar, Nr Bhid Gate* and **Dena Bank** *Sea Eagle Talkies Rd, Nr Azad Chowk.*
FOREIGN EXCHANGE **Regal Apex Forex,** *Sea Eagle Talkies Rd.*
MONEY TRANSFER **Western Union** is available at the General Post Office.

Communication
INTERNET **Vivek Computer Centre** *Nr Azad Chowk, Opp Hotel Krishna* is closed on Sunday afternoons.

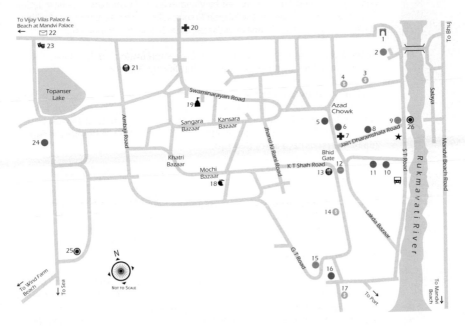

Mandvi
Legend

Accommodation
2   Rukmavati Guest House
9   Hotel Sea View
12 Sahara Guest House
15 Maitri Guest House

Food & Drink
13 Zorba The Buddha
21 Sarovar Restaurant

Places of Interest
1   Fort Tower
26 Shipbuilding

Nuts & Bolts
3   Regal Apex Forex
4   Dena Bank ATM
5   Rajeshwari Medical Store
6   Vivek Computers
7   Dr. Rana Surgical Hospital
8   Bharat Bicycle Rental
10 Sahajanand Travels
11 Swaminarayan Travels

14 SBI ATM
16 Book Shop
17 SBI Bank
18 Vegetable Market
19 Old Swaminarayan Temple
20 Dr. C. P. Sadhu Hospital
22 General Post Office
23 Tagore Open Theater
24 Laxmi Cinema
25 Light House

ACCOMMODATION

The Beach at Mandvi Palace *295725, Vijay Vilas Palace, www.mandvibeach.com* is a charming resort with luxury tents. Its multicuisine restaurant on the beach offers Indian and continental buffets and a-la-carte snacks, barbecue dinners with a campfire, and cultural performances. **Facilities** western toilets, attached baths, running hot water and AC. **Package** (3 days 2 nights incl. all meals) 11,000.

Hotel Sea View *224481, ST Road* faces the Rukmavati River and has clean rooms, some with a view of the shipbuilders. It has a multicuisine vegetarian restaurant. **Facilities** western toilets, running hot water, AC options, laundry service, TV. **Single** 400-1200 **Double** 300- 1200.

Rukmavati Guest House *223557, ST Rd, Nr Bridge across Rukmavati River* is a friendly and spacious guest house managed by Vinod Bhatt and is probably the best option for backpackers. You can use the kitchen to cook at Rs. 2/ minute for the gas. **Facilities** western toilets, laundry. **Dorm** (10 beds) 125 each. **Single** 200 **Double** 235.

Maitri Guest House *223283, Bunder Rd, Nr Kanthavalo Gate* has basic rooms with squat toilets. **Dorm** 50 **Single** 200 **Double** 350 **Extra Bed** 70.

Sahara Guest House *223272, Lakda Bazaar, Bhid Gate Chowk* has a friendly manager and great service. It is another good option for backpackers, but the surroundings can be noisy at times. **Facilities** western toilets, bucket baths. They arrange for money exchange and car rentals. **Single** 100 **Double** 175 **Family** (up to 5 persons) 250 **Extra Bed** 140.

FOOD & DRINK

Sarovar *Shyamaprasad Mukherjee Shopping Cmplx, Nr New Municipality Bldg* serves tasty Punjabi and Chinese food. **Zorba the Buddha** *Nr Bhid Gate* is locally known as Rajneesh Hotel. It is a busy dining hall that serves tasty and sumptuous *thalis*. This is probably the closest you will get to Kachchhi cuisine in a restaurant in Kachchh.

LOCAL SPECIALTIES ***Dabeli*** is a popular snack in Mandvi with vendors selling them in every corner of town. Most people flock to **Mr Gabba** in the **Kansara Bazaar**. Another local specialty is the ***khajli pakwaan***, a flaky, unsweetened pastry commonly eaten for breakfast; it is available at many sweet shops. There are more *dabeli* vendors opposite the post office.

EXCURSIONS

Koday
50 km from Bhuj, 10 km from Mandvi
This village has a Jain complex known as **Bohter Jinalay** that consists of 72 shrines, each with its own spire and deity. The marble temple spreads over 32 hectares. Accommodation is available in the local *dharmashala*.

Bada

22 km from Mandvi

The **Kachchh Vipassana Kendra** or **Dhamma Sindhu** is a meditation retreat based on a Buddhist technique that was promoted by the Buddhist scholar S N Goenka. *Details can be obtained from Ishwarlal Shah at 02834 223076 in Mandvi.* Only one bus leaves for Bada from Mandvi daily. The center has a strict code of conduct for the 10-day course, during which you isolate yourself from the external world to focus internally. For more information on Vipassana visit www.dhamma.org.

Navjivan Nature Cure Centre

Navjivan *02834 281430 Bhuj-Mandvi Rd, Punadi Patia,* which means new life, is a holistic naturopathy retreat that treats ailments and diseases using various therapies, natural diets, massages, yoga and baths. Dr Jay Sanghvi, the founder, and his team of doctors, also use therapies such as reflexology, acupuncture, acupressure, and the traditional Indian technique Panchakarma, which detoxifies the body and balances the internal systems. The center is spread across two hectares with an additional 40 hectares of farmland used to cultivate fruits, vegetables, and ayurvedic herbs—all organic.

Rayan

65 km from Bhuj, 7 km from Mandvi

Nu Tech Farm *02834 288361, nutechfarm@yahoo.com* is an organic farm based near Rayan village. The owners, Vijay and Kusum Shah, belong to the international group of **WWOOFers** (Willing Workers on Organic Farming), an organization that aims to spread awareness about organic farming by connecting individuals with organic farms across the world. The Shahs grow dates, aloe vera, tamarind, sesame, pulses, vegetables, oilseeds and many varieties of medicinal plants.

Mundra

52 km from Bhuj, 44 km from Mandvi

This port town is famous for its salt and spice exports. It is renowned for seafarers like **Kanji Malam,** who is credited with guiding Vasco de Gama on the direct route across the Indian Ocean (verses sailing up the east coast of Africa and down the west coast of India) from the Cape of Good Hope to India; and **Dhamji Ladha,** who went to Zanzibar as an advisor to its Sultan. Many memorial stones near the **Mahadev Temple** are dedicated to the unsung seafarers of Mundra. The town is now famous for block printing and tie-dye.

The **Darya Pir Shrine** honors Darya Pir, the patron saint of the Kachchh fisher folk. He arrived around 1660 as an exile from Bukhara (in present-day Uzbekistan). The friendly locals and Rao Tamachiji welcomed him to Mundra. He won a place in the hearts of the people, taught them the canons of Islam, and came to be revered as a saint. The *dargah* in his honor, built by Raydhanji I, successor to Tamachiji, attracts people of all faiths to invoke his blessings. The Mughal Emperor Jahangir, hearing of Murad's service to Islam, built a beautiful stone gate in Mundra. The *dargah* was badly damaged in the earthquake and is being renovated, but the **Mughal Gate** still stands. During the renovation, several of the Pir's belongings were unearthed and have been kept on display, including a 400-year-old chariot.

Dawood Kaka, a national award winner for his elaborate Bandhani designs, lives opposite the Darya Pir Shrine. He has been practicing this family tradition since the age of seven and stocks a variety Bandhani items for sale. He has held on to his award winning *sari* and unties a single knot from his masterpiece each time a visitor comes.

About 8 km from the main town, **Mundra Port** is one of the busiest in Gujarat. The main exports are salt, spices, onion and bentonite (clay used as a lubricant and a coolant in the oil rig industry). The annual turnover easily exceeds one million metric tons (one billion kg).

Bhadreshwar
76 km from Bhuj, 25 km from Mundra

This town is mainly famous for the **Vasai Jain Tirth**, one of the most important Jain pilgrimage sites in Kachchh. Built about 1600 years ago, it was added to and renovated several times. The Jain temple has beautiful marble idols of the *tirthankars* and intricately carved columns. Check to see if it is still under repair before visiting.

GETTING INVOLVED

Kachchh Nav Nirman Abhiyan *02832 221379, Dr Rajaram Campus, Nr St Xavier's School, Bhuj, www.kutchabhiyan.net* is a network of local NGOs in Kachchh working towards the rehabilitation and sustainable development of the region. Its members are working in different areas such as natural resource management, watershed development, micro-credit, craft preservation, women's empowerment, health, education and drought management.

Bhojay Sarvodaya Trust *02834 278687, Bhojay Village, Mandvi* was formed to provide medical services in areas that lack basic facilities. Shri Bhojay Sarvodaya Trust hospital was inaugurated in 1998 and houses a 24 hour out-patient clinic, basic diagnostics and a full fledged operation theatre.

Hunnar Shala *02832 221379, Kachchh Nav Nirman Abhiyan, Dr Rajaram Campus, Nr St Xavier's School*, works to help secure the livelihood of local masons while promoting eco-friendly, cost effective and low energy building materials that incorporate local resources and aesthetics. They also aim to build housing facilities at affordable cost for the marginal communities.

Kala Raksha *02808 277237, Parkar Vas, Sumrasar Sheikh, www.kalaraksha.org* has been working since 1991 to preserve the traditional arts of the region by making them culturally and economically viable. The Trust's activities are artisan driven and focus on their total development.

Khamir Crafts Resource Centre *02832 329247, 11 Nootan Colony, Bhuj, www.khamir.org* works for the revitalization of and innovation on traditional craft forms in the region by offering R&D and marketing support to the artisans. They aim to ensure that artisans can depend on their traditional skills as a source for sustainable income. Khamir also sells a variety of unique local crafts.

Kutch Mahila Vikas Sangathan (KMVS) *02832 222124, 11 Nootan Colony, Bhuj, kmvs@india.com*, established in 1989, works primarily with rural women collectives in 160 villages and focuses on a range of empowerment and development issues focused around handicrafts, savings and credits, legal aid, environment, health, education and citizen rights. They also run a unique grassroots radio program. As part of an income generation effort for artisans, KMVS sells a variety of embroidery products under the label QASAB at their Bhuj and Khavda locations.

Sahjeevan *02832 251814, 104/A, Lotus Colony, Bhuj, admin@sahjeevan.org* was established in 1991 with an aim to facilitate the development process in Kachchh through sustainable use of natural resources. Its primary activities are eco-restoration and regeneration of land.

Shree Bidada Sarvodaya Trust *02834 244444 Bidada Village, Near Mandvi, www.bidada.com* was established in 1974 and is one of the oldest charitable health institutions for the underprivileged in Kachchh. The organization works on a range of health activities, including health camps and awareness. **Contact** Bachubhai V Rambhai.

Shrujan Trust *02832 240272, Behind GEB Substation, Bhujodi, www.shrujan.org* was established in 1968 after a serious drought to help artisans sustain themselves by providing them with design, marketing and training support. Today Shrujan works in 80 villages and supports 2000 craftswomen in the district.

Vivekanand Gramodyog Society (VGS) *02834 220934, 9825235790, Nagalpur Rd, Near Jain Ashram, Mandvi, vgsbatik@rediffmail.com* was initiated in 1988 by the Vivekanand Research and Training Institute to provide design and marketing support to Kachchhi artisan communities. It supports over 250 craftspeople involved in block printing and batik art and runs a marketing outlet on their campus.

Vivekanand Research and Training Institute (VRTI) *02834 223253, Nagalpur Rd, Mandvi, vrti-mandvi@yahoo.com* was formed in 1975 to make village economies self-reliant and sustainable. It works on a range of issues such as watershed management, agriculture, animal husbandry and eco-restoration. The institute also conducts experiments and research on bio-gas and alternative farming.

NUTS & BOLTS

NUTS & BOLTS

CLIMATE

The **best time to visit** Gujarat is between late October and early March, when the temperatures are pleasant. Gujarat experiences three distinct seasons: summer, monsoon and winter. Gujarat's **summer** is between April and mid-June, when daytime temperatures can touch 45° C towards the end of this season. The **monsoon** in Gujarat is generally between mid-June and late August and can bring anything from sporadic showers to flooding, but there are always a few days of heavy rains. The weather varies between pleasant and humid. The northwestern region of Gujarat remains relatively dry with less than 500 mm of annual rainfall while the southern parts, from the coastline to the mountain crests, receive up to 2000 mm. The period just before and after the monsoon is characterized by humidity and heat; post-monsoon also brings mosquitoes. During **winter**, the climate is pleasant and average temperatures range between 12° and 27° C, although it does get cold in some areas such as the Ranns of Kachchh.

PACKING CHECKLIST

You can find just about everything you need in Gujarat; however, the following is a list of items you should pack from home.

- ☐ Loose fitting, cotton clothing (It is comfortable, suitable for the climate and easy to wash. Women and men dress modestly in Gujarat, so avoid shorts and sleeveless tops.)
- ☐ A light sweater or shawl (Nights in the desert and hill areas can be chilly.)
- ☐ Comfortable walking shoes
- ☐ Sunscreen and a hat or scarf to protect you against the sun
- ☐ Any medication that you need (Inhalers, anti-malarial drugs and birth control pills.)
- ☐ If you wear contacts, bring a pair of glasses (Gujarat can be dusty and may irritate your eyes.)
- ☐ Tampons and floss (These are also good for mending bags and shoes.)
- ☐ If you absolutely need toilet paper, pack some.
- ☐ A clean cotton sheet (This is for the dirty linen you are likely to come across. It also doubles as a cover during overnight train and bus journeys.)
- ☐ Flashlight and batteries (Available in India but not always long-lasting.)
- ☐ Specialty film and relevant camera equipment
- ☐ Insect repellent
- ☐ A water bottle
- ☐ Some strong string or rope to use as a makeshift clothes line.
- ☐ A sports bra (It is more comfortable in the heat and supportive on bumpy roads.)
- ☐ A good combination lock (Cheaper hotels may not have locks on their doors.)
- ☐ Pocket knife
- ☐ Hand sanitizer
- ☐ Multivitamins
- ☐ Ziplock bags
- ☐ Universal plug adapter

IN & OUT

You can fly into India from most continents around the world. Generally, international flights land in Mumbai or Delhi with connecting flights across the country. However, Air India, Kuwait Airways, and Singapore Airlines fly directly into Ahmedabad. Indirect flights are generally cheaper but add extra hours to the journey. Customs clearance happens at the city of arrival. If you are traveling light, you can also take a train into Gujarat (see **Getting Around, Trains**) from your point of entry.

Shop around for the best price since your ticket into India is likely to be the most expensive part of your trip. To book a ticket online try:

www.kayak.com   www.ebookers.com
www.cheaptickets.com   www.travelocity.com
www.expedia.com

Discount agents sell extra seats at cheap prices, sometimes only specializing in youth, student or budget travel.

Council Travel	www.counciltravel.com
STA	www.statravel.co.uk
Usit	www.usitcampus.co.uk
Trailfinders	www.trailfinders.co.uk

Airline regulations are constantly changing. To avoid emptying and repacking your bags at the airport, ask your ticket agent or the airline for the latest rules.

Overland Travel to India

If you are looking for an adventurous route into India, try the classic Istanbul-Iran-Quetta-Lahore-Amritsar overland journey, which combines trains and buses. Be sure to check the current political situation in the transit countries as well as visa requirements for your nationality before choosing this alternative. Another option is to take the Trans-Siberian express to China, then travel down the Karakoram Highway into Pakistan and then into India. Again, check the current political status of these places to avoid any danger.

VISAS & DOCUMENTS

All foreign nationals require a valid passport and an appropriate visa to visit India. In order to apply for a visa, you must have a passport that does not expire within six months, two passport size photographs and an application form, available at your nearest Indian mission or download one from www.visatoindia.com. Visas are available from Indian consular offices around the world and visa fees vary according to nationality. Most embassies and consulates will not issue a visa to enter India without proof of an onward ticket.

Types of Visas

Your visit on a tourist or business visa cannot exceed a period of six months.

TOURIST VISA Multi-entry visas, valid for a period of six months from the date of issue, are granted for the purpose of tourism. A less popular option is the three month visa, valid from the date of first entry into India, which must be within two months of the issue date.
BUSINESS VISA Valid for up to one year from the date of issue, this visa requires a letter from the visitor's sponsor stating the nature of the business to be conducted.
EMPLOYMENT VISA Validity of visa depends on the employment contract. An appointment letter, contract letter, resume and proof of the organization's registration in India are required.
STUDENT VISA Valid for the period of study, when accompanied by a letter of acceptance from the Indian institution. A health certificate may be required.
ENTRY VISA Valid for a six-month to five-year stay with multiple entry options. It is given only to persons of Indian origin. Members of the family of a person employed in India are also eligible for entry visas.
TRANSIT VISA These are granted by Indian missions abroad for a maximum period of 15 days. Confirmed airline ticket for an onward journey and a valid visa for the final destination are required.

Visa Extensions

Fifteen day extensions are possible under circumstances deemed exceptional by the local Foreigners' Regional Registration Office (FRRO). Since there is no FRRO in Gujarat, the Superintendent of Police in the district headquarters can be contacted for immediate help. FRROs are located in New Delhi, Mumbai, Kolkata and Chennai.

PIO Cards
Non-resident Indians (NRIs) holding Person of Indian Origin (PIO) cards are allowed entry into India without a visa. However, PIO card holders must register with a FRRO if the planned visit exceeds 180 days. For more information regarding the PIO card, contact your local embassy or consulate.

Indian Embassies & Commissions
For a comprehensive list of Indian Embassies and High Commissions abroad or Embassies, High Commissions and Consulates in India visit www.mea.gov.in.

Australia, Mumbai +91 22 5669 2000, www.ausgovindia.com

Canada, New Delhi +91 11 4178 2000, www.india.gc.ca

France New Delhi +91 11 2419 6100, www.france-in-india.org

Germany New Delhi +91 11 4419 9199, www.new-delhi.dip10.de

Israel New Delhi + 91 11 3041 4500, www.delhi.mfa.gov.il

Italy New Delhi +91 11 2611 4355, www.ambnewdelhi.esteri.it

Japan New Delhi +91 11 2687 6564, www.in.emb-japan.go.jp

Netherlands New Delhi +91 11 2419 7600, www.holland-in-india.org

South Africa New Delhi +91 11 2614 9411, www.sahc-india.com/g_maite.html

UAE New Delhi +91 11 2687 2937, embassymirates@bol.net.in

UK New Delhi +91 11 2687 2161, www.britishhighcommission.gov.uk

USA New Delhi +91 011-2419-8000, www.newdelhi.usembassy.gov

Copy your Documents
Keep copies of your passport and visas with you as you travel. Extra passport photos may also come in handy. Report any lost or stolen documents to your country's embassy or consulate as soon as possible. You can also scan important documents and email them to yourself so that they are handy in the case of theft or an emergency.

Driver's License
The International Driver's License (IDL) is recognized in India. You will need a license if you plan to drive a scooter, motorbike or car.

Insurance
Travel insurance provides medical coverage and insures your belongings against loss and theft. Most policies provide protection against the loss of baggage, tickets and a certain amount of cash and travelers checks. Sometimes it insures against the cancellation of your journey. It is important that you research which policy works for you and read through the fine print. Premiums vary according to the policy. In the case of medical coverage, clarify if benefits will be paid during the time of treatment or through policy reimbursement after you return home. Make sure the insurance covers emergency trips home. To make a claim, you need to keep all medical receipts. In case of theft, you must obtain an official police report. Also look into your current insurance policy, you may find that medical coverage and theft while traveling are already covered.

HEALTH

Taking care of your health is crucial to enjoying your travels in Gujarat. The right vaccinations and proper precautions with food, water and mosquitoes can protect you from both minor irritants and major diseases.

Immunizations
No immunizations are required for entry into India, but taking the time to get vaccinated

can prevent unnecessary health problems on your journey. Before departure, make sure you are up-to-date with routine immunizations such as tetanus, polio, measles, mumps, and rubella. Visit your doctor at least six weeks before your departure to allow enough time for vaccinations that cannot be administered at the same time or those that need to be given in multiple doses.

For the most current information on vaccinations, outbreaks and other travel health information, visit the following sites:

US Centers for Disease Control (CDC)
www.cdc.gov
World Health Organization (WHO)
www.who.int
Medical Services for Travelers (MASTA)
www.masta.org
Travelers Medical & Vaccination Centers
www.tmvc.co.au

Most sources strongly recommend that you take vaccinations against hepatitis A, hepatitis B, typhoid, tetanus, meningitis and Japanese B encephalitis prior to arrival in India.

General Precautions

Contaminated water and food are the leading causes of most health problems you may experience in Gujarat. Although diarrhea and upset stomachs are common problems while traveling the subcontinent, they can be avoided or minimized by observing a few simple precautions.

Wash your hands regularly to avoid bacterial infection.

Drink clean water (see **Water Purification)** and stay hydrated. Make sure you water is boiled or filtered and only purchase trusted brands of bottled water. Make sure the seal is intact before buying a bottle. Always crush bottles before discarding them to prevent others from refilling and selling unsafe water.

Water Purification

Contaminated water can be a major health hazard in India. In remote areas, where bottled or filtered water is not available, the best option is to boil water for at least five minutes before consuming. Strain the water through a cheesecloth to remove larger particles. Water can also be treated with purification tablets, but the quick-dissolving varieties of these may not be readily available in handy packs. It may be best to bring these with you. If you do buy these tablets in India, be sure to check their expiration date. Another option is to bring a portable water filter, but be sure to research your options and ask about a suitable model for your needs while in India.

Avoid ice and anything containing ice as it could be made with unsafe water. Make sure your *chaas* (buttermilk) is mixed with filtered water.

Wipe wet plates and cups dry before using them. Wash and dry fruit and vegetables thoroughly before consuming them; when water is not available, peel them.

As a rule, the hotter the food, the safer it is. Practice caution when eating street food and avoid places with questionable hygiene and sanitation practices. When not careful, street food is one of the easiest ways to contract a bacterial infection or worse.

Stomach Related Problems

DIARRHEA This is the most common ailment for many visitors to India. It is caused by a number of factors including excessive heat and spicy food, but the main source of contamination is through food and water. Follow the information under **General Precautions** to prevent most cases of diarrhea. If your diarrhea is accompanied by a fever or persists for several days, visit a physician.

Diarrhea

What to Eat	What to Avoid
Boiled potatoes	Raw vegetables
Plain rice	Most fruits
Plain bread	Heavy dairy products
(*rotis* without ghee)	Spicy and greasy foods
Chaas (Buttermilk)	Caffeine
Bananas and	Alcohol
Pomegranate	
Dry biscuits; salty	
or unsweetened	

CONSTIPATION Also a common health problem for travelers, constipation is often induced by immobility, inadequate fluid intake and/ or change in diet. To prevent constipation, increase fiber intake and include some form of exercise in your daily routine. For treatment, drink plenty of water and eat lots of peeled fruits (except bananas), vegetables, nuts and dried fruits. Try to cut down on meat in all forms.

Mosquito Borne Illnesses

The best way to avoid mosquito borne illnesses is to prevent mosquito bites as advised below. Anti-histamine tablets, calamine lotion and cool baths help soothe the itching in case you are bitten. Avoid scratching to prevent infection.

Preventing Mosquito Bites

Mosquitoes bite most often between dusk and dawn. To minimize bites, wear long sleeves, pants, and light socks to protect your body. Avoid dark-colored clothing as it attracts mosquitoes. Sleeping under a mosquito net, burning mosquito coils (available at most local shops), using electrically heated liquid repellants (like All Out, a popular local brand), wearing insect repellant cream (Odomos is widely available locally), or any repellant containing DEET (higher concentrations last longer) are all effective ways to protect against mosquito bites.

MALARIA Generally it requires several bites from infected mosquitoes to contract malaria. The disease is always serious and can be fatal in the absence of timely treatment. Symptoms may include fever, chills, headache, muscle aches, and fatigue. Fever in your first week of travel is unlikely to be malaria, but it should still be promptly evaluated by a physician. A variety of anti-malarial drugs are available in the market, each with a range of benefits and drawbacks. Discuss the options with your physician. **Note:** Chloroquine is NOT an effective anti-malarial drug for India.

DENGUE FEVER This viral illness is transmitted by a mosquito that bites only during the day. Symptoms usually begin with the abrupt onset of a high fever and headache. Severe muscle and joint pain is followed by a red splotchy rash that can resemble measles as it progresses. The disease can only be diagnosed through blood tests. There is no treatment, but high fluid intake and plenty of bed rest are critical to recovery.

JAPANESE B ENCEPHALITIS Mosquitoes that breed in rice fields are the main carriers of this viral illness, and while Gujarat has few rice fields, it is possible to contract it in other areas of India. If you experience an abrupt fever accompanied with headache, vomiting, stiffness of the neck, sensitivity to light, altered mental state, and drowsiness, seek immediate medical attention.

Environmental Hazards

Hot climates can lead to heat rash, exhaustion, sunburn, or worse. The best policy is to drink plenty of fluids and consume salty foods, while avoiding caffeine and alcohol. Eating onions also minimizes the possibility and severity of heat rashes. When spending time under the sun, try to use SPF 30 sunscreen. If you do get sunburned, drink plenty of water and apply aloe vera if available.

RABIES This potentially fatal infection can be transmitted through the saliva of any infected animal, even through something as harmless as a lick. In Gujarat, the most common hazard comes from stray dogs. Foaming at the mouth is a sign of rabies, so avoid any animals fitting the description. Seek out rabies treatment under medical supervision immediately if bitten by any animal.

FUNGAL INFECTIONS Usually brought on by the combination of hot weather and moisture, these infections can occur anywhere on the body with the scalp, pubic area, and feet being the most common places. To avoid fungal infections, wear loose, non-synthetic clothing, bathe yourself frequently and dry yourself thoroughly. If you contract an infection, it is important to follow through the full course of anti-fungal shampoos, creams, or tablets as prescribed by your physician.

INTESTINAL WORMS Parasites can enter the body through skin, contaminated food and/or contaminated water. Common symptoms include rectal itching, rashes on the body, fever, weight loss and chronic fatigue. To minimize your risk, avoid walking barefoot in tropical areas or places with open sewage and take proper precautions against contaminated food. If you contract intestinal worms, visit your physician for the proper course of de-worming medication.

HIV/AIDS

The HIV virus is most commonly contracted through sexual contact and blood. It is strongly advised to have safe and protected intercourse with new partners. If you require any shots in India, the best practice is to ask to see the syringe unwrapped in your presence. Diabetics should carry pre-packaged sterile syringes in the event of emergency. If you require a blood transfusion, only go to hospitals where blood is screened for the HIV virus. You should also take sensible precautions against body piercing, tattooing, and street-side shaves by asking for sterile needles and new blades.

Women's Health

MENSTRUATION Local brand sanitary napkins are readily available in Gujarat. If you prefer tampons, you should bring your own supply. Disposing of sanitary pads and tampons in rural areas can be difficult in the absence of a centralized waste management system. The best option is to wrap them in newspaper, pack them in a tightly sealed bag and discard them when you reach a larger town. During travel, it is normal for periods to become irregular as a result of mental and physical stress. In case of heavy bleeding, consume extra iron to avoid anemia.

BIRTH CONTROL Your regular brand of contraceptive pills may not be available in Gujarat, so pack enough to last the whole trip. Major stomach infections (diarrhea and vomiting) decrease your body's ability to absorb the pill, so use condoms to guard against unwanted pregnancy. You may want to bring your own condoms, as the quality of those available on the local market varies.

VAGINAL YEAST INFECTIONS If you are prone to yeast infections, they can recur in warm, moist climates. Packing extra medication from home is the quickest possible treatment. Birth control pills, tight clothing, and nylon underwear can all encourage yeast infections.

Home Remedies

DIARRHEA Buttermilk taken with a pinch of salt three or four times a day can help settle the stomach. Another remedy is to mix one spoon of *rai* (mustard seeds) with a drop of oil or ghee. Swallow the *rai* with a glass of water. Do this two to three times a day until the diarrhea passes.

COMMON COLD At the first sign of a cold, cough or sore throat, boil *tulsi* leaves, a few black pepper corns, crushed cloves, and some crushed ginger in water until the mixture becomes dark brown. Then add a little honey or jaggery. Drink it while hot.

COMMON FEVER Boil several *tulsi* leaves in a half liter of water, and mix with a half cup of milk, one teaspoon of sugar and a quarter teaspoon of powdered *elaichi* (cardamom). Drink this mix twice a day to bring down the temperature.

CONSTIPATION Take a spoon of Isabgol (psyllium husk) with a bowl of yogurt. Otherwise eat one to two guavas with the seeds or a medium sized papaya at breakfast to clean out the colon.

CUTS, SCRAPES AND SPRAINS Pack cuts with turmeric powder and for sprains, apply a paste of turmeric and salt and wrap it with a bandage. Turmeric actually has an infinite list of medicinal value, but in this case it is used to clot blood and doubles as an antiseptic.

Replenish your Body's Water Loss

All medical stores carry oral rehydration salts (ORS), which effectively replace lost minerals and salts. In case these are not available, mix half a teaspoon of salt and eight teaspoons of sugar in a liter of mineral water. Add lemon or lime to improve the taste.

Know your Drugs

Some doctors in India prescribe a handful of pills even for the common cold. It is a good idea to ask your doctor about what he is prescribing and why. Get a second opinion if you are uncomfortable with the diagnosis. The following is a list of generic names for medicines so that you know what you are taking. Most drugs can be bought over the counter for a fraction of the price back home. These may come in handy for some of the more basic health ailments.

Drug Names

Acid Reflux
Bismuth Subsalicylate (Pepto-Bismol)
Esomeprazole (Nexium)
Antibiotics
Azithromycin (Zithromax)
Erythromycin

Antidiarrheals
Bismuth Subsalicylate (Pepto-Bismol)
Diphenoxylate (Lomotil)
Loperamide (Immodium)
Travelers Diarrhea
Ciprofloxacin (Cipro)
Metronidazole (Flagyl)
Antifungals
Butoconazole (Femstat)
Clotrimazole (Clotrimaderm, Canesten)
Griseofulvin
Miconazole (Monistat, Mozazole)
Nystatin
Oral fluconazole (Diflucan Oral)
Terconazole (Terazole)
Tioconazole (GyneCure)
Antimalarial
Mefloquine (Lariam)
Proguanil/Atorvaquone (Malarone)
Chloroquine (Not very effective)
Doxycycline
Primaquine
Cold, Cough, Runny Nose Meds
Ceftrizine (Zyrtec)
Fexofenadine (Allegra-D vs normal Allegra)
Loratadine (Claritin vs Claritin D)
Headache, Fever
Acetaminophen (Tylenol)
Muscle & Joint Pain, Headache
Ibuprofen (Advil and other derivatives)
Steroid Creams
Hydrocortisone

TOILETS

The toilet can be a point of contention for many travelers. Although western toilets are commonly found in newer buildings and hotels, the squat toilet is what you will encounter in villages, public restrooms and older buildings. With a little practice and an open mind, you can grow to appreciate the benefits of the squat toilet.

On the first encounter, some people are not exactly sure how to maneuver the squat toilet. Prior to starting, always pour some water down the toilet bowl to help with the flushing afterwards. Then get into position by placing your feet on the two footrests with your back towards the larger end of the hole. Balance yourself as you get into a squatting position.

The balancing becomes easier with more practice. After you are done, pour a bucket of water down the bowl to flush. All bathrooms are generally equipped with a tap or a bucket of water and a small mug. Although many people prefer to keep toilet paper with them, the local way is environmentally friendly and more sanitary once you master the technique. After filling the mug of water, rinse with your left hand while using your right to pour. Once you are content, allow your behind to air dry for a few seconds. Wash your hands thoroughly with soap. When using public toilets in India, squat toilets are more sanitary than the western toilets since you avoid contact with all surfaces in the former.

MONEY

India's currency is the *rupee*, abbreviated as Re/Rs. One *rupee* is equal to one hundred *paise*. Notes are issued in denominations of Rs. 5, 10, 20, 50, 100, 500 and 1000. Coins are available in denominations of 50 *paise* and Rs. 1, 2 and 5, although the 50 *paise* coins are decreasingly used. Do not accept torn, disfigured or heavily soiled notes because they will be difficult to use later. Some authorized bank branches have signs indicating that they exchange disfigured notes. The American dollar, the Euro and the British pound sterling are the most commonly accepted forms of foreign currencies in India.

Foreign Exchange

There are no restrictions on the amount of foreign currency or traveler's checks tourists may bring into India, so long as a declaration is made if the amount exceeds 10,000 USD or its equivalent. Any money in the form of traveler's checks, drafts, bills and checks should be exchanged only through authorized moneychangers and banks that will issue encashment certificates, which will be needed to exchange left-over rupees at the time of departure. These moneychangers can be found at airports, major hotels and most banks. The State Bank of India (SBI), Thomas Cook India and Bank of Baroda branches are easily accessible in major cities. The process to change money at the bank can be long and tedious, so it is advisable to change large sums at a time. Request notes in denominations of Rs. 50 and Rs. 100 since higher denomination notes may be difficult to tender outside the major cities. Authorized private dealers offer faster service, but at higher commission rates.

All major brands of traveler's checks are accepted in India; American Express and Thomas Cook are the most commonly traded. If your traveler's checks get lost or stolen, they are replaceable. Be prepared to present receipts and serial numbers for the missing checks and possibly a photocopy of the police report. Always keep some dollars, pounds or euros on you in case of an emergency.

ATMs & Credit Cards

Most major cities in Gujarat have a number of 24-hour ATMs that accept Cirrus, Maestro, MasterCard and Visa cards. While this is a convenient source of cash, it should not be relied upon if you are planning to travel to smaller cities and villages in Gujarat. Check with your local bank for access and fee information before departing.

Credit cards are increasingly accepted at major retail outlets, restaurants and upscale hotels in the major cities of Gujarat, but always carry some cash with you. MasterCard and Visa are the most widely accepted.

Money Transfer

There are a number of facilities that allow international money transfer. Thomas Cook's Moneygram service and Western Union, which has a partnership with the General Post Offices in Gujarat, are the most reputed and have plenty of locations.

Tipping

Tipping is still not that common a practice in Gujarat outside of high-end establishments. In general, Rs. 10-20 is sufficient for a bellboy and Rs. 20 per bag is acceptable for porters at train stations. At fancier restaurants, tip ten percent of the bill. Leave a few extra rupees at most other places.

Entrance Fees

Some places of interest charge different entry fees for Indian citizens and foreigners. These are usually displayed on a signboard or printed on your entry ticket.

TOURIST INFORMATION

Gujarat Tourism Offices in India

Gujarat Tourism (www.gujarattourism.com) has a number of offices in the state as well as in Chennai, Mumbai and New Delhi. Be sure to ask employees for special brochures and recommended sites, as this material is not always stocked in the display shelves. The quality of service and information varies, but these facilities at least offer a basic orientation to the state. They also offer affordable package tours of different regions in Gujarat, the cost of which include transportation, accommodation and a guide fee.

Ahmedabad *079 26589172, HK House, Ashram Rd*

Rajkot *0281 2234507, Bhavnagar House, Jawahar Rd, Behind State Bank of Saurashtra*

Surat *0261 2476586, 1/847, Athugar St, Nanpura*

Vadodara *0265 2427489, Narmada Bhavan, C-Block, Indira Ave*

Chennai *044 25366613, Mount Chambers, 2nd Flr, 758, Anna Salai*

Kolkata *033 22438357, Martin Burn Building, Shop, Shop No 28, Ground Flr, 1, R N Mukherjee Rd, Opp Lal Bazaar*

Mumbai *022 22024925, Dhanraj Mahal, Apollo Bandar*

New Delhi *011 23744015, A/6, State Emporia Bldg, Baba Kharak Singh Rd*

GETTING AROUND

Air

Although Gujarat has seven domestic airports, they only connect to cities outside of the state. There is a flight between Ahmedabad and Vadodara, but the frequency is inconsistent.

Ahmedabad is well connected with Mumbai and Delhi. It also has regular flights to Bangalore, Chennai, Goa, Hyderabad, Pune and Kolkata. In recent years, several new airline companies and no-frill operators have surfaced, making travel between Ahmedabad and other parts of India much easier.

DOMESTIC AIRLINES For domestic ticketing you can visit any travel agency, but online reservations are the easiest option. Always check the cost of taxes since these can often exceed the ticket price.

Spice Jet www.spicejet.com
Indigo www.goindigo.in
Go Air www.goair.in
Kingfisher www.flykingfisher.com
Indian Airlines www.indian-airlines.nic.in
Jet Airways www.jetairways.com
Air India www.airindia.com
Deccan Air www.airdeccan.net

Road

Gujarat has one of the best road networks in India, making travel by car and bus to most destinations fast and smooth.

CAR RENTAL Renting a car (locally called "hiring a car") gives you the convenience and freedom to explore village areas and smaller towns at your own pace. During night halts, drivers mostly sleep in the car. Some hotels, especially on highways, will have dorm facilities for them at no extra charge. However, you are expected to cover the cost of their food and tea during the trip. Cars for hire are often found outside the main bus and train stations; these are good for travel within the city and nearby places. Mid-range to high-end hotels and travel agencies can help organize more dependable transportation for longer distances. For an economy car, the rate starts at Rs. 5.50/km with a minimum daily mileage requirement, usually between 200-300 km for long distance trips. You can average out the mileage over the number of days you travel. If you are renting a car to use in the same city and outlying areas, one day is usually measured as 7-8 hrs and charged for 70-80 km. Each additional kilometer costs extra. Gas is included in the rates, but all road tolls are additional. Self-driven rentals are not an option in Gujarat since all agencies rent out cars with drivers.

BUS TRAVEL THE STATE TRANSPORT (ST) buses run on an extensive network throughout the state connecting almost every town and village to major junctions. This is a great option for short distances and out of the way destinations, although buses can get crowded. For longer journeys it is advisable to travel by private bus or train when the option exists. A challenge with ST buses is that signs are in Gujarati and information desk attendants at most bus terminals do not speak English. Keep mentioning the name of your destination and people will point you in the right direction. Tickets are usually paid for on the bus except at the starting point of several inter-city bus routes, where you have to buy your ticket before boarding. Avoid traveling in the afternoon, since the heat and dust can prove exhausting. There are few toilet and food stops in between, so take care of business before boarding.

"LUXURY" BUSES are not luxurious by any means. They are private buses that run the same route as ST buses, but pack in even more people. Prices and travel time are about the same, so these make for good alternatives if you miss the ST bus.

A number of **private buses** (locally known as "travel" buses) move between major destinations and offer several options. Basic buses with reserved seats are less crowded

but not anymore comfortable than ST buses. Volvos, which often travel through the night, have reclining seats, AC options and Hindi films that blare throughout most of the trip. Sleeper buses travel overnight and have berths that you sleep on through the journey. Be sure to check your seating assignment as some of these buses have double sized berths, which could mean sharing with a stranger when traveling alone.

SHARED JEEPS are commonly found in rural areas and between smaller towns. They run the same routes as ST buses and charge about the same fare. Travel can be faster or slower depending on your luck and the driver. Sometimes they run more frequently than buses, but are often crammed with people hanging on all four sides. Although it can be an adventure, avoid shared jeeps if large crowds and tilting vehicles are not your thing.

RICKSHAWS are the most convenient way to move around within cities and towns. Except in Ahmedabad and Vadodara, they are generally unmetered, which means you should agree on a price prior to getting into the rickshaw. The seating capacity is usually three passengers per vehicle.

SHARED RICKSHAWS (locally called "shuttles") are essentially rickshaws modified to accommodate more passengers. Some are larger versions of the rickshaw that run on set routes. The tariffs are fixed and usually cost between Rs. 5-10 depending on the distance of your destination. Be patient though, shuttles will leave only after the vehicle is full.

CHHAKADAS are diesel fuelled vehicles made with a motorcycle front-end, Kirloskar engine and a fabricated body. In rural areas of Kachchh and Saurashtra, this is the chief form of transportation for travel between towns and villages.

Train
Train travel is one of the quintessential Indian experiences. From the friendly people you

will encounter while sitting in your cabin to vendors who sweep through the train singing *garam chai* (hot tea) and *singh dana* (roasted peanuts*)*, it is a great place to connect with the country. The Indian Railways, the world's largest employer, is made up of an efficient network that connects the entire country. Although trains run late on occasion, the overall system is very dependable.

Intercity trains have several categories: super fast, express (mail) and local. **Super fast** options include the **Rajdhani**, which transports you between Ahmedabad and Delhi (14 hrs) in a luxury cabin with meals included. The daytime **Shatabdi** travels between Ahmedabad and Mumbai (7 hrs). **Express trains** are usually the best option between most destinations. **Local trains** are good for short distances, and tickets for these can be bought at the station just before departure. When booking an unreserved ticket, remember that you have to pay according to the type of train you are boarding, otherwise you will be fined.

Of the eight classes available (though no single train will have them all), the most common options include second class unreserved, sleeper class, second class AC 3-tier, second class AC 2-tier and first class AC. **Sleeper class** is the best option if you want to enjoy the Indian rail experience. In this class you are guaranteed a seat during the day and a sleeper berth at night. If you book an upper berth, you can sleep all day. Women travelers can opt for the women's compartment, which is offered on long-distance trains. **Second class AC** is comfortable for long journeys in summer and includes bedding. AC options, however, isolate you from the scenery as you pass through different places. **First class AC** is relatively expensive—a better alternative would be to fly. Other options, generally on daytime trains, include **AC chair,** which has reclining seats, and the comfortable **Executive class**, which is the equivalent of the business class on airplanes. Second class unreserved tickets are an incredibly cheap

option. They allow you to board a train but do not guarantee a seat, which means that you might end up standing for the entire journey.

The Indian Railways website (www.indianrail. gov.in) offers online booking, but you need an address to register. The site lists all timetables, fares and updated information regarding train travel. Your other option is to book tickets at the reservation center, located in or around each station. In Ahmedabad, Mumbai and all other major cities of India you can take advantage of the **foreign quota**— a few seats reserved for foreign tourists, but you need your passport and proof of currency exchange (an ATM receipt works). You must fill out a form to purchase a ticket. During holiday seasons such as Diwali, reservations are nearly impossible.

Travel between Mumbai and Ahmedabad (8 hrs) is convenient, especially if you board one of the several night trains. Mumbai to Vadodara is about six hours. If you plan on extensive railway travel, invest in a *Trains at a Glance* (available at news stands at the railway stations). It lists all the main trains, their routes and fares.

A **reservation against cancellation** (RAC) ticket will get you on the train, but without a guaranteed seat unless a reserved passenger fails to show up. Wait listed (WL) means that you may get a seat after all the RACs have been accommodated, but if you are still wait listed on the day of departure, you are not allowed to board the train. You can approach the ticket inspector and ask him to find you an unreserved seat, but it is illegal for anyone to guarantee you a seat in exchange for a bribe or a "tip".

Addresses & Directions
Finding an address can be its own adventure. Most streets have several names, usually based on the most popular destination along the road. Road names are also likely to change without any notice. Almost all

addresses will include a number and a street along with several prepositional phases to help you locate your final destination—opposite the yellow house, next to Kanu's Restaurant, above One World Bank. Just follow the clues. If you ask for directions, most people are unlikely to turn you away without an answer, even if they do not know the correct information. Always ask more than one person to save yourself time and grief. Also, five minutes generally means ten, and close could mean two kilometers away. Just remember, it's all relative. Always try to keep a written version of the address you are looking for so that you can show people as you try to locate your final destination.

ACCOMMODATION

There is an eight percent luxury tax added to accommodation rates exceeding Rs. 500. Nominal taxes are then taken based on the amount of the luxury tax. These figures are likely to change.

A **dormitory** generally consists of a several beds in a shared room. It is wise to carry your own linen and lock your luggage.

Budget Hotels in Gujarat usually include a bed, bathroom (may or may not be attached) and some minimal furniture. Amenities, quality of linen and cleanliness vary. If hot water is not available 24-hours a day, you will probably get it in the morning. Otherwise request a bucket of hot water, which may be an additional cost. Toilets may be squat (see **Toilets**) or western.

Guest Houses offer basic rooms at budget prices with an attached or neighboring restaurant. They do not have many additional services.

Forest Rest House (see **The Dangs, Forest Rest Houses**)

Railway Retiring Rooms have varying standards of cleanliness but are convenient for those arriving or departing at odd hours. Available only at a few major stations.

Mid-Range Hotels usually offer AC options, and often have a TV and phone.

Three to Five Star Hotels have all major amenities and various frills (swimming pools, courtesy transfer, etc). The STD/ISD and Internet facilities cost substantially more at these hotels than at other places around town.

Heritage Hotels are former palaces or stately mansions converted into hotels that usually combine modern amenities with lavish decor. Sometimes the owners personally host their guests. Prices and quality vary.

Dharmashalas are generally for religious pilgrims of particular castes and communities, although some are open to all. A few of the popular pilgrimage places, such as Palitana and Ambaji, offer higher-end options.

Good hotels and restaurants can also be found along the major highways, which are slightly out of the way but convenient for those traveling by private vehicle. Places near the seaside often have salt water in the taps and will supply drinking water separately. Most hotels have 24-hour check-out and for those that do not, it is negotiable during off-peak seasons.

BUSINESS HOURS

Traditional banking hours are 1030-1430 (Mon to Fri) and 1030-1230 (Sat). However several banks have introduced 12-hour banking, and some even offer Sunday morning services. Similarly, shops usually operate from 0930 to 1800 (Mon-Sat), but with increased competition, many stores, especially chains and large department stores, have longer hours and stay open on weekends. It is important to note that cities like Ahmedabad and Vadodara have longer, more convenient hours of operation, while rural areas and many of the cities in Saurashtra and Kachchh, shut down for an afternoon break. Also, it is difficult to find restaurants that are open in the morning for breakfast. Most restaurants start after 1030 and close between 2200-2300.

The **General Post Office (GPO)** is open 1000-

1700 (Mon-Fri) and Saturday mornings. **State Government** offices operate from 1030 to 1810 (Mon-Sat) and are closed Sunday, every 2nd and 4th Saturday of the month and on public holidays. **Central Government** offices are closed every Saturday.

SHOPPING

There are plenty of great gifts and souvenirs to buy from Gujarat. The state has a rich craft culture (see **Resource Guide, Craft**) and no end to the beautiful hand-made articles available. If you buy directly from the artisan when possible, you help support the local economy and sustain the handicraft culture. You also get to learn the story behind the craft. Many non-profits also market various products that are often of excellent quality and proceeds from their sales are used for a good cause. Under the relevant places we have listed recommended shopping outlets. Gujarat is known for its silver costume jewellery and textiles (Bandhani, block printing, weaving). *Haats* are weekly bazaars where people from surrounding areas come to buy and sell hand-made pottery, bows and arrows, ornaments, and forest resources. A *gujari* is essentially a flea market and a great place to find hidden treasures. Although we have not listed commercial complexes or malls, Ahmedabad, Vadodara and Surat have plenty of boutiques and department stores selling western and traditional clothing such as *saris, chaniya cholis* and *salwar kameezes*. There are also plenty of Khadi Bhandars, which sell handspun cotton fabric alongside handmade soap and more. The open bazaars and specialized markets are great shopping experiences. Between the two you can find just about anything.

Bargaining
Bargaining is part of the local experience and expected in traditional open markets. As for the art of bargaining, first start by asking the price of an object you do not want. Then slip in a nonchalant query about what you really want without appearing too eager. Move on to other things before returning to the item of your choice. State a price lower than what you want to pay. Then exchange in a back and forth with the vendor until you reach a compromise that both sides are happy with. There are no rules of thumb, but generally, you can quote a price about a third of the original. You should aim to spend what you feel the item is worth to you. Once you start bargaining it is understood that you are committed to buying the article if you can agree on an acceptable amount. Remember that prices will automatically inflate if you have a different skin color or a western accent. Just enjoy the experience, and remember that at the end of the day a few rupees more will mean nothing to you.

COMMUNICATION

Telecommunications
To call India dial the international access code of the country you are in + 91 + area code (minus the initial zero) + local number. To call abroad from India dial 00 + country code + area code + local number.

To call any city from within India, dial 0 + the city area code + the number.

PCO/STD/ISD (public call office / subscriber trunk dialing / international subscriber dialing) allow you to call local / interstate / international numbers. These phones run on a digital meter so you know how many minutes (or rupees worth) you have spoken. These kiosks are always highlighted by a yellow sign with the words PCO/STD/ISD painted on them. Some STD kiosks have a callback option where you can give a local number to someone and have them call you back. However, this often costs you between Rs. 3-10/minute. Calling from a hotel telephone is generally more expensive. Many PCO/STD/ISD kiosks have fax and copy facilities. In general, STD/ISD booths are declining in numbers as cell phones become standard.

NET-2-PHONE is an international calling service operated through the Internet for much cheaper rates. The charges vary depending on the country you are calling. Calls to cell phones in certain countries cost more than triple the landline rates, so be sure to ask before dialing. Net-2-Phone facilities are usually found in cybercafés.

Although **mobile phones** are common in India, it is difficult to get a pre-paid SIM card without a local residential address.

Internet & Wi-Fi

Internet is available in all major destinations and increasingly in smaller towns. Most cybercafés charge an average of Rs. 20-40/hr. **Reliance World** and **Sify Iway** are found across the state and are reliable chains with fast internet connections. Reliance requires you to open a membership account, but at reasonable rates. You can then access and recharge your account from any Reliance World in the country. They also provide services such as international calling, eTicketing and video conferencing.

At most cybercafés, the quality and connection speed vary. Wireless service is increasingly found in Ahmedabad and Vadodara and is identified by a Wi-Fi sign hanging next to the establishment. Most places charge for the service.

Mail

India has the largest postal network in the world. Although it is generally reliable, mail delivery to and from India can take anywhere from a few days to a couple of weeks; count on an average of 10 days. The postal service is more dependable from larger cities. For important or valuable documents, registered mail is a better option.

Typically you will find vendors outside the post office to help with the required cloth packaging. Be sure to fill out and attach

a customs declaration form on which you should specify "no commercial value" to avoid paying duties. Request a registration slip when you are done. Cost will depend on the weight of the package and the means of delivery. Sea mail is slower and cheaper than airmail. The maximum dimensions accepted are 1m x .8m.

POST RESTANTE Most general post offices will hold on to your mail for one month. You must ask the sender to address it with your surname underlined and in all capitals, followed by the words "post restante" and "GPO" and the name of the destination. You will have to show identification to collect mail.

BOOK POST This service is much cheaper than regular post, but it is only for sending books and paper, which are delivered via sea mail. This service is not available at every post office, so ask to find the one nearest you. You have to get the package wrapped by one of the informal vendors outside, and be sure to keep one or both sides of the package open for inspection.

COURIER Private couriers, such as **Blue Dart** and **DHL**, offer dependable international courier services and are available in major cities. This option is faster, but also more expensive.

ELECTRICITY

India's electric supply is 230-240V AC, 50 Hz. All major appliances and sensitive electronics require a stabilizer to regulate the current and to prevent frying your equipment. You can purchase a universal AC adapter before coming.

SAFETY

Gujarat is generally very safe. You should still padlock your room in cheap hotels and hostels and secure your passport and any extra cash. In the case that something is stolen, file a complaint with the police, a copy of which you will need to keep for insurance claims. If you lose your passport, report the loss to the police, who will issue you a complaint form that will enable you to continue your travels. After this, contact the nearest embassy or consulate in India. You can request an emergency passport, which is cheap and only valid for a few days within your departure date. To get a full passport, you must go to Delhi or Mumbai.

LEGALITIES

If you get caught up in a legal mess, immediately contact your embassy. In recent times the police have started cracking down on foreigners for drug use, and if convicted, a minimum sentence of ten years without parole and a hefty fine could apply. If you get into a medico-legal situation, the best place to head is a government-run hospital; private hospitals may be reluctant to take you because of the hassles involved with the police.

PROHIBITION & LIQUOR PERMITS

Gujarat is a dry state, which means alcohol is illegal. However, it offers liquor permits to foreigners and to Indian citizens of other states. To obtain a permit, visit a Wine Shop or Permit Shop, usually found in high-end hotels across major cities. They are also available at the airport and Gujarat Tourism offices. A prohibition officer will issue the proper document after you present your passport. Technically the permit is free for foreigners and costs some Rs. 220 for Indian citizens, but the officer may hint at a "tip". Although you can legally buy alcohol with a permit, you must consume it in the privacy of your room. You will also get a list of shops where liquor can be purchased. There is a monthly limit of how much you can purchase, so ask for details.

DISABLED TRAVELERS

Gujarat does not have the proper infrastructure for travelers with disabilities. Current public transportation is not wheelchair accessible, while roads and sidewalks are full of potholes, high curbs and uneven levelling. Steps can often be steep and not all buildings have elevators. However, private transportation is relatively affordable and can make travel possible. It helps to travel with a companion or to come through a tour operator specializing in tours for the disabled.

GAY & LESBIAN TRAVELERS

Homosexuality is illegal in India and sodomy is punishable with a ten-year sentence. It is common to see men holding hands as an act of friendship, but anything more would not be taken so lightly. In general Gujarat is conservative and public displays of affection between any two people are considered inappropriate. The following are active gay and lesbian support groups in the state.

Lakshya Trust *0265 2331340*
lakshya121@rediffmail.com, Vadodara.
Contact *Silvester Merchant.*
Parma *0265 5535610 (Mon-Fri 10-4 pm),*
parma@hotmail.com, Vadodara.
Contact Indira Pathak.

TRAVEL WITH CHILDREN

India caters to travelers with children and locals are usually more than happy to accommodate to their needs. The main areas of concern for children are health and heat. Try to avoid travel during the peak of summer. Keep children hydrated, and carry packaged snacks as alternatives to spicy food. Diarrhea and vomiting are two of the most common health issues children face. You can purchase most baby products in India, but carry a portable changing mat, dried milk, baby food and wet wipes.

WOMEN TRAVELERS

Although Gujarat is relatively safe for women, you are still likely to encounter uncomfortable stares and catcalls. The local term, "eve teasing" refers to a group of men harassing a woman or a group of women. Dressing like local women in *salwar kameez* (a long tunic with loose pants and a scarf) helps decrease some of the unwanted attention. The *dupatta* (scarf) comes in handy when you have to cover you head to enter a mosque or a *gurudwara* and to protect you against the sun. Avoid baring your legs and midriff since this is seen as immodest and can be interpreted in a negative way. It also helps to say you are married and may be worth wearing a ring. Most men are less likely to harass a married woman. Light hair and light skin will unfortunately always attract attention, so take proper safety measures and avoid being out late at night by yourself. Always lock your hotel room. When riding public transport, place your bag or purse between you and other passengers to prevent groping or grabbing. You can always move if you are uncomfortable and never hesitate to scold somebody or tell him to stop if he is being inappropriate. It is best to avoid eye contact and conversation with male strangers, especially about personal matters, since this is sometimes taken as a sign of mutual interest. If you feel uncomfortable while talking to somebody you can always walk away.

PHOTOGRAPHY

It is not permitted to take photographs of airports, train stations, bridges, military installations, train interiors or in the vicinity of sensitive border areas. Most religious places also do not allow photography. It is becoming increasingly common for tourist destinations and archaeological monuments to charge a photography fee.

The best way to make friends in India is by pulling out your camera. In general locals love to have their photos taken and pose without hesitation. You will quickly learn that snapping a shot of a building becomes impossible if people, especially children, are nearby. If you have a digital camera, people will persist to see their photo, but even if it is a manual, they will be content to know that somebody has a photo of them.

Try to bring along all special equipment for your camera. It is also a good idea to buy a UV filter and pack any specific type of film that you may want, since it will be hard to come by in India. Avoid purchasing film from street vendors since their quality is questionable. Remember that heat affects the quality of film, so try to store it in a refrigerator if possible.

Most major cities and towns have good photo processing labs. Places such as **One Hour Photo** offer digital printing at very affordable prices. If possible, it is always a nice gesture to give copies of pictures to the people you photograph—they will cherish it long after you leave.

LAUNDRY

Although the washing machine is available in India, most people still wash clothes by hand or employ a *dhobi*, a traditional laundry man or woman, to take care of the task. The process begins with soaking clothes in soapy water, beating them clean with a wooden paddle and then rinsing out the soap. The clothes are dried in the sun. Then with a steam iron and some starch (sometimes too much) the wrinkles are removed. The clean and crisp clothes are returned a few days later. The beating and the sun, however, do lead to fading, fraying and the occasional lost button. If your accommodation does not offer laundry service, ask around to find the nearest *dhobi*. The charges are nominal. There are also plenty of drycleaners in most major cities and towns.

WILDLIFE SANCTUARIES & NATIONAL PARKS

These rates apply to all wildlife sanctuaries and national parks in Gujarat except for the Gir Wildlife Sanctuary and National Park in Junagadh District (see **pg 260-261**).

Entry Fee	
Mon-Fri	
Indian Rs. 20	Foreigner 5 USD
Sat-Sun	
Indian Rs. 25	Foreigner 6.25 USD
Small Four-Wheeler (up to 6 persons)	
Mon-Fri	
Indian Rs. 200	Foreigner 20 USD
Sat-Sun	
Indian Rs. 250	Foreigner 25 USD
Mini Bus/Van/Light Motor Vehicle (up to 15 persons)	
Mon-Fri	
Indian Rs. 500	Foreigner 50 USD
Sat-Sun	
Indian Rs. 625	Foreigner 62 USD
Bus/Heavy Motor Vehicle (up to 60 persons)	
Mon-Fri	
Indian Rs. 1750	Foreigner 175 USD
Sat-Sun	
Indian Rs. 2150	Foreigner 219 USD
Photography/Videography	
Amateur	Free
Professional Still	
Indian Rs. 100	Foreigner 10 USD
Video Documentary	
Indian Rs. 5000	Foreigner 500 USD

Feature Film	
Indian Rs. 25,000	Foreigner 1000 USD
Guides (In Gujarati)	
Rs. 50 for the first four hours	
Rs. 20 for each additional hour	

CITY NAMES

There has been a political move to change city names around the country back to their original pre-British designations. Hence, Baroda is now Vadodara, Bulsar is Valsad, Broach is Bharuch, Calcutta is Kolkata, Madras is Chennai and Bombay is Mumbai.

CULTURE & COMMUNITY

Public Displays of Affection
Besides holding hands it is considered offensive for couples to indulge in public displays of affection. You will, however, still find young couples loitering in gardens and along highways, hiding behind their scooters or under a tree with their backs turned towards the public.

Beaches
The Gujarati people generally dress very modestly and almost never expose their legs. Although swimwear is acceptable on beaches, you are still unlikely to find a local woman in a bathing suit, let alone a bikini. In Gujarat, beaches are generally used for family picnics and evening walks, not as a place to take in the sun or the waves.

The Right Attitude
Chaale literally means "to walk" in Gujarati and is used to indicate a carefree attitude. It is important to be laid back when dealing with things like customer service, government offices and ticket reservations. India works at its own pace and to get frustrated with it will only demoralize you and irritate those

around you. Learn to curb your expectations and learn from the process when dealing with little things that require large chunks of your time, or when somebody decides to take their tea break just as you reach the front of the line. India and Gujarat alike are developing quickly, and improving in the quality and efficiency of service, but these changes will take time, and more often than not, you will have to test your patience.

Hospitality

Athithi Devo Bhava is a Sanskrit term that means the "Guest is God". It is a living philosophy that is one of the unifying elements of the country and a big part of its identity. Gujaratis are extremely welcoming and hospitable and will quickly befriend you and invite you into their homes. Whether rich or poor, people will always offer their guest water and food, even if it means passing on their own ration for the day. Eating as a guest is a great experience. Inevitably, the host will insist on putting more into your plate and your stomach, and refuse to believe that you could possibly be full after just having had a third helping. It helps to eat what you like first, so that the refills are foods you enjoy. If not a meal, you will be offered tea or a cold drink. Hosts will go out of their way to help you. Although it is not customary, it is considerate to return their grace by showing up with a box of sweets, helping clean up afterwards or any other number of creative ways.

Beggars

Everyone has a different reaction to beggars, often because it is uncomfortable and guilt provoking to see poverty at such close proximity. There is no right or wrong solution to poverty, but you should remember a few things. Giving money can be dangerous since it encourages begging as a living and since you do not actually know for what or whom the money will be used. Once you give something to one individual, it is very likely that a crowd will build up around you asking for the same. Passing out food is also questionable since it

only supports the habit, especially in children. One of the best things to do is acknowledge them, talk with them and give them respect without necessarily giving them anything else. The most sustainable option is to contribute money and or time to non-profit organizations that work directly with the community.

The Right Hand

In India everybody eats with their right hand since the left is associated with cleaning yourself after visiting the toilet. Always remember to follow this etiquette as it is otherwise offensive and considered polluting. Always accept *prasad* with your right hand as well. In fact most things are done with the right hand, including shaking hands. If you are offered a gift, however, it is respectable to accept it with both hands.

Shoes Off

It is customary in most Indian households to remove your shoes as a sign of respect. This is also expected before entering a religious space. Pointing your feet at somebody or stepping on books or paper (seen as forms of Sarasvati, the Goddess of knowledge) is also considered offensive.

Holy Places

Each place of worship has its own implicit set of rules. Always remove your shoes before entering any religious space in India. In Hindu and Jain temples, *gurudwaras* and mosques, women and men are expected to dress modestly and not expose their upper arms or legs. Sometimes non-Hindus are not allowed into the inner sanctum of the Hindu temple. Before entering a Jain temple, remove all leather (belts, shoes, etc.) since the production of it is seen as an act of violence against animals. Men and women must cover their heads (with a handkerchief, scarf, hat) before entering a mosque or a *gurudwara*. There is also a water tank just outside mosques where followers partake in ritual cleansing before praying. Women are usually not allowed into functioning mosques. Always ask before taking a picture of any idol or interior of a place of worship.

Pushing Personal Limits

Locals will love to test their English out on you and quench their curiosity about you by making conversation. More often than not, the first questions asked will include whether or not you are married and what you do. If you look Indian, you will also be asked your last name, so that the person can gauge where in India you are from and what community you belong to. The questions will get progressively more personal; however, this is not considered rude and is actually a friendly Indian inquisition. Take the opportunity to ask questions back and gain insight into local culture.

Do not be put off by the long stares you may experience during your travels. Indians often stare beyond a point of comfort for most westerners, but it is culturally acceptable and usually not intended to be harmful. Of course if a man is ogling at a woman, take it for what it is.

Personal space is a foreign concept to the Gujarati and Indian cultures. This means that people may rummage through your stuff, stand in close physical proximity to you and always insist on giving you company, even if you want alone time. Often, an entire family lives in a one-bedroom house and forty people cram into an 8-person jeep. Although this can be uncomfortable initially, it is easy to get used to, and even miss once it is gone.

RESOURCE
GUIDE

CRAFT

Craft in Gujarat was already highly developed 4000 years ago, when the people of the Indus Valley Civilization made earthen pots and terracotta beads. Around the 1st c. AD Gujarat traded a variety of goods and exported fine textiles to the world. Over the centuries traders, seafarers and each invader introduced new ideas that influenced the creative expression of local craftspeople.

The artisan and the user had a social equation, so the artifact was never for a faceless customer. A craftsman generally knew the exact number of pieces needed each year by his community, which was also his market. Designs changed every 100 miles based on local resources and creativity. Craftspeople were respected for their role in fulfilling the functional and aesthetic needs of life.

Today, machine-made products are rapidly displacing local craft traditions. As people's appreciation and awareness of the skill underlying craft dwindles, many artisans have to struggle to earn from their trade. Despite these challenges, craft remains strongly embedded in the Gujarati culture and continues to enhance its ethos. Here is a look at the major crafts of Gujarat and some of the places where they are predominantly practiced.

MUD CRAFT

Clay Relief Work Bhirandiyara, Dhordo, Hodka, Ludiya
Every year before Diwali, some communities in Kachchh plaster their *bhungas* with *lipan*, which is then embellished with mirrors and *okli* (textures created by hand imprints). Artisans also use the local clay to mold intricate designs of people, flowers, animals and geometric motifs along the walls, doors and windows. In some villages this clay work is combined with beautiful paintings in mineral rock colors on the exterior of the huts.

Painted Pottery Khavda, Lodai, Bhuj
Pottery skills in Gujarat date from the Indus Valley Civilization. Like all traditional handicrafts, the subtleties of pottery change from village to village. Each vessel is shaped by hand or on a wheel, baked in the sun and coated with a thin wash of *geru* (an earthy red color). The potter's wife uses a frayed bamboo twig to paint various motifs in clay-based black and white colors. The piece is then fired in a kiln to set the colors.

Terracotta Chhota Udepur, Devgad Baria, Patan, Poshina
Many tribal communities place clusters of hand-crafted terracotta animals, such as elephants, camels, and horses, at their places of worship. Each region has its own distinct style of figures. Terracotta ware lined with lacquer is also used to store food and *tadi*, local liquor.

TEXTILE CRAFT

Ajrakh Printing
Dhamadhka, Khavda

This block printing technique, a shared heritage of Kachchh in Gujarat and Sindh in Pakistan, creates intricate geometric designs in shades of madder red, natural rust, black, and indigo among other natural dyes. Indigo is believed to have a natural cooling and warming effect depending on the season, an important feature in semi-desert regions. Ajrakh is a meticulous technique that involves 16 different processes. The resulting piece retains a beautiful depth of color otherwise impossible with surface printing alone. Traditionally, the men of the Maldhari, Ahir and Meghwal communities used Ajrakh prints for their *lungi*, headscarves and shoulder throws.

Bandhani
Bhuj, Jamnagar, Mandvi, Mundra

Bandhani remains one of Gujarat's most prominent textile crafts. Artisans first tie sections of the cloth with waxed thread and then dip it into vats of dye. When removed, the tied sections resist the color, creating the tie and dye effect. The quality of Bandhani is based on the fineness of the dots and the design. The base cloth (gajji silk, cotton, muslin or wool) combined with the colors and design of the Bandhani reveals the identity of the community that wears it. Bandhani is an important element in the wedding ceremony of Hindus, Muslims and Jains alike. The Gharchola, a traditional Hindu and Jain wedding sari, always uses multiples of 12 or 52 squares, each filled with various tie and dye motifs.

Block Printing
Ahmedabad, Dhamadhka, Jetpur, Khavda

Gujarat is the birthplace of India's oldest printed textiles. In block printing, the artisan first mixes the dye, dips the block in the color and then neatly impresses it in an ordered sequence on the fabric. The fabric is processed with a chemical wash to bind the final color. Today chemical colors have replaced most natural dyes.

Embroidery
Across Kachchh, Saurashtra & North Gujarat

Different styles of embroidery developed as pastoral communities migrated to various parts of Gujarat. Each community is identified by its own distinctive style of embroidery. The finest examples come from the northwest of Kachchh and the west of Saurashtra. This needle-and-thread tradition is passed from mother to daughter. They usually work on it during the long, hot afternoons. In many communities, women embroider intricate blouses and purses for their wedding dowry, and bring vitality to an otherwise monotonous backdrop in the semi-desert regions of Gujarat.

Mata ni Pachedi
Ahmedabad (Mirzapur and Vasna)

This ritual cloth-painting is identified by an image of the Mother Goddess battling demons in one of her several manifestations. The cloth is printed and painted with strong, bold forms filled with natural red and black dyes. The Vaghari community paints the Mata ni Pachedi for other communities who commission the piece as a ritual offering. The art form originated when poor migratory groups needed to set up temporary temples to honor their Goddess. The painted fabrics hung as walls and canopies, simulating a worship space while also serving as an offering. The printing, done either with wooden blocks or *kalamkari* (hand painting), begins with the borders and moves inward towards the Goddess. Certain elements of the ritual cloth remain fixed; the sun and moon are depicted in the top right and left corners of the cloth while Ganesh always sits on the upper left.

Mashru Weaving   Patan

Mashru is a mixed fabric woven with silk, cotton, and a satin weave. Initially, only Muslim men used this fabric since Islamic law prohibited them from wearing pure silk, but Hindu communities began to use it soon after. Silk yarn constitutes the outer face of the fabric while the cotton yarn is worn close to the body. Most Mashru contains vibrant stripes of tie and dyed yarns. In addition to being exported to Turkey and the Middle East, the fabric was used by women in some Kachchhi communities to stitch garments for their dowry. As the export market declined, Mashru was replaced by cheaper rayon. Once woven throughout India, including Bhuj and Surat in Gujarat, today Mashru is crafted in just a few places.

Namda Work   Bhujodi, Mundra

This felt-making craft, practiced only by the Pinjarar and Mansuri communities of eastern Kachchh, originated in Iran and Turkey. Wool is processed into felt and rolled into small slivers that are then laid out in a pattern. The technique of Namda relies on the natural matting and compression properties of wool to bind the various parts.

Patola Weaving   Patan

Patola is one of the most difficult weaving forms in the world. It employs the double-ikat technique, which incorporates binding and dyeing cloth fibers according to a preset pattern before the threads are set on the loom. The process of coloring the threads alone takes more than 70 days, while weaving one Patola *sari* requires about 25 days. Only three families in Patan still practice this skill-intensive craft.

Quilting   Bhuj, Banni & Pachchham, Across Saurashtra

Quilting originated as an effective method to recycle and strengthen old pieces of cloth, while creating utilitarian products with aesthetic appeal. In many communities, quilts are representative of the family's wealth and prosperity. Some clans consider quilts an essential part of a girl's wedding trousseau. Popular quilting techniques include patchwork (sewing together various scraps of material), appliqué (cut work in cloth with other fabric placed behind it) and *tanka* (using the running stitch in concentric circles to hold material together). In Kachchh, women also use *khambira*, a stitch sewn in a step-like grid to create a semblance of texture throughout the quilt.

Rogan Painting
Nirona

This colorful textile craft involves painting fabrics with a thick, purified castor oil and natural-dye paste. The artisan draws a design onto the cloth with a *kalam* (iron stylus) and fills in the outlines with the colored paste. Today only one family in Nirona practices this craft. Rogan was once an affordable substitute for embroidered textiles; however, the intense skill and labor demanded by the process has made this art form almost obsolete and quite expensive.

WOODEN CRAFT

Block Making
Pethapur

The block makers of Pethapur, who belong to the Suthar community, are reputed for their skill in making color separation blocks, of which one prints a background, another the outline, and the third fills in the remaining space. The artisans etch a design on a seasoned teakwood block and carve out the negative space. Designs usually include geometric motifs, flowers, plants, fruits and animals. Each block is fitted with a wooden handle, and drilled with a few holes to enable free air passage and the release of excess printing paste. New blocks are soaked in oil for about two weeks to soften the grain in the wood. The arrival of screen printing has challenged the art of block making in Gujarat.

Sankheda Ware
Sankheda

The Kharadi community has mastered the technique of Sankheda, which derives its name from its center of production. Pieces of teakwood are cut into required sizes, shaped on a lathe and smoothened before a coat of primer is applied. Designs vary from a lattice of geometrical shapes to floral motifs, and are painted onto the pieces with a squirrel-hair brush. The lacquer is applied onto the pieces through heat and friction, and then polished with a leaf. The patterns change color once heated and coated with lacquer. Finally the pieces are assembled to create furniture. As limited materials are used, the products have a fixed range of colors, mostly blends of brown and orange.

Wood Carving
Ahmedabad, Patan, Palanpur, Vaso

In Gujarat's architecture you will find wooden carvings that are unparalleled in India. Ironically, most of Gujarat had to import its structural timber from other parts of the country. Wood carvings can be seen on beams and doors throughout the state, and also on furniture and traditional storage units. Most wood carving in Ahmedabad reflects patterns of block printing, an indication of the once-thriving textile industry and its influence on the city. Although artisans occasionally painted the carvings with colors, Ahmedabad's craftsmen coated their work with oil that acts as a preservative while enhancing the wood's rich, natural color. Wood carving in this capacity is no longer practiced.

Woodwork
Hodka, Khavda, Ludiya, Navavas

The Kachchhi Meghwals make beautiful wooden items with geometrical carvings that imitate motifs found in local embroidery and clay work. The male artisans use lathes and chisels to shape and engrave the product. They make traditional furniture, boxes, book holders and coasters among other products.

TRIBAL CRAFT

Bamboo Work
Ahwa, Dharampur

Tribal communities in southeastern Gujarat make several woven bamboo products such as baskets and sieves used for agricultural purposes and fish traps. They also design intricate bamboo toys that demand dexterity and time. The artisan splits bamboo stems into smaller pieces, sets them into a pattern and weaves the components together to form the desired object.

Beadwork
Ludiya, Hodka, Dahod

Women make vibrant jewelry and other crafts by sewing together colorful beads into geometric and floral patterns. Beadwork originated in the 19th c. with the introduction of Venetian beads and it became an alternative form of embroidery. Today, it is a component of the regional dress for several communities, especially in tribal areas. In Kachchh, women also make *kanjaris*, (open-back blouses) with intricate beadwork sewn onto the cloth.

Lacquer Work
Nirona

Lacquer is a natural resin, heated and then mixed with color dyes. The artisan smoothes the surface of a wooden object and then turns it on a lathe while pouring lacquer onto it. The natural heat and friction created in the process fixes the vibrant colors. This finishing is done on a variety of items including ladles, boxes, wooden furniture and rolling pins.

Silver Work
Bhuj, Jamnagar, Moti Virani, Patan, Rajkot

Gujarat has a rich tradition of silver ornaments, which in some communities, function as a woman's portable assets. The particular style of or the distinctive designs engraved onto the ornaments reveal the identity of the owner's community. In pastoral and tribal communities, men as well as women wear silver. In some customs, women wear up to three kilos, including earrings, anklets, neckpieces, waistbands, toe rings and bangles. Some people believe that ornaments possess medicinal, protective or magical powers.

OTHER CRAFT FORMS

Agate Stone Work
Khambhat

Agate craft in Khambhat goes back several thousand years. The city is home to agate artisans who process the brilliantly striped, semiprecious stone into a variety of jewelry and decorative pieces. Traditionally these were made only for export as local tastes in jewelry favored gold and silver. Today, a burgeoning middle class has created indigenous demand for the affordable craft. The stone is also believed to possess magical powers that balance the energies of a person or a place.

Bell Work
Nirona, Zura

This trade, which originated in Sindh, is practiced by the Lohar community. Traditionally hung by pastoral communities on the necks of grazing animals to keep track of them, the bells are finding a growing place in urban homes as decorative pieces. The artisan shapes and colors the bell through a meticulous process and then sets its pitch with the aid of an instrument called *ekalavai*. The bells come in 14 different sizes and pitches. Bell makers also make the *jhummar*, a single piece comprised of several bells.

Kite Making
Ahmedabad, Khambhat

A single traditional fighter kite passes through as many as 15 hands and 23 processes before it is complete. Bamboo splints come from West Bengal and the kite paper, from Karnataka. The paper is cut in Ahmedabad and sent to Mahuda for artisans to thread its edges to strengthen them. Craftspeople in Ahmedabad heat and insert the *dhadho* and *kaman*, the splints that make up the spine and the bow-shaped truss respectively. These help the kite withstand the wind. Other artisans affix tags and a tailpiece. *Manjo*, the string used to fly the kite, is thread coated with colored glass powder and paste, elements that aid in the tradition of cutting down kites of opponents, lending to the name "fighter kite".

Leather Craft
Bhirandiyara, Dhordo, Gorewali, Hodka, Khavda, Nirona

Leather goods are crafted by the Meghwal community, who live and work closely with Maldharis (cattle owners, herders). From these neighbors the Meghwals source the raw hide of dead animals. The men shape the leather into products such as shoes and mirror frames while the women adorn the pieces with colorful embroidery. These artisans also produce a distinct style of leatherwork where they punch the leather with different shapes and then line it with colorful cloth to create an effect similar to reverse appliqué.

Metal Ware
Ahmedabad, Shihor, Wadhwan

Traditionally metal ware was associated with the occult, and the blacksmith was held in esteem for his sacred ability to shape metal. Later the craft developed into the science of metallurgy.

As more metals became available, vessels became more diverse. Artisans took inspiration from shapes in nature and in clay forms. They molded vessels to suit their intended use, such as the water pot that fits into the curve of woman's waist, supported by her hip. Today the Kansara community in Gujarat shapes copper and brass by alternately heating and hammering sheets of these metals. The hammer strokes leave behind patterns, which accentuate the texture. Copper and brass work involve hard physical labor and is only practiced by men. Women usually polish the metal objects with tamarind to enhance the luster.

Stone Carving
Ambaji, Dhrangadhra

The stonemasons of Gujarat, the Sompuras, trace their origin to Aparajita, the son of heaven's own architect, Vishvakarma. Stonework came much later than wood and ivory carving, but artisans quickly grew adept and emulated designs from the former mediums onto stone. The act of carving the likeness of a deity was considered a sacred ritual and stone carvers were revered. The Sompuras are among the few remaining communities of traditional temple builders in India, and are sought across the country for designing and building temples.

CUISINE

Gujarat offers a diversity of cuisine, influenced by variations in climate and soil across the state and the cultural differences between communities. The Jains, Vaishnavas, Rajputs, Muslims and Parsis each has a distinct culinary repertoire. In Kachchh you will also find subtle influences of Sindh, which lies just across the border in southeastern Pakistan.

The Case For Vegetarianism

Gujarat has a higher proportion of vegetarians than almost any other part of India. This is due to two major factors. First, between the 6th and 13th c. a number of Jain religious leaders wielded strong influence on society, propagating non-violence and prohibiting the killing of animals. The 15th c. saw the beginning of the equally influential Vaishnav Movement, which denounced eating meat. These legacies pervade the Gujarati ethos to this day.

The Gujarati Thali

At the center of the state's rich gastronomic range lies its quintessential experience—the Gujarati vegetarian *thali*. The word means "metal platter" and also refers to the meal served in it. The *thali* is composed of a range of preparations, with some of them served in *vaatki* (little bowls). The concept of courses does not exist, so you can switch back and forth between the items as you please. Usually a glass of *chhaas*, which aids digestion, accompanies the meal and helps take the tang off anything spicy.

Some restaurants offer Unlimited Thali, which comes with limitless refills. While the mix of dishes may vary by restaurant or region, a typical *thali* includes *farsan* and *nasta* (steamed or fried snacks), one or more kinds of bread (see **Gujarati Flat Breads**), a salad of diced vegetables, two or three kinds of *shaak* (cooked vegetables), *kathor* (beans in a gravy), a *dal* (lentil soup) or a *kadhi* (yogurt-based soup) served with *khichadi* and sweets. Different communities across the state boast their own variation of *khichadi*, a healthy and light lentil and rice mixture. The *thali* also includes hot, spicy, sweet and sour chutneys, pickles and relishes. Gujarat is famous for its array of pickles and relishes, which adorn the shelves of household pantries and restaurant tables. Just as you begin to finish your meal, the waiter will come around to refill your dish. At the end of the meal, you can choose from a tray of mouth-fresheners called *mukhwas*, such as *variyali* (fennel), *khati-mithi kharek* (spiced dried dates), *amla* (dried gooseberry) or *churan*.

Paan is also a popular breath freshener. It consists of a heart-shaped betel leaf layered with *chuna* (lime paste), mixed spices such as cardamom and anise, grated coconut and *katha* (a red substance extracted from the katha tree; it is what causes the saliva to turn red). *Paan* made with *supari* (areca nut) has a narcotic effect. The leaf is then folded into a triangular shape and secured by piercing a clove into it.

Gujarati Flat Breads

Rotli, made of whole wheat dough, is rolled very thin and usually cooked on an iron griddle.

Skillfully hand-patted out of *bajra*, *jowar* or corn dough, *rotlo* is roasted on a clay griddle, which gives it a sweet flavor. This village staple is thicker and heavier than *rotli*.

Thick and slightly grainy, *bhakri* is smaller in diameter. Made from wheat flour, it is cooked on an iron griddle, and then topped with a touch of ghee.

Thepla, also known as *dhebra*, is prepared like *bhakri* but the dough is made with wheat and *bajra* flour, mixed with a variety of shredded vegetables and mildly spiced.

Puran poli, prepared on special occasions, is rolled out of whole wheat dough, stuffed with sweet *mung dal* filling and cooked on a flat iron griddle. A thicker, smaller version is called *vedhmi*.

Puri, though not flat, is a very popular bread rolled out of whole wheat dough and deep fried, causing it to puff up.

Kathiawad (the Saurashtra Peninsula) is a semi-arid region that grows excellent chilies—one reason for the extra spice in its cuisine. Green leafy vegetables are scarce, so staple *shaaks* often use ingredients that are not strictly vegetables, as in *ganthiya nu shaak* (a crisp fried flour snack cooked in a curry), *sev-tamata nu shaak* (tomato curry with *sev*), *paanchkutiya shaak* (a curry with five ingredients) and *panch dal* (a mix of lentils). In both Kathiawad and Kachchh, known for their prime quality milk-yielding cattle, ghee and curd are an important part of the cuisine.

Kachchhi food is similar to Kathiawadi fare, but more moderately spiced and has Sindhi influences. Specialties include *dal-pakwan* (large and crispy *puris* served with chickpea *dal*), *sai bhaji* (spinach and lentils cooked with spices) and *bhea* (lotus stems cooked in spices). Sindhi *kadhi* is thicker with vegetables and *pakoras* added, giving it a special flavor.

The South Gujarat coastline has fertile soil and heavy rains, which shape its cuisine. The famous "Surti jaman" or Surat feast features more leafy vegetables and beans. A regional specialty is *undhiyu*, a popular winter dish made with green beans, unripe banana, *muthia*, purple yam and mixed vegetables cooked in a spicy curry that sometimes includes coconut. A classic treat is *matla nu undhiyu*, which is cooked in an earthen pot (usually inverted, which means "undhu" in Gujarati) buried in the ground and fired to give it a smoky or baked flavor. Unfortunately this is a rare practice now and the commonly available *undhiyu* is cooked in liberal amounts of oil. The sweets in this area include *ghari, ghevar, sutarpheni* and *halavasan*. A popular snack in the harvest season is *ponk* or fresh roasted millet.

During the summer months in Gujarat, *ras*, a rich mango puree, becomes an essential part of most meals.

Beyond Meals...

Gujaratis are known for their *farsans*, which are steamed items served as snacks, starters or accompaniments. These include chickpea rolls called *khandvi* and savory cakes known as *dhokla*, made from ground rice and mixed lentils, and served with chutney. *Muthia* ("fist") is named for the way the dough is gripped in order to make it. *Paatra* is colocassia leaf rolls stuffed with a mildly savory paste. Some *farsans*, such as *handvo*, a spicy baked chickpea and lentils cake with grated vegetables, can be a light meal on its own.

Fried snacks or *nasta* include *ganthiya, chevdo, sev* and *sakkarpara*. Wholemeal low-calorie versions of some of these are also available. *Khakhra*, a popular and healthy breakfast item, is a thinly rolled, crisp and dry flat bread that lasts for days without spoiling. It comes in a number of flavors.

Bhajiya (pakora) and *vada* are battered vegetables, deep-fried and eaten with chutney. *Gota* and *dalwada* are batter mixed with different spices and deep fired. The *vada pav* is a bun sandwich with a *vada* filling and a spread of chutney. *Kachori* and *samosas* are rolled dough stuffed with various fillings and then fried.

Fafda (fried chickpea flour strips served with green chilies, chutney and raw papaya salad) and *jalebi* (a thin batter deep-fried into spirals and dipped in syrup) is a popular savory and sweet breakfast combo, customarily eaten hot and fresh at a street side vendor.

Sweets

Gujarat has many mouth-watering sweets. One of the more popular is *shrikhand*, a thick, yogurt base garnished with saffron, nuts, cardamom and dry fruit. *Basundi* is milk thickened over a slow fire, sweetened and topped with nuts, cardamom and saffron. *Doodhpaak*—similar to rice pudding, is another milk-based treat. Several sweetmeats are prepared with a flour base. *Mohanthal* and *magas* are made from roasted chickpea flour, ghee, sugar, and nuts while *ladva* consist of different types of flour, roasted and sweetened with sugar and shaped into balls. *Kansar, laapsi* and *seero* are variations of roasted whole oats or coarse-ground semolina and grains cooked with ghee and sugar. Gujarat also has many kinds of nut and dried fruit confections, such as *kaaju katri*, made from cashews, *badam puri* from almonds and *pista* rolls from pistachios

Non-veg Food

Contrary to the popular vegetarian image, some Gujarati communities are traditionally non-vegetarian and their cuisine can be an unparalleled experience. Meat dishes particular to Muslims are found in Ahmedabad in areas such as Mirzapur and the popular street alley known as Bhatiyar Gali near Teen Darwaza.

With the population of Parsis declining and dispersing, restaurants serving their distinctive food are few and far between. The signature Parsi dish is *dhansak*, meat kebabs in *dal* served with rice. Other favorites are *bhaji dana gosht* (spicy mutton, fish or prawn curries) and *sali gosht (*tender mutton cubes in ground spices garnished with crisp potato straws). *Sali murg* uses chicken instead of mutton. *Murg farcha* (fried chicken) and *patra ni machhli* (steamed fresh fish cooked with green spices in a banana leaf wrap) are particular delicacies. Parsis also prepare delicious varieties of vegetables with fried egg toppings, such as *papeta par eenda* made with potatoes.

Gujarat's long coastline yields excellent marine catches but finding good sea-food at local restaurants can be difficult. At Veraval and Porbandar, the major fishing ports on the Kathiawad coast, you may get lucky at some of the eateries. In Diu and Daman, literally a hop and a skip across the state border, many places do good fish and prawns.

Street Food & Dhabas

Gujarat has an exciting culture of street food that offers cheap and good fare in an informal setting. Street vendors specialize in any number of food items ranging from *chaat* (generic name for small plates of savory snacks such as *pani puri, bhel,* and *dahi puri*) and *dosas* to sandwiches, Indian-Chinese and localized pizza (spicier tomato sauce and unmelted, grated cheese). Be cautious when eating at these places, since some of them lack proper hygienic practices. The *dhaba*, a round-the-clock highway eatery that evolved to serve the needs of passing truck drivers now caters to a wider clientele. The essence of the *dhaba* is that the fare, though spicy, is always made fresh and tasty. The sheer volume of turnover assures that there are no leftovers. This could be the original "fast food".

Modern Trends

In the last decade, continental and Chinese cuisines have caught on in Gujarat. While the Chinese fare at many restaurants is delicious, most continental options are local adaptations, not particularly recommended for everyone's taste buds. Some popular western chains have also popped up in the major cities, but local alternatives offer tasty options at reasonable prices and patronizing them supports the local economy.

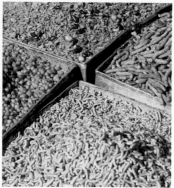

Chai

Chai cuts across class, caste and religion as a favorite pastime for most Gujaratis. This sweet tea brewed in half milk and half water is garnished with ginger or a mix of spices in the winter and with mint in the summer. It is served in small glasses and enjoyed alone or with a snack.

Vegans

Vegans should note that a lot of Gujarati cuisine depends heavily on milk products and yogurt in its cooking. Chai is always served with the milk already added.

Mangos

Indians are passionate about mangos and Gujaratis are no exception. The season in Gujarat starts in March and runs up until the monsoon. Regional mango loyalty in India can be as fierce as wine loyalty in Europe. Although most mangos are sweet and succulent, Alphonso (*hafus*) and Kesar are considered the best in quality and are the most expensive variety in Gujarat. There are two kinds of mango—the firm fleshy ones that you cut, and the softer ones that you can squeeze and suck directly after removing the stem.

Native Fruits

One of the pleasures of India is the variety of tropical fruits available in different seasons. The following are common in Gujarat:

Keri	Mango (summer)
Jaamfal	Guava (winter and spring)
Sitafal	Custard Apple (winter) - Messy to eat, but worth the trouble.
Chikoo	Sapota (winter and spring)
Jamoon	Java plum (summer through monsoon) - Nice with rock salt.
Bor	Jujube (winter)
Amla	Indian gooseberry (winter) - Full of vitamin C.
Shingoda	Water chestnut (winter)
Falsa	Small sour purple berry (summer)

LANGUAGE PRONUNCIATION GUIDE

The Language

Gujarati, which belongs to the Indo-European family of languages, also represents one of the 24 official languages spoken in India. It is written using the Gujarati script, a form very similar to Devanagari script (used for Sanskrit and Hindi), but without the line across the top of the characters. Gujarati emerged during the Solanki era in the 12th c. It continued to develop, incorporating elements of various languages into its lexicon for the next five centuries. Under the rule of the Delhi Sultanate, and then under the Mughal Empire, the court language was Persian. Meanwhile the influential mercantile class conducted business with many Arab traders. As a result, both Persian and Arabic words evolved into the Gujarati vernacular. Most Gujarati words dealing with administration, trade, navigation and emotions have roots in these two languages. Of course, after the Portuguese invaded, they also left their imprint on the local dialect, while the British introduced several English words that have taken a permanent place in the local vocabulary. The Parsis and the indigenous tribal communities have also lent generously to the language. Today, Gujarati is spoken by over 46 million people around the world. The dialect of Gujarati changes almost every 12 km across the state. Portuguese and English influence the southern vernacular while Arabic and Persian affect the language of the central and northern regions. Gujarati is also spoken in parts of Pakistan. Kachchhi, which combines Sindhi, Gujarati, Punjabi, and Marwari is spoken throughout the region of Kachchh.

Namaste

A respected and universal greeting throughout India, "Namaste" is said while placing both palms together and lowering the head. Namaste translates into "I bow to the divinity within you", and represents a mutual respect between two individuals.

This language guide has been developed to help you pronounce basic phrases so that you can communicate with local people. To keep it simple, the guide disregards certain rules of the language. For anybody interested in learning the language properly, there are several instruction books available at local bookstores. The transliteration in this section is different from the rest of the book.

Pronunciation Guide

a as in *'fun'*
aa as in *'calm'*
e as in *'bet'*
i as in *'fit'*
ee as in *'heat'*
u as in *'pull'*
ai as in *'nice'*
au as in *'saw'*

o as in *'hotel'*
ch as in *'bench'*
chh as in *'pitch'*
t as in as in *"ticket"*
th as in *"thumb"*
d as in *"dog"*
dh as in *"then"*
kh as in *"come"*

COMMON PHRASES

Yes	Haa
No	Naa
Hello	Namasthe
How are you?	Kem chho?
Good	Saaru
Bad	Saaru nathee

So, so	Theek Theek
Ok	Baraabar
Goodbye	Aavjo
Nice to meet you	Maleene aanand thayo
Thank you	(Khub) aabhaar
(very much)	

Please	Kripayaa
Sorry	Maaf karjo
Good (morning, night)	Shubh (prabhaath, raatri)
What is your name?	Aap nu naam shu chhe?
My name is_____.	Maaru naam _____chhe.
I (do not) understand.	Hu samajyo/samajee (nathee).
I do not know.	Mane khabar nathee.
I know.	Mane khabar chhe.
How do you say this in (Gujarati)?	(Gujarati) maa aa kevi rithe kaho?
Do you speak (English)?	Aap (angreji) bolo chho?
I am from (America).	Hu (America) thee aavyo/aavee chhu.
How	Kevi rithe
When	Kyaare
What	Shu
Why	Kem
Who	Kon
Family	Parivaar
Wife	Patni
Husband	Pati
Daughter	Putaree, deekaree
Son	Putara, deekaro
Mother	Maa, maataa
Father	Peetaa
Friend	Mitra

GETTING AROUND

Where is the _____?	_____ kyaa chhe?
Toilet	Toilet/sandaas
Public phone	STD
Hindu temple	Mandir
Jain temple	Deraasar
Sikh temple	Gurudwaaraa
Mosque	Masjid
Parsi temple	Agyaaree
Pharmacy	Davaanee dukaan
Hospital	Davaa khaanu/Hospital
(Vegetable) Market	(Shaak) maarket
General store	Karyaanaa
Laundry man	Dhobi
Store	Dukaan
I am lost.	Hu bhulo/bhuli padyo/padee chhe.
How much is the fare?	Bhaadu ketlu chhe?

One ticket to (Ahmedabad), please.	(Ahmedabad) javaa maate ek tikit aapasho.
Departure	Upardvaano samay
Arrival	Aavaano samay
Can I see the (room)?	Room joy shakun?
Reservation	Anaamath
Are there any vacancies (for tonight)?	(Aaj raath maate) jagyaa chhe?
No vacancies	Khaali jagyaa nathee
Key	Chaavee
Extra Bed	Vadhaaraano bistar.
Blanket	Odhvaanu
Hot	Garam
Cold	Thandu
Left (side)	Daabee (baaju)
Right (side)	Jamnee (baaju)
Straight	Seedhu
Up	Upar
Down	Neeche
Front	Aagal
Back	Paachal
Near	Najeek
Long	Laambu
Short	Tunku
Map	Naksho
North	Uttar
South	Daksheen
East	Purva
West	Pashchim
Here/there	Ahiyaa/thyaan
This/That	Aa/the
Open	Khullu
Closed	Bandh
Street	Sheri/rasto
Crossroads	Chaar rastaa
Square	Chok
Garden/park	Baagh
Mountain	Parvat
Hill	tekree/tekro
Ocean	Dariyo
Lake	Sarovar, talaav
River	Nadee
Bridge	Pull

TIME

What time is it?	Ketlaa vaagyaa?
7:13, Seven thirteen	Saath ne ther
3:15, Three fifteen	Thran ne pandar
3:15, Quarter past three	Savaa thran
11:30, Eleven thirty	Agiyaar trees or Saadaa agiyaar
1:45, One forty-five	Ek ne pistaalis
1:45, Quarter till two	Ponaa be
1:30	Dodh
2:30	Adhee

Hour	Kalaak
Day	Divas/din
Week	Athavaadiyu
Month	Mahino
Year	Varsh

Monday	Somvaar
Tuesday	Mangalvaar
Wednesday	Budhvaar
Thursday	Guruvaar
Friday	Shukravaar
Saturday	Shanivaar
Sunday	Ravivaar

Today	Aaje
Yesterday	Gayee kaal, kaale
Tomorrow	Aavthee kaal, kaale
Day after tomorrow	Param divas
Morning	Savaare
Afternoon	Bapore
Evening	Saanj
Night	Raat
Now	Atyaare
Later	Pachhee
First	Pahelo
Second	Beejo
Next	Pachhee
Last	Chhello

SHOPPING

How much does this cost?	Aanu/aanee kimmat shu chhe?
Do you accept credit cards?	Credit card sveekaaro chho?
What is this?	Aa shu chhe?
I'll buy it.	Hu khareedeesh.
I would like to buy _____.	Maare _____ khareedvu chhe.

Do you have _____?	_____ malshe?
Soap	Saabu
Clothes	Kapadaa
Handicrafts	Hastakalaa
Medicine	Davaa
Handkerchief	Rumaal
Envelope	Parbidiyu
Water	Paanee
A little	Jaraak
A lot	Khub
All	Badhu
Enough	Purtun
Big	Motu
Small	Naanu

NUMBERS

Zero	Shunya	૦
One	Ek	૧
Two	Be	૨
Three	Thran	૩
Four	Chaar	૪
Five	Paanch	૫
Six	Chha	૬
Seven	Saat	૭
Eight	Aath	૮
Nine	Nav	૯
Ten	Das	૧૦
Eleven	Ageeyaar	૧૧
Twelve	Baar	૧૨
Thirteen	Ter	૧૩
Fourteen	Chodh	૧૪
Fifteen	Pandar	૧૫
Sixteen	Sol	૧૬
Seventeen	Sattar	૧૭
Eighteen	Adhaar	૧૮
Nineteen	Oganees	૧૯
Twenty	Vees	૨૦
Twenty one	Ekvees	૨૧
Thirty	Threes	૩૦
Forty	Chaalees	૪૦
Fifty	Pachaas	૫૦
Sixty	Saahit	૬૦
Seventy	Sither	૭૦
Eighty	Enshee	૮૦
Ninety	Nevu	૯૦
One hundred	So	૧૦૦
One thousand	Ek hajaar	
One million	Das laakh	

Other helpful phrases

Volunteer work	Sevaa
I am married.	Mara lagnaa thaygayaan chhe.
I am single.	Hu kuwaaro/kuwaari chhu.
I like it.	Mane game chhe.
Children	Chhokaraa
Let's play.	Ramat ramiye.
Beautiful	Sundar
I am having fun.	Majaa aave chhe.
The food is great.	Khaavaanu masth chhe.

Gujaratis in general are very open and welcoming people. One of the best ways to connect with the people and the culture is to make friends with their children. Although language is not required to bond with most kids, here are a few phrases that will help and can make for great ice breakers with people of any age.

Want to play?	Maari saathe ramasho?
Will you be my friend?	Maara mithra bansho?
What grade are you in?	Kayaa dhoran maa chho?
Want to see magic?	Jaduu jovu chhe?
Will you sing a song?	Aap geet gaasho?
Good job.	Saras.
Can I take a picture?	Photo layshaku?
Do you know a joke?	Joke aavde chhe?
Your kid is cute.	Teneeyo majaano chhe/ tenee majaanee chhe!
I can teach you _____.	Hu thamne _____ shikhavaadhi shaku chhu.

Health

Health	Tabiyat
Where is the hospital/clinic?	Davaakhaanu kyaa chhe?
I am sick.	Hun maado chhu.
My (head, stomach, throat) hurts	Maaru (maathu, pet, gadu) dukhe chhe.
I have nausea.	Ultee thava jevu thai chhe.
I am allergic to _____.	Mane _____ ni allergy chhe.
I have a cold/fever.	Mane sardee/thaav chhe.

I have diarrhea/ diabetes/asthma.	Mane jaada/dhiabetes/ dam chhe.
I was bit by a dog.	Kutaraae mane bachku bharayu.
Medicine	Davaa

Emergency

Stop!	Ruko!
Help me.	Madad Karo.
Help!	Bachaavo!
Police!	Police!
Fire!	Aag!

Restaurant Phrases

What is in this?	Aamaa shu chhe?
Is this water filtered?	Aa paanee filtered chhe?
Boiled water	Ukaalelu paani
No chilies	Marchaa vagaar
Is it spicy?	Theekhu chhe?
Vegetarian	Shaakaahaaree
Please bring the bill	Bill laavsho?
Snack	Naasto
Spoon	Chamchee
Knife	Chappu
Fork	Kaanto
Glass	Pyaalo
Plate	Thaali
Napkin	Rumaal

Food & Drink

Food	Khaavaanu
Salad	Salaad
Dessert	Dhesart
Yoghurt	Dahee
Boiled	Ukaalelo
Fried	Tharelu
Lentils	Daal
Rice	Baath
Bread	Rotli
Sweet	Mithai
Clarified Butter	Ghee
Oil	Tel

Vegetables	**Shaak**
Bittergourd	Dudhee
Cucumber	Kaakdee
Cabbage	Gobee
Peas	Vataanaa
Eggplant/Aubergine	Ringan
Onion	Dungalee

Garlic	Lasan		
Potato	Batetaa	**Spices**	**Masaalaa**
Cauliflower	"Flower"	MixedSpices	Garam Masaalaa
Carrot	Gaajar	Salt	Meetu
Lady Fingers/Okra	Bhindhaa	Sugar	Khaand
Corn	Makai	Black Pepper	Maree
Spinach	Paalakh	Turmeric	Haldar
Radish	Mulo	Chili Pepper	Marchu
		Cardamom	Elaichee
Fruits	**Fal**	Cinnamon	Taj
Apple	Safarjan	Carom Seeds	Ajmo
Orange	Naarangee	Mustard Seeds	Rai
Custard apple	Sitafal	Cumin	Jeeru
Watermelon	Tarbuch	Asafetida	Hing
Coconut	Naariyal	Bay Leaf	Mitho Limado
Mango	Keree	Green Chilies	Leelu Marchu
Sapota	Cheeku	Dry Cloves	Laving
Banana	Kelaa	Fenugreek	Methi
Tangerine	Mosambi	Ginger	Aadu
Guava	Jaamfal	Nutmeg	Jaifal
Papaya	Papayu	Tamarind	Aamlee
Grapes	Draaksh	Saffron	Kesar
Cantaloupe	Tetee	Cilantro	Kothmir
Tomato	Taametaa	Mint	Pudinaa
		Basil	Dhamru
Dry Fruits	**Suko Mevo**		
Almonds	Badaam	**Meats**	**Maas**
Raisins	Draaksh	Chicken	Murgi
Walnuts	Akhrot	Lamb	Matan
Pistachios	Pistaa	Fish	Maachalee
Cashews	Kaaju		
		Drinks	**Peevaanu**
Food Grains	**Anaaj**	Milk	Dudh
Pearl Millet	Baajraa	Water	Paanee
Barley	Jowaar	Juice	Ras
Maize	Makai	Tea	Chaa
Whole Wheat	Ghon	Buttermilk	Chhaas
Rice Flour	Chokaa no lot	Liquor	Daaru
All Purpose Flour	Mendo		

GLOSSARY

aarti	worship offered to a deity or saint with auspicious articles such as incense and lamps
adivasi	'original inhabitant', refers to a tribal or indigenous person
agiari	Parsi Fire Temple
Agni	God of fire, in the Vedic/Hindu context
ahimsa	non-violence, esp. as articulated by Mahatma Gandhi under influence of Jain philosophy
alphonso	variety of mango called 'Hafus' in Gujarati
Amba	a benign form of the Mother Goddess
amli	tamarind
apsara	celestial nymph
Arjun	third and the most heroic of the five Pandava brothers, to whom Krishna narrated the Bhagavad Gita
Ashapura	a form of the Mother Goddess who fulfils desires
ashram	a commune for spiritual development or social service
asthi visarjan	Hindu death rite of dispersing ashes in a river or sea
Aurangzeb	last of the first six 'Great' Mughal Emperors
Ayurveda	one of the ancient Hindu medical systems, which emphasizes natural remedies
bagh	garden (from Persian)
bajra	pearl millet; a major Indian cereal crop
bangdi	bangle
banyan	a species of fig tree with an extensive spread and aerial roots descending from the branches, considered sacred by Hindus
ben/bahen	'sister'; used as an informal but respectful suffix after female names
beyt	island. As proper noun, abbreviation for Beyt Dwarka.
Bhagavad Gita	a discourse on duty vs. ethics that govern action given by Krishna to Arjun on the Mahabharata war battlefield
bhai	brother'; used as an informal but respectful suffix after male names
Bhairav	Shiva in his fierce form
bhajan	devotional song
bhajiya	vegetables mixed in a batter and deep-fried
bhakharvadi	fried roll stuffed with spiced savory filling and sprinkled with sesame seeds
Bhakti Movement	medieval pan-Indian movement that challenged the role of the priest as intermediary between devotee and God and fostered a loving devotion of God
bhandar	repository or storehouse
Bharatanatyam	a classical dance form of South India
Bhil	a tribal community found in several pockets along the eastern stretch of Gujarat
Bhima	second of the five Pandavas known for his physical prowess
bhunga	round mud houses with thatched roofs, traditional in north central Kachchh
bidi	small Indian 'cigarette' with tobacco wrappped in a leaf
Bisleri	a brand name of bottled water, used generically
bodhisattva	an enlightened being who helps others to achieve enlightenment
Bollywood	the Mumbai (Bombay) Hindi film industry and its melodramatic productions, coined to rhyme with Hollywood
Brahma	the Creator among the Hindu trinity
Brahmin	traditional priestly class, considered the top tier of the caste hierarchy

burqa	head-to-toe garment with netted peepholes for the eyes, worn by orthodox Sunni Muslim women
cantonment	exclusive army township, usually more spacious and green than civilian settlements
caste	a social division of Hindu society, in theory based upon merit, but in practice determined by birth
cenotaph	monument to a dead person whose last rites were performed elsewhere
chaitya window	horseshoe shaped window motif, used as ornament in Hindu and Buddhist architecture
chakra	a razor-edged wheel, used as a beheading weapon, associated with Vishnu
Chamunda	a folk form of the Mother Goddess
chana	chickpea
chaniya choli	colorful petticoat and blouse combination worn by women, especially when dancing Garba
chhakada	hybrid motorized vehicle made with the front end of a bike attached to a pickup-like two-wheel trailer fitted with seats
chhatardi	literally 'umbrella', a memorial pavilion with a domed roof resting on pillars
chho Rasta	an intersection of six roads
chowk	a courtyard or a piazza, depending on the context
chowki	a police post or other control point on a highway
chulah	stove, usually fueled by wood or charcoal
Civil Disobedience Campaign	protest through non-violent means
crore	ten million, written 1,00,00,000
cupola	dome-like structure
dada	'big brother'; used as an informal term of respect for anyone older, wiser, stronger etc.
Dakshinamurti	Shiva as the giver of knowledge
dal	thick spiced lentil soup eaten with bread or rice
darbar	a royal court; also a minor royal personage or a courtier
darbargadh	the building where the court meets; also the royal residence, usually in the heart of the capital city
dargah	a tomb, ususally of an important person (a spiritual or secular leader)
darshan	literally 'sighting' or 'viewing' of a deity or a holy person
darwaza	gateway in a fort wall; also a door
Dattatreya	the Trinity of Brahma, Vishnu and Shiva depicted as a single body with three heads and six hands
derasar	Jain temple
district	the smallest state-administered governing unit headed by the district collector
dhaba	roadside eatery, usually on a highway and patronised primarily by truckers
dharma	ethical duty; the intrinsic quality of self that sustains one's integrity as a being
Dharmaraj	An alternative name for Yudhishthira, the eldest of the Pandavas
dharmashala	a basic lodging facility for pilgrims, may be attached to a temple or stand alone
dhol	a drum-like percussion instrument with leather tightly stretched across both ends of a hollowed out wooden cylinder
dhow	a sea-going vessel in the Arabian Sea, Persian Gulf and Red Sea region fitted with sails and commonly used for cargo
diwan	high official in a princely state, similar to a prime minister

doli	small palanquin or other form of trasport, fitted with a poles projecting front and back, which rests on the shoulders of two bearers
dosa	crepe-like South Indian snack made from fermented rice flour dough
dowry	wedding gifts given by a bride's family to the newly married couple, now often extorted by the groom or his family
duha	fast-paced, high-pitched couplet preceding the main song of a Raas or Garba
dupatta	a long scarf that women usually wear with a salwar kameez
Dwarapala	gatekeeper, represented as an idol at the entrance to a temple or palace
fakir	a man detached from worldly attachments, often living a nomadic life, seeking higher existential truths
Farsi	the Persian language
filigree	delicate and intricate ornamentation, usually in twisted wire of gold or silver
gadh	fort or citadel
Ganesh	elephant-headed god, remover of obstacles and bestower of good fortune
ghat	steps built on a river bank or lake, sometimes for ritual functions
gopi	a young milk-maid. Krishna lore abounds in stories of his romantic involvement with the Gopis of the Mathura region
gramudhyog	village industries in general, formed on the basis of Gandhian principles
gufa	cave
guru	spiritual teacher or enlightener
haat	an open-air market, traditionally on fixed days of the week
haj	pilgrimage to Mecca prescribed at least once in life for a Muslim
Hanuman	the monkey-God, a yogi in his own right, popularly revered for his devotion to Rama
Hari	one of the names of Krishna
harijan	'people of God', term coined by Gandhi for the castes traditionally treated as untouchable
haveli	(1) any grand house; (2) a temple of the Pushtimarg sect among the Vaishnavas
hijra	eunuch
ikat	weaving technique involving previously tie-dyed thread, which forms regular patterns on the finished fabric
Jain	a follower of Jainism, the religion with a large following in Gujarat
jalebi	a spiral-shaped sweet dipped in a thick syrup
jali	grille
Jari	gold or silver thread embroidery on expensive garments, most commonly used on sari borders
jharokha	balcony window enclosed by a stone grille to cut out glare and to allow a person to look out without being seen
ji	suffix added to the name of a person as a mark of respect
Jyotirlingas	the twelve most revered shivalingas across India
kachori	dough filled with stuffing and fried
kalasha	pot-like motif, forming the summit of a temple spire
kanjari	hip length, heavily embroidered, backless blouse traditionally worn by Meghwal women
Kathak	a classical dance form originating in the Gangetic Plain, mainly Uttar Pradesh
Kathiawad	the peninsula of western Gujarat also known as Saurashtra
Khadi	handspun, handwoven, pure cotton fabric
kichaka	gargoyle-like motif in temple ornamentation
killo	fort

Krishna	eighth incarnation of Vishnu, vanquisher of evil, a ladies' man, philosopher, strategist and founder of Dwaraka
kulfi	Indian version of ice-cream, made from condensed milk and often garnished with nuts
kund	ritual bathing pond, rectangular in plan with steps leading down all sides
lakh	one hundred thousand (written 1,00,000)
Lakshmi	Goddess of prosperity, wife of Vishnu
Lakulish	Shiva as the teacher of Yoga
lari	wheeled handcart, often doubling as a portable vending stall
lassi	slightly thick, homogenized version of buttermilk, either sweet or salty
linga	a phallic representation of Shiva, symbolizing energy
lipan	mud and cowdung plaster used for periodically surfacing floors and walls, decorated with hand and finger impressed pattens
lungi	sarong for men, usually with checkered color patterns
madrasa	Muslim school for religious instruction
Mahabharata	longest epic in the world, based on the power struggle between two branches of the same ruling clan
mahadev	literally 'the great god', an alternative name for Shiva
Mahakali	a fierce form of the Mother Goddess
mahal	palace
Maharaja	emperor, great king
Maharao	title adopted by some maharajas, especially of Kachchh
maidan	a large unpaved outdoor space
mandap	a pavilion, open or closed on the sides, usually preceding a temple sanctum
mandir	temple, house of god
maqbara	tomb of an important person
maratha	a person from Maharashtra, south of Gujarat
marg	road; way
masala	spices in general; a mixture of dry spices
masjid	mosque
mata	mother; also a suffix added to the name of any mother goddess
Meghwal	a formerly nomadic community of Kachchh, known for their leatherwork, woodwork and embroidery
mela	fair
minar	tower, usually attached to a mosque
monsoon	climatic conditions forming the cycle responsible for the rains from June to September
Mughals	dynasty of Turko-Mongol descendants of Timur and Changiz Khan; reigned from 1526-1857
namaz	prayer offered by Muslims, prescribed to be performed five times a day
Nandi	the bull associated with Shiva
navagraha	the nine planets according to Indian astrology
Nawab	(1) a Muslim ruler; (2) a Muslim noble or aristocrat
niwas	residence; lodge
om	sacred sound and symbol representing the ultimate; the primordial sound
otlo	outdoor platform at the entrance to a house
Pali	one of a group of related languages that succeeded Sanskrit and preceded the Modern Indian Languages

pandava	the five princely brothers whose struggle for power against their cousins the Kauravas forms the storyline of the epic Mahabharata
Parvati	wife of Shiva; the original Mother Goddess
pendas	dehydrated milk-based sweets, made in many different ways all over northern and western India
pol	enclosed neighborhood with row houses and a hierarchy of streets and open spaces, accessed by a gate
prabhatiya	a morning hymn, usually addressed to Krishna
prasad	food ritually offered to a deity for blessing
puja	ritual worship at home or in a temple
pushtimarg	Vaishnav sect founded by Vallabha
Rabari	one of the communities of Gujarat, traditionally cattle rearers
Radha	the young Krishna's romantic interest and devotee
Raj	reign or rule; when capitalized it refers to British rule, including both the East India Company and Direct Rule periods
raja	king
Rajput	warrior caste, claiming roots in Rajasthan
Rama	seventh incarnation of Vishnu, worshipped by some Hindus as the ideal of righteousness
Ramayana	epic based on the life of Rama, composed by Valmiki; a morality tale about good vs. evil
rangoli	colored powder used to create geometric designs on floors during festive occasions
rani	queen
rann	the saline marshy desert along the northern and eastern boundaries of Kachchh
rasta	road
rishi	a sage, a person with outstanding spiritual or intellectual attainment
rotla	hand-patted bread made of bajra, jowar or corn flour
roza	enclosure including a tomb of an important person and a mosque found mainly in Gujarat
rudraksha	rosary beads
sadhu	a holy person; an ascetic
salwar	a loose, stitched, pant-like garment
samadhi	stage of yogic meditation in which the mind realizes the Ultimate Truth
samosa	spiced vegetable or meat wrapped in dough, sealed and deep fried
sampradaya	sect
sanctum sanctorum	the innermost chamber of a shrine, where the idol of the presiding deity is installed
sangam	confluence
sapota	a sweet fruit locally called chikoo
sarai	a dormitory or guest house
Sarasvati	Goddess of learning, wife of Brahma
sari	a woman's garment consisting of 5-meters of cloth, which is hand-pleated and draped; worn in many different styles across India
sarovar	lake, natural or man-made
Sati	(1) woman of high moral fibre and the virtue of chastiy; (2) immolation of a bride on her husband's funeral pyre
satyagraha	'pursuit of truth', philosophy of non-violent resistance most famously employed by Gandhiji to force an end to the British rule in India
Shaivite	a devotee of Shiva

Shakti	the feminine energy personified by Goddess Parvati in her several attributes
Shetrunjaya	hill in Bhavnagar district, the holiest place of pilgrimage for Jains
shikhara	summit; spire of a temple
Shiva	the Destroyer in the Hindu trinity; God of the arts and learning
Shivalinga	phallic symbol of Shiva
Sita	Rama's wife
sluice	an artificial water channel fitted with a gate to control the flow
Solanki	The dynasty that presided over Gujarat's Golden Era 11th-14th c. AD
sri/shree	Mr
srimati/shreemati	Mrs
stupa	dome-shaped masonry mound believed to contain a relic of Buddha
Sultanate	region or period of rule by a dynasty of Sultans
Surya	the Sun; the Sun God
swadeshi	'of one's own land'; using only indigenous made goods to support and strengthen the local economy
Swaminarayan	a Vaishnav cult with a massive and influential following among Gujaratis
swaraj	'self rule', independence
swastika	mark of good fortune and of cosmic truth; misappropriated by the Nazis
tabla	a pair of drums, one tuned and the other a bass, untuned
talav	natural or man-made pond
tazia	bamboo and paper replicas of the mausoleums of the martyrs Hasan and Hussain, which are paraded on Muharram
thali	a metal plate; a full course meal in such a plate
tirthankar	one of the 24 'enlightened gurus' of the Jains, the last of whom was the founder of the Jain religion
topi	cap
toran	an ornate free-standing gateway, with a beam resting on two pillars
tribal	indigenous people
tulsi	holy basil
UNESCO	United Nation's Educational, Scientific and Cultural Organization
untouchable	one outside of the caste system, whose mere physical contact was considered ritually polluting by Hindu caste
vad	banyan tree, see banyan
Vaishnav	a devotee of Vishnu
vav	stepwell
Vedas	the four principal Aryan canons of universal knowledge
Vedic	pertaining to the Vedas; one of the adjectives used by Hindus to describe their own faith until the end of the 19th c.
vihara	Buddhist monastery comprised of cells for monks to stay in
vipassana	Buddhist method of meditation and self-purification to gain insight
Vishnu	the Preserver among the Hindu Trinity; the primary deity of the Bhakti Movement that pervaded India in medieval times
wala	a suffix denoting occupational, geographic or other association with the root word to which it is attached
yagna	a sacrificial rite, usually involving fire, part of a mass prayer invoking divine intervention in a calamity or celebration
Yaksha	a celestial being attendant or a god, most often Kubera, the God of wealth
yatra	'journey' or 'travel', a pilgrimage

INDEX

BOXED TEXT

MAP INDEX

Regional Maps

City Maps

District Road Maps

Other Maps

USER GUIDE

In this book, the state is divided by its districts, which are then clustered together based on their geographic location. Under each district, the book highlights a major city (usually the district headquarters) as the main hub. These cities offer access to accommodation, restaurants, Internet, and a good transportation network. We have listed all other destinations within each district as excursions from the major city. In a few places where it makes sense, we have listed an entire district as the excursion itself.

At a Glance is a brief introduction to the region. The regional section is then broken down into districts. Each district section begins with an introduction and brief history of both the district and the major city highlighted.

Places of Interest are compiled under each major city section to help you build an itinerary according to your interests. They include descriptions of the destination along with a historical background when appropriate and contact information when necessary.

Nuts & Bolts (Tourist Information, In & Out, Getting Around, Money, Communication, Medical, Photography, Markets, Bookstores, Entertainment, Activities, Accommodation, Food & Drink) are listed for each city where the information is available. Semicolons are used to seperate different addresses for the same chain.

Excursions highlight the other interesting destinations within the district, which are accessible from the main city. Accommodation and restaurants are listed below a few of the excursion destinations where a longer halt is a good option. Approximate distances to the excursion site from the main city are given for most places.

Getting Involved is the final section of each district that highlights non-profit organizations throughout the region where you can volunteer. Please contact them ahead of time if you plan on visiting or volunteering your time.

Maps

Regional maps highlight a cluster of districts within a region.
The **city map** is designed to help you navigate each main city.
The **road map** helps illustrate how different places within a district are connected.

Abbreviations used in this book

Bldg	Building
c.	Century
Cmplx	Complex
Flr	Floor
Km	Kilometer
Nr	Near
Nxt	Next
Opp	Opposite
Stn	Station

THE INDIA GUIDE GUJARAT TEAM

Chief Editor
Anjali Desai

Assistant Editors
Vivek Khadpekar
Amishal Modi

Map Editor
Prashant Pednekar

Designer
Jayesh Patel
Tiffany Treweek
Anirban Dutta Gupta

Map Designer
Mahesh Panchal

Consultant
Kirti Thaker

Lead Photographers
Vivek Desai
Maria Durana

READER FEEDBACK

This is just the beginning! We invite and encourage you to send in your own discoveries as you travel through Gujarat so that we can improve this book and share new experiences. Please send your anecdotes, travel hints, advice and feedback to gujarat@indiaguide.in.

**To purchase India Guide Gujarat
visit www.indiaguide.in**

ACKNOWLEDGEMENTS
We would like to thank everyone who made this book possible.

The India Guide Gujarat Editorial Support Team
Ami Desai, Amit Shukla, Anand Shah, Anarben & Jayeshbhai Patel, Arpna Mansi, Avani Shah, Dharmesh Mistry, Deepa Panchang, Heena Patel, Guru Randhawa, Kokila & Ramesh Shah, Lakshmi Iyer, Margie Sastry, Nainesh Joshi, Nishant Shah, P S Seshadri, Pakka Bhai, P K Ghosh, Prashant Shah, Prem & Harshad Desai, Rahul Brown, Roopal Shah, Rupal Soni, Shilpa Shah, Swadha Majmudar, Zachary Grinspan.

Contributing Travel Writers and Researchers
Prashant Pednekar (lead travel researcher). Ajay Bhatt, Ajay Mayor, Anil Mulchandani, Ankur Patel, Arpit Shah, Ashish Ghadiali, Avani Parekh, Bina Shah, Falgunsinh Zhala, Hemang Desai, Jagdeep Dhebar, Kshitij Banker, Lalit Kumar, Nishant Shah, Palak Gandhi, Param Tevar, Parth Shastri, Pratik Shah, Vijay Ramachandani.

Krishna illustrations by Vijay Shrimali.

Contributing Photographers
Amul Parmar, Ashit Parekh, Dinesh Shukla, Divyesh Sejpal, Ketan Modi, Mahendra Mistry, Manish Chauhan, Milap Jadeja, Mukesh Acharya, Paren Adhyaru, Sanat Shodhan, Vinay Panjwani.

SPECIAL THANKS

We acknowledge the support of Gujarat Tourism and the Government of Gujarat.

Kanubhai Chaiwala and Naresh for the endless cups of tea and coffee.

Achyut Yagnik, Amit Gupta, Amit Tripati, Anjali Kadam, Ankur Dholakia, Ashok Desai, Atul Pandya, Ba, Bashir Ahmadi, Bhavesh Pipalia, Bhamini Mahida, Bhupendra Safi, Bimal Shah, Binjan Sheth, Bipin Shah, Bipin Vaghela, Camille Durand, Chirag Panchal, Dalpat Bhai Danidhariya, Dhara Bhatt, Dhun Karkaria, Dhvani Vaghela, Dilip Patel, Dinkar P Mehta, Dipak Thakor, Divendra Bhai, D V Ekbote, Envirokleen, Gandhi Smarak Sangrahalaya , H C Kapasi, His Highness Harshwardan Singh Rathod, Jagat Bhai, John Carpenter, Jugal Kishor Tiwari, Kailash Pandya, Kanchan Rabaria, Krishna Shukla, Krupa and Lenin Ventrapati, Kunal Shah, Mayur Patel, M K Jadeja, Mahipendrasinh, Mario D'Souza, Meena Shah, Meera Masi, Montu, M Qamar Shaikh, Mukund Brahmakshatriya, Nirali Shah, Nirmala Khadpekar, P K Shah, Palak Jhaveri, Pandya Sahib & L D Dhamel, Pankaj Shah, Paramjit Kaur & Sukhcharan Sing Sandhu, Patel Bhai, Pinno Chioxx, Pramod Jethi, Prasanaben & Ravendrabhai Shah, Princess Urvashi Devi, Purvang Rawal, Rajendra & Rita Mehta, Rajeswari Namagiri, Raju Thakor, Raju Mama, Raman Chitale, Ramesh Desai, Ramesh Shah, R I Patel, Rishi Dholakia, Rohini Patel, Sachin Desai, Saifee Kadiwala, Sandeep Virmani, Sangeetaben & Krishnakantbhai Patel, Shamrrat Patel, Sheel Mohnot, Sheetal Lawrence, Shruti Patel, Simon Mistry, Sonal Shah, Subrata Bhowmick, Suryakant Bhatt, Vibhakar Pandya, Vinod Bhatt, Vivek Sheth, Yatin Pandya, Yusuf Shaikh, Ravindra Vasavada. The Netlink team. The Manav Sadhna family.

To the kindness and hospitality of strangers, rickshaw drivers, bus conductors, government officers, NGOs and professors, shopkeepers and street sweepers, visionaries, spiritual leaders, teachers, timeless dreamers, to the people that give life to this country and feed the spirit of this book. We love you India.

INDIA ⊙ GUIDE

NOTES